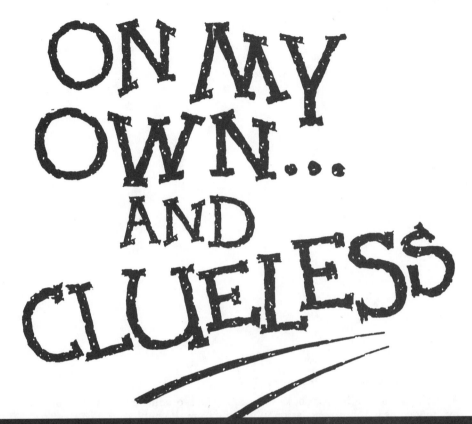

ON MY OWN... AND CLUELESS

An LDS Guide to Independent Life

Clark L. and Kathryn H. Kidd

BOOKCRAFT

SALT LAKE CITY, UTAH

Library of Congress Cataloging-in-Publication Data

Kidd, Clark.
  On my own and clueless / Clark L. and Kathryn H. Kidd.
    p.   c.m.
  ISBN 1-57345-650-0
    1. Young adults—Life skills guides.   2. Latter-day Saint youth—Life skills guides. I. Kidd, Kathy H.   II. Title.
HQ799.5.K53 2000
646.7'00842—dc21   00-025337

Printed in the United States of America   18961-6642
10   9   8   7   6   5   4   3   2   1

ON MY OWN... AND CLUELESS

To our parents—
Lloyd, Beth, Karma, Ed, and Pat—
who taught us to fly on our own,
and taught us that the flight
is as important as the destination

Contents

Acknowledgments

We thank Jeff and Louise Wynn for watching over us, with particular gratitude to Jeff for sharing his insights on the challenges faced by today's young adults;

Emma Gene Gentry, for a secret family recipe (that was a secret to Kathy only because she lost the cookbook);

Judy Willis, for her friendship and knowledge of all things related to real estate;

The folks at Debt-Free America, for some of the excellent tables in the chapter on finances. They have a whole lot of information about getting and staying out of debt. They can be contacted at:

Debt-Free America
3645 Ruffin Road
San Diego, CA 92123
(858) 268-2926
info@debtfreeamerica.com
www.debt-freeamerica.com;

Mike Mitchell, for his opinions on topics as diverse as ketchup and toilet repair;

Various federal and state governments, for making the results of their research available on the Internet;

Emily Watts, who saw an inscription become prophecy—happily for us;

Cory Maxwell, who held our hands during difficult times;

Aaron Taylor, whose cartoons are so much fun he's worth his weight in M&Ms;

Peter Gardner, who had the finesse to cut out 20 percent of the manuscript without eviscerating it (although Kathy still whines about the priceless recipes that were heartlessly omitted);

And Scott Card, who can decipher a publisher's contract or entertain us at dinner with equal aplomb, and who threw Kathy a life-preserver when one was desperately needed.

Introduction

Cutting the Apron Strings

It is a sad fact that most people spend the first half of their lives wishing time would speed up and then spend the second half wishing time would slow down. When we're young, we can't wait for the next phase of life to begin. We look forward to that first bicycle, because a two-wheeler sets us apart from the "little kids." We count the days until we're eligible for a driver's license, because we can have more freedom and be less dependent upon Mom and Dad as chauffeurs. We're even excited to get our first part-time job, because that paycheck gives us the ability to buy our own stuff—some of which our parents would never get for us!

Now, as you prepare to leave home and start life on your own, you're at the brink of another one of those giant steps in life. The day you achieve this milestone is the day people will know you have "arrived." You will no longer be just a kid living with your parents. You'll be your own master—your own boss—the queen or king over your own castle and kingdom. You can stay up as late as you want! No more vegetables for dinner, but pizza and ice cream every night! You can pick your own clothes, choose your own friends, play your music (as loud as you want), and never make your bed again!

Is it any wonder your parents are a little apprehensive about seeing you leave? They have invested as many as twenty or more years in training you to be a lady or a gentlemen, and they're afraid of seeing that hard work go down the drain as you devolve into an unhealthy, unmannered, and unsanitary Neanderthal with pizza breath.

Okay, that was probably a little strong. If you're old enough to leave home, you probably have enough sense to know that—at least in some ways—the time has come for you to start acting more like your parents, or at least more like people your parents' age. You've earned the right to be viewed as an adult by the rest of the world; but with that right comes the responsibility of actually acting like one during a good portion of your waking hours (we all need to act like kids on occasion, no matter how old we get). Although your parents may be concerned about seeing you go, they probably also understand that this is an important rite of passage and that you cannot remain a child forever. They know that you will probably push the bounds of your newfound freedom for a little while, but they are hoping that enough of the good habits they taught you will stick with you, even though they won't be there to tell you what to do.

Moving on Out

Although there are probably as many reasons for leaving home as there are people, chances are good that you will be leaving home for one of the following reasons:

- Education
- Military service
- Religious mission or volunteer service
- Employment
- Marriage
- Age (you want to be on your own)
- Family disputes

As you might expect, the difficulty you will experience adjusting to life on your own will vary based on the circumstances of your departure. For example, those entering military service will usually not need to worry about housing, cooking, or health care, since the military will provide those. On the other end of the spectrum, those leaving home because of marriage will have to learn many new things, including how to get along with a spouse twenty-four hours a day.

Even two people leaving home for the same reason need to learn different things. One college student may live on campus, have no car, and eat all his meals in a cafeteria. Another student may live off campus, drive to school, and eat "home-cooked" meals—which will require an understanding of housing, automobiles, and cooking.

Although not everything in this book will apply the day you leave, you will definitely need to know most of this stuff by the time you reach the age of thirty. Yes, we realize that may seem a century away right now, but trust us—the day will arrive before you can say "over the hill."

Why You Need This Book

Regardless of your reason for leaving home and of how much you think you know, we guarantee you will find living on your own more complicated than you expect. You may find yourself looking at your parents or guardians and saying, "How difficult can it be?" In a way, you're right to think that way. Thousands of folks move away from home every year, and they seem to survive. No matter how ill prepared you may be for life on your own, somehow you will make it.

Although anyone can start living on his own without special training, knowing what you are doing will save you a lot of grief along the way. Experience is the best teacher, but it is not always the most painless teacher. It isn't the end of the world if you ruin a shirt because the iron was too hot, but wouldn't it be better if you knew what you were doing before you picked up the iron? Using a bank that charges you more than the bank right next door will not cause you to go bankrupt, but wouldn't it be nicer to have that money in your pocket for an extra dinner or date each month? Sure you can eat peanut butter and jelly sandwiches every night for dinner, but wouldn't it be great to have some homemade lasagna? It certainly will not kill you to sleep on the same sheets for three months, but it sure feels nice to lie down on a crisp set of clean sheets. So, although anyone can *survive* living on his own, our goal is to help you enjoy life—not just endure it.

What we will try to do is provide you with a course that will teach you all you need to know about enjoying life on your own. Unlike a school course, there will be no tests, and you can study at your own pace and even jump around from chapter to chapter if you wish. You may want to read through the whole book, or at least thumb through the pages to see what's there for future reference. You can always come back later and use the index or table of contents to find a particular subject.

You will soon learn there are a lot of things associated with running a household that you didn't know about. These are things that somebody must have been doing when you lived at home—you just never realized it. But now you are the head of the house, and the responsibility to do all these things falls on your shoulders. Our goal is to educate you about these things so that they don't come as unpleasant surprises.

As we said earlier, not everything in this book will apply to you immediately. That is fine. The book will still be around in five years when you have decided you are tired of apartment life and are ready to buy a "starter" house to fix up.

Although this book addresses serious subjects, we don't believe that learning has to be dull. We'll use lots of examples and humor and tell you about dumb mistakes we made, so that you can avoid them.

Chapter Organization

We've tried to supply chapters that will teach you all of the basics you will need to at least get started on your own. As you start living on your own and gaining more experience, you may want more detail than what we can provide in one book. Thus, in ten years you may find your library filled with dozens of books about cooking, medicine, home repair, automobiles, and finances. What we have given you is a book to get you started, a book to answer your basic questions.

We have tried to present the materials pretty much in the order we think you will use them. For example, your first priority will probably be finding somewhere to stay; so in chapter 1 we teach you how to find and secure housing. Once you are settled, your thoughts will probably turn to your stomach; so we will teach you how to cook and use the kitchen in chapter 2. You will probably be anxious to use those new cooking skills, so we have included a lot of tasty, foolproof recipes in chapter 3.

But there's more to feeling good than just having a full stomach, so in chapter 4 we'll discuss your health and how to keep it.

In chapter 5, we turn our attention to such household tasks as purchasing and maintaining clothes, cleaning, and shopping. Chapter 6 teaches you to fix things around the house, perform common home-improvement projects, and handle home emergencies.

There is more to owning a car than knowing where to put the gas, so you'll learn about cars in detail in chapter 7. We'll cover your money in chapter 8 and how to make it in chapter 9.

To one degree or another, we all crave the company of others. You'll learn all about these social relationships in chapter 10.

In many of the chapters, we have included a final section called "I'm Still Clueless." This will address some of the questions that may have popped into your head as you were reading the chapter.

Also, look throughout the book for small sections titled "Sneaky Secrets." These identify an idea or tip that we have found to be particularly ingenious or clever.

There is one final point we would like to make. When many of us get older, we have conflicts with our parents over their rules and their advice. When we move away from home, we treasure our independence and insist on making our own decisions. There is nothing wrong with that, but be sure you make informed decisions—don't just do things to rebel against your parents. This book will give you advice that we think will lead to long-term success and happiness in your life. We were not bribed by your parents to do this even if some of our advice sounds similar to that which your parents would give. Yes, this is difficult to admit, but sometimes your parents are right despite their advanced age and their generally boring attitudes towards life.

Although there are a few crocodiles in this pond called life, you can avoid most of them with the proper training and preparation. We hope this book will be a trusty companion for you as you begin the adventure of living on your own.

CHAPTER 1

Your Own Place in the Sun

★ **IN THIS CHAPTER**
- ✔ Exploring Housing Options
- ✔ Understanding Apartments and Rental Properties
- ✔ Deciding Where to Live
- ✔ Finding That Perfect Place
- ✔ Dealing with Forms and Fees
- ✔ Keeping the Utility Companies Happy
- ✔ Staying Friendly with the Landlord
- ✔ Surviving Moving Day

The first step in living on your own is finding a place to call home. There are many things to consider when making this important decision, because your housing arrangements will have a great deal to do with how much you enjoy life. Life isn't a bowl of cherries if you find yourself in a depressing neighborhood, living in a place with leaky plumbing and cockroaches under the sink.

If arrangements have already been made for your housing, it may be that you won't need parts of this chapter right away. This may be particularly true if you're going away to school and plan to live in a dormitory. If your housing reservations have already been made, you won't have to worry about landlords or rental agreements. Yet. But before you skip this chapter, you may want to read sections that apply to campus living and moving.

Most people move several times during a lifetime. And nobody is more portable than is a single person, who has fewer connections to tie him to one place. Even if you aren't looking for housing now, eventually you'll do so. *Keep this book.* When you're ready for the rest of the information in this chapter, it will be waiting for you.

Most people moving away from home are likely to land in a dormitory or a rental property, so this chapter will concentrate on those options plus a few others. If you decide your housing arrangements will involve roommates, chapter 10 will teach you how to keep from killing your roommates or losing your sanity.

Housing Options

First, let's look at the various options you have when selecting a place to live. If your housing is already arranged, this section will help you understand a little bit more about your future living environment. If you haven't yet found a place to live, this may give you some options you had not previously considered.

School Housing

If you're going away to college or boarding school, this will probably be the first time you've lived away from home for an extended period. You'll find that staying in school housing is a unique experience, so enjoy it while you can. (If you hate campus living, at least you can take some consolation in the knowledge that you won't have to endure it forever.)

There are numerous different types of housing arrangements that are available for students, and there are nearly as many variations on those arrangements as there are different schools. The information you'll find here is a good general guide, but you may want to contact your particular school to get more specific information. If you haven't selected a school, make sure you investigate the housing options at all the schools on your list. After all, you don't spend all your time in the classroom. At least half your life will be away from classes, and the first place you'll want to go when you're not in class is home.

You may also find that school housing regulations will vary according to your seniority level and marital status. At many colleges, freshmen living away from home are required to live in on-campus housing during their first year. Other schools reserve their larger housing units and on-campus apartments for married students.

Let's look at some of the more common living arrangements that schools provide for their students.

▶ On-Campus Residence Halls

Back in the old days, residence halls were referred to as dormitories. The word *dormitory* is an anagram for the phrase *dirty room*. Residence hall rooms may or may not look like pigpens, but they do have several common features. They're usually on campus (or close to it) and are owned by the school. You may want to think of a residence hall as being like a prison—a building designed to house a maximum number of bodies in a minimum amount of space. This is particularly true of residence halls that were built before the 1980s.

Your room is probably the only place in the facility where you can be alone and where you'll have storage space for your clothes, toiletries, and other personal belongings. The standard furniture consists of a single bed, a desk and chair for studying, a dresser, and a closet. That's if you're lucky. Some facilities have private rooms, but it's more common to find rooms designed for two to four people. If you grew up in a large family, you'll probably feel right at home with this arrangement. If you value your privacy, sharing a room could be a bit of an adjustment.

There is much variation in the segregation of men and women in residence halls. Some schools have entire residence halls devoted to only one sex. More commonly, specific floors of a residence hall will be designated for either men or women. Some schools allow men and women to live on the same floor, but usually require all students sharing a room to be of the same sex.

Although your room may be small, most schools try to compensate for this by providing a number of public areas in the residence hall. For example, there is usually a lounge area where you can read, watch television, or play games such as Ping-Pong and billiards. Examples of common areas you may find include the following:

Bathrooms. Most dormitory bathrooms are equipped with toilets, sinks, and shower stalls. If both sexes live on the same floor, there will nevertheless be separate bathroom facilities for men and women.

Dining Area. The fare may feature "breaded surprise," but this is where you'll eat if there are no cooking facilities in the rooms.

Kitchenettes. Small kitchens allow you to prepare snacks and heat food. Don't expect more than a microwave and perhaps a refrigerator. Anything else is gravy.

Laundry facilities. Mom doesn't live here. If you want clean clothes, it's up to you to wash and dry them in coin-operated machines.

Lounge. If you're an extravert with time on your hands, this is where you'll watch television, play games, and visit with other students.

Music rooms. These are always handy if you want to listen to music or practice playing an instrument without annoying your roommates.

Post office. Without a post office, you'd receive no checks from home.

Snack bar. Whether it features vending machines or a real snack bar with a staff, the snack bar provides sustenance students crave (especially on "breaded surprise" days).

Sports facilities. Courts, swimming pools, picnic areas, and fitness centers allow you to work off your frustrations.

Storage facilities. This is the place for all that stuff that won't fit in your room.

Study rooms. A studying alternative to your bedroom if you need to go off someplace for a little peace and quiet.

If you're assigned to a residence hall with no cooking facilities, you'll need to investigate your meal options. Some schools give no option, and your meals from campus food services will be automatically included in the housing bill. Other schools require that freshmen purchase on-campus food plans, but allow their older classmates to choose for themselves whether to purchase plans or provide their own meals. If you decide to do the latter, keep in mind that many schools do not allow cooking appliances in the sleeping rooms and may even have restrictions on the types and amounts of foods that may be kept there.

If you participate in a campus food plan, you will find that each school has its own unique system. Some plans give you unlimited food, so you can eat all day long if that's what you want to do. More commonly, plans allot students a certain amount of money for the term or semester. If you subscribe to this plan you will receive a meal card that looks like a credit card, complete with a magnetic strip. Every time you purchase a food item on campus, your card will be run through a cash register and the cost of the item will be deducted from your balance. If you run out of money before you run out of school, you can usually pay extra and have that amount added to your card.

Residence halls built in the past twenty years are typically a little more civilized in terms of the amenities they offer. Some provide sinks in sleeping rooms, so you can at least have a glass of water or brush your teeth without having to walk down the hall. Other dorms are designed so that two or three sleeping rooms share a common bathroom that contains one or two sinks, a toilet, and a shower stall. Some campuses even provide kitchen units, where three or four sleeping rooms share a kitchen, storage area, and a bathroom.

NOTHING LIKE GOOD COOKIN' THAT I DON'T HAVE TO COOK!

Although living in a residence hall may take some adjustments, it has some advantages. On-campus housing is convenient to your classes and other campus activities. Living in a residence hall is probably the cheapest housing option, unless you decide to share a place with several roommates. There are multiple supervisors on each floor who look out for you—substitute parents, if you will. There are lots of programs and activities to keep you busy and happy, and lots of opportunities to meet other people and build friendships and social skills.

▶ On-Campus Apartments

Although not as common as residence halls, some schools own and maintain on-campus apartments for the use of students and faculty. These facilities tend to be similar to those of apartments that are not maintained by the school, but the rent will usually be cheaper because the apartments are provided by the school as a service to the students, rather than being operated to make a profit.

As you might expect, the demand for on-campus apartments typically far exceeds the number of available units. Consequently, you'll find that most schools restrict the types of students who are eligible to live in the apartments. At many schools, apartments may be rented only to married students or single-parent students whose children are living with them.

This only makes sense, since standard dormitories can't accommodate spouses or children.

Some schools reserve a small number of apartments for unmarried students, but this is usually done with the provision that the students must find and maintain their own roommates to share the housing unit.

▶ Fraternal Organizations

Many fraternities and sororities maintain residence houses close to campus. The costs and living arrangements vary widely, but don't overlook this as an option if you plan to be involved with such organizations. Keep in mind, however, that many social units are better known for their party atmosphere than for their academic standards. For this reason you may want to look at more traditional living arrangements, at least for your early years of school.

▶ Off-Campus Housing

Most universities are surrounded by apartments and rental properties that cater to students. The university doesn't own or control these properties, but it may provide information about them as a service to the students.

Some school administrations have established aggressive programs to make sure off-campus housing will meet student needs. Landlords who wish to have their property included on the school's list of approved off-campus housing units must follow a list of guidelines and specifications. These guidelines help ensure that you will be provided with a certain level of comfort no matter where you choose to stay off campus.

Other schools take a less-aggressive approach to off-campus housing, simply compiling information about the housing options available near the campus. The school will usually warn you that it makes no guarantees about whether the housing matches the descriptions or is even suitable for student occupancy. If your school provides no guidelines for off-campus landlords, continue reading in this chapter to learn how to find the housing that's best for you without making costly mistakes.

In no case should you arrange for off-campus housing without first learning if underclassmen are restricted to on-campus living. Otherwise you may be in for a rude surprise, as you find yourself stuck with an apartment you're not allowed to live in.

No matter what your requirement for housing while attending

school, you should first contact the school housing department to see what rules you'll need to follow and to get assistance in helping you find housing that suits your needs. Just remember you're not the only student who needs help. When thousands of students descend on the housing office at the same time with similar needs, not everyone is going to end up in a perfect situation. You can increase your odds by being pleasant and cooperative, no matter how much you are tempted to rant and rave.

Staying with Others

It may be that your first experience away from home will occur when you move in with relatives or friends. This type of arrangement usually works out pretty well because it allows you to save some money and become acquainted with the surrounding community before moving out on your own. Maybe you'll be staying for just a week or two, until you can find your own apartment. Or perhaps the hosts have offered to give you a more permanent arrangement by allowing you to live in their home while you work or attend school. It may be that you or your parents are paying rent to allow you to live with your hosts. Sometimes the friend or relative is gracious enough to offer you a room for no charge or to request that you do some minor chores around the house in exchange for the roof over your head.

Whatever the arrangements, your biggest responsibility is to be a good houseguest. In fact, you'll be more successful if you don't think of yourself as a "guest" at all. Guests are privileged characters. If you start acting like a guest, there will almost surely be trouble. Think of yourself as a resident or a roommate—someone who shares the house and the responsibilities of maintaining it. If you assume some of the household responsibilities, your host is probably going to want to keep you on the premises. If you turn into an albatross around your host's neck, however, you may soon find yourself out on the streets.

If you're expected to help around the house, make sure to do your tasks well and without being asked repeatedly. Do extra chores and lend a hand to keep the house clean. Don't tie up the telephone lines or the televsion for hours on end, and don't listen to your stereo late into the night. Give your hosts an occasional evening to themselves, even if that means you have to spend extra hours at the library.

Unlike your parents, your hosts are not there to wait on you, pick up your socks, make your bed, or clean your bathroom. This may be difficult

Sneaky Secret

Even if your hosts refuse to accept any rent, you can do little things to thank them for their hospitality. Bring home occasional sacks of groceries to help feed the family. Offer to take them out for dinner or to cook a special meal at home. Fill the tank with gas if you borrow the family car. Offer to watch the kids on occasion so the parents can go out on a date. These types of thoughtful acts will show your hosts that you appreciate their kindness and will make your stay a joy for them rather than a burden.

for you to understand—especially if you see your hosts waiting on their own children. But you are not an adopted child in the house, even if the host's children are the same age as you. As a boarder, you are being treated as an adult and are expected to act as an adult.

Never forget that your hosts make the rules for their home. They may restrict the hours that you can be away from home and may even require you to be in bed by a certain time each night. In fact, your hosts' rules may be even stricter than the rules your parents used to make. All of this may seem terribly unfair to you, but it isn't. Your hosts are giving you the privilege of sharing their house, so they have the right to set the rules that apply in their own household. Your only real option is to leave if you can't abide by the rules.

If you see that your presence is putting an undue strain on the host family, do your host a favor and find other housing accommodations. You don't want to put your hosts in the awkward position of having to ask you to leave their house. When you move out, do it graciously. Pack your belongings and clean your living quarters. Then shake your hosts' hands, apologize that things didn't work out better, pay them any money you owe them, thank them for their hospitality, and be on your way.

Apartments

An apartment is probably the most common type of housing arrangement for adults who are away from home and not attending school. Many students are also apartment dwellers. Apartments are popular because there is a wide range of accommodations in all price ranges, making it possible for young adults on a tight budget to find suitable lodgings. In addition, the convenience of apartments also matches the single lifestyle. Most young adults are involved in school, work, and social events and have little time for such things as lawn maintenance and home improvement projects. Living in an apartment suits them fine until they get older, start to establish roots, and have more time for projects around the house.

For many years apartments were viewed as a temporary measure—somewhere you stayed until you could afford your first house. But more people are thinking of apartments as permanent residences that don't require the same level of maintenance as a house. As a result, apartments have become more and more upscale, resulting in larger apartment complexes with many new services for apartment dwellers. Some of the newer apartments include amenities such as swimming pools, tennis courts, fireplaces, on-site stores and restaurants, computer rooms, fitness centers, cable and satellite television, maid service, shuttle buses, and large private rooms for parties and meetings.

▶ Unfurnished Apartments

When searching for an apartment, the first decision you need to make is whether you want one that is furnished or unfurnished. The majority of apartments are unfurnished, which means you will be expected to provide your own furniture. This doesn't mean the apartment is totally bare. Typically, an unfurnished apartment includes sinks, toilets, and the major kitchen appliances. Period. Everything else is up to you.

▶ Furnished Apartments

If all you've got to sit on is your suitcase, you might consider the option of looking for a furnished apartment. These are usually harder to find and will be more expensive than an unfurnished apartment. In theory, a furnished apartment has everything you'll need to move right in and start living. The living room has couches, chairs, a coffee table, and probably a television set. The bedroom has a bed, blankets, one or more dressers, and possibly a night table or two next to the bed. The kitchen will have dishes, glasses, pots and pans, and other cooking utensils.

Despite its name, you will probably find that your furnished apartment is not furnished nearly enough. We once lived in a furnished apartment for a few months while we were waiting for a house to be built. Even though we'd been promised the apartment was fully equipped, we still had to go out that first evening and spend nearly a hundred dollars on items for the apartment.

Sneaky Secret

If you are moving into a furnished apartment, the landlord may have you make inventory of all the provided furnishings at the time you move in. If your landlord provides you with such an inventory, go through and check that everything on the list is in the apartment. If you find that something is missing, bring it to the attention of the landlord, or you may be forced to pay for it when you move out. If your landlord doesn't provide an inventory, take one on your own, give a copy to the landlord, and keep a copy with your important papers. The inventory will help you remember which items should remain in the apartment, and which ones you purchased and should be taken with you.

When renting a furnished apartment, you will probably have to furnish your own sheets, pillowcases, and perhaps even pillows for the beds. Unless you do only basic cooking in the kitchen, you might soon find you need a particular cooking tool that hasn't been provided. Obviously, you'll have to furnish personal items for the bathroom, such as toothpaste and toilet paper. Also, you will be responsible for providing your own cleaning supplies, such as dishwasher soap, kitchen cleaner, bathroom cleaner, and paper towels.

Common sense indicates you should not go out and buy a lot of items until you've seen the inside of the apartment. But keep a little cash in reserve during the first few weeks of occupancy to purchase things that weren't provided that you can't live without.

Before you rent a furnished apartment, you may want to consider the "yuck factor." This is the unknown variable in the equation when you're moving in on someone else's used furniture. How clean is the furniture? What was spilled on that furniture? Are there residual smells inside the furniture? Chances are pretty good that the previous owners smoked cigarettes on it or threw up on it or did any one of a number of disgusting things to make the furniture fail the "yuck" test.

If you're not squeamish about a piece of furniture's history, go right ahead and rent a furnished apartment. But if the yuck factor is a problem for you, you may want to think about getting an unfurnished apartment and then renting from a furniture rental store. Rental furniture is new. It will not contain souvenirs of someone else's usage. You can rent to own, or you can return the furniture to the company when you're finished with it. After you've finished renting the furniture, it will be sold as secondhand furniture to someone who will then have to contemplate what *you* may have done to make the furniture fail the yuck test.

▶ Apartment Sizes

➔ Once you answer the "furnished or unfurnished" question, the next thing you must decide is the size of apartment you want. This will make a difference in terms of how much space is available to you and will also affect the amount of rent you pay. As you might expect, more space means higher rent. When looking for an apartment, it is common to see the size described using these common terms:

Bedrooms. The most common way to describe apartment size is by the number of bedrooms. A one-bedroom apartment typically consists of a bedroom, bathroom, living room, and kitchen area. There is usually a small dining area between the kitchen and living room where you can place a dining table and chairs. The layout is usually the same in a two-bedroom and three-bedroom apartment, except for the extra bedrooms, and sometimes a second bathroom.

As you would expect, the cost of the apartment increases with the number of bedrooms. There is no law saying that a single person can't rent a two-bedroom apartment. If you want to use the second room for hobbies or storage and you're willing to pay the rent, most landlords are more than happy to take the extra money. Conversely, it's possible to fit more than one person into a bedroom, assuming your rental agreement does not prohibit this. Thus a three-bedroom apartment could be shared by six roommates, who split the rent. But in most cases, both the landlords and the tenants are more satisfied having one tenant per bedroom. This situation allows you to be social or reclusive, based upon your mood.

Dens. In some newer apartment buildings, certain apartments come furnished with an extra room called a den. This can be used as a TV or computer room, a hobby or work area, or a storage room. Apartments with dens usually cost a bit more, but they are often cheaper than renting an apartment with an extra bedroom. It may be possible to use the den as a bedroom for a roommate, but check first to make sure this is allowed.

Efficiency or convertible. If you see an advertisement for an apartment in a great area at an unbelievable price, the odds are good that you will see the word "efficiency" or "convertible" somewhere in the ad. When you visit the apartment, you'll see why the rent is so reasonable. These apartments usually consist of just one room. They feature a bed that folds out of either the wall or the couch. There are no cooking facilities, so you either eat all of your meals away from home or cook them on a portable hot plate in the one room (some landlords won't allow even that). It's possible that you will even have to share a common bathroom.

Efficiency apartments are not necessarily bad. If you use your apartment only for sleeping, this sort of accommodation will meet your needs without breaking your budget. If you're waxing nostalgic for the cramped dorms and shared bathrooms of your college days, this type of apartment will make you feel right at home.

Lofts. Many newer apartments also feature second-story open areas known as lofts. These usually don't offer enough privacy to be used as a bedroom, but they are often used for activities such as watching television or reading.

In some large cities it is possible to find "loft apartments," which are different from apartments that have lofts. Loft apartments are made from the attic area of a warehouse. With the addition of plumbing and cooking facilities, these attics have been converted into housing units. Loft apartments range from cheap to luxurious. If you're interested in a loft apartment, scan the newspapers early every morning. Loft apartments go fast.

Studio. A studio apartment is one step up from an efficiency. The difference is that a studio apartment usually has a small kitchen or cooking area attached to the main room.

Don't ever rent an apartment without looking at it first, but this is doubly true for efficiency and studio apartments. There is a wide variety of rooms offered under such labels. Some of these offer nice, although compact, living areas. Others are barely one step up from a jail cell.

While you're contemplating apartments, another thing to consider is the length of time the landlord expects you to lease the apartment. Even though you'll pay for your apartment with a monthly rental payment, most landlords will not rent you the apartment unless you sign a lease for a minimum number of months. There are valid reasons for this. Tenants' moving in and out is hard on apartments and landlords, who have to fix the damaged walls, scratched floors, and chipped paint. Also, the landlord has to spend money cleaning an apartment for new tenants, as well as advertise a vacant unit. You can see why the landlord wants you to stay once you've moved in.

The most common lease lengths for apartments are six and twelve months. If you rent an apartment for $500 a month with a six-month minimum lease, you're really promising the landlord you will pay a minimum of $3,000. If there is a chance you will not be in the area that long, or if you have concerns about being able to make that much money, give some serious thought before signing a lease.

The technical name for a lease is a "rental agreement," and we will tell you much more about them later in the chapter. For now, just remember that the length of the lease is something to consider when looking for an apartment.

Rental Property

Although the idea of renting is most commonly associated with apartments, there are other types of housing that can be rented out. Here are a few things to expect when you see these types of properties for rent.

▶ Houses (Entire)

Occasionally you may be able to find a house for rent. A house doesn't have to refer to a single, detached dwelling. It can also refer to townhouses, condominiums, and a unit of a duplex or triplex. A duplex refers to two living units that are connected together, while a triplex consists of three connected units.

Renting an entire house will usually give you more space than an apartment, but the rent will probably be higher, too. You can offset this rent by sharing the house with several roommates. If you're planning to do this, you need to check with the owner to make sure he will allow multiple renters. If the home is in a community with a homeowners' association, you should also read their rules and bylaws to check for possible roommate restrictions. Parking may be a problem if you have more vehicles than the neighborhood allows.

Depending on the rental arrangement, a house rental may involve more work for you than living in an apartment. As part of renting, you may be agreeing to do things such as mow the grass or shovel the snow. Granted, you can always hire people to perform such tasks for you, but make sure to include the price of these services when calculating how much it will cost you to live there. If utilities are not covered by the rental payment, remember that the rates for such services may be higher than what you are used to paying, particularly if the property is old and the appliances are not as efficient.

Although living in a rental house can be quite enjoyable, make sure you fully understand the rental contract and the extra costs that may be associated with living in the house. If the agreement you are being asked to sign is a sublease, please read the cautions listed in the "Apartment subleasing" section below.

▶ Houses (Partial)

It is common to find arrangements where the owner wants to rent just a portion of a house or townhouse. Here are some situations where that will happen, and some suggestions for questions you should ask before agreeing to rent:

- The house may be rented by other people who are looking for roommates to help share the monthly expenses. Make sure the owner agrees to this arrangement, because many rental agreements prohibit this without specific permission. Don't just take the word of the potential roommates—talk to the owner or ask to read the rental agreement. Also, make sure you fully understand the extra expenses you'll be asked to share and how the monthly bills will be divided among the roommates. *Get everything in writing.*

- Someone may be living in the house, but renting out a portion of it. As with any rental, you should ask to see the rental agreement and make sure it's clear in terms of what extra costs you will have besides your rent. You should also understand whether you will be expected to share bathrooms, kitchens, and other facilities. Will the owner expect you to do yard work, shovel walkways, or do other chores? Regular houses typically are not designed to be shared, so you may find there will be more of a problem with noise carrying between different areas of the house.

- An older person with physical limitations or a family with specific needs may be looking for someone to live in the house and help with certain duties. Such arrangements may result in you paying little or no rent, but you will be expected to perform certain tasks in exchange for your lodging.

If you are thinking of living as a hired companion in a household, avoid confusion by getting a written agreement. Make sure the agreement specifically spells out the tasks you'll be expected to do and sets a limit on the maximum time per week you will be expected to devote to these tasks. Don't enter into this sort of living arrangement unless you have the necessary skills and the time to perform the tasks that are required.

If any of the details of the rental involve a sublease arrangement, make sure you read the cautions outlined in the next section.

▶ Apartment Subleasing

You may be a little confused here, since we already talked about apartment rentals. An apartment sublease, however, is a special kind of arrangement where someone has already rented or leased a property from the owner or landlord and now is trying to lease it to someone else. Thus, the person who originally leased the apartment will hold the lease, and you will hold a sublease.

There are numerous reasons why someone would want to sublease an apartment to you. The person who leased the property may want to share it with several roommates. In a legal sense, most courts would rule that the first roommate leased the property and then entered into a sublease agreement with the other roommates. The original tenant may be out of the area on a job assignment and doesn't want to break the lease. He simply subleases the apartment while he is away. Or the tenant may have been forced to leave the area before his lease agreement expired. The solution is to sublease through the end of the lease period. After that, many landlords will agree to continue the lease in the new tenant's name if he is interested.

Picking up a sublease might be a good deal for you, but there are a number of ways that you could get into real trouble. Use the following checklist to make sure everything is locked up as tightly as a drum before you sign:

❑ 1. Get the landlord's written permission to assume the lease or be added to it. Don't let the current renter talk you out of doing this. This is equally important for people who are coming into a rental as a roommate. Make sure your name is added to the lease, and the name of any previous roommate is removed.

❏ 2. Get a copy of the original rental agreement from the landlord, as well as the agreement the current renter is asking you to sign. You will be bound by both agreements, so make sure you understand them.

❏ 3. Make sure the current renter is not charging you more than he's paying. It may be acceptable to pay a slight increase, such as 5 to 10 percent, but don't go much beyond that. The only exception might be if the property has fluctuating rates during the year, such as beachfront properties. Make sure the lease price you are being charged is fair for the season in which you are renting.

❏ 4. Make sure no laws are being broken. For example, some areas in New York have rent controls, where a landlord has to keep rents artificially low for tenants who have lived there a long time. Such tenants may then turn around and sublease the apartment to you, collect higher rates more typical for the apartment being rented, pass the base rent onto the landlord, and pocket the difference.

A sublease can be a good deal, but make sure you approach the situation with caution to avoid some of the pitfalls. If the lease holder will not cooperate, or if he seems suspicious, walk away and forget the deal.

Choosing a Location

Experienced business owners have a saying: "When starting a business, the three most important factors to consider are location, location, and location." You can have the best product and sales team in the world, but you won't be successful unless your business is located where it is visible and convenient to your customers. Similarly, even the most luxurious apartment with the best amenities could be downright unpleasant if located in a bad neighborhood or light-years away from the nearest grocery store.

The previous section about different types of housing should have given you some ideas about the types of properties that are best suited to your needs—at least at this point in your life. In this section we will coach you on factors to consider in deciding where your housing should be located. Some of these factors may be important to you, and some may not.

Cost

Many of your housing decisions will be based upon money and how much of it you are willing to pay for housing. Real estate is a business, and the market is driven by supply and demand. Every desirable feature of a housing unit will jack up the cost because there are always people who have money to pay for amenities.

For example, since every student looking for an apartment would like to be near campus, you'll always find that such housing is more expensive than units located five miles away. Housing that has on-site laundry facilities will be more expensive than housing that does not. Housing that features private bedrooms will be more expensive than housing with three to a room. It's up to you to decide which amenities are important enough to pay extra for them.

There are options that allow you to cope with high costs, however. You might compromise on a property that is not as large or as elegant as you had hoped. Or you could live with several roommates and divide up the cost of an expensive property. Some rental properties charge you reduced rent or sometimes none at all if you work as a maintenance person or an assistant manager. Some government programs allow you to qualify for low-income housing if your income is below the poverty level. Look at all the options before choosing a place to live.

Neighborhoods

Another factor to consider is the type of neighborhood in which you would like to live. Everyone wants to live in a "good" neighborhood, but the definition of "good" will vary from person to person. Some people place a lot of emphasis on having a quiet environment, so living in the middle of Manhattan would probably not be a good option for them. For others, the noise and diversity of life make a hectic place like Manhattan ideal. It is important for some people to have parks and sports facilities nearby, while other people have no interest in such things. Some feel more at home surrounded by young families with lots of children, while others crave a quiet neighborhood where most of the residents are retired.

Even if the place where you're moving is some distance from your current home, you can still do research on the neighborhoods before you arrive. If you have Internet access you can research neighborhoods online through many of the national real estate companies' websites. You usually enter a zip code and a street name, and the site will provide you with a map, as well as some interesting statistics about the neighborhood. This is what Clark learned when he researched the neighborhood where he grew up in Ogden, Utah:

- The median yearly income of the residents is $45,924.
- That income ranks in the 75th percentile of all incomes in Utah.
- The average age of those living in the neighborhood is 37.1 years.
- 65.8 percent of households contain married couples.
- 34.1 percent of households have children at home.
- There are twenty schools in the local school district, with 616 teachers and 13,011 students.
- The average teacher-to-student ratio is 21.1 to 1.
- The market value of the average home is $125,000.
- 88.8 percent of the dwellings are single-family houses, 5.4 percent are duplexes, 4.2 percent are apartments with three to nine units, 1.2 percent are townhouses, and 0.4 percent of the dwellings are mobile homes.
- The average temperature in July is seventy-seven degrees, but the high temperature can creep up to ninety-two.
- The average temperature in January is twenty-nine degrees, but it can dip down to a chilly nineteen.
- The Utah state tree is the Colorado Blue Spruce.

You probably aren't going to consider the state tree when you're deciding what neighborhood to choose, but this list gives you an idea of what you can learn about a neighborhood before you sign a lease. Using the Internet to find the information about a potential neighborhood can give you a pretty good idea about the people who live there and about the type of houses and schools you will find. If you don't have Internet access, you might want to visit your local library and see if you can find similar information in the reference area. Or visit your local real estate agent and ask for help. As we discuss later, most real estate offices offer many services that are free of charge.

No matter how much you study, there's no substitute for actually spending some time in the neighborhood you're considering. Before you make a final decision on a property, visit the neighborhood and make sure it will be a pleasing place to live.

While you're at it, you may want to visit the local church congregation where you'll be attending if you move into the neighborhood you're considering. Your church community is your family away from home, and some of those "families" will fit your needs better than others.

Proximity to Other Areas

People have different ideas about the things they want to have convenient to their homes. Some want to be close to work, while others are more concerned about living in a scenic area or living close to friends.

When calculating proximity, think in terms of travel time rather than distance. When we moved to Virginia, we bought a house that was about fifteen miles from Clark's office. We made the drive with the real estate agent in the middle of the day, and it seemed like a pleasant twenty-minute drive. It was only after we moved into the house that we discovered the same drive done during rush hour was a frustrating forty-five-minute nightmare. When selecting a place to live and considering travel times, conduct your experiments during the same days and times that you will typically be traveling.

Availability of Public Transportation

Depending on where you're moving, you may find that a car is more of a liability than an asset. Driving in big cities can be a frustrating experience. In addition to traffic jams and tolls, parking in such cities is often impossible, and you will pay a fortune for a parking spot or park illegally and pay a fortune in tickets. Either way, you may eventually decide to leave the car at home and use the train, bus, or subway.

If you think there's any chance you will be needing or using public transportation, take that into account when looking for a place to live. Even if you drive on most days, it is nice to have an alternate way to get around when the car is in the shop.

Resources to Locate Housing

Once you've determined the location and the type of housing you want, the next step is to see what's available.

In this section, we'll describe some of the resources you can use to locate housing that meets your needs. These general tools apply to any housing search, whether you are looking for an apartment to rent or a house to buy. In later sections, we'll go into more detail about the differences between finding an apartment and finding a house. Just keep in mind that although all of these sources may not apply to you this very moment, you can always come back to them when you're ready to plan your next move.

School

When looking for housing, students should contact the school to see what resources are available and what rules may be related to the housing you'll be allowed to choose.

Associates

If you live near the area where you want to live, talk to some of your work, church, or school associates. Some of them have probably lived in the area for a while, and will be able to recommend specific neighborhoods or subdivisions. Perhaps they can also recommend the name of a good real estate agent.

For those who are working, contact the human resources or personnel office of your company. Some companies provide services to help employees imported from different parts of the country find proper housing and get settled in the community. Perhaps your company will consent to cover some of the costs related to your move. Your employer wants to make sure that you are happy at your job, and he can often be helpful in answering your questions and getting you connected with the proper people.

Home and Apartment Guides

In many large cities, you'll find free guides that advertise available houses and apartments. You'll usually find separate guides for houses and apartments. These are usually published about once per month, and are available in such public places as busy street corners, the entrances to grocery stores and video stores, and public transit stations. If a search of these places doesn't turn up any guides, visit the local public library or a real estate office to see if they can help.

Even if you don't find your dream home in one of these guides, they're useful for getting you acquainted with the area. The guides will show you the different cities, counties, and neighborhoods, plus the properties available in each area. Most of the advertised properties will include pictures and a listing of dwelling sizes, amenities, and prices. The guides may also have other useful information, including a list of important phone numbers and a map of public transportation routes.

Before you look for your own specific property, consulting such guides will give you an indication of the places that look good and are within your price range.

Newspaper Classified Ads

The classified ads section of the local newspaper is still one of the best sources for housing leads. The classifieds section got its name because the ads are classified according to what they are trying to buy or sell. As you look through the headings on each column, you'll see classifications such as "Furnished Apartments for Rent," "Unfurnished Apartments for Rent," "Houses for Sale," "Houses for Rent," and "Roommate Wanted."

Once you've used some of the other sources in this section to determine the kind of property you're seeking, the daily classified ads should be your bible. Grab them as soon as possible each day and scan the ads for new listings that fit your needs. Remember, other people are doing the same thing, and if you're not quick you could lose out on a great property.

In most cities the best classified ads for property will run in the weekend editions of the paper. That is because the weekends are the most popular time for looking at housing. Get an especially early start on the weekend ads.

If you're moving to another city, your local library may have copies of a newspaper from that city. It may be that the paper arrives a couple of days late, but it will still give you a pretty good idea of what is available. Also, some of the larger newsstands sell an assortment of papers from various major cities across the country.

Some people turn up their noses at classified ads, preferring to put their fate in the hands of realtors. This is a mistake. When we moved to Virginia, we read a copy of the *Washington Post* as we waited for our realtor to pick us up. We found an ad for a house that looked good. When we showed it to the realtor, she said that with a price that low, there must be something wrong with the house. But she took us to see it anyway, and that was the home we eventually bought.

Real Estate Agent

When you're moving to a new area, one of your first stops should be at a local real estate office. A real estate agent will usually question you about your current housing and financial situation, plus your housing preferences. Based on these questions, he or she will give you some options and show you some available properties that might meet your needs. Unless you decide to buy (rather than rent), the realtor will probably not drive you around to look at properties. But most agents will be more than willing to load you down with guides and pamphlets galore, so they can also be a good source to develop housing leads.

You'll probably have the best experience with a real estate agent if you go into the office without having made a lot of decisions. Explain that you're new to the area and that you're looking for a place to live. Then let the agent interview you and make some suggestions. Agents have a lot of tables and formulas that can help you decide which options are available based on your income. If you go into the meeting with no preconceived ideas, you might be in for a pleasant surprise. You may have come expecting to rent an apartment only to find that you can rent or even purchase a house for the same cost.

Sneaky Secret

Now for a little secret about the real estate business. Real estate agents earn their living from fees and commissions, but those who are selling the property almost always pay this money. Thus, as a buyer you are entitled to all kinds of attention and service from the agency without paying a penny. Now that you know this little secret, please don't be unreasonable. Real estate agents need to make a living, and every minute they spend with those who are "just looking" is a minute they could have spent with a paying customer. If and when you know that you are not going to be buying, have pity on the agent and don't take any more of his or her time.

Real estate agents like to deal in sales rather than in rentals because that's where they make the bulk of their commissions. Although they often earn a small commission by arranging rentals, most agents believe it isn't worth their time. If you have a particularly good agent, he might take some time searching the agency computer listings for rentals. But don't expect him to drive you around to see rental properties.

Yellow Pages

Find a copy of the telephone book for the area where you will be living, particularly the yellow pages or the business section of the phone book. If you're looking for the phone book of a distant city, try the local library. Look under "Apartments" to find larger apartment complexes and apartment locator services. These are services that can do computer searches to locate apartments in the area that meet your specifications. Apartment locator services are usually free because they are operated by the apartments that are available on the service. Look under "Real Estate" to find the real estate companies operating in the area. You may prefer a national company or one operating just in that area.

Internet Resources

We've already mentioned the valuable services that can be found on the Internet. If you have access to this tool, you'll find that it can be used to put a lot of good information right at your fingertips.

Many of the national real estate companies have websites. These can be used to teach yourself about the buying process, to research neighborhoods, to search the listings of that company, or to find a local agent that is affiliated with them.

Many cities where there are a lot of apartments for rent have established websites that allow you to search for available properties. The sites will often show such things as pictures and floor plans so you can decide for yourself if it is the kind of place you are seeking. One caution with using this type of site is that it often features only those apartments that pay to be part of the service.

The developers and owners of many large apartments, condominiums, and housing projects will often develop websites to advertise their properties. These sites are used mainly to convey such information as prices, amenities, and floor plans. Use them for information, but remember that they are really just on-line advertisements.

You can find on-line newspapers as well as other sites that allow you to post or search classified ads.

There are sites available that allow you to search the yellow pages for a particular area. This is easier and probably more current than visiting the library.

Hints When Renting

There are differences between finding a property to buy versus finding a place to rent. Although some of the tools and steps are the same, some are different. In this book we'll concentrate on rentals. After all, if you're rich enough to be buying a house at your tender age, you're probably so sophisticated that you don't need this book.

Finding a Rental

In the previous section we listed a number of tools that are useful when looking for housing. But now let's put them together into a specific procedure that you can follow when looking for a place to rent:

1. Determine how much you can afford to spend. In most areas, figure that your rent should not be more than a third of your monthly salary. An easy way to calculate this is to divide your yearly income by 36. If you make $36,000 a year, look for a place that will cost you no more than $1,000 per month. You may have to adjust this number up or down slightly, based upon the cost of living and your own personal financial situation.

2. Determine where you want to live and what type of rental unit (house, studio apartment, and so on) you want to rent. Also, consider things such as proximity to work or public transit.

3. Identify the available rentals that meet your requirements. If there aren't any, you'll need to change your options and try again. Perhaps you'll need to consider a different neighborhood or another living arrangement, such as living with a roommate.

4. Be aware that rental ads can put a positive spin on even the trashiest apartment. For example, you might see something called a "Garden" or "English" apartment. These quaint terms simply mean an apartment that is on the first level or even in the

basement. Similarly, a "Coach House" apartment is usually a remodeled portion of a garage or barn. Although there's nothing wrong with these types of apartments, be sure you understand the meaning behind the words.

5. Make a list of important questions you wish to ask each landlord. Call each of the rental properties that meet your initial criteria and use your list of questions as a script. Write down the answers next to the name of the property or the address so you will not get confused after talking to several landlords.

6. Narrow your list down to a manageable number of possibilities. Now it's time to actually visit the places on your list. Call the landlord first to make an appointment to come and see the property.

7. Make sure you avoid the temptation to rent the first property you see. Sometimes the process of finding your own place is so exciting that the first place looks glamorous and perfect. You need to look at several different places to get a feeling for the different possibilities in your price range. Don't sign a contract with any landlord who tries to pressure you to rent his or her property.

8. You might find that locating the right place takes longer than you expected. When you go out to visit properties, you may not be able to visit more than three or four in one afternoon. Be patient and reserve enough time so that you can visit several properties before having to make a decision.

9. When viewing each property, ask any questions that may come to mind. If you think of something later, you can always call back and ask other questions. If you think you may be interested in that rental, ask for a copy of the rental agreement. Read it carefully and ask about anything in the agreement you don't understand. Be polite to the landlord and thank him for showing you the property. If you still want to consider that rental, ask the landlord to hold it for you until the end of the day.

10. Rather than make a decision on the spot, go back home and take some time to consider each of the places you saw. Evaluate the good and bad points of each, and eliminate different properties until you are down to the one you want. Check the rental agreement again, just to make sure everything looks fine. Contact the landlord, tell him of your decision, and indicate that you would

like to proceed. (It wouldn't hurt to contact the other landlords afterwards to tell them you've found other accommodations. After all, you won't stay in that first apartment forever. If you keep good relationships with the other landlords, they'll want to see you again.)

11. After you have decided on a specific apartment, it is possible that the property is no longer available. If this happens, ask the landlord if he knows of any similar properties that are available now or in the near future. If not, don't be discouraged, but go back to your list of possible properties and start the process over again.

Assuming the place you want is still available, the landlord will accept your offer and the process will continue. The property isn't yours yet, but you're at least a step closer. Now it's time to move on to the next step of the process.

Rental Application

This is something that was not required when we were renting apartments but seems to have become more popular lately. It is becoming more common for landlords to require you to submit a rental application much as you would submit an application for a bank loan. The application will ask you questions about your credit history (salary, debts) and may ask for a rental history so the landlord can check with previous landlords.

Complete the application as accurately as possible, but make sure to include any information that will make your application look more favorable. For example, if your parents have agreed to help pay a portion of your rent each month, include that money as a source of your income. Or, if you have secured a job but have not started yet, you could ask your future employer to write a letter that confirms your employment and the salary you will be receiving. If you don't have a good rental history, the landlord might require you to pay extra fees to secure the rental. The landlord might require you to pay an extra month's rent up front or double the security deposit (we'll talk about all of these fees in a minute). Although it may be inconvenient to have to raise this extra money, you will eventually get it back, either as a refund, or as an extra month's rent.

Some states allow landlords to charge a non-refundable credit check fee when you submit your application. This is used to cover the cost of contacting a credit agency and getting a copy of your credit report. (Don't worry—we'll explain a lot of this stuff in the chapter on finances.) The law may allow the landlord to keep this fee even if you didn't get the apartment. Yes, this is unfair, but so is life.

If the landlord rejects your rental application, the law gives you the right to know why. Politely ask him why the application was rejected so you can remedy the situation. Although he is not required to give all the details, he must tell you the source of any negative information, such as a credit agency, an employer, or a former landlord.

If the bad information was from a credit agency, you have a right to get a free copy of your credit report. See the chapter on finances for more information about this. If the information came from an employer or former landlord, and you feel the information is incorrect, contact the person who provided the information and make sure that a mistake has not been made. If you can show the landlord he was given bad information, he may change his mind and rent the apartment to you.

Rental Agreement

Once you've been accepted for the apartment, you're almost ready to move in. As soon as you

Sneaky Secret

Your experience renting your first apartment may also be your first exposure to a legal document. Legal documents are hard to understand and boring to read, but if you don't read them you're leaving yourself open to trouble. Despite what the landlord may have told you in person, the document constitutes the legally binding agreement between the two of you. If there is ever a question about your agreement, the answer will be found in the document you signed— not in anything that someone may have said. The landlord is promising to provide you certain things (namely an apartment) and you are agreeing to provide things in return (money). If either of those promises is broken, the judge will make his ruling based on the signed contract. Judges aren't very sympathetic to statements such as "I didn't read the agreement before I signed it" or "I didn't understand what I was signing." It's your responsibility to read and to understand, or you face the consequences.

Sometimes you will get pressure to sign something quickly without reading the full document. **Don't do it**. In fact, the more someone pressures you to sign without reading, the more likely it is that there's something in the document he doesn't want you to see. You have every right to understand the agreement and to know the promises you are making before signing your name. Even though we have signed a lot of contracts over the years, it still makes us a little nervous when we pick up that pen to sign on the dotted line. But that's probably the way that it should be.

sign the rental agreement and pay some fees you'll officially have your own place.

If you followed our advice during the search process, you should have already asked for a copy of the rental agreement, read through it, and resolved any questions with the landlord. If you didn't do that, now is the time. Yes, the rental agreement (sometimes called a lease) is boring and hard to understand, plus it uses small print and goes on for pages. But it is important that you understand it before you sign it.

Rental agreements vary from landlord to landlord and from state to state. Each state has different laws protecting both the landlords and the tenants, and these will be reflected in the contract. But based on the lease contracts we have seen, you should expect to find most of the following in your rental agreement:

The names of the parties involved in the agreement. This will be your name and the name of the landlord or the company that owns the rental property. Make sure there is an address and phone number for the landlord or rental company.

The description of the property being leased. Make sure the correct address is listed—including the apartment number, if applicable. This description should also state that all fixtures, appliances, and equipment already in the apartment are being leased as well. (Otherwise, you're likely to move into an apartment that doesn't have a refrigerator.) If you've been promised other items, such as a specific parking place or storage closet, make sure these are listed in the property description.

The terms of the lease. It should include the starting and ending dates for the lease, the total amount of money you will pay, and the details about each monthly payment and when it is due. Make sure this information is accurate.

The address where monthly payments should be sent, and the types of payments that are accepted. Most landlords expect your rent to be in the form of a check or money order.

The penalty for a late payment or a bad check. It is not uncommon to be charged fees as high as $40 for either of these offenses.

The names of the persons who will live in the apartment and the rules for how long guests can stay. This section usually says that you cannot allow anyone else to live there without the landlord's permission (you cannot sublease the apartment). If you plan on having roommates, make sure the landlord agrees in writing before you sign the contract.

Details about who is responsible for maintaining the fixtures in the apartment. Usually, the landlord will maintain the major systems (plumbing, electrical, ceilings, walls, floors) and the major appliances that come with the apartment, and the tenant will be responsible for such items as curtains and blinds. The contract usually excludes repair to items damaged by the tenant due to fault or negligence. If your buddies decide to put an old shoe in the garbage disposal, don't expect the landlord to come and replace it.

The policy related to pets. If the apartment allows pets, the agreement may specifically list the pets you may have on the property. It might also specify an additional fee you must pay for your pet and additional cleaning you must perform before moving out of the apartment. You will also usually agree to pay for any damage caused by the pet and to follow any state, local, or apartment laws or rules relating to pets.

Specifications for terminating the lease to serve in military or on certain government assignments. Special laws relate to people in such circumstances. The agreement will give the details for terminating your lease and specify the maximum fees you must pay to end the lease early if you are in such an assignment and are transferred out of the area.

The amount of any security deposit that must be paid before you can move in. There will be details about what will happen to this money while you are living in the apartment and what you must do to get this money back when you move out. *Read this section carefully, because many arguments with landlords are caused by misunderstandings related to security deposits.*

Preoccupancy inspection specifications (in some agreements). A preoccupancy inspection happens before you move in, to identify damaged items or things in need of repair. *You should receive a copy of the inspection report.* Make sure to add any items that were missed, so you will not be required to pay for them when you move out. If the rental agreement does not require such an inspection, you should do one on your own. Write a letter to the landlord, listing all the items that were broken or damaged when you moved in. For those items the landlord is obligated to fix by the rental agreement, request that he repair them. Date and sign the letter. If possible, ask the landlord to also sign the letter. Give a copy to him and keep a copy for your files.

The renter's obligations to keep the property in good repair. This means the renter must regularly clean the apartment and must maintain the plumbing and appliances. Even though the landlord is usually responsible for appliance repair, you must notify him when repairs are needed or risk having problems when you move out. If you find the property infested with insects or rodents, report it immediately, or you may be liable for the expense. You may also be responsible for such things as yard maintenance, snow removal, drain cleaning, replacement of lightbulbs and appliance filters, testing of smoke detectors, and the cleaning of carpets.

The landlord's rights if you don't pay your rent or if you damage the apartment. *Read this section carefully and make a vow that you will always pay your rent on time. The law is solidly behind the landlord on this issue, and he can cause you a lot of grief if you don't pay as promised.*

Details about what will happen when your lease expires. Usually the landlord has a certain number of days to notify you in writing of what your options may be. This is when he has a right to do things such as raise your monthly rent or terminate your lease. Many agreements specify that the lease will change to a month-to-month lease when the original lease expires. This is good news for you because it doesn't lock you in for another six or twelve months. You will also be told how many days' written notice must be given to terminate the lease without paying an extra month's rent.

Limitations on the kinds of items you may keep on the property. Some agreements prohibit water-beds or wood-burning stoves unless you have written permission. You may also not be allowed to have eyesores or hazards on most properties, so don't expect to have your car up on blocks in front of your apartment.

Conditions when the landlord is allowed to enter your property. This is usually allowed when repairs need to be made or if you are leaving and he is showing the property to another potential renter. He may be authorized to enter at other times to perform inspections or if he suspects a problem such as a broken pipe.

Renter's agreement to not knowingly break the law and to avoid doing things that would bother or endanger the neighbors. Violations of this agreement would include making excessive noise or improperly disposing of trash, as well as more serious violations, such as using illegal drugs and possessing explosives or flammable chemicals. These restrictions apply not only to the renter but to all persons on the property. The language is usually quite strong in this part of the contract and typically allows immediate eviction if the landlord thinks there is excessive danger.

Rules for vehicles that are to be stored on the property. Your car must usually be properly registered, licensed, and in good mechanical condition.

Rules regarding changes to the apartment. Although you are certainly free to hang posters and paintings on the walls, you must usually get permission before making changes such as painting, wallpapering, carpeting, or adding or changing locks.

Specifications for proper trash disposal. Large apartments typically have a trash chute that can be accessed on each floor. Other properties may require you to put out garbage cans, leave the garbage next to the door, or place it in a dumpster.

Responsibility for payment of utilities. The contract will describe which utilities will be paid by the renter and which ones are included as part of the rent. Make sure you have a good understanding of this section, because utilities can significantly increase your monthly expenses. Many utility companies will help you estimate what your typical monthly charges will be.

Rules for extended absence. Often, you must notify the landlord if you are going to be away from the property for an extended length of time. The landlord usually has the right to enter your property while you are gone to check for problems and to protect it from such things as weather damage.

Renter's insurance requirements. Although the landlord will have insurance that protects his property, it will not cover any damage that may occur to your belongings that are stored within the rental. You can purchase renter's insurance, which will insure your possessions and also give you liability coverage if someone is hurt on the property. Some rental agreements require you to show proof of such insurance. Even if this is not required by your agreement, you should strongly consider it.

As you can see, rental agreements include a number of issues and can be extremely complex. If you and the landlord have decided upon any changes to the agreement, you can either make the alterations right on the contract (both you and the landlord should initial any changes) or attach a separate document with the changes to the agreement. If the latter option is used, make sure both signatures appear on the attached documents. If other people are renting the apartment with you (such as roommates or a spouse), they must also sign all the documents. Make sure each renter is given a copy of the contract, preferably at the time the agreement is signed. Keep your copy in a safe place. You will need to refer to it when you have questions or if there is a dispute with the landlord.

Required Deposits

The rental agreement will specify any deposits or fees you must pay before you are allowed to move into the property. Here is a short explanation of the fees you will commonly find. Such fees may greatly increase the cost of getting into the rental, so make sure you have budgeted enough money to cover these costs before signing the rental agreement.

Rental application fee. Some landlords will charge a small processing fee to be paid when you submit your rental application. This fee should hold the apartment until you decide whether to take it. Make sure you get an explanation of what will happen to these fees, based on the outcome of your application. If you get the apartment, will the money be counted as part of your security deposit? If you don't get the apartment, will you get all, some, or none of the fee back? It is reasonable for a landlord to keep some money to compensate him for processing your application, but the amount shouldn't be excessive.

Advanced rent. Just about every rental agreement will require you to pay rent in advance—usually just one month's rent, but sometimes two. While this may seem like a lot of money to pay up front, remember that you will eventually get it back.

Security deposit. The security deposit, also known as a cleaning deposit, is required for most rentals. It provides a safety net for the landlord in case you leave before the full term of the lease or in case you leave the apartment dirty or damaged. The landlord keeps the security deposit until you move out. At that point he will inspect the rental and make sure it is free from damage. If the property is clean and well maintained, you should get your full security deposit back. If there is damage to be repaired or cleaning that needs to be done, the costs of this work will be deducted from the security deposit, and you will get the remaining amount.

If you don't have a very good rental history, there is a possibility the landlord will increase the amount of the security deposit. As with advanced rent, this is money you should get back when you leave, assuming the rental is clean and undamaged.

Often, state laws limit the maximum security deposit that may be charged, require the landlord to pay your refund within a certain number of days, and require a written accounting of any charges subtracted from the security deposit.

Other deposits. You may also be assessed fees if you have a pet, if you have rented an extra storage room on the property, or if you want access to an on-site pool, fitness center, or parking facilities. The rental agreement should specify how these deposits will be used. Sometimes they are nonrefundable, and sometimes they are added to the security deposit, and will be refunded if the rental is left in good condition.

Association dues. If you are renting a condominium, there are regular dues that each owner must pay to the condominium association to cover the costs of maintenance. Depending on how the rental agreement is written, you may have to pay these fees and may have to prepay the first payment. Those renting homes in communities with homeowners' associations may have to pay similar monthly fees to the association. Such fees are not refundable.

Utility Bills

Perhaps when you were growing up you didn't give much thought to the electricity and running water. They were part of the house—sort of like the floors. If you still believe that, you're in for a big surprise. Items such as electricity, telephone, and water service are known by the collective name of "utilities," and paying monthly utility bills is another one of the joys of adulthood.

Lucky for you, many apartments include some of the utilities as part of the rent. But there are some utilities that you almost always have to pay. Let's take just a minute to discuss the most common types of utility payments. Even if you don't have to pay for all of these in an apartment, you'll need to get a feel for them if you plan to move into a house some-day.

Many utility bills are cyclical in nature. Natural gas bills are low in the summer when you're not running the furnace. If you have a lawn to water, you can count on your water bill being higher in the summer. Some utility companies give you the option of averaging your bills out over the year. For example, your natural gas bill could range anywhere from $5 to $100 per month, depending on the season. But if you enroll in an averaging plan, you'll be charged the average amount each month. Having uniform payment sizes helps those who have limited funds and those who are trying to stick to a budget.

▶ Electricity

Most apartment complexes are designed so that each unit will receive an individual monthly electric bill for the electricity used. This can be done if each apartment is wired to its own electric meter. The electric meter is designed to measure power consumption in *kilowatt hours*—the use of 1,000 watts of electricity for one hour. Each electrical appliance consumes a certain amount of power, measured in watts. For example, a 100-watt lightbulb consumes 100 watts of electricity for each hour it is used. Thus, ten 100-watt bulbs would consume a kilowatt for each hour they are used.

The electric meter records the total number of kilowatt hours that have been used since the meter was installed. Subtracting that reading from the previous month's reading will show how many kilowatt hours were consumed during the month. Most power companies charge a flat fee for each kilowatt hour used, although different billing schemes may be employed that can either reward or punish the heavy power user. Some companies will also charge you a monthly customer service fee of a few dollars, even if you have used no power that month.

If you see the word "estimated" on your bill, it means the meter wasn't read this month; the bill was based on the estimated usage. The next time the meter is read, the power company will adjust for any miscalculation.

If your rental unit does not have its own electric meter, the landlord may suggest you pay a portion of the total electric bill, such as 25 percent. If you agree to this type of situation, make sure you're being treated fairly. Ask to see copies of previous electric bills so you can estimate how much you'll be paying.

▶ Gas/Oil

If your rental is electrically heated and cooled, those costs will be included in your electric bill. But some rentals may use natural gas or heating oil to heat the rooms; there are even some air-conditioning systems that are powered by natural gas. If this is the case with your rental, there's a possibility you will also be receiving a gas or oil bill in addition to the electricity bill.

Gas and oil bills are computed similarly to electric bills. There is a meter that will measure your fuel consumption (in terms of gallons for heating oil and cubic feet for natural gas). As with electric bills, you may also see estimated bills and minimum customer service fees.

▶ Telephone

Because telephone charges vary drastically from person to person, just about every rental will require you to pay for your own telephone service. Although your apartment may come with phones connected to the walls, that doesn't mean the line has been activated. You will usually have to open an account with the phone company before you can make any calls.

The utilities we have covered up to now have been fairly standard in terms of how they compute charges. They measure how much of their product you've used and bill you accordingly. But when we get to telephone service, billing works a little differently. There are a number of different telephone rate structures, some of which will save you money and others that will cost you money. The rate structure that's best for you depends on your telephone usage. Find out about the different rate structures by referring to the front of your phone book or by calling the business office of your local telephone company.

Another complication when ordering phone service is to decide which long-distance company you'll use. Don't just pick up your phone and start making long-distance calls or you might have an unpleasant surprise when the bill arrives. If you didn't specify a long-distance company when you installed your local phone service, one was probably selected for you. But there's no guarantee you got the best company or that their plan is the cheapest one for someone with your calling habits. As with local phone service, you need to do a little investigation and find the company and plan that's best for you.

▶ Cable TV

Most modern apartments are wired for cable TV these days, and some even include cable as part of your rent. If you wish to have cable but it isn't included, it's your responsibility to contact the cable TV company and establish an account.

As with telephone service, there are all kinds of different plans depending on the number of stations you wish to receive. The cheapest plan will give you the local stations and perhaps a couple of others. More expensive plans will usually add specialized stations, including sports, science fiction, weather, and shopping channels. You will also have the option to add one or more premium channels, which show first-run movies and specials available on only those channels.

The cable company may also charge a monthly rental fee for equipment such as channel selector boxes and remote controls. You might be able to save money by buying your own equipment, but make sure the kind you buy is compatible with the cable system to which you subscribe. Many televisions these days are "cable ready," which means they can bypass the tuner box (except for premium stations, which are scrambled).

▶ Water/Sewer

We never had to pay a water bill while living in an apartment, but water bills are a regular fact of life for those who own or rent homes. As with many other utilities, there is usually a meter attached to the water line, and you are billed according to how many cubic feet of water you use during the month. Sewer charges are a little tougher. Take comfort from the thought that no one will be measuring the volume of stuff you flush down the pipes—at least not directly. If you are attached to a regular municipal sewer system, you're usually assessed a flat charge, or are billed as a percentage of the water you consume.

If your residence is not connected to a municipal sewer system, you will have the joy of owning a septic tank. This is an underground tank used for the storage of wastewater. On a regular basis, you'll need to call a septic service to come and pump out the tank.

▶ Garbage Collection

Once again, those who live in apartments will probably escape this charge. Those who live in homes may or may not have to pay it, depending on where they live. Some cities offer their residents garbage collection either free of charge or for a nominal fee that is usually added to another municipal bill, such as the water bill.

Some areas do not offer garbage collection at all, and individual homeowners must contract with garbage collectors to come and haul away the trash on a regular basis. Those who live under homeowners' associations or condominium associations will often have garbage collection included in the monthly fee paid to the association.

After signing the rental agreement, you'll need to contact and set up accounts with the utility companies. You should do this in advance so that the utilities will all be working when you move in. There is nothing more frustrating than moving into a place that has no electricity or running water.

If this is the first time you have established an account, some utilities will require you to pay an extra security fee. This is like the security deposit on your apartment, in that it gives the utility company something to cover your bill if you move out in the middle of the night. If you have had a utility account open somewhere else, you can often ask that company to give you a letter of reference that may be used in place of a security deposit. Ask about other options for avoiding this security deposit.

Once you're a regular customer, you'll start getting bills from the utility companies. These usually arrive every month, but they sometimes come less frequently. Pay attention to the dates the bills are due so that you can avoid extra charges and fees for paying late. If your utilities are ever turned off for lack of payment, you will pay a pretty stiff reconnection fee to get them turned back on again.

When you're planning to move out of a rental, many landlords require proof that your utilities have been paid in full. Keep copies of receipts, bills, and canceled checks so that you can prove this. Otherwise, the landlord may hold your security deposit for an extra month or two to make sure no new bills arrive.

Being a Good Tenant

Living out on your own is not all fun and games. Yes, it gives you freedom, but it also adds to your responsibilities. Your parents probably nagged you about being responsible. Life on your own will quickly teach you why: *People who are not responsible end up throwing away a lot of money.*

Do you believe that? If not, please back up and reread the sections about utilities and rental agreements. You will be signing papers that obligate you for the next six to twelve months to do many different things—things that will cost you a lot of money if you neglect your responsibilities. What could you have done with the $35 you had to pay because your rent check was late? Or how about that $50 reconnection fee you were charged when you didn't pay the phone bill? And how much will it hurt to lose that $100 from your security deposit because your buddy put his fist through your window?

Mature individuals of any age act responsibly because it's the right thing to do. If you learn the concept of responsibility as it applies to rental agreements and utility bills, responsibility may be ingrained in you by the time you enter into life's more important undertakings. Marriage, for example. The habits you make now will last for the rest of your life. You might as well begin your life as an adult on the right foot by honoring your commitments.

Landlord Disputes

We hope that you'll be lucky enough to always get along with your landlords and that you'll never have a moment of trouble getting things repaired and getting deposits refunded. Most of the landlords in our experience tried their best to be fair with the tenants. But be on guard; landlords are people too. And in any group of people you'll find some who are negligent and a few who are dishonest.

But before you point fingers at your landlord, make sure that your rent is current and that your landlord doesn't have any cause to be upset with your conduct. If your dwelling is a continual mess or if neighbors have repeatedly complained about the noise coming from your apartment, the landlord probably isn't going to be very receptive to your requests. If your conduct isn't the problem, conflicts with landlords are usually caused by simple disagreements or forgetfulness on the part of the landlord. Perhaps he has failed to do something that the lease requires him to do, such as repair a broken appliance. Another common problem with landlords arises over the issue of how much of the security deposit, if any, should be returned to the tenant at the end of the lease.

Sneaky Secret

We said earlier to make sure your name appears on the lease when you rent a place with roommates. This way you have some legal rights. The reverse of this rule applies when you move out. Make sure the landlord gives you a written, signed statement that you will no longer be a tenant and that you have no future financial obligations. If you fail to do this, the landlord could hold you accountable for damage done after you moved out.

▶ Conversations

If you have a problem with your rental, first see if you can resolve the problem by talking it out with the landlord. It may be best to talk to him in person, although a phone conversation may have to suffice if he does not live in the same area. Be considerate but firm. *If you're not sure of your rights, read your rental agreement and ask the advice of others before you contact the landlord.* This does not mean you have to hire a lawyer at this point. You may want to discuss the dispute with an older friend or a coworker to get feedback as to whether your request is reasonable and within your rights as a tenant.

▶ Letters

If you're sure your request is reasonable and talking in person did not solve the problem, the next step is to write a letter. Use the address that appears on your lease; it may give you better results than writing to the property manager located on the premises. It could be that the landlord is just managing the property for another company and that sending a letter to the home office will get the attention of someone higher up. As in your phone conversation, the letter should be friendly and yet firm, laying out the reasons why your request should be honored. Include any facts that would help substantiate your request, such as quotes from your rental agreement and copies of any previous written correspondence.

Give the letter a little time to do its work—at least one week and preferably two or three. If that doesn't get results, you may wish to write a second letter. Remind the landlord of your legal rights and state that you are willing to defend those rights in court if necessary. If you rent from a large company, try sending a copy of the letter to a different person in the organization. Call the management office to get the name and address of the president of the company and send a copy to him as well.

When sending letters, be sure to date them and keep copies for your files. You should send all such correspondence via certified mail. This costs more to send, but it proves that the letter was delivered and provides stronger evidence if you have to appear in court.

▶ Research

If none of these steps produces any results, it's time to evaluate the situation. There are still further steps that can be taken, but now you're getting to the point where you'll have to devote a great deal of time and potentially a considerable amount of money to continue the fight. You need to decide if it's worth the time and the aggravation to get the results you're seeking. It's not worth spending $5,000 on court costs over a $30 dispute. Sometimes you have to take a loss and write the money off as a lesson learned the hard way. There are better things to do with your life than sit in court.

Before you consider using the court system, you should also keep in mind that the law tends to side with the party who is following the rental agreement. If you're trying to weasel out of an agreement but the landlord is following that agreement, you won't get very far in court.

If you decide to pursue the matter despite the costs and the time involved, the next thing you must do is research the laws in your particular state. Most states have laws designed to protect both landlords and tenants, but the laws vary greatly from state to state. Look in the phone book for the numbers of the state attorney general and the Office of Consumer Affairs. Most states also have several free or low-cost publications that explain your rights in certain areas. Doing some research will help you decide if your claim has merit or if you are wasting your time. The research might also help you decide the next step in pursuing your claim.

▶ Arbitration

Many states have arbitration services that can help to settle disagreements. An arbitrator is like a judge but usually has no legal authority. He is a neutral party who tries to reason with both sides in a dispute, hoping to reach a compromise that is acceptable to both. Seeing an arbitrator is much less expensive than going to court; arbitration services are often free. Look in your yellow pages under *arbitration, dispute resolution,* or *mediation.*

If your landlord will agree to arbitration, you and he will meet with the arbitrator and try to work out a compromise. You will probably not get all that you want, but whatever you get will be better than nothing. Besides, it will save you from going to court. In fact, some states require you to try arbitration before going to court.

▶ Court

When you have tried everything without success, you have two choices—forget the issue or take the landlord to court. Again, the types of courts available to you will vary by state. Most states have a small-claims court, where the parties represent themselves (attorneys are optional), and the maximum amount of money you can collect is limited, commonly $5,000.

Depending on the amount of money at stake, perhaps you will want to contact an attorney to have him review the merits of your case. Some states even have court advisors who will help you prepare your case. These services are available for free or for a reasonable fee.

If you have a dispute regarding a security deposit refund, it may be difficult for you to collect evidence to prove your case if you have already moved out. If you suspect you will have a problem, take pictures before you leave and keep any receipts for cleaning supplies and cleaning services. You may also have an unbiased source come in and look at the apartment. Depending on the state, the source may have to testify in person, so select someone local to your area. Bring to court copies of all written correspondence to the landlord, and also note the dates when you talked to him.

If you are accused of damaging property, make sure the depreciated value of the item is being used when calculating the replacement cost. For example, assume you stain some curtains that are nine years old. If they have only a ten-year life expectancy, then you should only have to pay back 10 percent of the replacement value.

There are no guarantees in life, but if the law is on your side and you have done your homework, then you may win your case and be able to tell your friends about your masterful performance in court.

When It's Moving Time

When you first move away from home, you probably won't have much control over when you leave. Since you'll be going to school or starting a job, you won't have the luxury of sitting around at home waiting for inspiration.

But you will probably have more control over subsequent moves. You may want to switch to a better apartment or move from an apartment into a rental home. If you have the flexibility to plan your move, it will be to your advantage.

Looking for an apartment in a college town? If possible, avoid moving to town when the students are moving in, when you will have more competition for apartments. Conversely, moving in when the students are leaving for the summer may give you many options. Moving late in the year is also usually bad, because no one wants to be moving over the holidays. The best and worst times to move can vary by location, so rely on a real estate agent or someone in your area that understands the housing market.

Moving out of an apartment may be tricky because you have to plan your move around the expiration of your lease. Most leases automatically renew themselves when they expire, although the landlord might take the opportunity to raise the rent or make other changes. In fact, if he has found someone he thinks would be a better tenant, he is probably within his rights not to renew your lease. Review the lease carefully before it expires. You'll usually have to give at least thirty days' advance notice that you will be moving out and not renewing your lease when it expires. Sometimes the lease requires a written notice that must be in the landlord's hand thirty days or more prior to the expiration of the lease. Include some extra days if you are going to mail the notice and mail it using registered mail.

Some leases automatically become month-to-month leases when the original period of the lease expires. This is good for the renter, who can then move out at the end of any month—providing the required advance notice has been given. If you plan to move and your lease does not do this, try to get your landlord to consider this type of lease conversion, even if it will cost you a little extra for a monthly lease.

Consider that you may need some extra money to pay deposits on the new place before you get your refunds from the old place. You may need to pay a security deposit and an advance payment on your new apartment before you get the security deposit back from your current apartment.

Making Repairs

If you're moving out of an apartment, you'll need to repair any broken items that might reduce your security deposit. Also, some agreements specify that you will be held responsible for any repairs that were not done before you move out. This may even apply to repairs that the landlord is obligated to make, such as those on appliances or plumbing. Thus, a clogged toilet reported to the landlord while you are yet living in the dwelling will cost you nothing; if you fail to inform the landlord of the problem before moving out, the repair costs can be deducted from your security deposit.

Preparing for the Move

Moving time is a great time to inventory your possessions and make some hard decisions about what is worth keeping. As you get older you will find that people, yourself included, tend to accumulate a lot of unnecessary stuff. Moving time is a good time to draw a line in the sand and send all that junk to a better place.

Ask yourself, Have I used this item in the past year? If the answer is no, throw it in the trash, give it to charity, or put it in the garage sale pile. All that wonderful stuff that you just couldn't bear to throw away will become a real burden when it has to be moved. Take advantage of this opportunity to simplify your life.

▶ Packing It In

To protect your property from damage and loss during the move, it's important to use the proper packing materials. In general, avoid the standard cardboard boxes found behind grocery or drug stores. Locate a local moving or packaging company that can provide reinforced boxes designed for moving. If you do insist on using discarded boxes, try to find sturdy ones with lids and without holes in the cardboard. In addition to the boxes, it is useful to get packaging material such as bubble wrap or foam peanuts, although crumpled newspapers will also do in a pinch.

Do not overload the box with too many items, especially if they are heavy and could break through the bottom of the box. Use plenty of packing material to cushion the contents, particularly if you are moving a long distance. When packing dishes, wrap each dish separately, and then turn it on its side, much as you would if you were loading plates into a dishwasher.

When packing items, separate your possessions into one of three groups:

Things to take with you. These are the items you will take with you as you travel to your new residence, or things that are too valuable to just dump into a box. Consider items such as your travel clothes, the keys to the new place, personal items (medicines and eyeglasses), valuable or fragile items, important documents, plants, pets, travel cash, and maps or directions to your new location.

Things to unpack first. These are the items you will need soon after arrival. Put them in specially marked moving boxes that you can open first. Include in this category such items as cleaning supplies, bathroom and kitchen supplies, important addresses and phone numbers, and basic tools needed for home repair. Also consider items useful when moving in, such as a tape measure, a knife, blankets (for padding), and marking pens.

Things to unpack when you get around to it. These are the things you will take that you will not need for the first month or two. Just put them into moving boxes to be unpacked when you have the time.

Try to pack items based on where they will be stored in your new dwelling. For example, pack all kitchen items together in the same box.

Then label each box clearly so that it will be taken to the proper area of your new dwelling.

▶ Leaving Gracefully

Most people end up cramming several days' worth of tasks onto their last-minute list. Following are a few things you can do in the week prior to your departure to make sure moving day will go smoothly and be relatively free of headaches:

Accounts. Shortly before you leave, you'll need to contact any of your current utility companies to terminate your account. Tell the company the date you are leaving so the meter can be read on that day. Have them send the final bill to your new address. Be sure to contact the utility companies you will be doing business with in your new area to establish new accounts.

You should also identify all of your other local accounts, such as those at banks and department stores. If the business has a branch or store at your new location, you might be able to transfer the account. Otherwise, you should probably close it.

Car tune-up. If you will be driving a long distance, have your local mechanic give your car a quick once-over before you hit the road.

Mail. If you're interested in getting mail when you arrive, be sure to go to the post office and request that your mail be forwarded to your new address. You will complete a change of address form, which will specify your old address, your new address, and the date that mail should start being forwarded to the new address. Do this as soon as you know your new address—the postal service prefers to have it at least thirty days before you move.

First-class mail will be forwarded to your new address for up to a year, and second-class mail (magazines and newspapers) will be forwarded for up to sixty days. Third-class mail (advertising, catalogs) will not be forwarded at all, and fourth-class mail (parcels) will be forwarded for up to a year, although you may have to pay a forwarding charge if you moved a long distance from your old residence.

Having your mail forwarded does not take care of telling the senders that you've moved. In most cases, you will have to contact all the people and organizations that send you mail and inform them of your new address. When forwarded mail starts arriving, it will contain a yellow sticker with your new address on it. When you see a piece of mail that has this forwarding sticker, contact the sender with your new address. Most bills and business letters make it easy to change addresses by including a "change of address" section on each billing statement or letter. Just fill out that section, and include it when you mail in the payment or the return letter. The post office can also supply you with "address change notification" postcards.

If you filed federal tax returns from your old address, you might also want to notify the IRS of your move so that future forms and correspondence will be sent to the right address. As with most everything the IRS does, there is a form to notify them of your change of address.

Remember groups such as employers, schools, churches, and clubs that may have your address but rarely mail you anything. This is especially important with former employers, as they often have to mail you tax forms at the end of the year.

Consider taking a phone book from the area you are leaving. It may come in handy if you have to call friends, doctors, businesses, or utility companies. No matter how much you try to plan ahead, you will probably still have to make a phone call or two to resolve something you forgot to take care of before moving.

Moving Options

For most people moving away from home for the first time, the physical move is no big deal. You will probably have only a few boxes of possessions and perhaps just one or two large pieces of furniture. If you are moving only a short distance, you can probably get by with borrowing a van or a truck from a friend or family member. Ask a couple of friends to help move the larger pieces, and then make several runs until all the big stuff is moved. This is the kind of move that can probably be done in a day or so. Once the larger pieces are moved, you can move the rest in the car. Move the more important items first. When moving short distances, many people take several weeks getting totally moved, picking up less urgent items on weekends or on the way home after work.

If you have accumulated a lot of stuff or if you are moving a long distance, it will be better to move everything in one shot. Your best bet is to rent a large truck or trailer large enough to hold all your furnishings. This will not be cheap, but it will be cheaper than using a professional moving company or making multiple trips over long distances. Compare the prices of several rental companies. Some companies charge a flat daily fee, with an additional charge for each mile driven. Others may charge you a penalty if you don't return the truck to the same location where it was rented. Make sure you understand all the charges before agreeing to a rental.

On moving day, get as many friends and family members as possible to help load the truck. The more people you have, the faster the loading will go, and the sooner you can be on the road. When you pick up the truck, inspect the tires and the brakes to make sure everything is in good running order. When loading the truck, try to keep in mind the unloading process, so that things are loaded in the opposite order from the way you would like to unload them. Although it is not always possible, try to load the smaller items first, and then the larger items. This will allow you to place the larger items in your dwelling first and then to fill in with the smaller items that you unload towards the end.

Balance the items in the truck so that the weight is spread evenly across the length and width of the cargo area. Keep in mind that items may shift when you drive around corners, so pack them to be resistant to such movement. Use blankets, sheets, and other padding material to keep furniture from rubbing against other items.

Make sure you express your gratitude to the family and friends who help with the move. Most of these people would refuse your money, but we've never found an amateur mover who doesn't appreciate a slice of pizza, a fresh doughnut, or a cold soft drink. If different sets of friends help on each end of the move, don't forget to reward both groups for their help.

Fewer than 10 percent of those who move use professional movers, but here are some guidelines for those of you who are among that lucky 10 percent. There are few federal or local laws regulating movers, so you must take care to find one that will meet your needs. Check with friends and business associates to get recommendations. Call several different movers and ask for a "binding estimate." Make sure the movers actually come out and survey your goods, not just give you an estimate over the telephone. Inquire about extra charges for packing materials or for moving large or fragile items.

Make sure you understand the moving company's policy regarding damage. No matter how careful the movers are, there are always a few things that get broken, dinged up, or scratched during the move.

Determine the conditions under which the moving company will pay for damage you discover after your move.

Once you have selected the best company for you, check with the local Better Business Bureau (BBB) or the state Consumer Affairs office. These organizations keep track of complaints against businesses, and they can let you know if the company you selected has had problems in the past.

When you have arrived, inspect your goods as soon as possible for damage and report that damage in writing to the moving company. Most companies will ask you to sign a document freeing them from any future obligations for damages. Make sure you don't sign this until you have inspected your goods and identified any damage that occurred during the move.

Some moving expenses can be deducted from your income tax, so you will save money on taxes if you keep track of your expenses. Keep all receipts, invoices, related to your move. This is especially important for expensive moves.

Once You've Arrived

Reaching your destination, unfortunately, is not the end of your move. You've still got to unpack, organize, and clean—all without losing your sanity. If you find yourself becoming tired and frustrated as you try to settle into your new home and neighborhood, kick off your shoes, make yourself a cold drink, sit down on your coziest packing box, and take a break. Unpacking isn't something that has to be done the first day.

But before you get too comfortable, consider a few things you'll need to arrange now that you are a new resident in this dwelling and community. Some of these things are urgent, while some can wait until you are settled in.

Insurance. If you are buying a house, the mortgage company will require you to buy homeowner's insurance. Renters may or may not be required to buy renter's insurance, depending on the rental agreement. Even if you are not required to purchase insurance, you might consider it if you own anything of value. Renter's insurance is usually quite reasonably priced, and it will replace your goods if they are stolen or destroyed. If you had insurance in your previous dwelling, be sure to contact your insurance agent to get the insurance transferred to your new property.

Change locks. If your new residence had a former occupant, there is a possibility that spare keys are still in the possession of that former occupant—or the occupant's friends. If you are worried about your security, contact a locksmith and have the locks changed.

Motor vehicles. If you moved from another state, contact the Department of Motor Vehicles (DMV) and determine what you must do to register your car and get a new driver's license. Many states provide this information on the Internet.

Voting. Check with the local board of elections to see what you must do to get registered to vote in your new neighborhood.

Know the neighborhood. Use local maps and tourist guides to find the area parks, schools, libraries, and shopping centers, as well as nearest hospital, fire station, and police station. Keep copies of these maps at home and in the car until you become familiar with the area.

Travel around the neighborhood looking for merchants that sell groceries, tools, furniture, and other things you will need to buy. Also look for service establishments such as banks, cleaners, movie theaters, gas stations, post offices, and restaurants. You will probably also want to locate a doctor and a dentist, and establish yourself as a new patient.

I'm Still Clueless

? *Can I request that my school find me a roommate with certain attributes?*

Although schools consider some attributes such as gender and smoking preference, they usually don't have the time or the inclination to find a roommate that is up to your lofty standards. For one thing, it's against the law to ask questions about such things as race and religion. Also, the school usually has enough to do without finding a roommate that matches your specifications.

Part of the reason for going away to school is to learn new things. This is not just learning about things such as math and science, but also learning about other people and other cultures. Unless your roommate has homicidal tendencies, it will probably not kill you to live for a short time with that person. You might even learn something in the process.

? *Do you think my dog will adapt to living in my small apartment?*

Your dog's tender psyche may be the least of your worries. Most apartments have severe restrictions on pets, and many will not allow dogs at all. Usually, contained pets such as tropical fish will not be a problem, and apartments often allow cats. But many apartments will not allow dogs, and those that do tend to fill up quickly because of the demand. Look for apartment advertisements that say pets are allowed, or at least do not say that pets are prohibited. Even when you find such a place, make sure you understand the restrictions before signing the rental agreement. Many landlords will require you to pay an additional pet deposit that can be as much as one month's additional rent.

An exception to the "no pets" rule is if you own a guide dog or another type of dog required for medical reasons. The law specifies that you cannot be denied housing if you can prove the medical need for such animals.

Even if you meet the requirements for keeping a pet, your responsibility does not end there. You need to clean up after your pet, and make sure it does not disturb the other tenants. And yes, there's a possibility that your dog may not adjust to apartment living, especially if he used to live in your backyard. If you take a dog into a new environment, it's your responsibility to keep the dog happy. If you don't have the time, it may be best to leave the dog home.

? *What if I have no furniture but can only afford an unfurnished apartment?*

One option is to throw yourself on the mercy of friends and family, asking that they loan you some spare furniture until you can afford your own. Then, as you buy each new piece of furniture, you can return the borrowed stuff to its original owners.

Another option is to visit thrift stores or look for yard sales and used furniture advertised in the classified sections of the daily newspaper. This won't be the sort of furniture you see in *Architectural Digest,* but you can get it for a bargain price, and it will do until you can afford new stuff.

Some larger cities have furniture rental companies that will rent you the furniture you need for a monthly rental charge. Before doing this, investigate the quality of the furniture, the cost, and the minimum rental time required.

If all else fails, you can live in an unfurnished apartment until you can afford to buy furniture. You can sleep on the floor on pillows or a sleeping bag until you can afford a bed. Then decide what you need next, and start saving your money for that item.

? *Why didn't I get all my security deposit back when I moved?*

Landlords will keep all or part of your security deposit if you left something damaged, or if you didn't clean the rental appropriately. The earlier section on landlord disputes gives some suggestions for getting your deposit back.

But before you waste a lot of time and money, honestly ask yourself if you did meet the requirements to get the deposit back. A friend of ours who does property management can tell you horror stories about how people will destroy a rental and then splash a little paint around and expect to get a full security deposit back.

When you have finished cleaning prior to your move, ask yourself two questions: Am I leaving the place in equal or better condition compared to the way I found it? If I were the incoming tenant, would I be satisfied with this cleaning job? If you can't honestly answer those questions in the affirmative, it's time to get out the soap, water, and paint and give it one more try.

CHAPTER 2

Life after Pizza and Fast Food

One of the first things most people realize when they leave home for the first time is that they no longer have to eat what Mom puts on the table for dinner. One of the next things people realize when they leave home for the first time is that they no longer *get* to eat what Mom puts on the table for dinner.

As you'll soon learn, being on your own at mealtime is a mixed blessing. The temptation to have pizza for every meal is a strong one, and we recommend you succumb to this temptation. Eat exactly what you want to eat—for about a week. Then, after the euphoria has worn off, sit down and decide whether you can afford to spend at least five dollars per meal, week in and week out, for the rest of your life. If you ate only two meals a day and never touched a snack, eating fast food would cost you roughly $310 per month. And that's if you always ate from the bottom of the menu. Can you afford that much?

Equally important is to ask yourself how long your body will let you get away with eating a hundred to two hundred grams of fat a day, day in and day out, for the rest of your life. You may not gain weight during that trial week, or even during the first month, but sooner or later you *will* gain weight. Your health will suffer in other ways, too. Your blood will have the consistency of applesauce, and your heart will have to work overtime to push it through your corpulent frame.

Right now you're young. You probably have your looks and your health. (If you don't have your looks by now, forget about it. It's all downhill from here.) But trust us, your looks and your health are going to fade all too fast, and they'll fade years earlier if you don't take care of your body.

But your desire to remain lithe and lovely isn't the only reason to learn your way around the kitchen. You're at the age, or will soon be at the age, where you'll be looking for someone with whom to share your life. Just as important is that you are at the age where people are looking at you and evaluating you to see if you measure up. Whether you're male or female, being able to put dinner on the table is going to make you more attractive to the people you date. The way to a man's heart really is through his stomach, and one way to a woman's heart is to be a man who isn't afraid of a spatula or a dishrag.

Fortunately for most of us, it's easy to fake people out about one's culinary expertise. As long as you know some of the basics, you can fool people into thinking you know a lot more than you do. And it's not just trickery—once you learn the basics, you'll pick up the intermediate stuff without even thinking about it.

If you were lucky, you had a mother who made you help her in the kitchen. You helped clean up after dinner, and sometimes you even helped her put a meal together. But for the sake of this book, we're going to assume that besides peanut butter and jelly sandwiches and cold cereal the only food you've consumed at home was food prepared by someone else. Don't worry, because you're about to have the grand tour. We're going to tell you how to use the major kitchen appliances and let you know which tools you'll need to have in your own kitchen inventory. In fact, by the time we get finished with you, you're not only going to be able to impress people with your cooking talents, but you're going to have a lot of fun doing it, too.

The Tour de Kitchen

You're probably thinking, "This is dumb. I've been in a kitchen millions of times. Why would I need a tour of the kitchen?" But in the past, you've been only a *user* of the kitchen. As long as the cabinets were full of

clean plates and the refrigerator was full of food, you were
happy. But now you are the
owner of a kitchen, and you
will control how it is arranged
and what items it will contain. The kitchen is a place
where you will be spending a
certain amount of time each
day, and you will want the
kitchen to be a place that will
be designed and equipped to
meet your needs.

Every kitchen is as
unique as is its owner. We
have appliances and tools in our kitchen that you would never use and
that would just be a waste of your money and kitchen space. And you
probably can't afford a kitchen that would rival the one you left at home.
Start with the basics and acquire kitchen equipment as you find a need
for it. This section should at least give you some ideas as to the types of
items you might want to consider acquiring for your kitchen. The average
person would never go out and buy all these items, unless he had an
unlimited budget and a kitchen the size of a football stadium.

Major Appliances

We'll start with those appliances that are common enough to be
found in just about any kitchen. Some of these, such as the microwave
and garbage disposal, were once considered luxury appliances. But they
are now inexpensive enough to be found in the majority of kitchens. You
can certainly survive without some of these appliances, but we're betting
you'd miss them, especially if you used them in a previous life.

▶ The Refrigerator

Your tour starts at the refrigerator, because it's the appliance you've
probably used most often before. Throughout your life, your experience
with the refrigerator has probably been limited to taking things out of it.
Now that you're on your own, you're also responsible for putting things
into it—and for keeping those things fresh until you eat them. It's not as

easy as it seems. A refrigerator (including that handy freezer compart-ment) is only designed to be a temporary stopping place for foods. Other than such condiments as mayonnaise, salad dressing, peanut butter, and jelly, you shouldn't count on food in your refrigerator lasting much longer than a week. Food in the freezer will be good for about a month.

The typical refrigerator has a door where items can be stored. This isn't just for looks. The temperature in those refrigerator doors is con-siderably warmer than the temperature in the body of the refrigerator. That means the refrigerator door is best for keeping condiments or soft drinks or butter or bottled water. Even if a refrigerator door is wide enough for a carton of milk, or if there are nifty little holes where you can put your individual eggs, you're probably better off putting that milk or those eggs in the body of the refrigerator. They will keep longer there.

The temperatures are also different for the vegetable crisper and the meat compartment. Other than the freezer, the meat compartment should be the coldest place in the refrigerator. The vegetable crisper should be almost as cold but more humid. (Humidity is good for fruits and vegetables.)

There are several unsavory things that can happen to food after you put it in the refrigerator. Some things such as meat or cheese can be damaged by air, so they should be properly closed up or wrapped to keep the air away from them. Those handy plastic zipper bags are helpful for keeping air away from your food, but be sure to squeeze out the air as you seal the bag.

Also, smells can move from one food to another. If you've got a dish of leftover salmon sitting on your refrigerator shelf, you may find out that you have chocolate pudding that tastes like fish. Unless you happen to like such effects of odor migration, items that were sealed when you bought them at the supermarket should be kept sealed. Also, be sure all pungent leftovers are covered with plastic wrap or are stored in a sealed plastic bag. The top that comes on your milk bottle isn't there just for decoration; it's there to keep the milk tasting like milk as long as pos-sible. An open box of baking soda in your refrigerator will absorb some refrigerator odors if you remember to change the box every month or so.

Even if your groceries are properly wrapped, time is the worst enemy of the food in your refrigerator. Even under the best of circumstances, raw meat won't keep for more than a few days. When you buy meat there should be an expiration date on the package. If you can't cook your meat by the expiration date, keep it in the freezer until you can cook it. Just don't forget about it; if it stays in the freezer too long it will get "freezer burn," which is just as bad.

While we're talking about expiration dates, here's something you may not know. Expiration dates are guidelines, not law. People who package food can estimate how long the food will last before rotting, but they have no idea what conditions that food will be kept in after it has been packaged. If the temperature in your refrigerator is too warm, milk could turn sour days before the expiration date. Conversely, meat can be good several days after the expiration date—depending on the care that was taken in the grocery store and after you took the meat home. And foods such as yogurt or eggs could keep for months beyond the expiration date. So don't use the date written on the top of the package as your sole guide to a product's freshness. But if the date has expired, give your food a good inspection before sinking your teeth into it.

It's easy to know if a product has gone bad. When Kathy was in college, she took a class in sanitation and public health. She spent a whole lot of tuition money to learn something that will help you every time you open the refrigerator. Here is that vital piece of advice: "If it smells like it's dead, don't eat it."

That's an easy piece of advice to remember. Every time you crack an egg or open a package of meat or unwrap a package of leftovers or open a bottle of milk, do the sniff test. If the food you're smelling smells bad, throw it away. If you do that, you'll catch most of the germs that can contaminate your food.

Another way to tell if meat is going bad is to feel it. If uncooked meat or deli meat feels slimy, it's probably at the point where you should throw it out. And it's a good idea to wash that sliminess from your hands with an antibacterial soap.

Fruits and vegetables are easy to judge. You'll be able to tell they're bad just by looking at them. Nobody—not even a novice like you—would be tempted to eat rotten lettuce. But if a fruit or vegetable starts to go bad on you, you can usually cut out the bad part and eat the rest without any real deterioration in quality.

Although it's easy to see when fruits and vegetables have gone bad, it's not so easy to detect when they're past their prime. From the moment a fruit or vegetable is picked or harvested, it starts to deteriorate. For instance, corn loses its sugar over time, so corn that is sweet today may be tasteless tomorrow. When buying fruits and vegetables, purchase only as many as you think you'll need during the coming week. You'll soon learn which items can be stored longer in your refrigerator, and which will barely last until your next shopping expedition.

Cheese is another product that may be salvageable even if it looks bad. Cheese is susceptible to mold, but in almost all cases the mold can be cut off without any loss of quality in the rest of the cheese. This is because mold exists only where there is air; it doesn't permeate down below to the rest of the food. Thus you can scrape mold off cheese or yogurt without worrying about the food underneath. The only exception to this is cheddar cheese. If you get mold on your cheddar, cut it off and then smell the cheese. If the cheese still smells like cheddar, it's okay. But more often than not it will have a strong, odd odor. That means the whole brick of cheese should be thrown out. Next time use the cheese before it goes south on you.

Now that you're living on your own, you're responsible for making sure your food stays edible. Researchers have estimated that as much as 40 percent of the food that Americans buy ends up in the garbage can. That means that if you're like everyone else, every time you have $100 to spend on food, you might as well spend $60 on food and throw the other $40 away. One way to prevent food from spoiling is to keep your refrigerator fairly empty so that you can see what's inside. That way, items won't get lost and die. Another way is to keep the temperature of your refrigerator correctly regulated. If you notice food items going bad before their time, try lowering the temperature by adjusting the dial inside your refrigerator. If you start seeing ice crystals in your lettuce, raise the temperature just a little. This isn't brain surgery, but it's something you may not think of doing if this is the first time you've ever been on your own.

The freezer compartment is probably responsible for more wastage than any other part of the refrigerator. Because things in the freezer are out of sight, you may tend to forget them until they aren't good anymore. Don't overpack your freezer or things are even more likely to get lost—to say nothing of the pain they cause when a frozen roast falls out of the freezer and lands on your toe.

To extend the shelf life of food in your freezer, you can put it—package and all—in a zippered freezer bag. Be sure to squeeze all the air out before you zip the bag. This will give added protection against freezer burn. Even if you store food in this way, don't count on it lasting more than a month or two in the freezer compartment of a refrigerator. Just remember that freezers are temporary storage places rather than the food equivalent of the safe deposit box, and you should be fine.

Ice cream has a short life in the freezer once it's opened. It will develop ice crystals, drawing water out of the ice cream so that the remaining ice cream turns into a greasy sludge.

Even ice isn't safe from freezer burn. Ice can easily pick up odors that are lingering in the refrigerator. You may want to keep an open box of baking soda in your freezer as well as in your refrigerator, but it's just as easy to throw out your ice when it starts to pick up an off taste and make a fresh batch of it. Also, watch out for stinky plastic ice trays—they can pick up bad smells and tastes, too.

Putting stuff in your freezer is only half of the process of freezing foods—you've still got to thaw it before you can eat it. The best way to thaw meat is to move what you want to eat for dinner into the refrigerator in the morning. By the time dinner comes around, the meat should be ready to cook. If you forget to thaw meat in the refrigerator, you can thaw it on the counter for a couple of hours or so. Don't leave meat on the counter all day to thaw, though, or the outside may spoil while the inside thaws. This is especially problematic for thick pieces of meat, such as roasts and whole turkeys.

▶ Home on the Range

Our grand tour now takes us to the range. You probably don't call it a range; you probably call it a stove. Your junior high home economics teacher would probably disapprovingly remind you that stoves are devices for burning wood, not food. We're not that picky, but we'll go with range for consistency. Your typical range is composed of two parts—the "cooktop," where you heat pots and pans, and the oven, where you bake potatoes and cook the Thanksgiving turkey.

When we were growing up, the consumer had two choices in a range—gas or electric. Today, there are many other enhancements from which to choose. The chances are next to zero, however, that you will ever see anything extraordinary in your first apartment or dorm kitchen, so we'll stick to the basics. If you can afford to purchase a $20,000 range, you can also afford to read the owner's manual or to hire someone to teach you to use it.

You probably won't be able to choose between gas and electric in your range. But in case you can choose, know that both options have their advantages. For one thing, gas is cheaper than electricity. Also, with gas you know exactly what you're getting. You can see the fire right there, so you know which burner is on and can guess how hot it's going to be.

Baked items cooked with gas usually yield better results than items that are baked in electric ovens. Another plus with gas is that you can cook even if the power goes out. (You use a match to override the electrically operated ignition system.) With electricity, once the power goes out you're not cooking anything.

The big advantage of electric ranges is that they get hotter faster. You can boil a pot of water several minutes faster on an electric cooktop than on a gas one. Electric controls also allow for more precise temperature settings. This is important if you're doing such delicate work as keeping chocolate melted but not burned or keeping gravy hot but not congealed.

A disadvantage of electric ranges is that they are electrical, which means they have circuits that can short out on you, leaving you with burners that work sometimes and don't work at other times. You may have a pot of water on the burner for half an hour before you realize the water isn't boiling, or even warm, for that matter. We speak from experience. Right now our electric range has two burners that work and two that usually don't. Kathy longingly remembers the days when she cooked with gas.

A bigger problem, though, is that it's hard to tell when an electric burner is off. If you forget to turn off the heat and then put something on that burner—or even worse, touch the burner—you're looking for property damage or personal injury. Even after a burner has been turned off, it's unsafe for at least five minutes afterwards because, unlike gas, there's no immediate cooling of the heating element. Electric burners are like loaded guns—treat them with caution, and you should be fine.

Unless you have a self-cleaning oven, your oven probably has two major options. These are *bake* and *broil*. Baking is what you do to biscuits and cookies and cakes. When you cook a piece of meat on the bake setting it's called *roasting,* but it's essentially the same thing. When the oven is set on "bake," the heating elements at the bottom of the oven are activated. When you bake, first arrange the shelves inside the oven so that the food will be roughly at the center of the oven. This allows the heat to circulate evenly around that food that is being cooked. After the shelves are in place, you preheat the oven by turning it to the temperature you want. When the oven reaches the desired temperature, a light goes out. (This takes five to ten minutes.) Because the cooking time on the recipe will depend on the food being in the oven at the proper temperature for the specified amount of time, it's important to preheat the oven when you're baking products such as cakes, breads, and cookies. If you're roasting meats, the whole process is less scientific and preheating is unnecessary.

When baking, you can usually just set the timer and wait until you hear the buzzer, which lets you know your food is finished. However, some ovens tend to cook hotter and others cooler than the temperature dial indicates. If your food is coming out too dark for your tastes, it may be that your oven is cooking too hot. Or maybe your cakes aren't cooking all the way through; your oven may be cooking too cool. A few under- or overcooked meals will let you know if your temperature dial is not accurate. To improve your chances next time, simply add or subtract a few degrees from the recipe's cooking instructions.

The "broil" option is a different ball of wax. Broiling is a way to barbecue thinner cuts of meat indoors. Hamburgers and pork chops lend themselves to broiling. Broiling is also useful for melting cheeses on nachos or quesadillas. When you broil, the top heating element is what gets hot, and the shelves should be arranged so that the item being cooked is about four to six inches from the heating element or the open flame.

The other big difference is that when you broil, you'll leave the oven open just a little so the hot air can escape. Broiling is done at a high heat for a short amount of time, but the heat is supposed to come only from the top. If you leave the oven door shut, the oven will quickly get hot all over and you'll be baking, not broiling. Most oven doors are designed so that they can be kept open a couple of inches for broiling. If your oven door doesn't have such a setting, you can prop it open with a wooden spoon.

With broiling there's no set time so you don't need to set the timer. Simply put, items cooked in the broiler are done when they're done. This means you have to constantly watch the item you're broiling, or you're going to end up with a burned mess.

When you're broiling meat, you should use a *broiling pan*. This pan usually comes with the oven. It may be found in the drawer below the oven. The top part of a broiling pan has handy slots in it so that juices from the meat will drip into the bottom portion of the pan, a solid drip pan for catching the juices. Broiling pans should be thoroughly cleaned after every use. Once you see what a pain in the neck it is to clean a broiling pan, you may be forever cured of your passion for broiled meat. And the broiling pan is the least of the cleaning problems you'll have with broiling. Read on and weep.

Ovens usually come with one of three cleaning options—self clean, continuous clean, and clean-it-yourself clean. Self clean is the best option because when your oven gets dirty you can turn a couple of knobs and let the oven clean itself. Continuous clean ovens allegedly clean themselves every time they are used, but that's a fairy tale. What a continuous clean oven really does is spread the grease around until the oven is uniformly dirty all over. With continuous clean, you can't even use oven cleaners to get rid of the mess. You just have to reconcile yourself to the idea that every time you use your oven, it's going to be just a little bit dirtier than it was before.

If you don't have a self-cleaning oven, hope for one you have to clean yourself. However, you should be warned that cleaning an oven is the most horrible job in a household—even worse than unplugging a toilet. You can make it easier on yourself by noticing every spill that occurs in your oven and immediately pouring a whole lot of salt over it. Once the oven cools down, you can lift off most of the mess with a spatula.

Before you broil that first piece of meat, think twice. Broiling meat spits grease everywhere. Only a masochist would actually broil meat in any oven except a self-cleaning oven. Remember—if you get your oven dirty you'll eventually have to spend hours inhaling the dangerous fumes of oven cleaners just to get the oven clean again. If you have a craving for flame-kissed animal flesh, either cook it on a barbecue grill or go to Burger King.

▶ The Microwave (They Don't Call It "Nuking" for Nothing)

Despite persistent rumors that microwaved food may be unhealthful, microwaves are here to stay. Your new place of residence probably has one, and if it doesn't you can pick up a nice one for less than a hundred dollars.

Microwaves are so convenient that we're not even going to tell you that food tastes better when it's cooked by conventional methods. There are going to be nights when you will be half-dead after school or work. On those occasions, you won't be thinking about the possible long-term health effects of microwaved food or that what you fix would taste marginally better if cooked on stovetop or in an oven. Your only concern will be getting something in your stomach and then crashing. Microwaves are perfect for that scenario.

Microwave ovens have their uses. They're great for thawing frozen food and for softening hard butter. They're terrific for reheating any leftovers you may have sitting in your refrigerator. And nothing beats Orville Redenbacher's white cheddar microwave popcorn—especially if you don't see the label that says how much fat is in it. Additionally, microwaves are much faster than the conventional oven if you're cooking a TV dinner. Use the microwave whenever you want a quick fix. But if you're cooking for company, use the friendly neighborhood range. When you have company you're trying to impress, pull out the metal pots and pans and cook the old-fashioned way.

Microwave ovens have lots of different options and come in lots of different strengths (in wattage). Read the owner's manual that came with your oven. If you don't have the owner's manual, you'll have to find out what your microwave does through trial and error. But don't experiment by putting the cat in the microwave, and just take our word that you do not want to put any sort of metal in it.

▶ The Garbage Disposal

In a fair world, a garbage disposal would do everything it's designed to do. It's designed, of course, to grind up every bit of food you don't want to eat—potato peels, pork chop bones, eggshells, bacon grease, and the science experiment (formerly a casserole) in your refrigerator. But life isn't fair, and garbage disposals are temperamental beasts that quite often don't do what they were designed to do. At this very moment, the authors' household garbage disposal is backed up because Kathy dared to put watermelon rinds in it. If the garbage disposal is backed up, the whole sink is useless until the disposal has been unplugged. This is almost as nasty a job as cleaning an oven and is considerably more difficult.

Common sense probably tells you that garbage disposals would have a hard time grinding up chicken bones, but would be able to handle a carrot peel without any problem whatsoever. Unfortunately, garbage disposals do not think the way we do. Garbage disposals actually "like" small bones and eggshells and other hard things, which sharpen the blades of the garbage disposal. The potato and carrot peels and other vegetable matter cause you the most trouble; they form a paste that prevents water from draining from the disposal. Depending on the quality of your garbage disposal, you'll want to grind these items cautiously or not at all.

The novice garbage disposer should keep the following two rules in mind: Always have the water running when you use the garbage disposal; and if you like your fingers, never reach down into a garbage disposal.

We'll discuss fixing minor garbage disposal problems in chapter 6.

▶ The Dishwasher

Depending on how much you're spending on your new abode, it may come with one dishwasher or two. If you have a cheaper place to live, it probably has two dishwashers—your two hands. We're going to concentrate on the one-dishwasher home—the home with a mechanical dishwasher.

Like all the other appliances in your new home, your mechanical dishwasher was purchased by someone who may or may not have had your interests at heart. More than likely, your dishwasher is a bottom-of-the-line model without many bells or whistles. It may not actually clean your dishes unless you prewash those dishes, which sort of defeats the purpose of a dishwasher.

When you move into your new residence, read the manual that comes with your new dishwasher—if, indeed, such a manual can be found. Even if you do read the manual, though, you'll have to use trial and error to determine exactly how well your dishwasher is going to clean your dishes.

Loading a dishwasher is so easy that a child can do it. There are only two things you must remember—first, that the dishwasher will wash only the surfaces it can reach, and second, that liquid tends to collect in dishes that are left face-up. Therefore, you should make sure things aren't piled too closely together in your dishwasher. Everything should have a little space around it so the water can get between the items and clean all the available surfaces. And you should always put glasses and bowls upside down in the dishwasher so they won't collect water and grime.

Eating utensils are put in baskets that hold small items. Some people say you should group all your forks together, and so on, in order to make a faster job of unloading the dishwasher. Other people say if you stack like utensils together they will "nest," and the water won't get to items that are nested together. Now that you're an adult, you can make your own decision in this important matter. Experiment.

You may find that your dishwasher leaves spots on your glasses and silverware, or even a film over shiny surfaces. If you watch television commercials, you know that spots or film on your glassware show that you are a horrible person. But aside from your inherent goodness or badness, there are several reasons why you may have spots on your glassware or film on your dishes. First, your dishwasher may be dirty. Try running it without any dishes, using a cup of vinegar instead of soap. If that doesn't help, your problems may stem from having hard water. Or you may have an impossibly cheap dishwasher that just doesn't do a good job. If all else fails, there are dish detergents and additives you can use in your dishwasher that may eliminate the problem. Or, unless you're entertaining important dinner guests, you can just live with the spots.

If you substitute liquid dish soap for the powdered stuff, be careful. Liquid dishwashing soap is far more concentrated than soap that is designed for dishwashers, and a little bit is more than enough. Clark learned this in his first apartment with a dishwasher, when he decorated his new kitchen with mountains of suds. He didn't even realize you needed a special kind of soap for dishwashers. But now he knows better, and so do you.

By the way, although it's possible to wash clothes using liquid dish soap, it is not advisable to use washing machine detergent in your dishwasher. Washing machine detergent is highly concentrated and makes vast quantities of suds. If you try using washing machine detergent in your dishwasher, you'll be mopping up bubbles till next Friday.

Furnishing Your Kitchen

Now that we've covered the appliances that will probably come with your kitchen, it's time to consider the pots, pans, plates, household gadgets, and basic foodstuffs that will occupy the drawers and cabinets of your kitchen. These are the things you'll be buying, so read about everything and then just buy what you think you'll use. The kitchens of most homes and apartments have a surprisingly small amount of space devoted to the storage of such items. Kathy has a theory that this is because most houses are designed by men, most of whom have no idea of the number of gadgets even an average cook needs to perform her daily magic. But because there's only a finite amount of storage space, you need to fill that space judiciously.

Optional Appliances

Other than the floors and the cabinets and the major appliances that come with your kitchen, everything else in your kitchen will be chosen by you or by someone who lives with you. This is a big responsibility. As a young person, you're in the acquisition stage of life. But before you buy that first kitchen gadget, realize that everything that sits on your counter will sit there at the expense of workspace you would otherwise have. On top of that, every small appliance has to be dusted and—worse—cleaned. This is one area where you should consider the way your parents have done it, and do just the opposite. Don't buy a blender, or even a toaster, just because you grew up with one in the house. Unless you don't think you'll be able to live without a blender or a toaster, you'll probably be happier without. Even then, don't go out and buy an appliance until you find yourself in need. You may realize that if you don't have one, the need will never present itself.

We can't tell you how to furnish your kitchen, because your kitchen will be *your* kitchen, not ours. We can, however, give you a list of small appliances that may come in handy for single people who are away from home all day and who want to spend as little time as possible cooking dinner or dusting unused appliances. Pick and choose the things that sound good to you.

Blender. There isn't a blender on the market that works as well as blenders are supposed to work. But if you know the limitations of blenders and are in the habit of using them anyway, consider getting one. Blenders are especially handy for mixing fruit drinks. Several of our recipes in chapter 3 call for a blender, although you can often get away with using a hand mixer instead.

Breadmaker. We used our first breadmaker until it fell apart, but subsequent breadmakers have been dustcatchers on the kitchen counter. It takes only three minutes of your time to make a loaf of bread, but you have to keep viable yeast on hand to make the bread, and then you have to slice the bread after you make it. Using a breadmaker is one way people can get fantastic results with a small amount of effort (impress your friends!), and if you use a breadmaker consistently you'll save money over buying store-bought bread. You'll have funny-shaped sandwiches, but if you can live with that, a breadmaker may be a good investment.

Crockpot. This is one thing that may come in extremely handy, but only if you use it. If you're cooking for only one or two, you don't need a big crockpot. Buy a small one if the idea appeals to you. We'll give you easy recipes for the crockpot in chapter 3. Crockpots are never-fail appliances that require little food preparation time. They are the only way you'll be able to walk through the door after a long day at work or church and have dinner hot and waiting for you.

Electric can opener. Manual ones don't clutter up your countertop, and you don't have to use them near an electrical outlet. Unless you open a lot of cans, buy a $2 manual one, and give your wrists a little exercise.

Mixer. This small and inexpensive appliance may come in handy if you like to cook brownies or cakes or if you mash a lot of potatoes or want to whip cream. However, you may be just as happy with the good old wire whisk and the friendly neighborhood potato masher. Depends on how much you plan to use it.

Rice cooker. Here's a handy contraption if you eat rice every day of your life and if your rice of preference is that short-grained Oriental rice that sticks together when you cook it. If you don't eat that much rice, or if the rice you cook runs toward American tastes, it's just as easy to make it in a two-quart saucepan with a lid.

Toaster. If you use a toaster every morning of your life, by all means buy a toaster. Get one with a wide slot if you toast bagels or English muffins. But if you make toast only on rare occasions, consider buttering your bread, putting it on a cookie sheet, and putting it under the broiler for a minute. This is called "oven toast." If you were to sprinkle sugar and cinnamon over the butter before you put the bread in the oven, it would then be called "cinnamon toast." There you are—your first recipes in this book. Don't thank us yet. There will be plenty more where these came from.

Toaster oven. This contraption is like a toaster and broiler combined. Fans of toaster ovens will tell you they use far less electricity than conventional ovens, and they don't get the house as hot in the summer. They're right on both counts. However, toaster ovens get as dirty as both appliances put together. If you just love a toaster oven, don't let us stand in your way. But remember that toaster ovens are hard to clean, they take up counter space, and they perform the same functions as you could get in a regular oven.

Waffle iron. Most waffle irons are exclusively designed for making waffles. If you're an entertainer who wants to have friends over for midnight breakfasts, owning a waffle iron may be on your agenda. Your only other option if you're a waffle-eater is to buy the frozen variety, or cook pancakes instead.

Pots and Pans

▶ Oven Baking Pans

Baking pans come in several standard sizes. There's the "oblong pan," whose dimensions are roughly 9x13 inches. There's a smaller oblong pan, whose dimensions are roughly 7x10 inches. You can get square cake pans and round cake pans. You can also get muffin pans, as well as cookie sheets. Thicker oven-proof bowls and containers are known as "casserole dishes." These come in a variety of shapes.

If you intend to use the kitchen, you'll probably want to start off with one large oblong pan, two square cake pans (square is better than round for the purposes of making brownies), two cookie sheets, and a casserole dish. Buy the other items as you need them.

The big question in purchasing ovenware is to determine what material you want to buy. To the novice cook, nonstick sounds like the ideal way to go, but nonstick pans generally do not perform as advertised—cakes produced in nonstick pans are almost as likely to stick to the bottom as are cakes produced in non-nonstick metal pans. But that's not the only problem. All too quickly, the nonstick finish comes off such pans, leaving the metal to become discolored and to rust.

You can purchase effective (and expensive) nonstick cookware through such vendors as Williams-Sonoma, but there is another alternative. Glass bakeware called "Pyrex" is available in your supermarket or discount store, at the same place where nonstick pans are found. Pyrex is just about the same price as nonstick baking pans, but is pretty near indestructible. Yes, you'll have to grease the pans before you bake cakes or brownies in them. But you'd have to do that with the nonstick cookware, too. And Pyrex cookware will look the same in twenty years as it does when you bring it home from the store, so it's far cheaper than nonstick in the long run. Trust us. We spent twenty-five years replacing nonstick pans over and over again, and have now gone back to Pyrex. Start off with Pyrex, and you'll be glad you did.

The one place where inexpensive nonstick bakeware actually works is in the area of cookie sheets. Cookies really don't stick to nonstick cookie sheets, probably because there are no corners to hold the dough. According to our confirmed bachelor friend, cookie sheets that have a cushion of air between the top and bottom layers of metal are the best of the bunch, because cookies baked on these sheets don't burn. This is a real plus for those of you who want cookies but who are uncertain of your culinary abilities. If you tend to forget about cookies in the oven, you may want to invest a few extra dollars in this handy innovation.

▶ Stovetop Pots and Pans

The pots and pans you use atop your range are more expensive—and harder to buy—than the pans that go inside the oven. There's such a huge variety of cookware available that a little more thought is needed for this sort of purchase.

There are two pans that will account for most of your cooking needs—the one-quart saucepan and the two-quart saucepan. (Cookware sets should always supply two two-quart saucepans and forget about three sizes of frying pans, but no manufacturer has done it yet.) You'll also want one all-purpose frying pan and a larger pot that's called a "Dutch oven." Once you decide to add pastas and soups to your cooking itinerary, it's nice to have a stockpot as well. But if you start off with a one-quart saucepan, a two-quart saucepan, a frying pan, and a Dutch oven, you'll be covered for most of your basic stovetop cooking needs. All these items, with the possible exception of the frying pan, should have lids.

High-quality cookware is made of stainless steel (never aluminum!), which conducts heat in a uniform manner and also holds up to years of rigorous use. Cookware is made with or without nonstick coatings. Nonstick coatings perform well in pots and pans that are used outside the oven, and if you buy a good-quality nonstick pot or pan it should give you years of service. But not all nonstick cookware really is nonstick. Kathy was once given an extremely expensive name-brand frying pan in which she tried to scramble eggs. The eggs never came out of the extremely expensive pan, which had to be thrown away.

Single people are especially vulnerable to the claims of salesmen who tell you to buy an expensive set of cookware that will serve you for the rest of your life. Kathy once squandered the equivalent of about two months' rent on a set of pans because she fell for a salesman's spiel. She never used the cookware and finally donated it to the kitchen of her church. (The purchase may have been worthwhile, though, because she has used the free deluxe food shredder that came with the pans for more than twenty-five years.)

By the way, the new breed of high-end nonstick cookware allegedly allows people to use metal utensils when cooking with it. In fact, Kathy purchased her current set from the good old Home Shopping Club after seeing a demonstration where an orbital sander was used on the finish and the omelet still came out of the pan perfectly. However, unless you're using top-of-the-line stuff—and even if you *are* using top-of-the-line stuff—you'd be wise to use only plastic utensils with your nonstick cookware. No sense in damaging that pan's finish before its time.

Dishes and Glassware

"Paper or plastic?" is an option you're given at the supermarket. But neither should be an option you consider when buying dishes and glassware. Paper is awfully expensive to use on a day-to-day basis. Plastic picks up old food tastes and odors, and the food you eat or drink from it eventually tastes vile. Acrylic (a form of plastic) melts and cracks under the heat of the dishwasher. Glassware should be made from glass. If you want to use jelly glasses, that's fine—but glass is the material of choice. Glass doesn't retain odors or tastes as does plastic. It can be relatively cheap, and glasses made from glass will last longer than plastic glasses if you don't drop them.

Plastic plates also retain old flavors and smells. Another problem with plastic plates is that when you use a knife to cut food on them the knife will cut into the plastic. This makes the plate ugly, and those crevices provide a breeding ground for germs.

You may not want to spring for stoneware (heavy, cumbersome, and easily chipped) or china (expensive) when you're first starting out. Fortunately, there's a compromise. This is Corelle, a glass product that's made by the Corning glass people. Corelle is relatively cheap and relatively indestructible. (If you drop a Corelle plate so it lands on its edge just right, you'll see why we used the word "relatively." When Corelle breaks, it *really* breaks.)

For years, Corelle came in four basic patterns. People got awfully tired of those four patterns, so the designers branched out. Unfortunately, they branched out too far. Corelle patterns no longer stay around long enough for you to be able to replace your broken pieces. You may want to choose the solid white, which never goes out of style. You can always bring color into your table setting through the use of placemats or napkins.

Utensils

→ *Utensils* is a fancy word for *gadgets,* and there are literally thousands of kitchen utensils available for you to consider. Your first trip into a cooking store will boggle your mind. If you're new to the kitchen, here's a scaled down roster for you to use as a shopping list.

By the way, you may want to check out the dollar stores in your area to see if they have any cooking supplies that may save you money when you're outfitting a kitchen. Kathy recently discovered a dollar store with merchandise of such high quality that she stocked the kitchen of our church building for less than twenty dollars.

Can opener. The best ones to get are the ones that have soft handles so you can get a good grip on your cans. Buy one that's dishwasher safe, and throw it into the dishwasher occasionally to kill germs on the opener blade.

Colander (strainer). There are two basic types of colanders: the ones with bodies that are made of wire mesh and the ones with solid metal or plastic bodies that have holes punched in them. The fine wire mesh ones are better because there are more holes to drain the water and also because they allow you to strain smaller items without having those items fall into your sink.

Cooking spoons (slotted and unslotted). If you're using nonstick cookware, by all means spring for plastic cooking spoons. Slotted spoons come in handy when you're trying to serve vegetables without getting a pool of cooking juices on your plate.

Cutting board. "Why use a cutting board when I can just as easily use my kitchen counter?" you ask. Your knife will make tiny cuts in the countertop—cuts where germs will lurk. So, for your health, buy a cutting board. Go for the ones made of tempered glass, since they don't breed germs like wood or plastic boards.

Flatware. Flatware is the accurate name for the stuff you probably call silverware. (Silverware isn't really silverware unless it's made of silver.) Most flatware sets consist of knives, forks, spoons, salad forks, soup spoons, and a couple of serving spoons. Wait to pick out your real flatware until you're more settled—perhaps when you get married. For now, buy a set of flatware in a discount store. Getting sturdy stuff is more important than getting beautiful stuff, so go for the heaviest pattern in your price range.

Knives. Unless you're a gourmet cook, you have no need for gourmet knives. A set of knives can cost hundreds of dollars, and then you have to worry about sharpening them all the time because they get dull so quickly. However, you can get excellent knife sets for about twenty dollars if you look for them. They come in a wooden block, complete with steak knives to round out the set. Best of all, they never need sharpening and they're sufficient for all your cooking needs.

Measuring cups. Start off with a set of plastic measuring cups. The world's best measuring cups are made by Tupperware. They're the only ones we've ever seen whose set includes a two-thirds cup and a three-fourths cup. For real cooking pros, consider getting a two-cup Pyrex (tempered glass) measuring cup for measuring liquids.

Measuring spoons. Cheap and plastic will do the trick.

Mixing bowls (in assorted sizes). It's always handy to have a few large bowls around the house. Although you need only one big one, sometimes the smaller ones come in handy as well. If you're planning to melt things in the microwave, make sure the bowl is plastic or glass. Otherwise, metal is the bowl of choice, because it resists being gouged and it doesn't warp in the dishwasher.

Peeler. Here's an item that's a must for women and a frill for men. If men are going to bother to peel potatoes or carrots, they can just as easily use a knife. So what if they occasionally lop off a digit? *Real* men can easily do without a full complement of fingers. Okay, so we're teasing. Peelers are a must, no matter what your gender.

Pot holders. Pot holders are a necessity. Buy more than you think you need, in case one gets dirty or wet. If you use a wet pot-holder to pick up something hot, the water will turn to steam and will severely burn your hand.

Spatulas. There are two types of spatulas. One of them is also called a "rubber bowl scraper," because it's the rubber implement that is used to get batters out of bowls. The other type of spatula is rigid and can be made of plastic or metal. These are also known as "pancake turners," because you can turn pancakes, hamburgers, and other things that are being cooked. Both types of spatulas are essential to a functional kitchen.

The Top-Ten Lists of Basic Food Supplies

The concept of outfitting a kitchen may be a little intimidating, unless you break it down to the different kitchen areas. There are four general areas in a kitchen—a spice cabinet for items that will provide flavor to your food; an area where you should store baking supplies (if, that is, you intend to bake); a cupboard where general foodstuffs should be kept, and a refrigerator for the perishables.

The following four lists will tell you the top ten items that are found in most household kitchens (as determined by the authors' whims). Read the descriptions and decide which of these things you'll need when you outfit your own cooking area. After you buy these basic needs, you can personalize your cupboards with pickled okra and smoked oysters and the other fineries of life.

▶ The Spice Cabinet

1. **Salt.** Salt is such a basic commodity of life that Roman soldiers used to be paid in salt. In fact, the word "salary" comes from that practice. We need salt in our diets, but most of us get far too much of it. One small way to reduce salt intake is to buy Salt Sense, which is real salt but with a third less sodium. It tastes and cooks just like high-octane salt, and it's found in the spice section of your supermarket.

2. **Seasoning salt.** Beginning cooks are especially dependent on seasoning salt to enliven bland foods. If you don't yet have a favorite, look for Jane's Krazy Mixed-Up Salt in the spice section of your supermarket.

3. **Pepper.** Pepper adds zing to foods and is a component of many recipes. A small amount of cayenne pepper will make even canned soups taste good, and lemon pepper gives food a whole different taste.

4. **Garlic salt/garlic powder/minced garlic.** After salt and pepper, garlic is the most commonly used seasoning. A bachelor friend of ours says that every bachelor's kitchen contains three things: peanut butter, ketchup, and garlic powder. Dehydrated minced garlic and garlic salt are also handy, but the garlic powder is a must.

5. **Parmesan cheese.** Most men love Parmesan cheese. Most of them don't even have to have the fancy stuff; the Kraft grated Parmesan that comes in the green shaker container is the stuff of male fantasies. Clark, who is a typical male, thinks Parmesan should go on everything but desserts. Kathy thought Clark was just being Clark until our ketchup-loving bachelor friend told her that Parmesan cheese is a staple in every kitchen that is run by a man.

6. **Oregano/Basil.** Dried oregano leaves come in handy if you like Italian foods. Add them to spaghetti sauce, shake them on sandwiches or salads, and use them in otherwise bland dishes to add a gourmet touch. A companion to oregano, basil is also an Italian staple. Dried basil leaves also enhance cooked vegetables, which makes them handy around the kitchen.

7. **Vanilla extract.** A flavoring for everything from cakes and cookies and frostings to ice cream and puddings, vanilla belongs on every spice shelf. Don't waste your money on artificial vanilla; buy the real thing.

8. **Cinnamon.** This favorite spice is great for making cinnamon toast, and it also tastes wonderful in cocoa and other treats.

9. **Onion soup mix.** This old standby from Lipton can turn you into a gourmet cook. All you need is a crockpot. Put your slab of beef in the crockpot, pour an envelope of onion soup mix on top, add about a half cup of water, and cook on high until the meat falls apart. This is no-fail cooking.

10. **Vinegar.** Every spice cabinet should have vinegar in it, although we're not exactly sure why. Vinegar can sit unloved in your cabinet for five years, but when you need it, you're really going to need it. Also, that bottle of vinegar will tell the people who open your cabinets that you're a person who knows what to do in a kitchen.

▶ **Baking Needs**

Here's a no-brainer for you: You'll use baking ingredients only if you do any baking. If you're not planning on doing any baking, don't buy any of this stuff except, perhaps, a small container of sugar. Most baking supplies have no conceivable purpose except to be used for baking.

1. **Sugar.** Although Americans eat so much sugar that it's among our most often consumed foodstuffs, you're not going to use a whole lot of sugar in your kitchen unless you do a lot of baking or eat cold cereal by the ton. Try buying a two-pound bag of sugar for starters. If sugar goes hard it doesn't have to be thrown away. You can use a grater to turn it into granules again, and it'll be as good as new.

2. **Powdered sugar.** It's used only when making frosting or candies, but when you need it, you need it. Purchase it in a plastic bag instead of in a box, so you don't have to deal with the pesky waxed paper liner.

3. **Brown sugar.** Brown sugar tends to get hard, just like granulated sugar. Because brown sugar is moister than granulated sugar, it turns into a regular brick when it gets hard. We've heard that the brown sugar will soften right up if you put it in a zipper bag with a slice of apple. But if you need brown sugar now, it might be faster to get out of your pajamas and go to the store . . . or forgo the cookies altogether. Brown sugar will stay soft longer if you buy it in plastic bags and keep it in zipper bags after it's open. Be sure to squeeze the air out of the bag as you reseal it.

4. **Chocolate chips.** A house feels like a home if it has chocolate chips in the cupboard. Men are especially fond of chocolate chips, as Kathy discovered when she saw Clark adding them to a tuna noodle casserole.

Sneaky Secret

Whenever you bring flour or other grains such as cornmeal into the house, watch out for hitchhikers. Meal products are often infested by meal moths or by weevils. Put the whole new bag of flour in the freezer for several days to kill any larvae that may be present. If you don't have room in your freezer for this preventative maneuver, put the flour or other meal product into a large plastic zipper bag. Keep that zipper firmly shut unless you're actually using the meal in question. This way, you'll be able to see if anything hatches out of your flour. If it does, throw the entire bag in the garbage (still zipped!) and replace it with a new container of flour.

5. **Raisins.** If you like raisins, go all out. Experiment with golden raisins or dried cranberries. (Dried cranberries are a spectacular addition to salads, as well as to cookies.) But if you don't like raisins, you don't have to put them in your cupboard. There aren't any raisin police waiting to put you in jail

6. **Flour.** Flour is used to thicken gravies and stews and for baking and other purposes. Unless you're doing a lot of baking, you shouldn't buy large quantities of flour. The two-pound sack should suffice, at least until you determine if you'll need to buy it in larger quantities. If you use whole wheat flour, keep in mind that it goes rancid very fast. Buy it in small quantities and store it in the refrigerator.

7. **Baking powder.** There is but one use for baking powder, and that's to make cakes and cookies and "quick breads" rise. (Quick breads are breads that are made without yeast.) If you aren't baking, you don't need baking powder in your kitchen. If you do use baking powder, watch out for the expiration date. Baking powder may be good beyond the expiration date—or it may not.

8. **Baking soda.** Baking soda is quite similar to baking powder, and in fact the two are often used together. However, baking soda can also be used as a toothpaste (or, more accurately, tooth *powder*). As stated earlier, its odor-absorbing qualities also make it a good candidate for use in a refrigerator or freezer (just place an open box in your refrigerator or freezer, and it should absorb odors for about two months).

9. **Cocoa.** Used in cakes, frostings, fudge, and old-fashioned hot chocolate, cocoa is one of those ingredients for which there's just no

substitute. If you need it, nothing else will do. Buy it if you think you'll need it.

10. **Yeast**—Unless you plan to make some sort of baked product that requires yeast, you'll have no need for it. If you do use yeast, buy it in small quantities and keep it in the freezer. Yeast loses its oomph so quickly that quite often it doesn't even last until the expiration date. You're much safer if you freeze it. Just remember that yeast must be used at room temperature or it won't work. Let it sit on the counter for a half hour or so before you use it in a recipe.

> **Sneaky Secret**
> After you've finished using a box of baking soda in the refrigerator or freezer, or if the baking soda you have in your cupboard passes its expiration date, dump it in the kitchen sink and flush it down the plumbing with water. This will help clean your pipes and keep them from clogging.

▶ Cupboard Fillers

When you first open those kitchen cupboards, they're going to look awfully big and awfully bare. But you're not just facing empty space; you're looking an opportunity right in the nose. All during your growing-up years, your kitchen cupboards were stocked by somebody other than you. Canned asparagus or hominy grits or other noxious foodstuffs took the place of the real food you wanted to eat—gourmet stuff such as Fritos and Vienna Sausage and Ding-Dongs.

Now that you're on your own, you can set things right. If you want an entire cupboard full of Oreos and Spam, it's up to you. But if you'd like to live past the age of twenty-one, we've got some suggestions for things you might want to put in your cupboards in the space that isn't occupied by junk food. Here's our top ten list.

1. **Bread.** If you don't eat bread fast, it's going to mildew. This is especially true when the weather is hot. You can slow down the process by storing your bread in the refrigerator, but bread quickly goes stale when it's refrigerated. If you

> **Sneaky Secret**
> If you have an unsliced loaf of bread that has gotten hard, put it on a cookie sheet with a very wet (but not dripping) paper towel over it. Bake it at 350° F. for ten minutes, and it should be good as new.

have a major problem with bread rotting before you eat it, keep part of the loaf in a zipper bag for you to eat now and freeze—not refrigerate—the rest. Bread freezes better than it refrigerates, especially if you force as much air out of the package as you can before you freeze it.

2. **Canned soup, chili, stew.** When you're hungry but too tired to cook, nothing beats a hearty can of chili, stew, or soup. If you haven't tried canned soups lately, you're in for a pleasant surprise—especially if you try some of the new brands. Branch out and see what goodies are in store and then doctor 'em up with seasoning salt or cayenne pepper or that garlic powder you have on hand. Although experienced cooks cringe when they think of using cream of mushroom soup as part of a gravy or casserole, it's a lifesaver for novices. There are plenty of recipes featuring cream of mushroom soup in chapter 3.

3. **Tuna.** Canned tuna is a mainstay of American cuisine. There are a couple of reasons for this. First, everyone knows that fish is good for you—but a lot of Americans don't like fish. Tuna is the compromise that mothers across America discover early in their mothering careers. A nice tuna salad sandwich meets the fish requirement, without the drawback of fins, bones, and scales. Second, tuna is dirt cheap. Tuna is the cheapest hit of protein that money can buy, with the possible exception of peanut butter.

   Tuna is packed in water or oil, either of which will have to be drained off before you do anything with the meat. Both varieties taste pretty much the same, so health-conscious people usually choose water-packed tuna. White albacore is the best tuna that comes in cans, and solid white albacore is the best of that.

4. **Jell-O.** The commercials say there's always room for Jell-O. Personally, we tend to doubt it. But if you grew up in some neighborhoods in the Intermountain West, chances are pretty good that Jell-O is a main staple of your diet. If Jell-O melts your butter, by all means stock your cupboards with it. It's cheap, it's filling, and every friend you have will be eager to share a great Jell-O recipe with you. Just don't invite us to share your dinner.

5. **Vegetable oil.** Even if you don't do a lot of frying, vegetable oil is something you always want to have on hand. It's used in a lot of recipes, and it's handy to have available for greasing cake pans.

(Yes, even so-called nonstick cake pans need to be greased before using.) Your parents grew up with corn oil, but in this sophisticated age there are many varieties available. The healthiest of the bunch is olive oil, but olive oil has a taste you may not like. (Get the lightest, highest-quality extra-virgin olive oil you can find; the lighter the color, the less taste it has to it.) If you want to be healthy, but not to the extent of having to use olive oil in your cooking, the next best oil you can use is canola oil. Canola oil is available even in your grocer's generic brand, and it doesn't have to be refrigerated. It doesn't have a taste to it, and unlike peanut oil, it will not kill your friends who have allergies to peanuts.

If you haven't used your open bottle of oil in a long time, smell it. If it has a funny odor to it, it's probably rancid. Rancid oil won't kill you, but it doesn't taste good. Next time buy a smaller bottle or keep your oil in the refrigerator.

6. **Baked beans (and other side dishes).** Man does not live by steak alone. There should be something else on the plate, if only to give your tongue some variety. Baked beans are a terrific staple item. These days, canned baked beans are just about as good as the baked beans Mom used to make. There are also great rice dishes that are available and that can be whipped up in twenty minutes or less.

Canned vegetables, particularly canned corn, come in handy if you forgot to buy fresh or frozen at the supermarket. And canned fruits make good side dishes as well, if you make sure to keep a can in the refrigerator so a cold one is always on hand.

7. **Oatmeal or cold cereal.** For stick-to-your-ribs goodness, nothing beats an oatmeal breakfast in the winter. Many people prefer cold cereals, however. Take care when eating cold cereals because the recommended size serving wouldn't feed a sparrow. Cold cereals are extremely high in calories, and you may stop eating them after you realize exactly how many "servings" you're eating every morning for breakfast.

8. **Cookies, crackers.** Cookies and crackers are great comfort foods. If you're sick, it's always good to have soda crackers on hand. If you're hungry but don't want a full meal, a handful of gingersnaps is a whole lot fewer calories than a couple of candy bars. Just remember that neither cookies nor crackers stay fresh

very long after they're put on the grocery shelves. Don't buy more cookies or crackers than you plan to eat in a month or so.

9. **Aloe vera gel.** Back when your parents were kiddies, their parents used to torture them by putting butter on burns. Grandma and Grandpa didn't realize that putting butter on a burn was the worst possible thing they could do for a burn, sealing in the heat and greatly increasing the damage that was done to the skin and the flesh underneath the skin.

Fortunately, we live in a more enlightened age. If you *immediately* put pure aloe vera gel on a burn, the burn will heal far more quickly than it otherwise would. Depending on the severity of the burn, one application may do it—or you may have to apply aloe vera as needed for several hours.

Do not confuse pure aloe vera gel with the numerous lotions and creams that contain aloe vera. It's found in the first aid section of your supermarket, and the label should read "100 percent aloe vera."

When using aloe vera, speed is of the essence. Make sure you always keep your aloe vera in the same place, so you can find it at a moment's notice.

10. **Small fire extinguisher.** If you're a novice cook, you probably have no idea how quickly a small kitchen incident can turn into a crisis. You may casually leave a pot-holder on an electric burner, forgetting that you left the burner on. Oil can boil over and cause a fire in the drip pan of your range. A grease spatter can ignite and wreak havoc in your kitchen.

Even if you don't have a fire extinguisher, you'll probably survive the conflagration. You can grab salt and pour it on the fire. Baking soda may do the same trick. But small fire extinguishers are available for around ten dollars, and they're designed to put out small fires like nobody's business. If you want the extra peace of mind a small fire extinguisher can give you, invest in one and keep it handy. You may never use it. Then again, it may save your life.

▶ Refrigerator Essentials

You're already expecting to fill your refrigerator with ice cream and soft drinks and other delectable treats. You may even have gone far enough to think that such frills as lettuce and tomatoes, fruits and sandwich meats may be good items to add to your inventory. But if you're looking for the top ten staples to keep on hand in your refrigerator, you can't go wrong if you consider the items on the following list:

1. **Cheese.** Cheese used to come only in slices or blocks. These days you can also get it shredded. Shredded cheese is extremely convenient to use, but it mildews quickly. Mildew can be cut away from blocks of cheese with the possible exception of cheddar. (If mildewed cheddar doesn't pass the sniff test, the whole block has to be thrown away.) But if you have shredded cheese that gets mildewed, you pretty much have to throw away the whole package. Decide whether convenience or longevity is more important, and choose your cheese that way.

2. **Milk.** Most people go for the lowest-fat stuff they can stand— starting out with whole milk, and then going down to 2 percent milk, before ending up at 1 percent or skim. These days, we know that it's great to cut down on fat wherever we can. However, there are two drawbacks to using extremely low-fat milk. First, skim milk loses most of its nutrients along with the fat; people in the dairy industry call it "blue milk." The second drawback is that the fat in milk keeps milk fresh longer. If you don't drink a lot of milk, you're going to be throwing out rotten milk a lot more often if it's 1 percent than you will if it's whole.

3. **Butter.** If you use health factors to decide between butter and margarine, your head will soon start spinning. In their infinite wisdom, the supposed experts on this sort of thing keep flip-flopping over whether it's better to use butter, which is all natural, or chemical-laden margarine, which is lower in saturated fats. You can't decide on the basis of calories, because butter and margarine are the same in terms of calories—both are equally bad. When deciding between butter and margarine, follow your taste buds. The only rule here is that if you're going to use butter or margarine in cooking, buy it in stick form rather than in the tub. Butter and margarine that's found in a tub has water whipped into it, and this wreaks havoc with recipes.

4. **Eggs.** When buying eggs in the store, check inside the carton to make sure none of the eggs is cracked. Then take them home and keep them in the carton in your refrigerator. Some people wash eggs before putting them in the refrigerator, probably because

they're remembering where eggs come from. Do not wash them; washing them gets rid of oils that protect the eggs in their shells. Eggs keep for a long time after the expiration date on the label. But just to be sure, never crack an egg into a bowl that has other ingredients in it. Crack it into a cup, sniff it, and if it doesn't stink you can throw it in with the rest of the ingredients.

5. **Peanut butter.** Believe it or not, a lot of people don't put peanut butter on their shopping lists. Peanut butter is notorious for being contaminated with aflatoxin, which causes cancer. (If you ever see a dusty black mildew on the shell of a peanut, it's probably aflatoxin.) Additionally, most peanut butter is "enhanced" with vegetable oil and with corn syrup to make it spread more smoothly and taste better. So, as you might guess, peanut butter is a major calorie-fest. If you want to eat peanut butter anyway, fine. Just be aware that it's not a high-quality foodstuff.

6. **Jam or jelly.** If you've got peanut butter in the house, you've got to have jelly. There are three major kinds of fruit spreads, by the way. Jelly is made by cooking the fruit and straining out the solids. Jam is made by squashing the fruit and cooking it. Preserves are made by cooking the fruit without squashing it first, trying to keep it as intact as possible. Jams and preserves have roughly the same consistency. Most jams and jellies do not need to be refrigerated until opened.

7. **Mayonnaise.** Stuff that looks like mayonnaise isn't necessarily mayonnaise. Mayonnaise is not sweet. The sweet spread that looks like mayonnaise is called "salad dressing." The most popular salad dressing is Miracle Whip. If you know what Miracle Whip tastes like, you know what salad dressing tastes like. Whether you prefer mayonnaise or salad dressing depends entirely on what you ate while growing up. By the way, both mayonnaise and salad dressing are about a hundred calories per tablespoon. If you can train yourself to eat sandwiches with only mustard, you'll be saving yourself a lot of hidden fat.

8. **Mustard.** You probably grew up on good old yellow mustard, but as you start shopping for yourself you're going to see that mustard comes in a cornucopia of varieties—from horseradish mustard to apricot mustard. Experiment. Some of those mustards taste terrific. If you decide you don't like the variety mustards,

you're allowed to go back to the yellow mustard you know and love. There's no particular stigma associated with eating yellow mustard as an adult.

9. **Ketchup.** Children and many men put ketchup on everything except ice cream. It's red, it's sweet, and—above all—it's familiar. But by the time you reach adulthood, if you still have a craving for ketchup you may want to keep that craving in the closet. If you slather your food with ketchup, the person who cooked for you will rightfully feel at least slightly offended, and the date you're trying to impress may wonder what *other* delightful surprises are hiding up your sleeve.

10. **Salad dressing.** We've already covered the salad dressing that looks like mayonnaise. The salad dressing you know and love—the stuff that goes over lettuce—is found in a bottle. If you're a salad-eater, you'll probably want to keep some salad dressing in your refrigerator. Some salad dressings (notably Italian and other oil-based dressings) are also good marinades for meat you want to throw on the grill.

Basic Cooking Terms

We can't give you a cooking course in the pages of this book. But if you familiarize yourself with these cooking terms, you'll be able to follow most recipes without having Julia Child in your kitchen. If you don't know a term used in a recipe, look it up here.

Baste—To pour melted fat or cooking juices over food as it cooks, using a brush or a spoon or even a squeeze bottle. Basting prevents foods from drying out and adds color and flavor.

Blanch—To plunge raw fruits or vegetables briefly in boiling water. Blanching will partially cook the food, but the cooking process is so brief that color and texture are preserved. One use for blanching is to remove the skin from tomatoes. If you blanch the tomato for about ten seconds and then remove it from the water, the skin should easily slip off.

Blend—To combine ingredients in a recipe. This can be done with a blender, with beaters, or with a fork or spoon. Blending is different from mixing in that, when blending, all you have to do is combine the ingredients so there are no pockets of flour and so the eggs are some-what evenly dispersed throughout. When you mix something, there's a little more enthusiasm involved.

Boil—To heat liquid until it bubbles. This is 212° F. at sea level, but you're not going to be tested on that. Another definition of boiling is to cook food in a liquid that is boiling. Thus, one boils an egg.

Bone—To remove bones from animal flesh. It's easier to do this after the food is cooked because cooked flesh doesn't adhere to the bones the way raw meat does. However, boning is more often than not done in preparation for cooking.

Braise—To cook food (usually meat) by heating it in a small amount of liquid in a tightly covered container for a long amount of time. This is usually done at low heat. Food that is cooked in a crockpot could be said to be braised, because meat fibers are broken down and the meat is tenderized. Occasionally foods are browned in fat before braising. Liquids that are used in braising include water or bouillon, which can then be used as the base for gravy.

Broil—To cook food near a heat source. Technically, food can be broiled with the heat source directly below it as well as directly above it, but food that is cooked with the heat source underneath is more com-monly referred to as grilled. See the previous section on ranges for instructions on how to broil.

Chop—To cut food into bite-size pieces. The most important thing is that the food should be chopped to a uniform size. Yes, a piece of potato that's a half-inch cube and a piece of potato that's an inch cube are both bite-sized—but one of them is going to cook a lot faster than the other.

Cure—A treatment process used to preserve foods. This can be done with salt or with smoking, as in ham, or with brine, as in pickles.

Dice—To cut food into pieces of less than about one-fourth inch. Diced food is smaller than chopped food but larger than minced food.

Drain—To remove the liquid or fat in which a food was cooked, usually by using a colander. If you want to drain the fat off fried foods, place the food on a bed of paper towels.

Dredge—To drag through flour or some other dry coating a food that is going to be fried. These days, it's easier to put the flour or breadcrumbs or cornmeal in a plastic zipper bag and shake everything together. This gives a more even coating, without turning you into the dough-fingered monster. Coating food that is going to be fried gives it a crunchy texture and a good taste. Cook dredged foods immediately, or they'll get soggy.

Fillet (pronounced fill-A)—To remove bones from fish. (If you miss a bone and swallow it, eat a piece or two of bread to help protect your stomach.)

Fold—To combine a light substance into a heavier mixture, such as adding beaten egg white to cake batter. This is done by gently mixing with a spatula or spoon.

Fry—To cook food in hot oil over moderate to high heat. When the food is submerged in the oil, this is known as "deep frying." Frying and sautéing are similar except that frying uses more oil or fat.

Grate—To convert a large piece of food into small pieces by rubbing it against a grater or shredding it in a food processor. Only hard foods are successfully grated. Soft foods stick to the grater and become a pulpy mess.

Grill—To cook food on a grill over an open flame or another source of heat. The food is placed close enough to the heat source that the surface of the food forms a crust that seals in flavor and juices. The grill should be hot before the food is set on it; otherwise the food will stick.

Grind—To use a grinder to convert large pieces of food to small pieces.

Knead—To work dough into a pliant mass. This is done by pushing and stretching the dough with the hands, and then folding it over on itself. Kneading allows gluten in the flour to stretch. Gas bubbles from the yeast then push on the dough and allow it to rise.

Marinate—To soak meat in a seasoned liquid. This process makes the food more flavorful and tenderizes the meat. Take care not to marinate food in aluminum containers. Glass is best. Food that is being marinated should be covered and refrigerated during the marinating process.

Mash—To crush a food with a masher or other implement until it is smooth and free of lumps. No, this has nothing to do with the old television show.

Mince—To cut food into tiny pieces that are even smaller than those that are made by dicing and are much smaller than those made by chopping.

Roast—To cook food in an oven, uncovered. The high heat seals in juices and browns the meat or vegetables being cooked.

Scald—To quickly dip fruits or vegetables in boiling water, and then immediately dip them in ice water. This loosens the skins so peeling is easier. Do not leave foods in the hot water for more than thirty seconds, or cooking will occur.

Scale—To take the scales from a fish. This is done with a dull knife that is run against the grain of the scales, from tail to head.

Sear—To brown meat over high heat quickly enough to seal in the juices and make the surface of the meat crisp. Once food is seared to keep the juices in place, the meat can be further cooked by another method.

Season—To coat the cooking surface of a new pot or pan with cooking oil and then cook the pan in a 350° F. oven for one hour. This is particularly important when using cast-iron pots or pans for the first time because seasoning retards rusting. If seasoned cast iron is washed with soap and water, it should be reseasoned before it is used again. Seasoning also prevents foods from sticking to the surface of the pan. The term *seasoning* may also, of course, mean to add spices to a recipe.

Seed—To remove the seeds from fruits or vegetables.

Shred—To cut food into thin strips, either by hand or with a grater.

Sieve—To put ingredients through a mesh colander or sieve in order to remove particles of food, seeds, or bone. To make for a more flavorful product, make sure to get all the juices out of the solids that are left behind.

Sift—To aerate flour or other dry ingredients by passing them through a mesh. This breaks up the ingredients and allows for the removal of foreign particles. Aerating flour by sifting it is recommended in many recipes because it makes the dry ingredients lighter, resulting in a lighter product. If you don't want to spend money on a sifter, use a wire-mesh colander.

Simmer—To cook at a consistent temperature (just below the boiling point) so that bubbles barely break the surface of the liquid.

Skewer—To hold food in place for cooking or serving by pushing a skewer through it. Skewers can be made of metal (for cooking) or plastic or wood (for serving fruits or other things that are not meant to be cooked).

Skim—To remove with a spoon any material floating at the top of a liquid. If you need to skim fat off a liquid and if time permits, you can refrigerate the liquid until the fat congeals, then remove the fat. If time doesn't permit, you can add ice cubes to the liquid. Fat will congeal around the pieces of ice, which can then be scooped from the mixture.

Skin—To remove the skin from food. Poultry skin can easily be pulled off the flesh. To skin fruits and vegetables, see **Scald**.

Smoke—To cook over smoky heat for a long time, so that the food that is being cooked absorbs the taste of the burning fuel. Wood chips for smoking foods are commercially available.

Steam—To cook food over (not in) a boiling liquid. The pan must be covered to hold in the steam. The advantage of steaming is that it retains flavor and nutrients that would be washed away if the food were boiled.

Sweat—To partially cook vegetables in seasonings and oil, uncovered, until they are wilted but not browned. This seals in the flavor so that the vegetables will have a better taste in soups and stews.

Planning Your Meals

When planning your meals, you may want to think of four factors—nutrition, variety, taste, and cost. The last three categories should come easily to you as you determine whether you want tonight's dinner to come from Burger King or Pizza Hut. But you're an adult now, and adults are at least supposed to remember that the primary function of food is not for entertainment. Food is meant to fuel your body, and the best fuels for your body are not necessarily going to make your taste buds' top ten list.

If you don't know how to plan meals, the government is more than happy to tell you exactly what to do. In fact, in its infinite wisdom the

United States Department of Agriculture occasionally comes out with the Only True Guidelines for how Americans should eat. Invariably these guidelines are completely different from the guidelines they replaced—the former Only True Guidelines for the ideal American diet.

The most recent Only True Guideline is the food pyramid, which is shown below. If you are to believe the USDA, all your meals should center around the information on this pyramid. Take a good look at this food pyramid. Concentrate on the shape of it, because if you plan your meals according to the food pyramid, this is how you will eventually look. You don't want a rear end that looks like the *Titanic,* do you? Well, if you center your diet around that many carbohydrates, that's exactly what you're going to end up with.

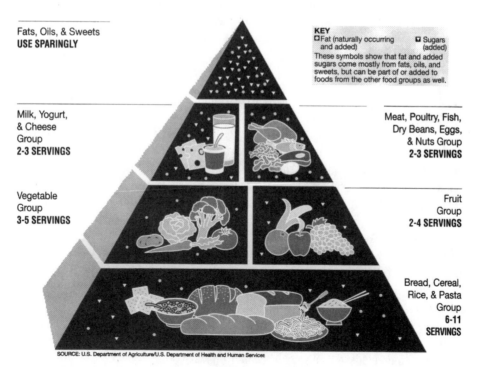

Food Guide Pyramid

A Guide to Daily Food Choices

Fats, Oils, & Sweets
USE SPARINGLY

KEY
☐Fat (naturally occurring and added)   ◪ Sugars (added)
These symbols show that fat and added sugars come mostly from fats, oils, and sweets, but can be part of or added to foods from the other food groups as well.

Milk, Yogurt,
& Cheese
Group
2-3 SERVINGS

Meat, Poultry, Fish,
Dry Beans, Eggs,
& Nuts Group
2-3 SERVINGS

Vegetable
Group
3-5 SERVINGS

Fruit
Group
2-4 SERVINGS

Bread, Cereal,
Rice, & Pasta
Group
**6-11
SERVINGS**

SOURCE: U.S. Department of Agriculture/U.S. Department of Health and Human Services

Figure 2-1

There have been so many recent news articles and medical reports focusing on Americans' continued weight gain under a carbohydrate-based diet that the folks at USDA are probably even now frantically coming up with America's next Only True Guidelines for eating. Until they do, study the pyramid and take the good advice from it without falling for its weaknesses. Don't eat a whole lot of red meat. Try not to eat a lot of sugar and fat, being careful to look out for the hidden quantities of fat and sugar found in processed foods. Tank up on fruits and vegetables. Eat dairy products, trying to avoid the high-fat varieties in favor of dairy products that are lower in fat. Eat carbohydrates, too—but unless you're bulking up to play college football, don't even think of eating carbohydrates in the proportions that are suggested by the food pyramid.

You couldn't drive very far if you didn't put gasoline in your car. Without gasoline, your car wouldn't run even if you'd just had your tires replaced and your engine tuned. Your body is like your car. If your diet focuses on any one food group to the exclusion of the others, your body is going to suffer. Daily variety is the key to a good eating program. But you shouldn't vary your diet just to keep your taste buds happy. When you plan your meals, try to determine what a particular food is supposed to do for you. For example, fruits and vegetables provide vitamins and minerals. They also provide roughage that may keep you from having to rely on Ex-Lax and, later in life, Preparation H. Protein nourishes the

Sneaky Secret

Clark hated okra when he was growing up because his parents always served frozen okra that had the slimy consistency of nose drippings. Needless to say, he was not too excited when he came home one evening early in our marriage to find okra on the table. But Kathy was raised in the South, and knew the Only True Way to prepare okra (fresh okra, cut into small pieces, boiled for seven minutes to get the slime out, drained, then dredged in flour and deep fried). After much persuading, Clark tried the okra and found it was nothing like the hated food of his youth.

Sometimes we dislike certain foods not because of the foods themselves, but because we didn't like the way the food was prepared the first time we tasted it. Mom may be the best cook in the world, but even good cooks have their weaknesses. She may have cooked some foods she didn't understand how to prepare. As a result, we may dislike something we would have enjoyed if it were only prepared in a different way. So when you move away from home (especially when you get married and someone else is doing the cooking), forget your former dislikes and be willing to give those hated foods a second chance. Maybe something you previously disliked will become a new favorite.

blood and the internal organs; dairy products strengthen the bones. Carbohydrates provide energy.

If the only fruit you like is apples, fine. Eat an apple a day and keep the doctor away. If corn is the only vegetable you can stand, eat a lot of corn and hope for the best. But if you do a little experimenting, you're bound to find some other representatives of each of the food groups that you can incorporate into your diet.

As for spending money on food, you're going to have to do it. Your body doesn't care whether your car payment is due, or if the rent is late. It wants food every day whether you're going through good times or bad. You can't escape spending money on food, but you *can* avoid spending a lot of money on food.

Shop at the cheapest grocery store in your area that has quality food. Don't listen to the commercials to tell you which store is the cheapest; find out which store is the cheapest for the foods *you* eat. Make a sample list of groceries you'd expect to buy in a week. Don't just put juice on the list, for example—make it brand-specific and size-specific. Come up with a list of about thirty things you regularly purchase, and then go to each store in your area with that list and a calculator. Figure out how much money it would take you to purchase each item on that list at each store. Then add up the costs, by store. You'll see a significant difference in the total cost from one store to another—and you may be surprised to learn which store is the cheapest. If money is an issue with you, the cheapest store is the place where you should shop.

Some people suggest that you use coupons when you shop, but coupons can be a trap in two ways. First, coupons tempt you to buy things you wouldn't ordinarily purchase. Maybe coupons will only entice you to change brands, but just as likely you'll buy products you wouldn't have purchased at all.

In addition, coupons are seldom found for natural foods. It's a rare ad that will feature a coupon for a pound of carrots. Instead, coupon items are usually highly processed foods. It only makes sense that processed foods are more expensive than foods that are straight from the farm—you're paying for the extra labor, additives, and processing equipment. But it's also worth remembering that except for the pasteurization of milk, every process that a food undergoes after it leaves the farm will probably leave that food less healthful than it was originally.

When you see a coupon, determine if you'd buy the food even without the coupon. Then determine whether you should be eating that food anyway. If the answer to both questions is yes, by all means use the coupon and save yourself twenty-five cents.

Another way to save money is to buy and cook in bulk. It's much more cost-efficient to buy three cans for a dollar than it is to purchase one can for fifty cents. Before you grab the first item you see on the shelf, determine if a different size or quantity would better meet your needs. If the mozzarella cheese and the lean ground beef are a lot more cost-effective if you purchased the two-pound packages than if you purchased one-pound packages, make two batches of lasagna and freeze one of them. Just remember to thaw and eat what you freeze; food that goes down the garbage disposal is money down the drain.

The rule of processed food also holds true with vending machines and fast food: the more human hands that have touched that food, the more expensive it's going to be. Avoid fast food and vending machines whenever possible. Now that you're out of high school, you're no longer considered a geek if you carry a sack lunch. Take advantage of that by fixing your own lunch instead of paying somebody else to do it for you. You'll save a lot of money in the long run, and your meals will probably be more healthful if your own loving hands have prepared them.

Leftovers

Once you've purchased the food, cooked the meal, and eaten your fill, you may still have a few servings' worth to go. If you're absolutely unable to eat leftovers—and some people just can't bring themselves to eat them—teach yourself to cook less food. You'll save money that way. If you tolerate leftovers, great. Wrap 'em up in a sandwich-sized zipper bag and eat them tomorrow night or take them to school or work.

But don't let the food rot in the refrigerator, or you're throwing money down the drain. In fact, that's why those plastic zipper bags are so handy—not only are

they cheap, but they also allow you to see what's inside the bag without having to open it and peek in. If you see that pork chop staring you in the face every time you open the refrigerator, you're a lot more likely to eat it before it rots.

If you open a can of cream of chicken soup, but only need half a can's worth, don't leave the remaining portion in the can when you store it in the refrigerator. The metal in the can will react with the air in your refrigerator and will affect the quality and taste of your leftover food. Once again, rely on those trusty plastic zipper bags to hold the food and give you a constant visual reminder that there's food in your refrigerator that should soon be consumed.

I'm Still Clueless

? *Is it really true that you can't refreeze any meat, poultry, or fish? That's what Mom says, but she also told me to treat burns by putting butter on them.*

Listen to your mother. This time, she's right.

As a general rule, meat (including poultry and fish) should not be re-frozen after defrosting. The big problem with refreezing protein is that it affects the taste and texture. Every step food takes between the farm and your mouth is going to affect the quality of that food—usually adversely. Freezing meat one time is fine. Freezing it a second time is going to result in meat that doesn't taste quite as good as it would have if you'd eaten it the first time around.

? *How do I know which foods need to be refrigerated?*

That's easy. Just look for the tiny print located somewhere on the packaging. Another answer is to remember where you found the food in the grocery store. If you found it in a refrigerated bin or a freezer compartment, then that's where it should go when you get it home.

Most products have directions printed on them such as "Keep Frozen," or "Keep Refrigerated." The ones that you have to watch for are the ones that say "Refrigerate After Opening." These can sit for weeks or months in your cupboard without causing a problem, but as soon as you open them, exposure to air will cause the product to begin spoiling. These products should be placed in the refrigerator after you have used them. Examples of such foods would include jams, jellies, ketchup, mustard, pickles, and most other condiments. But don't use our list—check the packaging to make sure.

By the way, if you forget and leave out a "Refrigerate After Opening" product overnight, don't panic. Despite the admonition on the label, most such foods will keep for weeks at room temperature after they've been opened. (The difference is that they'd keep for *months* if you refrigerated them.) If a "Refrigerate After Opening" product has been left out, take a good look at it. If the mustard has dried out and cracked or the mayonnaise has developed a rancid smell, you may want to throw it out just for the aesthetics of it. But generally these foods aren't rotten unless there's mold on them or they have an off taste—which isn't going to happen after a night out on the counter. Put them back in the refrigerator, and they'll be fine the next time you want to use them.

CHAPTER 3
Recipes Anyone Can Follow

★ **IN THIS CHAPTER**
- ✔ Learning Some Basic Cooking Skills
- ✔ Whetting the Appetite with Salads
- ✔ Feeding the Masses with Main Dishes
- ✔ Adding Variety with Side Dishes
- ✔ Saving Time with Crockpot Meals
- ✔ Giving Guests Their Just Desserts
- ✔ Entertaining with Snacks and Party Foods
- ✔ Greeting the Day with Breakfast

If you've never cooked anything in your life, *don't skip this chapter.* We're going to show you everything from boiling water on up. (Yes, there are secrets to boiling water!) You'll be surprised to learn that tasks such as baking a potato and roasting a turkey are ridiculously easy—and extremely similar.

We're going to start with kitchen basics. On top of that we'll give you a wide variety of tasty and easy-to-cook recipes to add to the favorites you got from your mom. (By the way, Mom's recipe box is a great place to start when building up a repertoire.) We'll also include a few recipes for the ambitious cook who wants to impress. These recipes will be categorized according to their function (main courses, breakfasts, snacks, and so forth).

Whenever you use a recipe, you should always read it through to the end before you start cooking. This way you can make sure that you have all the ingredients on hand, that you have set aside enough time to do the cooking, and that there aren't any instructions at the end of the recipe for which you'll need to prepare. For instance, the turkey recipe tells you to take the foil or the lid off the roaster during the last half hour of cooking. If you don't read the recipe first, you'll miss that vital piece of information.

As we placed these easy recipes in this chapter, we realized a lot of them featured a common main ingredient—canned cream of mushroom soup. We do not think of this as *haute cuisine*. In fact, in our own home we virtually never use recipes that feature this particular ingredient. Nevertheless, this chapter and the recipes in it are designed for the novice cook.

Before we get to the recipes, here's one final note for you. The recipes are going to look long and complicated. In fact, the opposite is true. The reason the recipes look long is that we're going to assume you know nothing about cooking and are going to walk you through it step by step. Thus, where a normal recipe would say, "Caramelize a half cup of sugar," we're going to assume you have no idea how to do that and will tell you exactly how it's done. Thus, "caramelize a half cup of sugar" might become "Caramelize one half cup of sugar. In order to do this, put a half cup of sugar in a saucepan and melt it over medium low heat, stirring constantly until the sugar is completely liquefied and is caramel in color. Do not touch the melted sugar or it will severely burn you."

We're also going to include notes (in italics) with many of the recipes, telling you what the ingredients are or giving you some other tidbit of information. This will make the recipe look even longer. *But do not be fooled into thinking a long recipe is a complicated one. In this book, the longer the recipe, the easier it will be for you to follow.* You should be able to cook any of the recipes in this book perfectly the first time, with no mistakes whatsoever.

Basic Recipes

How to Boil Water

You think we're kidding, don't you? Even you can boil water without instructions. You put the water in a pot, put the pot on the range, turn on the heat, and eventually the water boils.

There are three things that make a difference when you're boiling water, though. First, water seems to boil faster if you add salt to it. Whether you start off with hot water or cold, pour a little salt into the water when you put it on to cook. You don't need to measure, but a teaspoon or so should do it. Use common sense, though. The salt will affect the taste. Don't add salt if you're boiling water for, say, hot chocolate.

Second, water and other boiling liquids have a tendency to boil over—especially when the pot also contains something that would make your cooktop messy. Don't fill your pot too close to the top; use a big enough pot that you'll have room for the water, for whatever you're cooking in the water, and for several extra inches to allow for enthusiastic boiling. Despite all this, some things will want to boil over anyway. When you see that something is in danger of boiling over, pour in a little cooking oil. Oil has a way of calming the waters.

Third, water will heat faster if you put a lid on the pot. Of course, if you can't see into the pot you may not know when the water starts to boil.

How to Boil an Egg

Boiling an egg is just like boiling water, only you put eggs in the pot with the water before bringing it to a boil. But there are additional secrets you need to know when boiling eggs. First, you'll need to know whether you want your egg hard-boiled or soft-boiled. Hard-boiled is the way Easter eggs are cooked. Soft-boiled eggs are runny, but some people have a taste for them.

When you're boiling eggs, everything depends on the altitude where you're doing the cooking. At sea level, a soft-boiled egg usually takes three minutes. That's where the term "three-minute egg" comes from. For a hard-boiled egg, you can double that time. At higher altitudes, that "three-minute egg" is going to take considerably longer to cook, and a hard-boiled egg will take about ten minutes. You'll have to experiment to see how long to cook your eggs so they come out the way you like them.

The rules for boiling water apply when you're boiling eggs. You can add

Sneaky Secret

If you have hard-boiled eggs, leave them in the pan after you drain out the cold water. Bounce them around in the pan so the shells get broken all to pieces. After you do that, the shells will easily slip off the eggs. Rinse each egg afterwards to get rid of bits of shell, and there you have your hard-boiled eggs.

Also, if your eggs tend to crack when you boil them, you can add a little vinegar to the water. Sometimes that prevents cracks. If eggs do crack you can still use the eggs, although some that really break apart don't look very appetizing after they've been boiled.

salt to the water to make it boil faster, and oil to the water if the water is in danger of boiling over. The difference comes after the eggs are done. When the eggs are finished, take the pot to the sink and drain out the hot water. Add cold water and let the eggs sit for a few minutes. This will cause the inside of the eggs to shrink away from the shells, so you'll be able to shell them more easily. After the eggs have sat for a few minutes, drain off the water. If you have soft-boiled eggs, crack them by hitting them in the middle with a kitchen knife to cut them in half, and then scoop out the yummy insides with a spoon.

How to Brown Ground Meat

In these days of culinary diversity, something that looks like browned ground beef can actually be made of ground chicken, pork, turkey, or even such exotic meats as lamb, venison, or elk. Choose what you want. The cooking process is the same for any of them, but the results may taste a little different.

Ground beef and ground pork are "enhanced" with a lot of animal fat. Some varieties are leaner than others. Traditional medical wisdom says the leaner the meat, the healthier the meal. Lean meat is also more expensive, so you'll have to decide whether to go for health or money. Ground chicken and turkey have less total fat, so they're thought to be considerably healthier than beef and pork.

When browning ground meat of any variety, put the meat in a frying pan and set it on a burner at medium heat (medium-high heat if you have a nonstick pan). Use a spatula to break up the meat as it cooks. Constantly stir the meat so that every bit of it comes in contact with the hot surface of the pan.

Contrary to the name, "browned" meat never turns the color of, say, a cow's hide. Meat is "browned" as soon as it is no longer pink. Some people brown meat a little longer than others do, because the longer you brown a meat that contains added fat, the more fat you'll cook out of it. However, no browned meat should be cooked until it resembles a pile of BBs, which is what Clark did the first time Kathy asked him to brown some ground beef. The meat should still be juicy when it's browned. It should have some spring to it when you chew a piece of it. It should *not* be suitable for packing into shotgun shells.

After you've finished browning the meat, you're going to see the real difference between ground meat and ground poultry. If you've browned ground beef or pork, that meat is going to be swimming in a little to a whole lot of melted fat. Before you can do anything with your ground meat, you'll have to get rid of the fat. The best way to do this is to strain the meat through a colander. *But do not pour the fat down your kitchen sink drain.* Pouring grease down a sink is a surefire way to clog it up. You can pour the grease into a container or, better yet, pour it over a nest of paper towels that is sitting on a plate in your sink. As the grease cools it will congeal, and you can then dump the nasty towels in your garbage can.

If anything needs to be drained off ground poultry it will be water, which is considerably easier to dispose of than fat. Once you see how much easier it is to cook with ground poultry, you may want to use it in some of your recipes that call for ground beef. For one thing, the results taste pretty much the same in a lot of recipes, especially in ones that are highly seasoned. Additionally, when you finish browning poultry, you're going to end up with a much bigger pile of meat than you would if you browned beef or pork. A large percentage of ground beef or pork consists of the fat you'll be putting in your garbage can. With poultry, what you see before you brown the meat is just about what you're going to get after you're finished.

How to Sauté Vegetables

Sauté is a fancy French word that means "cook over low heat in a small amount of fat." (If you're not a Francophile, sauté is pronounced saw-TAY. In fact, it's pronounced that way even if you *are* a Francophile.) "Small amount" is the important phrase when you're sautéing something. We're not talking about a cup of cooking oil. The amount of fat you'll use will depend on the type of pan you're using, but for most pans you can start off with about a tablespoon and add more as needed.

Vegetables should be cut into pieces before you sauté them. This isn't an exact science, because the way vegetables are sliced or chopped will depend on what vegetable you're using, and the recipe itself. If you're making soup, carrots should be sliced into coin-shaped pieces. If you're adding carrots to potato pancakes (and we have no idea why you'd want to do such a thing), you may want to chop them up into tiny pieces. If you're slicing vegetables into coin-shaped pieces, the "coins" in question should be no more than about a quarter inch thick. Otherwise, the vegetables won't cook all the way through when you sauté them. If you're slicing vegetables into pieces, you may want to end up with pieces that are no bigger than a fingernail (you choose the finger). Uniformity is the key. If the pieces of food are roughly the same size, they'll cook to the same amount of doneness. If they aren't, you can count on some pieces of vegetable being mushy while others are still raw.

When you sauté something, you don't want to cook it until it falls apart. Onions should be cooked until they become translucent. If you eat a piece of onion that's been properly sautéed, it will taste sweet. Other vegetables should be cooked until they're starting to get soft, but should still give a little resistance to your teeth when you bite into them. Mushrooms should be cooked until they start to smell terrific, and then for about five minutes after that. You get the picture. Often, sautéing something is only a prelude to putting it into something else for additional cooking. If that's the case, don't sauté the food for too long or it will become mushy and unpalatable when you finally eat them in soup or something else.

After you're finished sautéing, you may want to drain off any excess fat (there shouldn't be much). If you have any, though, drain it off unless your recipe says not to. You don't need the extra calories.

How to Make White and Cheese Sauces

White and cheese sauces are made exactly the same except that one of them has cheese in it. Both are good to pour over vegetables, making them look and taste more appetizing. (Sauces also add a lot of calories, so don't go overboard on them.)

Making a white sauce or a cheese sauce is not an exact science. However, that's not good enough for some people. For the sake of those of you who must have exact measurements, here are some. There are four ingredients in a white sauce—butter, flour, salt, and milk—plus the optional pepper to taste. Use the ingredients in roughly the proportions shown in the accompanying chart, depending on the

> **Sneaky Secret**
> Do not ever cook with margarine or butter that comes in a tub. This "whipped" margarine or butter has a lot of added water and will ruin your recipe. Always use margarine or butter that comes in a block or a stick.

thickness of sauce you want to make. Remember, though, that this chart will yield only one cup of white sauce. If you want a larger quantity, enlarge the recipe.

Consistency	Butter	Flour	Salt	Milk
Thin	1 tablespoon	1 tablespoon	¼ teaspoon	1 cup
Medium	2 tablespoons	2 tablespoons	¼ teaspoon	1 cup
Thick	3 tablespoons	¼ cup	¼ teaspoon	1 cup

Start by melting the butter in a saucepan over medium heat. When the butter is melted, add the flour. The flour that comes in a shaker in your grocery store is called "instantized" flour (although it probably won't say that on the label), and is processed in a way that makes it perfect for making sauces and gravies. Stir up the two ingredients to make a gluey mess. Add salt. Add pepper to taste. If you're a purist you can use white pepper so there won't be black flecks in your sauce, but most people aren't purists.

Next, pour the milk in the pan. Continue cooking and stirring until the sauce thickens. (It will bubble when it thickens.) If it thickens too much, add more milk.

To turn your white sauce into cheese sauce, add some grated cheese and stir until it has melted. Cheddar is often used, but you may also want to experiment with white cheeses such as Monterey Jack. Once again, this isn't an exact science. Start off with a half cup or so of cheese to a cup of sauce. Then you can add more milk if the mixture gets too thick, or more cheese if you want a stronger cheese taste.

The biggest trick in making white sauce or cheese sauce is the timing. Once the stuff starts thickening, it just keeps getting thicker and thicker. You can always thin it out with milk, but it's easier just to time the cooking so the sauce is ready at the same time as the rest of the meal.

Making white sauce or cheese sauce is an easy process. It's almost foolproof, but there are two potential problems. Breathe easy—both of them are easily fixed. For example, if your sauce doesn't thicken after a reasonable time, it may not have enough flour in it. You can fix this by adding more flour. But don't just pour in more flour, or you'll end up with lumps. Instead, put a couple of tablespoons of flour in a cup that has a lid, along with about a half cup of cold milk. Put on the lid and shake the mixture until it's nice and smooth. Then add the liquid to your sauce. Keep stirring and cooking until it thickens.

The other problem is that you might end up with lumpy sauce. If this happens, you can get rid of the lumps in a blender, with a wire whisk, or with an electric mixer. If you don't have any of these, do the best you can with a fork. If you still can't get rid of all the lumps, you can dig them out with a spoon or live with them (no, lumps won't kill you).

How to Make Gravy

Recipe Notes: Gravy has the same tendencies as white and cheese sauces in that it tends to get lumpy and become too thick once it starts thickening. If you have problems with your gravy even after reading these simple instructions, go to the white and cheese sauces section and see how to deal with them.

Gravy is similar to white and cheese sauces, except that it's neither white nor cheesy. It also usually has meat juices of some kind in it, either in the form of drippings from the meat or from canned meat broth. If you're a vegetarian, don't despair. We'll give you a variation for mushroom gravy at the end of this section.

No experienced cook would ever use a recipe to make gravy. Once you've had a little experience, gravy is something you'll be able to do purely by instinct. But if you had a little experience you wouldn't be reading this, so we're going to give you some measurements that will help you until you can do it without our help.

Basic gravy. Basic gravy begins with the drippings that are left in the pan after the meat has been removed. Scrape the pan to loosen any remaining pieces of meat and stir them in with the juices. Then add about a cup of broth. (You can buy broth in the soup section of your local grocery store.) For beef, use beef broth; for poultry, use chicken broth. If you're adventurous you may even use canned onion soup. Be creative! Boil the whole mess over high heat until some of the liquid begins to evaporate and the rest of the meat becomes syrupy. (This is called "reducing" the liquid.) Turn off the heat, stir in one or two tablespoons of butter, and serve immediately. This recipe makes about 1½ cups of gravy. If you want more gravy, add more broth.

Pan gravy. Like basic gravy, this recipe begins with a pan where meat was cooked, but it features a major difference from basic gravy in the addition of flour. To make pan gravy, remove the meat from the pan and set it aside to cool. Pour all the liquid from the pan into a large measuring cup. Almost immediately the fat will start to float to the top of the cup, leaving the good juice on the bottom. If it looks as though there's a lot of fat in the drippings, you can add a few ice cubes to the measuring cup. Ice cubes will attract the grease; in a minute or two you can spoon out the greasy ice cubes and throw them away. In any case, you'll need to remove as much fat as you can from the cup before you make the gravy.

While the fat is rising to the top, scrape the pan to loosen the remaining pieces of meat. You'll need those scraps for the gravy. Then take about ¼ cup flour and put it in a jar with about 1½ cups of broth. Put the lid on the jar and shake like crazy until the flour is evenly mixed in with the broth. Try not to leave any lumps, or you'll have lumpy gravy. Set the jar aside and finish scooping the fat out of the cup of drippings. Throw the fat away and pour the drippings and the flour mixture into the pan. Stir over medium-high heat until the mixture reaches gravy consistency. Add salt and pepper to taste. Serve immediately. This recipe makes two cups of gravy. If you want to make more gravy, add more flour and broth in the same proportions that you used for the original two-cup yield.

Mushroom Gravy. If you don't have any meat on hand, you can make gravy anyway if you have fresh mushrooms. Wash and slice about half a cup of mushrooms. Then sauté them in about a half stick of butter. Mushrooms contain a whole lot of water, and as you cook, the water will leach out of them. Pretty soon it'll look as though you're cooking a mushroom soup. This is fine. You've just made mushroom broth.

Now proceed as you would for pan gravy. Like the recipe for pan gravy, this recipe makes approximately two cups of gravy. If you want to make more, add more flour and water in the same proportions that you used for the original two-cup yield.

How to Cook Rice

If you grew up in the United States, chances are pretty good that you think rice comes in a red box and takes one minute to cook. If that's the case, you probably believe that rice is a pretty tasteless commodity. In fact, you may have no plans to cook rice in this or any other lifetime.

However, although other varieties of rice are not as convenient as the rice in the red box, all of them taste considerably better. If you'll do just a little bit of experimenting, you may decide that rice is worth cooking. In fact, you may even decide that rice is worth cooking often.

For your purposes as a beginning cook, we'll talk about only three kinds of rice: brown rice, regular white rice, and pre-cooked white rice.

Brown rice has a good, nutty flavor. It's also the best for you to eat because the rice grain is intact. Keep your brown rice in the refrigerator, because it will go bad quickly if it isn't cooked. (Remember the rule—the better something is for you, the faster it'll go bad on you.)

White rice (we call it "regular" rice in the chart below) can vary in taste and consistency, depending on the length of the grain. Shorter grains tend to clump together, so they're good if you're planning to use chopsticks. Short-grain rice has a gummy consistency; long-grain rice, on the other hand, doesn't clump together or feel pasty in your mouth.

Pre-cooked rice is the stuff that comes in a red box—the rice that takes only a minute to cook. All the flavor—along with most of the nutrients—has been stripped away. The best you can say about pre-cooked rice is that it fills you up and it cooks up quickly. Unfortunately, pre-cooked rice is so convenient that most Americans think of this rice when they think of rice at all. After all, as the boxes so cheerfully proclaim, it takes only a minute to cook!

Rice is cooked by putting the rice in a pan, along with water and butter and maybe a little salt. Bring the water to a boil, put a lid on the pot, turn down the heat to medium low, and cook for the amount of time indicated on the package. When the time is up, take the rice off the burner and let it sit for five minutes without removing the lid. *The rice needs this time to soak up the remaining water and finish cooking, so don't omit this step.*

Here's a table that will help you cook rice in several different ways. Keep in mind that this is only a general chart. The brown rice we use takes only 25 minutes to cook, so be sure to use the chart on your rice container if it differs from our instructions.

Rice	Yield	Liquid	Salt	Cook
1 cup brown	4 cups	2½ cups water	1 teaspoon	45 minutes
1 cup regular	3 cups	2 cups water	1 teaspoon	14 minutes
1 cup precooked	3 cups	1 cup water	½ teaspoon	soak 5 minutes in hot water
1 cup regular	3 cups	2 cups broth	1 teaspoon	14 minutes
1 cup regular	3 cups	1½ cups water and ½ cup maraschino cherry juice	1 teaspoon	15 minutes
1 cup regular	3 cups	2 cups fruit juice	1 teaspoon	15–20 minutes
1 cup regular	3 cups	1 cup water and 1 cup tomato or vegetable juice	1 teaspoon	15 minutes

As you'll see from the above chart, you don't have to cook rice in water. You can do all sorts of interesting things with rice by cooking it in broth or in fruit or vegetable juice. Be creative with your rice, depending on how you're going to be serving it.

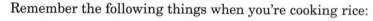

Remember the following things when you're cooking rice:

- Don't ever rinse rice before or after you cook it, because you'll wash the nutrients away;

- Don't use more water than is called for in the recipe, because too much water will make the rice soggy and will leach out the nutrients;

- Don't ever peek when you're cooking to see how it's doing. Rice cooks in steam that builds up in the pot. Every time you take the lid off the pot, you lose the steam;

- Don't stir the rice after it starts boiling, because that makes the rice gummy; and

- Don't let the rice sit in the pan for more than a few minutes after the cool-down period, or it will solidify into a pan-shaped doorstop. This is especially true with short-grained white rice, which gets gummy even in the best of circumstances.

By the way, cooked rice keeps for about five days in the refrigerator. If you don't know what to do with leftover rice, sauté it with a raw egg and some green onions and pieces of vegetable or meat with soy sauce to make a quick fried rice. Or for a speedy breakfast treat, break an egg or two into the rice, add sugar and a little milk, butter, and cinnamon. Whip it all together so the egg is thoroughly mixed in with the other ingredients. Put in the microwave until the egg sets and voilà! You have a quick rice pudding. It's not suitable for company, but it makes a nutritious and tasty breakfast.

How to Cook Pasta

Spaghetti is the mainstay of the single American male's diet. There's a reason for this, and taste has nothing to do with it. Making pasta is as easy as falling off a log.

Take a huge pot, fill it about two-thirds full of water, and bring it to a boil. Add salt to get it boiling faster and oil to keep it from boiling over. When the water is boiling at a good clip, add the pasta and cook until it's done.

"Done" is the operative word when making pasta. Some people like it so done that it turns to mush in their mouths. Other people like it *al dente,* which means there's still a little resistance to the pasta when you bite a piece of it with your teeth. One rule of thumb is that pasta is done when it sticks when thrown at a wall. If you rely on this method, make some sort of effort to remove the pasta from the wall after you've thrown it there.

When the pasta is done, immediately remove it from the heat and pour the contents of the pot into a large colander in your sink. The sink should be cleaned out when you do this. The water will drain off the pasta, and you're ready to eat. Just put sauce on the pasta, cover it with Parmesan cheese, and dinner is served.

If you're setting the pasta aside to use later in another recipe, you may want to rinse it in cold water to stop the cooking—or even soak it in cold water if it's going to be sitting for a while. This keeps it from drying out.

How to Deep Fry

Frying is an American tradition. Despite the modern fascination with low-fat eating, some regional cuisines still rely heavily on fried food.

Almost anything can be fried—meat or seafood, vegetables, pieces of dough, or even pieces of sliced fruit. Fried food tastes terrific, but don't get into the habit of frying too many things. If you're frying so many foods that a "Fry Baby" appliance sounds like a good idea, you may want to rethink your diet.

Deep frying means that your food is cooked completely submerged in oil. So the first thing you'll need is a pan that's several inches deeper than whatever you want to fry. Fill the pan with enough oil to cover whatever it is you're cooking, and set the burner on medium-high. The oil is hot enough when a droplet of water thrown into the pan will pop and sizzle.

Many foods should first be dipped in either a batter or an egg-and-milk mixture (one egg to one cup milk) and then in flour or cornmeal. There are few hard-and-fast rules as to which is best. For example, some people fry fish in batter, some by dipping it in flour, and some by dipping it in cornmeal. People have their own preferences. Follow the recipe for whatever you're going to cook until you have enough experience to experiment.

You should cook fried food until it's done. We'd give you more precise instructions, but the time differs greatly depending on what you're cooking. A whole piece of chicken with the bone inside is going to take a lot longer to cook than a slice of apple ring. Smaller items such as oysters or hushpuppies will float to the top when they're done, but pieces of chicken are more complex. When you're cooking a piece of chicken, you may want to take out a test piece and stick a knife into it. If the juice that comes out is still pink, the chicken isn't done yet.

There are a couple of things you need to remember when you're frying. First, food doesn't like to be taken out of hot oil and then put back in for more cooking. That makes it greasy. So don't get in the habit of checking every individual piece of chicken you cook. See how much time is recommended on your recipe and start with that as an estimate.

Another thing you need to remember is to drain your food after you cook it. Fried food should soak on a bed of paper towels to absorb the grease. Any grease that isn't absorbed by paper towels is going to be absorbed by your digestive tract. Don't skip this important step!

Salt will adhere to fried food only when the food is still hot. If you're a salt fiend, salt the food immediately after it comes out of the frying pan.

A big problem with frying is figuring out what to do with that cooking oil after you've finished using it. Cooking oil is expensive, and you can get by with using it more than once if you're frying similar foods. That's the key. Cooking oil picks up the taste of whatever you've cooked in it. If you've fried fish in oil today, you certainly don't want to be frying doughnuts in it tomorrow. If you think you'll be using the oil within the next month or so, remove the frying pan from the heat immediately after you've finished using it and let the pan cool for an hour or so. When the oil is no longer hot, use a fine colander to strain out all the pieces of flour or batter from the oil. Then the oil can be poured into a jar, covered, and refrigerated until you need it again.

When it's time to dispose of your oil, do not pour it down the sink. Find some sort of container for it and throw the whole container in the garbage can. It may be nastier to deal with that way, but it'll save you a whole lot of money on plumbers.

Salads

Sneaky Secret

When you start using recipes, you will find a wide variety of ways to list ingredients and directions. Words that are often abbreviated include teaspoon (tsp. or t.), tablespoon (tbl. or T.), cup (C. or c.), pound (lb.) and ounce (oz.). We will try to spell these words out completely in our recipes, but don't be surprised to see these abbreviations when you look at other cookbooks. Also, when a recipe calls for a "pinch" of something, put in about ⅛ teaspoon, or the amount you could probably pick up if you pinched it between your fingers. When you are told to add an ingredient "to taste," it means to keep adding that ingredient until the food tastes right to you. For example, when told to "salt to taste," it means to keep adding salt until the food tastes just salty enough.

If you're like most people, you grew up eating iceberg lettuce. Iceberg lettuce is the kind of lettuce children like because it has absolutely no flavor. You may not be familiar with other types of lettuce, because iceberg lettuce was the only type available in the supermarket when your mother was learning to cook. But today romaine lettuce is so common that romaine is giving iceberg a run for its money. And your supermarket should have other varieties, too. In fact, most stores carry cellophane packages of several different greens, mixed together so you don't have to eat a salad that has only one kind of lettuce in it. The most exotic of these consist of "field greens," which contain every sort of leaf but lettuce.

Buying prewashed and prepackaged lettuce may not be the most economical way to prepare a salad, but it's a great timesaver and there's less wastage than if you just bought a head of lettuce and had to tear it apart yourself. Another advantage is that when you buy these variety lettuce mixes you'll be able to determine which lettuces you like and which you don't without going to the trouble of buying a head of each. You may decide, for example, that you don't like the bitterness of raddichio. If that's the case, next time you can choose a salad mix that contains other ingredients.

If you're a die-hard iceberg lettuce fan, you're not going to impress your future sweetheart with your culinary sophistication. But if somebody's going to reject you because of the lettuce you eat, you might as well find out before you make an eternal commitment.

By the way, you're not supposed to cut lettuce with a knife. You're supposed to tear it into bite-sized bits. Kathy's home economics teachers, centuries ago, told her that cutting lettuce with a knife would kill the vitamins. This sounds pretty lame, but for whatever reason it's considered bad form to take a knife to lettuce.

Thousand Island Dressing/"Special Sauce"

mayonnaise (not Miracle Whip)
ketchup
pickle relish (for Thousand Island dressing)

In a small bowl, mix mayonnaise with enough ketchup to make a pale coral color. If you're making Thousand Island Dressing, add a spoonful of drained pickle relish. Store leftover dressing or "special sauce" in a jar or some other covered container, and keep it in the refrigerator door. Ideal for your iceberg lettuce salads, to use as a dip for French fries, or to give your hamburgers a McDonald's-esque taste.

Tuna Salad

There are only two things that must be included in every tuna salad—tuna, and some sort of glue to hold the tuna pieces together. The tuna isn't debatable; whether you use water-packed tuna, oil-packed tuna, or solid albacore, the salad must have tuna in it or it isn't a tuna salad. The glue is interchangeable. You can use mayonnaise, flavored mayonnaise, Miracle Whip, mustard, or anything you want. You can use Cool Whip, if that's where your tastes lie, although if your tastes lie in that direction we don't even want to hear about it. All that matters is that you mix *drained* tuna with your chosen glue, adding the chosen glue until the salad reaches the consistency you prefer. Then serve the whole mess over lettuce, on crackers, or between slices of bread. If there's any one meal that allows for free choice, tuna salad is it.

⟶   Although the only necessary ingredients of tuna salad are tuna and glue, most people add other ingredients. Here's a list of ingredients you may want to add to your tuna salad to give it the taste you like:

- chopped onion
- pickle relish
- hard-boiled eggs
- diced jalapeños
- olives (green or black)
- chopped celery
- chopped apple
- garlic or other spices
- raisins
- diced carrots
- frozen peas (thawed)
- croutons
- chives
- crumbled potato chips or tortilla chips

This list is by no means comprehensive. There are no tuna police to tell you that you can't add marshmallows, if marshmallows are what you want. Vary the recipe depending on your mood and the ingredients on hand. The ultimate variation, of course, is to substitute drained canned chicken or turkey, or even drained chopped ham, for the tuna. Then, of course, your tuna salad is no longer tuna salad, but is some other concoction altogether. Go for it.

Waldorf Salad

5 cups diced apple
3 cups diced celery
2½ cups broken pecans
1¼ cup raisins
½ cup mayonnaise
2 tablespoons sugar
1 teaspoon lemon juice
dash salt
1 pint whipping cream, whipped

Recipe Notes: This recipe makes a whole lot of salad—about nine cups of it. But when you consider that it keeps for days in the refrigerator, and that it tastes great for breakfast, nine cups doesn't seem like an insurmountable amount.

By the way, this recipe calls for mayonnaise, not Miracle Whip, and for whipped cream, not Cool Whip. If you've never whipped cream, this is a good time to learn. Chill your egg beaters and your glass or metal bowl in the freezer. When they're cold, put the cream in the bowl, add about a tablespoon of sugar and about a teaspoon of vanilla, and beat the cream with your mixer on the highest setting until it turns into whipped cream (but not so long that it turns into butter).

Blend mayonnaise, sugar, lemon juice, and salt. Set aside. Combine apple, celery, pecans, and raisins in a large bowl. Fold mayonnaise mixture into apple mixture. Fold in whipping cream. Chill, covered, for several hours before serving.

Main Dishes

Turkey

1 whole turkey, thawed
cooking oil
salt
turkey roaster (can use disposable aluminum foil ones, if you cover with aluminum foil)

Recipe Notes: Once you get your turkey thawed, the rest is so easy a trained seal could do it. You can read about the thawing part in chapter 2. Or better yet, buy a fresh turkey in the supermarket and don't even worry about having to thaw it.

After the turkey is thawed, notice that there are two large openings in it. One of them is the where the neck used to be and the other one is, well—where the turkey would sit if he had a chair. Inside each cavity you should find a wrapped packet of goodies. One of those is the turkey neck. The other consists of the "giblets," which include the liver, the heart, and the gizzard. If the idea of sinking your teeth into these treats doesn't make your mouth water, throw the packets away unopened or give them to the cat. If you like them, you can unwrap them and throw them in the roasting pan with the turkey for an hour or so. Later you can eat them or cut them up and put them in gravy or dressing.

Years ago, people used to fill turkeys with stuffing and roast both the turkey and the stuffing together. In these paranoid days, most people don't do that anymore, because of fears of salmonella. If you're a nervous cook, play it safe and cook it in your oven after the turkey is finished.

Take out the top rack of your oven and set it aside. Move the bottom rack to the bottom shelf. Shut the oven door and preheat the oven to 325° F.

While you're waiting for the oven to preheat, drain any liquid out of the turkey by holding it over the sink, holeside down. You may want to pat the skin dry afterwards with a paper towel, but that's optional. Another optional trick is to pour a little cooking oil on your hands to rub on the turkey. Then salt the outside of the turkey. If you're a skin eater, you'll like this because it makes the skin crispy.

Place the turkey in the roasting pan, breast side up. (The breast is the meatiest part.) If you're using a foil roasting pan, put a piece of aluminum foil loosely over the top of the turkey to keep it from drying out. If you're using a porcelain roaster, put the lid on the turkey except for the last half hour of cooking. Cook for the amount of time specified on the label. Some turkeys come equipped with a "tender timer" that allegedly pops up when the turkey is done. *These are not foolproof. Don't ever put your faith in a tender timer.* If the timer hasn't popped by the time the chart on the label says the turkey should be done, you can test doneness by moving a leg. When the leg is so loose in its joint that you could pull it off the turkey without using a knife, the turkey is ready.

Let the turkey cool for about twenty minutes before you carve it. This is a great opportunity to cook your stuffing and your gravy. (Look under the basics section to see how to make gravy. The stuffing recipe will come with the mix you buy.) Cut all the meat off the bones before you refrigerate the leftovers. Store the pieces in plastic zipper bags to keep them from drying out.

Easy Beef Stroganoff

1 pound ground beef
1 onion, sliced
salt, pepper, and garlic powder to taste
1 can cream of mushroom soup
1 8-ounce container sour cream
medium egg noodles, cooked and hot

Recipe Notes: This recipe lends itself to a lot of variation. You can use chicken instead of ground beef, for instance, by taking two or three boneless chicken breasts, cutting them into bite-sized hunks, and sautéing them in your skillet with the chopped onion and seasonings. Or add a box of frozen peas to the recipe when it's almost finished cooking. Or sauté some fresh sliced mushrooms with the onions and meat for a different taste.

Brown ground beef with chopped onion, salt, pepper, and garlic powder. Drain meat. Add cream of mushroom soup and a small amount of water to the skillet with the meat. Cook over medium low heat until heated through. Add container of sour cream, heat again until heated through. Serve over cooked egg noodles.

Fast Chicken Noodle Soup

15 cups chicken broth
2 cups chopped onion
1 tablespoon Paul Prudhommes's poultry seasoning
salt and pepper to taste
1 tablespoon dried basil, crushed
1 tablespoon dried oregano, crushed
2 bay leaves
4 large cloves garlic, pressed
3 10-ounce packages frozen mixed vegetables
6 cups cubed, cooked chicken
1½ cups uncooked small pasta

Recipe Notes: Paul Prudhomme's poultry seasoning is found in the spice section of your supermarket. This recipe makes a lot of soup, but soup keeps for days and days in the refrigerator. If it is too much soup for you, half the recipe.

In a large pot mix the chicken broth, the onion, the basil, the oregano, the bay leaves, the salt, and the pepper. (Start with about a tablespoon of salt and ¾ teaspoon of pepper.) Bring to boiling; reduce heat. Stir in the pasta. Return to boiling and reduce the heat. Cover and simmer about 6 minutes or until noodles are done. Add chicken and vegetables. Continue cooking till the vegetables are crisp-tender and the pasta is done. Discard the bay leaves and serve.

Grilled Cheese Sandwich

sliced cheese (cheddar, Swiss, Monterey Jack, American, etc.)
bread
butter

Grilled cheese sandwiches may not be health food, but they're easy to fix. All you need are the above ingredients, a frying pan, and a spatula.

First, butter *both* sides of *both* pieces of bread. The butter on the inside of the sandwich is necessary to help hold the sandwich together, and the butter on the outside of the sandwich is what causes the sandwich to get that nice grilled texture and flavor. If you don't butter the outside of the sandwich, all you'll get is burned bread.

Once you've buttered both sides of the piece of bread, put some sliced cheese in the middle of the sandwich and put the sandwich in your frying pan. Cook the sandwich at a temperature *no higher than medium,* or the sandwich will burn before the cheese melts. After the sandwich has cooked for a few moments, turn it over so it will brown evenly on both sides. You can turn the sandwich several times during cooking. As soon as the sandwich is pleasantly browned and the cheese is melted, dinner is served.

Tuna Melt

tuna salad
bread
sliced cheese

Here's an open-faced sandwich that combines the best features of tuna salad and grilled cheese sandwiches. Spread tuna salad on a slice of bread, put a slice of cheese on top of the tuna and place the sandwich on a cookie sheet. Cook the sandwich under the broiler until the cheese melts. You may want to put the sandwich closer to the middle of the oven than you would usually do with broiled food, and you may want to close the oven door even though the oven setting is still on broil. This is so the tuna salad will get warm before the cheese burns. You can experiment with different cheese varieties and use a variety of breads for the base.

World's Easiest Pasta

cooked pasta
1 large onion, diced
olive oil
1 can diced Italian stewed tomatoes
2 cloves fresh garlic, minced
1 teaspoon basil leaves
Parmesan cheese

Recipe Notes: For a spicier pasta sauce, use Ro-Tel brand tomatoes, which are found with the stewed tomatoes in the supermarket.

Put the pasta on to cook. Meanwhile, sauté chopped onions in olive oil. Add tomatoes. Add garlic and basil leaves. Heat to a simmer. Serve over cooked spaghetti or angel hair pasta, with lots of grated Parmesan cheese.

Barbara's Soup

1 pound lean ground beef
½ cup chopped onions
1 48-ounce can tomato juice
1 beef bouillon cube
1 teaspoon oregano
1 12-ounce package frozen mixed vegetables
¼ teaspoon pepper

Recipe Notes: The aunt who passed on this recipe to Kathy says that canned S&W brand tomato juice tastes better than Campbell's. Also, she prefers the mix of carrots, broccoli, and water chestnuts as her package of vegetables, but says you can use any combination that looks good. This recipe is an easy way to use leftovers such as corn, beans, rice, or whatever. Simply add the leftovers to the rest of the soup.

Brown hamburger meat with onions. Pour off any grease. Add remaining ingredients. Bring to a boil and simmer for about 15 minutes.

Tacos

1 pound ground meat
1 package taco seasoning (optional)
1 package flour tortillas or crunchy corn taco shells
1 jar of salsa or picante sauce

Plus any combination of the following:
- chopped tomatoes
- shredded lettuce
- grated cheese
- chopped green or white onions (or both)
- chopped olives
- sliced jalapeños
- sour cream

Recipe Notes: Tacos are Mexican sandwiches. Just as the only ingredient that has to be included in an American sandwich is bread, the only ingredient that has to be included in a taco is a tortilla. You can have a peanut butter and jelly taco if you want. As long as you use a tortilla instead of bread, it's still a taco.

For a traditional taco, brown a pound of ground meat. For a Mexican flavor, cook that meat with a package of taco seasoning (available either in the Mexican food or the spice section of your supermarket). If you choose to use taco seasoning, you'll find easy directions on the back of the package.

While your taco meat is cooking, assemble the optional ingredients. Put them in separate bowls unless you're the only one eating; that way people can customize their tacos at dinnertime. When your taco meat is draining, open your plastic bag of tortillas and warm them in the microwave. You can leave them in the open plastic bag as long as you don't cook them longer than about a minute, or you can wrap several of them in paper towels and cook them for a minute. If you don't have a microwave, heat the tortillas in your oven, with a damp paper towel over the baking dish to keep them from drying out. You can also warm them one at a time in a greaseless frying pan that's large enough to accommodate them.

Needless to say, if you've chosen to use the prepared corn taco shells, you don't need to heat them before you eat them.

Now you're ready to fill the tortillas with any of the ingredients that look appealing. Eat as many as you like, but don't throw away the leftovers. Seal the ingredients separately in those little zipper bags. Tomorrow you can heat up the meat, drain the juice off the tomatoes, and mix everything together for a taco salad dinner.

Taco Pizza

1 package Pillsbury Pizza Dough
1–2 pounds ground beef
1 packet taco seasoning
1 medium onion
2 cups chopped lettuce
2 chopped tomatoes
2 cups grated cheddar
salsa or picante sauce

Recipe Notes: Pillsbury Pizza Dough is found with the refrigerated biscuits in a pop-out container. Taco seasoning is found in packets with the spices or the Mexican food in your supermarket. This recipe can be made in a pizza pan or on a cookie sheet. If you're making it in a pizza pan, 1 pound of ground beef is sufficient. If you're making it on a cookie sheet, use 2 pounds.

Roll out your pizza crust in a pizza pan or cookie sheet, depending on how many people you're feeding. Brown the ground beef with the taco seasoning as directed on the package. Drain the meat and put it on the uncooked pizza dough. Bake according to the directions on the pizza container. After pizza crust is cooked, top with lettuce, tomatoes, onions, and cheese. Serve with salsa or picante sauce.

Mexican Casserole

1 good-sized bag Fritos
1 large can chili
chopped onions
shredded cheddar cheese

If you can squash a Frito, you can make this casserole.

Without opening the bag of Fritos, crush them into small pieces. Put a layer of chips on the bottom of a casserole dish. Put a layer of chili on top of the chips. Put a layer of chopped onions on top of the chili. Sprinkle a layer of shredded cheese on top of the chili. Repeat in the same order until you get to the top of the casserole dish. Bake in a 350° F. oven for about 40 minutes, until everything is hot and the cheese is melted.

If you don't like crunchy onions, you can sauté the onions before putting them in the casserole. But if you don't like onions, what are you doing eating Mexican food?

Spaghetti Casserole

1 pound lean ground beef, browned and drained
2 cups shredded cheddar cheese
3 14½-ounce cans stewed tomatoes, chopped
1 pound spaghetti

Cook spaghetti until it's at the *al dente* stage. (If you need an explanation of "*al dente*" see "How to Cook Pasta," p. 103). Combine all ingredients and place in a large casserole dish. Bake at 350° F. for 1 hour, uncovered.

Beefy Mac and Cheese

1 bag of corkscrew pasta
1 8-ounce can tomato sauce
1 pound cheddar cheese
2 cloves garlic, pressed
1 teaspoon basil
1 teaspoon oregano
½ pound lean ground beef
1 onion, chopped

Cook pasta according to package directions. While pasta is cooking, brown ground beef and onion together until onions are limp and meat is cooked. Drain meat mixture and add to cooked and drained pasta. Grate the cheese and add to the pasta mixture. Add the spices. Cook on medium-low heat until the cheese is melted.

Side Dishes

Baked Potato

Baking a potato is just like baking a turkey except that potatoes don't have any nasty guts to dispose of. In order to bake a potato, you must first choose your potato. Potatoes come in three major categories—red, white, and brown. Brown potatoes are the kind you want to bake. (Also, there's a new variety known as "Yukon Gold" that can be considered a baking potato.)

To bake a potato, set the oven for about 400° F. (You can go up to 450° if you're in a hurry.) While the oven is preheating, scrub your potatoes. If you're a baked potato fan, you may want to have a vegetable scrubber on hand just for this purpose.

When the potatoes are clean, take a big fork and stick it in each potato several times. This will keep your potato from exploding in the oven as the juices in the potato are heated. If you want a softer-skinned potato, coat the outside of the potato with vegetable oil before cooking it. This is an optional step. Not coating the potato skin will give you a crunchy crust. When you coat the potato skin, you're also adding extra calories that could otherwise be used in potato toppings.

Once you've coated or not coated your potato with oil, you're ready to throw it in the oven. Put potatoes on the middle rack, several inches apart. Let them cook for an hour or so, until a fork inserted into the potato doesn't meet any resistance when it goes in.

Baked Stuffed Potatoes

baked potatoes
shredded cheese
milk
salt
butter

Once you've learned how to bake a potato, you're three-fourths of the way through the process of stuffing it. Take your potatoes out of the oven. Trying not to burn off the tips of your fingers, lay a potato down on the counter and slice about the top third of it off. Use a spoon to scrape out the insides of the potato and the "lid" you just cut off, being careful not to break the skin. Put the potato scrapings in a mixing bowl and set the skin aside. Repeat for every potato you've cooked.

Once the potatoes are all scooped out, add a little milk (2 or 3 tablespoons per potato), a little butter (about a tablespoon per potato), and some shredded cheese to the mixing bowl. Mix it all together with salt to taste. You can use a fork, a wire whisk, or a mixer to accomplish this task, but it should be fairly easy to do if your potatoes are cooked through. If your mashed potatoes are too stiff, add a little more milk. Don't add too much milk, though, or they'll get gluey. Mashed potatoes should be light and fluffy.

Now take a spoon and scoop the mashed potatoes back into the skins. (You can throw the tops away or salt 'em and eat 'em.) Then put a dollop of butter on top of each potato. If the potatoes have cooled off, you can heat them in the microwave or put them back in the oven for a few minutes.

Garlic Bread or Parmesan Bread

baguette
butter
clove of garlic or garlic powder or Parmesan cheese
seasoning salt (optional)

Recipe Notes: Baguettes (pronounced bag-ETTS) are hard-crusted loaves of French bread that are sold in larger supermarkets. They come in paper bags, hence the name. Usually baguettes come in two sizes, fat and thin.

Slice your baguette either in half lengthwise or diagonally. However, if you slice the baguette diagonally, you may not want to slice all the way through. Slice the bread *almost* all the way through, so the bread stays in one loaf but the pieces will be easy to tear off.

If your bread is sliced lengthwise, you can make garlic bread by spreading butter on each half and then sprinkling a little garlic powder on top. (With Parmesan bread, you'd omit the garlic powder and use Parmesan cheese instead.) Then put it under the broiler until the butter melts and the bread is just starting to turn brown.

If your bread is sliced diagonally, melt some butter in a saucepan, add garlic powder or Parmesan cheese to the melted butter, and pour it between the cuts in the sliced bread, so that every piece of bread has a little butter on it. Then put the bread in the middle of the oven and bake it at about 400° F. for about 5 minutes, until the bread is warm.

Frozen Vegetables

frozen vegetables
salt or seasonings to taste
butter (optional)

If you've purchased frozen vegetables that come with a sauce, follow the recipe on the package. If, however, you've purchased plain old frozen vegetables, they're all cooked the same way. This is how to do it.

Using a saucepan that's bigger than the amount of vegetables you want to cook, put a little bit of water in the bottom of the pan. The operative phrase here is "little bit," because there's enough water in the frozen vegetables to provide most of the water you'll need. If you're cooking one of those standard boxes of vegetables, about ¼ cup of water should be plenty. (By the way, those boxes are just the right size if you're cooking for one or two.)

After you've put the water in the pan, put the frozen vegetables on top of the water. You don't need to thaw them first, but breaking up the vegetables in the box or bag before you dump them into the pan will help them cook evenly. Heat the vegetables, stirring occasionally, until the vegetables are heated through. Except for lima beans, most vegetables need a little cooking to be soft enough. Lima beans need a lot more cooking to be soft enough.

As the veggies cook, you can flavor them by adding butter or salt or seasonings. Butter always tastes the best, but face it—if you get in the butter habit you're going to regret it one of these days. Experiment with dried basil or oregano or some of the vegetable seasoning blends that are in the spices area of your supermarket.

When the vegetables have cooked, they're ready to serve. Drain off any liquid that is left, and you're ready to eat.

Corn on the Cob

Recipe Notes: The secret to cooking good corn is buying good corn. Whether you buy white corn or yellow corn doesn't matter, but the quality of each ear does matter.

Buy corn on the day you intend to consume it. Over time, corn loses sugar, and it doesn't taste as good the second day as it would have the day you bought it. If you buy your corn ear by ear instead of the package, look for the larger ears. They've been on the stalk the longest, and are naturally riper and more mature. Choose an ear from the stack, peel open the top of the ear, and smell it. If it smells like chemicals, that's because it's been sprayed with chemicals. Don't buy any corn that has a chemical smell, because it will taste just the way it smells.

Look at the kernels. The kernels should be firm and fat, rather than wrinkled and shrunken. If you're brave, you can dislodge a kernel with your fingernail and eat it. The kernel should be sweet rather than bland. All the corn in the grocer's display probably came from the same place, so you don't need to taste or smell every ear of corn you consider buying. If one ear of corn passes muster, you can choose the rest of the ears according to size or weight.

Corn on the cob is easy to cook—especially if you have a microwave oven. But even without a microwave, cooking corn is such a simple process that the hardest part is cleaning up after the meal.

The first thing you'll need to do is clean the ear of corn. This means "shucking" it, or taking off the outer leaves and the silky strands that cling to each ear of corn. If there are any bad pieces of corn, cut them out. Cut off the stem, and also cut a half inch or so off the other end to expose the cob for your corn-holders.

If you have a microwave oven, this is where it gets easy. Wrap each ear of corn in a white paper towel. Cook the wrapped ears one at a time in the microwave, for about three minutes. The corn is then ready to eat.

If you don't have a microwave or if you're cooking so many ears of corn that three minutes per ear would take a lot of time, you can boil corn by putting a large pot of water on the range and boiling the corn in it for about three minutes. Yellow corn will get just a little bit darker in color when it's done, so look for that slight color change. Turn the corn around in the pot so all sides get cooked.

Mashed Potatoes

potatoes
milk
butter
salt and pepper to taste

Recipe Notes: In order to get good mashed potatoes, you need to buy the right potatoes. Red and white potatoes are the potatoes of choice for mashed potatoes. Red and white potatoes are just alike except that one has a red skin on it, so choose the cheaper of the two. (There's also a new potato on the market, Yukon Gold, which is supposed to be similar to red and white potatoes.) Don't use brown potatoes for mashing—they are too grainy to make a good mashed potato.

First of all, you'll need to decide how many potatoes to mash. If there's only one of you, you don't need six or seven large potatoes. After all, you'd eat only one potato if it were baked. A good way to determine how to choose an appropriate number of potatoes is to figure out how many people you're cooking for and cook one large potato for each—plus one extra potato per four people.

There should be at least three or four inches of boiling room above your potatoes, so choose a pot that's big enough to hold your potatoes and still leave that amount of room. Fill the pot to about five inches from the top with water, throw in a little salt from the box (you don't need to measure, but keep it down to a couple of teaspoons), and turn on the burner so the water can start heating. Now peel your potatoes with a potato peeler. Then slice the potatoes into slices that are about ¼-inch thick. The smaller the slices, the faster your potatoes will cook.

Potatoes start going brown as soon as the insides are exposed to air, so you'll want to peel the potatoes quickly. But you'll also want to put them in the pot all at once so that all the potato pieces will cook for the same amount of time. When all your potatoes are peeled and sliced, put the potatoes in the water. There should be enough water in the pot for the potato pieces to move freely around as they boil. Now boil the potatoes until they're done. Test doneness by spearing out a piece of potato with a fork, letting it cool down, and biting into it. If it's still at all crispy, keep cooking. Underdone potatoes will yield lumpy mashed potatoes. Overdone potatoes will yield gluey mashed potatoes. Both are edible, but neither is as appetizing as potatoes that are cooked just right.

There are two things you need to know about boiling potatoes. First, because there's a lot of starch in potatoes, potatoes have a tendency to boil over. They will do this without a whole lot of warning. If the boiling seems to be getting a little too enthusiastic, pour about a tablespoon of cooking oil in the pot to calm the waters. (If the water does boil over, clean up the mess as soon as you turn off the burner. Boiled-over potato water is a pain in the neck to clean up once it's dry.)

The second thing you'll need to know about mashing potatoes is to watch the timing. Depending on how thick you've cut your potatoes, they'll be boiling for about ten minutes to get to the right consistency. As soon as your potatoes are finished, drain them into a colander that's sitting in your sink. Then transfer them into a mixing bowl. Add a little milk, a little butter, and a little salt and pepper. *This is not scientific.* Start off with about a quarter cup of milk and a tablespoon of butter and go on from there. Mash the potatoes with a mixer, a potato masher, a wire whip, or even a fork, adding more milk or butter until the potatoes reach the right consistency. Salt and pepper them to taste, and your potatoes are ready to eat.

Canned Green Beans Deluxe

canned green beans (the fat ones, not the skinny French-style beans)
butter
Parmesan cheese
seasoning salt
powdered garlic

Recipe Notes: These beans are so good you'll want to have them all the time. Resist the temptation. This stuff ain't health food. It'll clog your arteries faster than you can say "triple bypass." So eat it on rare occasions and enjoy it, but don't make a habit of it. We want you to live long enough to buy our other books.

Drain the green beans and throw away the liquid. If you're using a standard size can of green beans, put about 2 tablespoons of butter in a saucepan and turn the heat to medium. As the butter starts to melt, add the beans. Throw in about a quarter cup grated Parmesan cheese and several good-sized shakes of powdered garlic. Don't be skimpy with the garlic. Start out with about ⅛ teaspoon and go from there. Stir. The butter will melt and the cheese will turn into a sticky mess. Water will begin to cook out of the beans. That's fine. Keep cooking until the water evaporates.

As the beans cook, they'll start falling apart. Don't worry—this stuff tastes a whole lot better than it looks. Keep stirring, so everything gets equally cooked. Season with seasoning salt to taste. When ready to serve, stir in another couple of tablespoons of Parmesan cheese.

Daryl's Fried Corn

1 10-ounce box frozen corn
1 medium onion, diced
salt and pepper to taste
butter

Sauté the onion in about 3 tablespoons butter. When the onions are translucent and sweet, add the corn right from the box and cook it with no liquid but the butter. Cook, stirring occasionally, until the water from the corn has evaporated so that you're left with onions and corn and butter. Add salt and pepper to taste, and serve.

Hazie's Baked Beans

1 cup diced onion
butter
2 cans (1 pound) baked beans (small beans)
6 tablespoons dark molasses
¾ cup ketchup

Sauté onion in butter. Pour most of the liquid off the cans of beans and add to the onions. Add remaining ingredients. Bake at least 25 minutes at 350° F.

Super Easy Chili

3 tablespoons vegetable oil
1 medium onion, chopped
1 clove garlic, pressed
1 pound lean ground beef
1 14½-ounce can stewed tomatoes
1 large can kidney beans
1 tablespoon chili powder

Sauté onion in oil until the onion pieces are translucent and sweet. Add ground beef and cook, stirring often, for 5 more minutes. Add garlic somewhere along the line. Add stewed tomatoes, beans (including the liquid), and chili powder. Cook for 45 minutes stirring very, very often!

Crockpot Meals

Crockpots are so cheap and so easy to use that it's worth investing in one if you're away from home for most of the day and want to have dinner waiting for you when you return. You can fill the crockpot and refrigerate it the night before, plugging it in and turning it on before you leave the house the next morning. When you come home, dinner is served. All that, and there's only one pot to clean when you're finished. Such a deal!

There are two kinds of crockpots—crockpots that come all in one piece (except for the lid) and crockpots that have removable pots inside the cooking mechanism. At first glance, the removable pots are the way to go because they're lots easier to clean. However, these crockpots don't get nearly as hot as the one-piece units. Quite often your hungry authors have gotten home when a corned beef was supposed to be ready and waiting for them, only to find it had not yet begun to cook. If you must have a crockpot with a removable dish, make sure the dish is a thin one rather than one made of thick crockery.

Another advantage of the one-piece units is that they have a smaller capacity that is ideal for single people or couples. You may have trouble cooking the whole corned beef and cabbage extravaganza in a smaller crockpot, but smaller crockpots should have a sufficient capacity for most of the things you'll want to cook. When buying a crockpot, think small and you won't be sorry. You can always get a bigger crockpot down the road if your needs change over the years.

One thing you may notice about crockpot cookery is that it takes very little water. That's because there's a whole lot of water in the foods you eat. Crockpots take advantage of that, giving you a moist and tasty meal without a lot of added water. Crockpots also intensify the flavor of spices. Don't go overboard with the spices when you're cooking in a crockpot.

The secret to crockpot cooking is to keep a lid on it. Don't be tempted to open the lid and check on the progress of your food, or your food will take hours longer to cook than it otherwise would. Satisfy your curiosity by looking through the clear glass lid, and the food will be ready on time.

Finally, it's almost impossible to burn something in a crockpot. If something should cook on low heat for eight hours but you'll be gone for ten, don't worry about it. Everything should be fine when you get home.

Roast Beef with Onion Gravy

beef roast (any thick or round slab of beef without a rind of fat will do)
1 envelope Lipton's onion soup mix
salt, pepper, and garlic powder to taste

Put the meat in the crockpot. Pour the envelope of onion soup on top of the meat. Throw in a little salt, pepper, and garlic powder (less than a teaspoon of each). Pour about a half cup of water on top. Cover and cook on high setting for 4 hours, or low setting for 8 hours, until the meat is fork-tender.

No-Peek Beef Casserole

2 pounds beef stew meat
1 10¾-ounce can condensed cream of mushroom soup
1 package dry onion soup mix
1 soup can of water
hot cooked noodles or rice

Mix all the ingredients well, with the exception of the noodles or rice. Pour mixed ingredients into a crockpot and cook on low setting for 6 to 8 hours, or on high setting for 3 to 4 hours. If you don't have a crockpot, you can make this in an oven by putting the ingredients in a casserole dish that has a lid. Cover and bake at 325° F. for 3 hours. Serve over noodles or rice. Serves 4.

Cream of Mushroom Chicken/Pork

fresh mushrooms
1 onion
oil for sautéing
3–6 pork chops or chicken pieces (equivalent to one chicken)
2 10¾-ounce cans cream of mushroom soup
cooked pasta

Wash mushrooms, slice onion into rings, and sauté onions and mushrooms together in oil. Place in crockpot, together with pork chops or chicken. Add mushroom soup. Mix well and season to taste. (Try two cloves of garlic, salt, and pepper if you don't know what seasonings to use.) Cook on low setting all day. Serve over pasta.

Stew Meat Hot Pot

1½ pounds stew meat
½ teaspoon garlic powder
2 teaspoons salt
½ teaspoon pepper
6 medium potatoes, peeled and sliced
3 medium onions, thinly sliced
1 can cream of mushroom soup
½ cup water

Recipe Notes: This may seem like a no-brainer, but stew meat is meat that is cut up for stew. It is sold like that in the grocery stores.

Depending on the grocery store you use, stew meat may be ready to use right from the package, or it may need to be trimmed of fat and gristle. If you'd rather not use stew meat, cut up a few boneless chicken breasts or a large steak into chunks and brown that instead. Or brown 1½ pounds of lean ground meat. Maybe you'll want to try substituting an envelope of Lipton's onion soup mix for the cream of mushroom soup.

In a skillet, lightly brown stew meat; drain. Add garlic powder, salt, and pepper; set aside. Place half the potatoes and half the onions in greased crockpot. Add browned meat. Top with remaining potatoes and onions. Combine mushroom soup and water; spread over top. Cover and cook on low setting for 8 to 10 hours, or on high setting for 3 to 4 hours.

Barbecue and Other Grilled Foods

If it's seared animal flesh you want, nothing takes the place of the good, old-fashioned barbecue grill. These days, grills can be powered by electricity or by propane, in addition to the charcoal grills where Dad used to burn his sirloin. There are tabletop grills for indoors, so you can even barbecue throughout the winter.

Grilling meat is essentially the same process as broiling except that the heat source is below the meat rather than above it. Because the meat is cooked from below, meat should be turned frequently to keep the juices inside and to ensure adequate cooking.

The first thing you need to do if you want to barbecue is to decide what kind of grill you want. Charcoal grills include the traditional full-sized grill or the tabletop hibachi. These are the cheapest grills you can buy, and the hibachi is even small enough to be fairly portable. (Hibachis should never be used in an enclosed space, as more than one grieving relative has found out.)

Electric grills are convenient, but they can be the most expensive means of grilling food.

These days, propane grills are the most popular. If you want a propane grill, be sure to stock up on an extra propane container. Propane canisters always seem to run out at the most critical time of the barbecue.

Unless you have a strong personal preference for one method over another, we'd recommend some sort of charcoal grill as a starter. With a charcoal grill, you don't have to spend a lot of money to decide whether you'll use a barbecue grill often enough for it to be worth the expenditure. And these days there are so many fire-starting gizmos on the market that you don't need to set your hair on fire with charcoal lighter fluid to get your grill going. There are wands with a flame on the end to act as a charcoal starter; there are briquets with charcoal lighter fluid embedded in them so all you need to ignite them is a match. The most efficient method we've seen is an aluminum chimney where you wad up a piece of newspaper and put it on the bottom, then pour the charcoal on top. Light the newspaper with a match, leave the scene for ten minutes, lift off the chimney, and your charcoal is ready for cooking.

Because there are so many alternative types and brands of grills available, we're going to let you learn on your own how to operate the grill you prefer. They come with instructions, which you should read carefully and then keep for future reference.

For the purposes of this book we're going to assume you're cooking with charcoal. This is how to do it: Most grills require some type of filler on the bottom, such as sand or lava rocks, so that the charcoal doesn't touch the metal bottom of the grill. Place one layer of charcoal evenly on top of the lava or sand, close together and just touching at the edges. If you're not cooking a lot of food, you won't need charcoal completely covering the bottom—just enough to be under all of the food you will place on the grill. If you're using the older types of briquets, you will need to squirt lighter fluid on them. A couple of short squirts per briquet should do it. Then light a match and place it at the corner of a briquet until the flame jumps up and it starts to burn. Lighter fluid is not as flammable as gasoline, so unless you really soak the briquets, lighting them should not be dangerous. Use matches to start them burning in several different locations, so the fire will spread faster. Now just wait for ten to fifteen minutes. The flames will eventually go away, but the charcoal should start getting gray around the edges, and you may see specks of red coals in the center. Now all you need to do is put the grill in place over the charcoal (put it close but not touching), and you're ready to cook.

Sneaky Secret

Adding cornstarch to any marinade will do amazing things to tenderize beef. Don't just throw the cornstarch in the marinade; mix about a teaspoon of cornstarch to a teaspoon of water for each pound of beef you'll be grilling, and use your (clean) finger to make a smooth paste. Then add the cornstarch paste to your marinade, mixing well. Cornstarch doesn't change the taste of the marinade, but it will change the texture of your beef—for the better.

Now that you have your grill and know what to do with it, the possibilities are endless. Human beings are no longer restricted to cooking hamburgers, hot dogs, and an occasional steak. We're going to give you recipes for a wide assortment of things, including vegetables and bread. But because meat in one form or another is still the food of choice when cooking on the grill, meat will be our primary focus in this barbecue primer.

Barbecues and meat go so well together that you don't really need anything else except perhaps a little salt to make a great meal on the grill. But if that's all you do, you're vastly limiting the scope of tastes that are available with various recipes. The best way to treat a meat is to marinate it first. Marinating makes meat more tender, in addition to adding a variety of flavors to barbecued meat. For some unfathomable reason, marinating works best if you don't marinate in a metal container.

No-Brainer Marinade

Marinate your meat in salad dressing for a half hour before grilling. Try an Italian dressing first; then experiment after that. We don't need to tell you not to use Thousand Island dressing, do we? Use a dressing that has some flavor to it and is made with oil and not mayonnaise.

Other Easy Marinades

Create your own marinades. The best marinades contain a little oil and something for tartness. Once you have the oil as a base, add ingredients from there. Possibilities include:

- 1 stick butter and about 4 cloves of crushed garlic, heated until butter melts

- ½ cup cider vinegar, ½ cup lemon juice, ¼ cup soy sauce, 3 tablespoons vegetable oil

- ½ cup vegetable oil, ¼ cup rice vinegar, ¼ cup soy sauce, and 1 tablespoon sugar

- 1 cup barbecue sauce, ¼ cup brown sugar, juice of ½ lemon, ½ teaspoon ground horseradish, 2 tablespoons orange juice, ⅛ teaspoon cayenne pepper

Marinated Chicken

Several hours before grilling, rinse the chicken parts. Salt lightly while the chicken is still wet. Make enough marinade to cover chicken pieces, and place chicken in marinade until ready to grill. Grill over medium heat until done, 25 to 30 minutes per side.

Steak on the Grill

1¼-inch-thick rib eye steaks
1 tablespoon Montreal Steak Seasoning
¼ cup Worcestershire sauce
2–3 pieces of raw fat from the steaks

Recipe Notes: Montreal Steak Seasoning, made by McCormick, is a blend of coarsely ground black pepper and other spices and is available in the spice section of your supermarket.

Marinate steaks in Worcestershire sauce for 4 hours. Fire up the grill. Sprinkle generous amounts of seasoning on steaks and rub into the meat. When the grill is extremely hot, take the raw fat and rub it on the grill to coat it to a shine. Then add the steaks and cover the grill immediately. For rare meat cook 8 minutes on the first side and 3 minutes on the second side. For medium, cook 9 minutes on the first side and 4 on the second side. For well-done, cook 10 minutes on the first side and 5 minutes on the second side.

Smoky Chicken

1 chicken (cut up)
2 crushed garlic cloves
½ pound butter
½ teaspoon salt
½ teaspoon pepper
1 teaspoon parsley flakes
1 teaspoon lemon juice

Start up the grill. While the coals are heating, mix all ingredients except chicken in a small saucepan and cook until butter melts. Stir to mix the ingredients. When the coals are ready, place the chicken on the rack and immediately baste it with the butter mixture. Cover the grill. Every 8 minutes, turn the chicken over and baste again. When the last of the baste is used, the chicken should be finished.

Aluminum Foil Dinners

heavy aluminum foil
4 small steaks, 4 boneless chicken breasts, or 4 hamburger patties
2 sliced carrots
2 sliced potatoes
1 onion, sliced into rings
salt and lots of pepper
garlic powder
4 slices white cheese (Swiss or Monterey Jack)

Tear off 4 pieces of foil (about 18 x 18 inches). On center of each piece, place a piece of meat. Stack sliced carrots, potatoes, and onions on top of the meat. Add salt, pepper, and garlic powder to taste. Top with a slice of white cheese. Seal the foil tightly. Bake about 40 minutes on a barbecue grill or campfire, or 50 minutes in a 450° F. oven. Serves 4.

Campfire Potatoes

1 large red or white potato
⅓ cup cheddar cheese
½ teaspoon Worcestershire sauce
½ medium onion, sliced
sprig of parsley
¼ cup chicken broth
1 tablespoon melted butter
Pam spray coating
heavy-duty aluminum foil

Recipe Notes: This recipe serves only one, so make one batch for every person you're serving.

Slice the potato and the onion and put them in a bowl. Slice or grate the cheese and add it to the potato mixture. Add Worcestershire sauce, parsley, and about a tablespoon of melted butter. Mix the ingredients together until everything is well distributed. Take a large square of heavy-duty aluminum foil and spray one side with Pam. Place potato mixture on the sprayed side and wrap well. Add a second layer of foil for good measure. Cook on low heat until the potatoes are done. The potatoes will take longer than the meat, because they can't be cooked as close to the heat source, so give them about thirty minutes and then peek to see if they're done.

Corn on the Grill

corn, still in the husks

Leave the corn in the husks and soak them in water for about two hours. Place them on a hot grill until the outside husks get brown or even a little black. Serve them as is and let each husk his own. After all, barbecues are *supposed* to be messy.

Cheese and Bread

1 baguette
smoked cheese
butter
heavy-duty aluminum foil

Slice the baguette diagonally, but do not cut through. Take smoked cheese, sliced thin, and place between the bread cuts. Melt butter and brush the top and sides of the baguette. Wrap in foil and put on the top rack of the grill while cooking your other foods. Heat until the bread is warm and the cheese is soft.

Desserts

Although there are common elements in most treats (namely, sugar and fat), desserts vary widely in flavor and appropriateness. What dessert you choose for a given occasion should depend largely on what you just ate or in what activity you are engaged. Rice Krispies Treats are fine for picnics and casual meals, but they probably wouldn't do much to impress a prospective significant other—and they have no place at the conclusion of a four-course meal.

Haystacks

1 12-ounce package butterscotch morsels
1 12-ounce can cashews or 1 cup miniature marshmallows
1 3-ounce can chow mein noodles (2 cups)

Melt butterscotch morsels in the microwave or on the range over low heat. Stir cashews or marshmallows and noodles into morsels until coated. Drop by spoonfuls onto waxed paper to cool. These are so easy that even kids can make them.

Condensed Milk Fudge

1 can sweetened condensed milk
1 12-ounce package chocolate chips
1 cup nuts

Recipe Notes: Low-fat sweetened condensed milk works fine with this recipe, and nonfat may work equally well. The recipe calls for semi-sweet chocolate chips, but use milk chocolate if you prefer. If you don't want to put nuts in your fudge, think of substituting toffee bits, miniature marshmallows, or other treats. Another variation is to use mint chocolate chips and make mint-flavored fudge.

Heat chocolate chips and condensed milk over low heat until the chocolate melts. Stir in nuts or other treats. Pour in a square or round buttered cake pan and chill several hours, until hardened.

Kool-Aid Pie

1 can evaporated milk
⅔ cups sugar
1 envelope Kool-Aid
vanilla wafers

Chill evaporated milk in an ice tray until the milk is beginning to freeze at the edges. Put the beaters in the freezer while you're chilling the milk. Line a pie plate with vanilla wafer cookies. Put the milk into a large bowl and mix at high speed with chilled beaters until it's fluffy. Add sugar and Kool-Aid. Whip until stiff. Pour milk mixture over vanilla wafer crust. Freeze until firm.

Grape-Nuts Pie

¾ cup Grape-Nuts cereal
½ cup warm water
3 beaten eggs
¾ cup sugar
1 cup light corn syrup
3 tablespoons melted butter
1 teaspoon vanilla
⅛ teaspoon salt
unbaked 9-inch pie shell
whipped cream (optional)

Recipe Notes: This tastes exactly like pecan pie—without the pecans.

Pour the cereal into the water. Let stand until the water has soaked in. Meanwhile, blend the eggs with the sugar. Add the other ingredients except for the pie shell and whipped cream, stirring until the cereal is mixed evenly into the mixture. Pour into pie shell. Bake at 350° F. for 50 minutes, or until the filling is puffed completely across the top. Carefully remove from oven and cool. Garnish with whipped cream and sprinkle with additional cereal, if desired.

Fruit Cocktail Cake

1 cup all-purpose flour
1 cup white sugar
½ teaspoon salt
1 teaspoon baking powder
1 egg
1 (16-ounce) can fruit cocktail
½ cup brown sugar

Preheat oven to 325° F. Spray one 9" square baking pan with cooking spray. In a medium-sized bowl combine flour, white sugar, salt, baking powder, egg, and fruit cocktail, including the juice. Mix until just combined and pour into the prepared pan. Sprinkle the top with the brown sugar. Bake for 45 minutes or until golden brown.

3-Minute Cobbler

1 stick butter (not margarine!)
¾ cup milk
¼ teaspoon salt
2 teaspoons baking powder
1 cup sugar
1 cup flour
fruit for filling
whipped cream or ice cream (optional)

Recipe Notes: This is a pretty liberal recipe. The fruit you add can be canned pie filling, drained canned fruit, drained bottled fruit, or even frozen or fresh berries. About two cups of fruit should do it, whichever form you use. Fresh, sugared blackberries taste terrific in this, but drained bottled pineapple is also good. Be creative.

Melt the butter over low heat in a casserole dish. Stir in remaining ingredients except for the fruit. The mixture will be lumpy. Don't worry about the lumps. Pour in the fruit. *Do not stir!* Bake at 350° F. for about 50 minutes, or until the cobbler is puffy and brown on top. Serve hot or cold, with whipped cream or ice cream. Serves 4.

Snacks and Party Foods

Mild Chicken Wings

1 cup soy sauce
1 stick of butter
2 tablespoons garlic powder
chicken wings

Recipe Notes: You don't use whole chicken wings for this or for any other dish that features chicken wings. Prepared chicken wings are cut into pieces by the butcher, and the "finger" portion of the wing is discarded. The two pieces that are left are called "drumettes," even though technically only one of them is shaped like a miniature drumstick. If you can't find them in your supermarket, ask the meat department employee where to find the chicken wings for buffalo wings. They're probably tucked away in a freezer compartment somewhere.

Melt the butter and mix in soy sauce and garlic. Dip the chicken pieces into the mixture, making sure each wing is coated. Put on a cookie sheet and cook in a 350° F. oven, turning occasionally until golden brown.

Nachos

Basically, nachos consist of cheese that has been melted on tortilla chips. Anything else is a bonus. That being the case, all you really need for nachos is tortilla chips, shredded cheddar or Monterey Jack cheese to melt over them, and a cookie sheet on which to cook them. Cook them right under the broiler for just as long as it takes to melt the cheese. But be sure to watch like a hawk to make sure the cheese doesn't burn.

The most important thing you need to remember when cooking nachos is to spread the tortilla chips thinly on the cookie sheet. Only the tortilla chips that get cheese on them turn into nachos; the ones that don't get the cheese are cooked tortilla chips.

If you're a nacho fan, you know there are countless things you can put on your nachos before you cook them or dip your nachos in after they're cooked. Following is a list of a few things you may want to consider, so you can personalize your nachos to suit your taste. Place on nachos before cooking:

- sliced jalapeños
- refried beans
- browned ground meat, which may or may not be seasoned with taco seasoning
- fully cooked beef or chicken, cut in small strips or bite-sized chunks
- chili
- cheese sauce, or "queso" sauce (which is Spanish for the same thing)
- sautéed or raw onions
- sliced black olives

Have on hand after cooking:

- chopped green onions
- guacamole
- sour cream
- salsa or picante sauce

Quesadillas

Quesadillas are just like nachos except that they're cooked on flour tortillas instead of tortilla chips. Look at the recipe for nachos to find items you may want to put on your quesadillas, but remember that tortillas are too thin for you to be able to load up with heavy items. If you want to make a taco pizza with the same ingredients, use a regular pizza crust. Quesadillas can be made by putting your ingredients on top of one tortilla, or by putting a tortilla on the top and the bottom, like a sandwich.

Bird Seed

raisins
roasted, salted cashews
Rice Chex cereal
M&Ms
semi-sweet chocolate chips

Mix equal parts of all ingredients and store in an airtight container.

Fluffy's Punch

1 2-liter bottle ginger ale or 7-Up
1 12-ounce can of juice concentrate
ice

Mix all ingredients in a large pitcher. If it's too strong, add water to taste.

Cucumber Punch

2 2-liter bottles 7-Up (*not* diet, *not* Sprite), chilled
2 12-ounce cans frozen limeade concentrate, thawed but cold
1 liter cold water
⅓ cucumber, sliced thin
½ large pitcher ice

Recipe Notes: Eventually, you or a friend is going to get married. This is the ultimate wedding reception punch. It doesn't taste like cucumbers, but the cucumbers are essential to the taste. Don't leave them out or it isn't cucumber punch!

Mix ingredients. Right before serving, add cucumber to punch bowl and let the slices float. Eight batches of this does a wedding reception for 250 thirsty guests.

Velveeta Dip

1 2-pound block Velveeta
1 can diced Ro-Tel brand tomatoes
1 small can chopped chilis
chips or vegetables for dipping

Recipe Notes: Ro-Tel brand tomatoes are found with the stewed tomatoes in the grocery store. Chopped chilis come in a small can and are found in the Mexican food area of the grocery store. Leftover Velveeta dip is a good ingredient to add to casseroles.

Cut Velveeta into large chunks and put in a casserole dish. Add tomatoes (with liquid) and chilis. Melt together in crock pot or microwave, stirring occasionally. Serve with chips or chopped raw vegetables.

Shrimp Cocktail Sauce

ketchup
bottled horseradish

Recipe Notes: Look for bottled horseradish in the refrigerator case of your supermarket. It's usually located in the same area where you'd find Velveeta and refrigerated pickles and other gourmet delights. If you don't see it, ask for it. Try this sauce as a substitute for ketchup on your French fries, or serve it with boiled shrimp or cooked fish.

Mix ketchup with horseradish to taste. Start small and work up. Horseradish has a lot of bang to it.

Fruit and Dip

1 6½-ounce tub strawberry or pineapple cream cheese spread
1 10-ounce jar marshmallow creme
sliced fruit

Recipe Notes: Flavored tubs of cream cheese are found with the cream cheese in the grocer's refrigerator case. Marshmallow creme is usually found with the candy or baking supplies. This recipe looks like junk food, but the taste will be a pleasant surprise. It's especially good with slices of banana, apple, or mango.

Stir cream cheese spread and marshmallow creme until they're thoroughly blended. Serve as a dip with sliced fruit.

Breakfast Foods

Biscuit Treats

1 tube packaged biscuits
butter or margarine
jelly, sugar and cinnamon, raisins, chocolate chips, or nuts

Preheat your oven as specified on the biscuit package. Grease a cookie sheet if it doesn't have a nonstick coating. Take a biscuit out of the tube and mash it flat on the cookie sheet. You can use your hands or a rolling pin or even a glass drinking glass, but remember that flatter is better. Then coat the top side with a thin layer of butter or margarine. Put a dollop of jelly in the middle, or add sugar and cinnamon, raisins, or nuts. Don't get carried away. You don't want the biscuit so full you can't work with it.

Bring up the sides of the biscuit to cover the goodies inside. Pinch the edges together so they don't leak on your cookie sheet. Repeat for all the biscuits in the tube. Then bake the biscuits as specified on the package. This is so easy that kiddies can do it—and indeed the recipe has been included here to satisfy the palates of people who are still young at heart.

Scrambled Eggs

cooking oil
eggs
milk (optional)
salt and pepper
other optional ingredients (cheese, bacon bits, chives, onions, green peppers, jalapeños, Tabasco sauce, and so on)

The hardest part of making scrambled eggs is determining how much cooking oil you'll need. This will depend on the frying pan you use. If you use a nonstick coating, you'll be able to get away with using very little oil. If your pan doesn't have a nonstick coating, you'll use considerably more oil—and even then, you might be spending a lot of time scrubbing that pan after use.

Break the eggs into a bowl and beat them with a fork or other implement until the yolks and whites are well mixed. Add about a tablespoon of milk per egg and mix again. Add salt and pepper. You guessed it—mix again.

Pour your oil into the frying pan. If you're adding raw vegetables (such as onions or green peppers) to your eggs, you may want to sauté them in the oil. Then pour the egg mixture into the oil. Add other ingredients. Cook over medium heat, stirring to keep the eggs from sticking, until the eggs are done the way you like them. Serve them before they get cold and nasty.

Bacon

bacon
paper towels or napkins

Bacon isn't hard. Most people who mess up do so because they cook the bacon too quickly. When making bacon, patience is a virtue. Cook bacon over medium heat.

Before you start cooking, gauge your pan to see if it can hold the full strip of bacon. If it's too small, cut the bacon in half and make smaller pieces. Then put the bacon in your cold frying pan, crowding the pieces as close together as possible without overlapping them. Cook over medium heat, pushing the bacon down onto the frying pan so that all the ripples are forced into contact with the hot metal. Turn the bacon at least once and cook until the bacon is as done as you like it. Then drain for a few minutes on paper towels to get rid of the extra grease and to make the bacon crispy.

Do not pour the used bacon grease down the sink!

French Toast

bread slices
eggs
milk
cinnamon
cooking oil
powdered sugar and fruit or syrup

Crack a couple of eggs into a bowl. Add a tablespoon or two of milk. Shake a half teaspoon or so of cinnamon onto the eggs and beat well with a fork. Put a little bit of cooking oil in a frying pan and turn on the heat to medium. Quickly dip a piece of bread into the egg mixture so both sides get wet but not so soggy that the bread falls apart. Take out the slice of bread and cook in the frying pan until the eggs are cooked and the toast is golden brown. Repeat with as much bread as you want to cook, replenishing eggs, milk, and cinnamon as needed. Serve hot with maple syrup or powdered sugar and fruit.

CHAPTER 4

An Apple a Day

Right now you're probably as healthy as you'll ever be in your life. If you're in normal health for someone your age, your joints work without pain, your heart is in prime condition, your lungs are so strong that you don't even think about breathing, and your organs do exactly what they're supposed to do. And even though you think you could lose a pound or two, chances are the time will come when you'll wish you weighed what you do today.

If you're like most young people, you assume your body will always work just as smoothly as it does right now. We've got sad news for you, Sweetpea. It's all downhill from here. Enjoy your health while you can, because it isn't going to last forever.

Currently, the average life span for Americans is seventy-six years. You're at the point where you can't even imagine being thirty, so seventy-six may sound like an incredibly long time to live. But there are different standards of living. Some people are hale and hearty right up until they keel over dead on their seventy-sixth birthday. Other people start falling apart before they reach age forty, and struggle with pain for the rest of their lives. But there are ways to maintain your health, or some semblance of it, to your seventy-sixth birthday and for many beyond.

This chapter is going to focus on your health—how to keep it and what to do when it fails. We'll give you enough advice to be able to tell when you should go to the doctor and when you should save your money. We'll also give you information about health insurance to help you understand how you can use it to keep the costs of medical care at a manageable level. But it all comes down to this: An ounce of prevention is worth a truckload of extra-strength Excedrin. Trust us. We speak from bitter experience.

Planning for Good Health

Some health problems can't be avoided. Jogging every day of your life won't keep you from getting multiple sclerosis if that's your destiny. But many other health problems can be prevented by your lifestyle. If taking care of yourself today would keep you out of a wheelchair tomorrow, would you do it?

The Killers

First of all, there are a handful of maladies that will probably kill you if you live long enough. The tendency to acquire these diseases resides in all of us. You may have heard the saying, "Any man will get prostate cancer if something else doesn't kill him first." This is also true of several other afflictions. We compiled the following list of maladies not to depress you but to let you know what to watch out for in the future. Some of them may surprise you.

▶ Accidents

Yes, we realize that accidents are not diseases. However, they definitely fall in the category of problems that are inherent in the human condition. In fact, if you die between the ages of fifteen and twenty-five, the odds are three to one that an accident is what's going to kill you. And you're even more likely to die of an accident if you're male than you are if you're female. Males are natural risk-takers. This is the reason that although equal numbers of boys and girls are born, only 48 percent of adults are male.

If an accident doesn't kill you, it may incapacitate you to the point that you'll never again live a normal life. In fact, for every person killed in an accidental death there are ten people injured who will never fully recover. Looking at these figures may prompt you to fasten your seat belt next time you get in a car—as driver or passenger. Automobile accidents take more lives and cause more injury than any other traumas, so being a wise driver and passenger will go a long way to eliminate this killer in your life.

▶ Arteriosclerosis

Arteriosclerosis is the buildup of a gummy material known as "plaque" on the interior walls of your arteries. Arteriosclerosis usually kills people by causing a heart attack or a stroke, and it accounts for nearly half the deaths in the United States. *Arteriosclerosis is not a disease that affects only old people.* In fact, most people start accumulating plaque in their arteries at least twenty years before they ever show any symptoms of it. You probably have plaque deposits that are beginning to form in your own arteries even now—and if you have a family history of heart attacks and strokes you may have a whole lot of plaque. (People have been known to have their first heart attacks or strokes when they were still in their twenties.) However, there are ways to keep plaque from forming. There are also ways to shrink plaque deposits that have already formed, as you will soon see.

▶ Cancer

You probably already know that cancer is caused when a few renegade cells in your body go haywire and start producing more of these renegade cells. A clump of these renegade cells is called a "tumor," and tumors can progress until they take over and destroy the whole body. What you may not realize is that cells turn renegade only after they've been exposed to repeated injuries. Some of those injuries are unavoidable, but other injuries can be prevented. In fact, at least two-thirds of cancers can be prevented by your own actions.

▶ Cirrhosis

If you thought that cirrhosis of the liver is caused strictly by alcohol consumption, you were wrong. We all have a tendency toward cirrhosis, but cirrhosis develops so slowly that most of us are usually killed by something else before we ever see any cirrhosis symptoms. If you drink alcohol, you can change all that. In fact, 75 percent of cirrhosis cases are alcohol related. If you stay away from booze, cirrhosis will probably never be a problem for you.

▶ Diabetes

The human body loses its tolerance for sugar as it ages. This is especially true for people who are overweight. Diabetes is a potentially fatal illness that afflicts the pancreas, the part of the body that produces insulin. You may show symptoms of diabetes as a child, and if that's the case there's nothing you can do but control it with insulin treatment. However, adult-onset diabetes can usually be reversed without medical treatment. Your lifestyle is a big factor in whether diabetes will ever threaten your life.

▶ Emphysema

You're probably surprised to see emphysema on this list. Just as you thought cirrhosis was a disease only for drinkers, you probably assumed emphysema is a disease that affects only smokers. Guess again.

The lungs are fragile organs. The breathing tubes naturally fill with bacteria-containing mucus, which is normally flushed out of the lungs and into the throat by small hairs called "cilia." If the cilia get destroyed, lungs lose the ability to flush out the mucus. The lungs get clogged, and death can result in any one of a number of ways.

If you're hoping to destroy your cilia and ruin your lungs, smoking is the fastest way to do it. In fact, 90 percent of cases of emphysema are smoking-related. Some smokers beat the odds and never get cancer, but they will all get emphysema if they smoke long enough. There is no guarantee a nonsmoker will avoid lung disease, but smoking just about guarantees your lungs will be destroyed if you persist in doing it.

The Preventers

Believe it or not, you can almost eliminate your chances of dying of any one of the big diseases if you pay attention to five areas of your life. If you don't smoke or drink—and we hope you're smart enough to leave alcohol and tobacco alone—there are only three additional things you need to watch to safeguard your health from the major killers. These things are so obvious that you're going to be tempted to skip the sections after you read the headlines. *Don't do it.* We've got some interesting information here for you—stuff even you don't know yet.

▶ Diet

Most of us think that as long as we're healthy and we're not fat, we can pretty much eat whatever we want. This is not true. In fact, the night before we started writing this chapter, we had a conversation with a waiter in a Chicago tapas restaurant. This waiter tried to convince us to eat a whole lot more than we knew we could hold. We told him that in spite of what our plump bodies suggested, we didn't eat a whole lot of food. The waiter, who was a dashing and beanpole-thin Spaniard, went on to tell us how much food he ate. He ate a *lot.* He told us he stayed thin by drinking eight cups of espresso every day, and he went on to say that he knew we ate healthy food because we weren't thin. "The body doesn't like good food," he said. "You need to shock your system with bad things to keep your body in line." He went on to recommend we abandon our healthy lifestyle in favor of one that contained enough "bad things" to improve our appearance. No doubt his very arteries wept as he gave us this happy news.

The dashing Spaniard doesn't know it, but he's heading for disaster. One of these days, he will be a good-looking corpse. That's because it's your diet that determines how much plaque you're developing in your arteries. Your diet can help keep your body from developing certain kinds of diabetes. Your diet can even help reduce your chances of getting colon cancer or breast cancer. You owe it to yourself to eat foods that will make your body healthier and avoid foods that will hurt your body.

We already told you in chapter 2 to ignore the food pyramid as a dietary guideline. We're going to second that advice here. As you choose your diet, traditional medicine says there are certain guidelines you should follow to help your body fend off these killer diseases. In a nutshell, here they are:

Avoid saturated fats. Saturated fats are any fats that are solid at room temperature. These include butter and margarine, shortening, and lard. However, saturated fats are also found in such natural foods as red meat, cheese, eggs, and whole milk. Because of the milk fat it contains, ice cream is a big source of saturated fat.

Conventional medical wisdom says that fats are fattening and that saturated fats are the worst of all. For more than twenty years, the medical establishment has drummed the concept of a low-fat diet into our heads. Americans have swallowed this philosophy and have lessened the fat in their diets, but their health has continued to deteriorate.

The problem with conventional medical wisdom is that it assumes all people will react the same way to a diet low in saturated fats. If you come from a long line of healthy people who aren't overweight and who don't suffer from heart-related diseases, maybe a low-fat diet will work for you. But if you gain weight even on a low-fat diet or if you find yourself unhealthy in other ways, you owe it to yourself to do a little research.

Avoid sugar. The average American eats 152 pounds of sugar per year. When you compare this to how much you weigh, this should be cause for alarm. A big part of this sugar consumption comes from Americans' love of candy; we consume twenty-five pounds of candy per person, per year. Candy is one of the three most commonly purchased food items, and soft drinks are right up there with candy.

Sugar is found in almost every processed food you eat, including canned vegetables, canned soups, and other things you'd swear contained no sugar at all. There are lots of ways to say "sugar" on the label without writing the word. Read the labels. If food you're purchasing contains an ingredient whose name ends in "-ose," you're buying sugar. If food contains corn syrup, you're buying sugar. If food contains molasses, you're buying sugar. The fewer processed foods you eat, the better off you are.

Sugar causes weight gain, which engenders its own set of problems (more on that later). Sugar can also wreak havoc with the pancreas, and that causes diabetes. You're also well aware of the connection between sugar consumption and tooth decay, but because tooth-decay isn't one of the life-threatening diseases we won't go into that here.

Eat a lot of fiber. Fiber isn't even one of the food groups. That's because fiber isn't a nutrient. In order for something to be a nutrient, it must be absorbed by the body so it can pass through the blood and feed your internal organs. Fiber isn't absorbed by your body at all and can still help you avoid some serious illnesses.

Eating a lot of fiber is believed to help prevent colon cancer, which is one of the big cancer-type killers. It helps lower your cholesterol levels and can help you control the effects of diabetes. It will also prevent a lot of smaller health problems that may not kill you, but can be a big factor on your enjoyment of life. If you don't know where to find fiber, look for it in unprocessed foods. Raw fruits and vegetables are big on fiber, as are whole grains. Constipation may be a sign you're not getting enough dietary fiber. If you're constipated, don't rely on medicines to get you going. Constipation is just a symptom of a bigger problem, and the bigger problem usually is that your eating habits—whatever they are—aren't working for you.

Welcome a variety of good foods into your diet, but shun the bad stuff. Your body requires a wide array of nutrients to accomplish all its functions, and no single food can meet all your body's demands. (This is bad news for those who try to subsist solely on cold cereal.) Eating a variety of healthful foods will generally cover all the bases. If you refuse to get enough variety in your diet, dietary supplements may improve the quality of your life. If you are interested in dietary supplements, do a little research on the Internet or look for a good book at your bookstore or health food store.

But just as important as taking good foods into your body is avoiding things that may harm you. Some of these items are awfully hard to avoid. (Kathy learned this lesson when she found out she'd grown up in a city that had thirty-three carcinogens in the drinking water.) Unless you're sure the tap water in your area is free of chemical contaminants, you may want to consider bottled water. If you choose this route, be sure you use toothpaste with fluoride, because bottled water isn't fluoridated.

You may want to also think twice about consuming the chemicals found in most processed food. The average American eats fourteen pounds of chemical additives every year. The good old United States government assures us that these chemical additives are safe, but any research you do on the matter will quickly convince you otherwise. Many of these additives are thought to cause cancer. Stay away from food additives if you can, and don't buy fresh produce that smells of pesticides.

▶ Exercise

Exercise helps you in every facet of your life. It improves your sleep and gives you a better mental outlook. Exercise can even turn back your body's clock by shrinking the plaque you already have in your arterial walls. All other things being equal, a manual laborer who isn't killed by injury will probably outlive someone who works at a desk. Exercise is the deciding factor.

 There are three kinds of exercises:

Strengthening exercise. This is the kind of exercise done on those fancy exercise machines at the health spa. It doesn't do much for you except give you bulky muscles. If your goal in life is to look like Arnold Schwarzenegger, strengthening exercise is the kind for you. Otherwise, forgo the strengthening exercise and spend your time in a more worthwhile way.

Stretching exercise. This kind of exercise helps you by giving you more flexibility, which is something you may not be able to appreciate now—but which you'll appreciate once you get older. Ironically, stretching is more dangerous for the people who can most benefit from it. As you get older, take care not to overdo the stretching exercises.

Endurance exercise. This is the workhorse of exercise. This kind of exercise gets your heart pumping and your lungs moving. Endurance exercise is also called "aerobic" exercise, because the deep breathing that accompanies this kind of exercise takes oxygen to every part of your body. Aerobic exercise is the exercise that strengthens the blood vessels, the heart, and the lungs and that will help prevent arteriosclerosis. Because it increases sugar uptake by the blood, this exercise also works against diabetes.

Aerobic exercise is so important that a different theory about the best way to do it comes out every week or two. We're not even going to try to tell you how to do your aerobic exercise, because the information would probably be obsolete by the time you read it. The only thing that everyone seems to agree on is that it's best to diversify, finding at least two ways to get your heart pumping. If you jump rope one day and run the next, you'll benefit more than you would if you did either exercise exclusively.

If you want to learn more about aerobic exercise, look on the Internet or ask your doctor. And if you've got the money, bookstores are filled with publications on aerobic exercise.

▶ Weight Control

If you ever want evidence that life isn't fair, compare the eating habits of family members and friends to their physical appearances. Sure, some people get just what they deserve. But others seem to eat all the time and never gain an ounce. Some people hardly eat at all and are wider than they are tall. For many people, genetics is the deciding factor in whether they're fat or thin. You may wish with all your heart that you could change the situation, but in many instances the best you can do is to be warmed by the feeling of virtue you get from knowing you've done your best.

➡ A huge factor in successful weight control is your body type. There are three body types—ectomorph, endomorph, and mesomorph.

Ectomorphs. These are the lucky ones. They're lean, no matter how much they eat or how little they exercise. All of us would like to be ectomorphs, because ectomorphs never have to go on a diet. In fact, the only dieting an ectomorph might consider would be a diet to *gain* weight.

The biggest problem with being an ectomorph is that ectomorphs may seem healthy when indeed they are not. You can be as skinny as an asparagus and still be a prime target for heart attacks and strokes. If you're an ectomorph, be sure to watch your diet—not for weight control, but to keep the killers at bay.

Endomorphs. These are at the other end of the spectrum. Their bodies naturally put on fat. Endomorphs originally came from areas with cold climates and short growing seasons. The endomorph's metabolism is so efficient that it turns everything to fat, so as to keep the body alive during those long winters where there is no food.

Clark comes from a family of endomorphs. He is shaped like a pear and will likely always retain that shape. He walks for an hour every day, and at times he bicycles more than fifty miles a week. All this exercise only shapes him into a slightly smaller pear. Clark could fast for a year and he'd *still* look like a pear. Alas, this is all too often the case with endomorphs, who spend their lives dieting and have nothing to show for it.

Mesomorphs. The mesomorphic body type is probably the most common.This group includes the people who are right in the middle. They will probably gain weight if they overeat, but diet and exercise will cause them to lose the excess weight they've gained. The people featured in before-and-after shots on diet commercials are all mesomorphs—people who gained weight because they didn't exercise or had a baby or went on an eating binge, but who lost the weight as soon as they changed their ways. Diet and exercise books are written *by* mesomorphs and *for* mesomorphs. They blindly assume that because *their* appearance is governed by diet and exercise, that must be the case for everyone else.

Mesomorphs may be the luckiest of the three groups, because their bodies usually reflect the care they take of themselves. If a mesomorph seems out of shape on the outside, he knows he is probably in bad shape internally, too.

All of the three body types are subject to diseases that may drastically alter their appearance. Tumors in strategic places can turn mesomorphs or even ectomorphs into sumo wrestlers. Sometimes the body gains weight for reasons that nobody can explain, which happened to the mesomorphic Kathy. She doubled her body weight in six months, and no doctor ever figured out why. All she knows is that no amount of dieting or exercising will cause her to lose the weight.

All this is a long way of saying that when people tell you to control your weight for better health, they may be telling you something that isn't possible for you to do. You can probably follow that advice if you're a mesomorph, but if you're an endomorph or if you have other health factors, you may not be able to control your weight despite your best efforts.

Before you use this as an excuse to live your life as an overweight person, you should honestly determine what kind of body type you have and what the reasons are that you're overweight. *If you can lose weight, you owe it to yourself to do so.* Obesity is a major cause of heart attacks and strokes. Fat people are at a much higher risk for colorectal cancer and breast cancer. Adult-onset diabetes is largely weight related. But all that can pale in comparison with the social stigma that is heaped upon fat people. In these politically correct times, fat people are almost the only people who are still considered fair game for ridicule.

We've promised you the names of a couple of books that may help you in your quest to be a healthier person. Coincidentally, the books that give you an alternative way to lower your blood pressure and avoid diabetes and get rid of arterial plaque are also books that may help you lose weight. If you keep packing on the pounds despite your low-fat diet or if you're upset with the condition of your health, read *The Schwarzbein Principle: The Truth About Losing Weight, Being Healthy, and Feeling Younger* (Health Communications, Inc., 1999) by Diana Schwarzbein, M.D.; or *Protein Power: The High-Protein/Low Carbohydrate Way to Lose Weight, Feel Fit, and Boost Your Health—in Just Weeks!* (Bantam, 1996) by Michael R. Eades, M.D., and Mary Dan Eades, M.D. Kathy read both books and followed their advice, and almost immediately her blood pressure went down so much that she no longer needed her blood pressure medication. These diets are not for everyone, but no diet is for everyone. If traditional low-fat diets have failed you, you owe it to yourself to look for alternatives.

If it's impossible for you to lose weight, all you can do is to continue to eat right and exercise daily. Try not to hate yourself, no matter how much you're shunned or scorned. You are who you are. Hating yourself because you don't like the way you look isn't going to help you lose an ounce, and it could detract more from the quality of your life than does being overweight in the first place.

If you're able to lose weight, good for you. You're more likely to succeed (and keep the weight off) if you do it gradually and if you change your eating habits than if you go on a crash diet and lose a lot of weight all at once. Combining diet and exercise is the most effective way to reach a proper weight. Of course, the best way to live is to keep the weight off in the first place. As any dieter can tell you, it's far easier to keep the weight off than to lose it once you're wearing it around your waist.

Other Preventive Measures

We didn't go into the other two big factors in preventive medicine because we hope you're not stupid enough to drink alcohol or to smoke. Aside from the warnings found in section 89 of the Doctrine and Covenants (the Word of Wisdom) there is plenty of medical evidence of the dangers of using tobacco. Smoking is directly related to arteriosclerosis, lung cancer, mouth cancer, liver cancer, and cancer of the esophagus. It also causes emphysema. In other words, it greatly increases your risk of getting three of the five diseases that are responsible for most deaths. Any young person who starts smoking these days, when even the tobacco companies are admitting the risks of using their product, has to be just plain dumb. Don't be dumb. You owe it to yourself and your future children to be around when they graduate from college and get married and do all those other important things that you will want to see.

Alcohol is a cause of mouth and liver cancer. It's the biggest single factor in cirrhosis, and it causes more fatal car accidents than any other factor. It's a factor in three of the six major causes of death (including accidents, which are not considered a disease). If you're drinking or smoking, do your body and spirit a favor and quit while you are still young—while you still can. The same is true for other drugs. If you're taking anything harmful into your system, it's easier for you to stop now than it will be later.

Really, you should try to avoid dependence on anything—whether it be Gummi Bears or chocolate or chewing gum. If you find yourself constantly indulging in the same food or drink to the point that you can't even think about getting along without it, that's exactly the time when you should stop consuming it . . . if only to prove to yourself you can.

There are four other areas where your behavior can prevent early death. The first is to avoid risky behavior. If you speed, you're more likely to die in a car accident than you would be if you didn't. If you ride a motorcycle, your chances of dying in a vehicular accident are greatly increased. If you ride a bicycle without a helmet or ride in a car without a seat belt, the chances of any accident becoming a fatal accident increase exponentially. If you go rafting without a life preserver, all the swimming prowess in the world may not be able to keep you from drowning if the raft overturns. If there's a safe way and an unsafe way to do something, choose the safe way. That way you can avoid becoming a statistic.

The second preventive measure is to get proper rest. You're young, and as a young person you're accustomed to pushing your body to its limits. You probably think nothing of staying up all night to study or to visit with friends. If you happen to fall asleep at the wrong moment on the highway, this behavior could kill you. But lack of sleep can also cause you to get physically run-down, which lowers your resistance to disease. Diseases as minor as colds or as life-threatening as cancer can invade the body when it has been pushed beyond its limits once too often.

The third preventive measure is to school your emotions. There is increasing medical evidence to bear out the proverb, "As a man thinketh, so is he." If you're angry or depressed, you're weakening your resistance to disease. Ulcers and heart attacks are obvious results of emotional turmoil, but even cancer may be affected by our emotions. If you're a hostile person or you've been unable to deal with life's injustices, find a way to add joy to your life. Learn to forgive people who've wronged you, and refuse to hold a grudge. If you let life's problems eat away at your soul, you may find yourself on a mortuary slab decades before your time—and you won't even be a happy corpse.

The fourth preventive measure is to get proper medical attention. If you're young and healthy, you don't need to see a doctor every year. However, if you notice changes in your body, you owe it to yourself to get a thorough medical exam. There are many problems that give small warnings far enough in advance to save your life—if those warnings are heeded immediately. There are also some silent killers that don't give warning signs until it may be too late to cure you. These are the conditions you should be looking for, even if you're young and think you're going to live forever.

- High blood pressure is a condition that doesn't display any symptoms for most people, but it's a killer just the same. People who have untreated high blood pressure are at extremely high risk for heart attacks and stroke, because they quickly develop artery-blocking plaque. In addition, their artery walls are weaker and more susceptible to blowouts that could have fatal consequences. High blood pressure is easy to treat once it's detected. If you have a family history of heart attacks or strokes, you may want to have your blood pressure checked early and often. There are often free blood pressure machines in large supermarkets and drugstores.

- By the time women reach age twenty-five, they should be doing monthly breast exams and having Pap smears every couple of years. Breast exams can catch breast cancer before it spreads to other parts of the body, and Pap smears can detect cervical cancer while it's still early enough to be curable. Nobody likes going to a gynecologist, but these tests can save your life.

- If you want to keep your teeth, have a dental checkup at least once a year. Ideally, you should have your teeth cleaned every six months. Most of us aren't that diligent, but people who don't regularly clean their teeth are particularly susceptible to gum disease. If you take care of your teeth, you'll never have to suffer the inconvenience of dentures.

If you do preventive maintenance on your car, you're going to be able to drive that car for years longer than you'd be able to drive it if you didn't take care of it. Your body is exponentially more important than a car, because nobody can crank out replacement bodies on an assembly line. You get only one of them. Take care of yours, and it will serve you well all your life.

Getting Help When Sick

The previous section concentrated on preventing the big killers. However, there are diseases that may beset you despite your best efforts against them. Some of them are minor annoyances, such as colds or other seasonal bugs. Other diseases can cause long-term debilitation and may afflict you even if you rigorously watch your health in every area.

People often wonder if they are sick enough to see a doctor or if there is something they can do themselves to treat their symptoms. This section should help you know when you can combat the offending bug yourself and when you should throw in the towel and see a doctor.

Self-Help Techniques

By the time you're old enough to leave home, you've probably already established a pattern of medical care that will persist throughout your life. Some people make a doctor's appointment every time they get a cold or the flu. Colds and flu are not treatable by doctors because they're caused by viruses, but these people insist on medical treatment anyway. At the other end of the spectrum are people who refuse to go to the doctor unless someone else carries their unconscious body to the hospital in an ambulance. These people consider gaping wounds to be "just a scrape" and festering dog bites to be one of the hazards of living. They let infections persist until they're hard to cure, even with today's wonder drugs. You'd do well to let your own habits lie somewhere in the middle between these two extremes.

Although there are times when seeing the doctor is necessary, many common illnesses can be self-diagnosed and self-treated. This saves the cold or flu sufferer from the hassle of dragging his weary body to the doctor's office and from the expense he is likely to incur there.

Often your body will give you easily recognizable clues concerning its condition. It lets you know when it wants food and it definitely lets you know when you are ill. Sometimes, you know something's wrong with you but your body doesn't offer any hints. In such cases there are other ways to determine what's wrong with you and what your body needs. Research is an important diagnostic tool. These days there are amazing books on the market that can help you diagnose what's wrong with you. Some of these books even tell you how to correct the problem without seeing a doctor.

Here's an example for you. Because Kathy works on the computer all the time, she has problems with carpal tunnel syndrome. At one point several years ago, she began wearing braces around her elbows and her wrists. The braces didn't help, but she believed she was doing the best she could, short of having surgery. Then she looked in a book about vitamins and learned that carpal tunnel symptoms can be cut back or even eliminated by taking a B-100 vitamin every day. She tried this method and regained the full use of her arms and hands within a couple of weeks. The carpal tunnel syndrome stays away as long as she continues to take the B-100. In this case, it was a little research, not the doctor, that helped her find lasting relief.

With the advent of the Internet, any computer owner who has a modem hookup has a wealth of knowledge at his fingertips. You will find no shortage of people who have experienced the same symptoms and can give you suggestions. Be careful, however, because not all such suggestions are safe. Your best bet may be to find a few good books on the subject and go from there. A few of the outstanding books in this field include *Vitamins, Herbs, Minerals & Supplements: The Complete Guide* (Fisher, 1998), and *Complete Guide to Symptoms, Illness and Surgery* (Fisher, 1995), both by H. Winter Griffith, M.D.; and *Take Care of Yourself* (Perseus, 1998) by Donald M. Vickery, M.D., and James F. Fries, M.D. The first book tells you how nutritional supplements may help you treat various annoying conditions, from acne to muscle cramps to wounds. The other two books start with your symptoms to determine what may be wrong with you and tell you when you should think about seeking medical treatment. *Take Care of Yourself* goes into detail about finding doctors and getting medical treatment. The Griffith book is so exhaustive in its coverage of diseases that a lot of doctors benefit from using it. However, all of these books are so easy to read that you shouldn't have any trouble using them.

Even if you choose to see a doctor, you should still do your homework. You still need to determine whether to follow the doctor's advice. Doctors are human beings, and some doctors are better than others. Even the best doctors are entitled to a bad day now and then, just as you are.

In Kathy's long and colorful medical career, a doctor has prescribed antidepressants for her because, as he said, "you're depressed and you don't know it." She has been prescribed appetite suppressants even though she doesn't have a big appetite. She has been prescribed antibiotics on countless occasions for conditions the doctors told her were caused by viruses (antibiotics don't combat viruses). She has been told she was pregnant by a doctor who had put her on a drug that was notorious for causing false positives in pregnancy tests. She had a doctor try to put her on the Opti-fast diet after the doctor's own nutritionist told her Kathy should be eating more food, not less. And she'll have to watch her blood pressure for the rest of her life thanks to a doctor who put her on steroids for six months because the doctor didn't know what else to do. So it's a good idea to prepare in advance before you see the doctor. If you go to the doctor armed with a little knowledge, you're more likely to end up with the medical treatment that your body needs.

If a doctor gives you advice that doesn't make sense to you, ask him to explain his reasons. The doctor will probably be glad to explain his reasoning to you in a way you'll understand. (If the doctor gets defensive and surly, find yourself another doctor.) Even after the doctor explains his reasons, however, you might not agree with them. It's your body. If the doctor says something to you that doesn't make sense to you, cheerfully take his prescription and thank him for his help. Once you leave his office, he's not going to be watching to make sure you fill the prescription or follow his advice.

Getting Medical Attention

If you find yourself in need of medical attention, there are three places you can go. The first is to your own personal physician. If you don't already have a personal physician, the time to get one is before you get sick. Otherwise, you're likely to be told that the doctor can't see you for three months, which wouldn't be much help in your current situation.

When you choose a doctor, there are many factors to consider. In most cases, people choose a "primary care physician," who they see first when something inside is malfunctioning. It's the primary care physician you'll visit when you break your arm or get an infection in your ear. If your case warrants treatment by a specialist, it's the primary care physician who will refer you to that specialist.

As you choose a primary care physician, you'll probably be influenced by your health insurance. Not all doctors accept all insurance plans. In fact, you may have to look long and hard to find a competent doctor who will take your particular health coverage. (More on that when we get to health insurance.)

Once you've found the list of doctors who take your health insurance, you can narrow down the selection based on your own preferences. Would you prefer a female doctor? That's your choice. Would you like a doctor who is conveniently located (near your home or work or school)? You can choose that, too. You can choose doctors based on the recommendations of friends and co-workers, although you should be warned that your friends and co-workers may not have the same standards as you. You can choose a doctor based on his specialty; many women choose an obstetrician/gynecologist as a primary care physician.

In some cases, you may choose a group of doctors rather than one particular doctor. If a group of physicians work together in the same office, you may choose to visit anyone who happens to be working in that office on the day you need an appointment. (It's much easier to get an appointment that way.)

Be sure to choose a doctor who gets along with you. Doctors are people, and people have different personalities. Your best friend may get along just great with Dr. Frankenstein, but you and the good doctor may never see eye to eye. Your doctor may not like you because you look like his obnoxious cousin, or you may not like your doctor because he looks like the French teacher who flunked you even though you clearly deserved a C. It doesn't matter why you and your doctor don't get along—if you don't like each other, find another doctor.

But not all people have primary care physicians. If your health is so good that you don't plan on seeing a doctor more than once a year or so, you may opt for the next form of medical care, which is the fast care center.

Fast care centers have many names, but they're all pretty much the same. They're open every day and often far into the night. They're designed for people who decide after regular office hours that the sore throat they have isn't going to go away on its own or who fall down and sprain an ankle in the middle of the night.

Fast care centers are usually staffed by a group of doctors who devote a day or part of a day each week to help out in the fast care facility. This is good advertising for the doctors, because if you find a doctor you like, you're welcome to make that doctor your primary care physician. Unless you make a fast care center physician your regular doctor, don't go to a fast care center in the hopes of seeing the doctor you like. You may visit a fast care center a dozen times without ever seeing the same doctor twice.

For the most part, fast care centers don't deal with medical insurance plans. If you have medical insurance, keep the receipt and file for a claim yourself. One of the ways fast care centers keep prices down is to eliminate such frills as filing medical claims for you. The lower cost of fast care centers offsets the lack of services you may otherwise expect.

The third choice in medical attention is the hospital emergency room. Take a close look at the phrase *hospital emergency room.* Before you run

off to an emergency room, make sure your "emergency" is really an emergency. A sore throat is not an emergency. Constipation is not an emergency. Your stubbed toe—even if you stubbed it so severely the toenail is turning black—is no true emergency. In fact, if you go to an emergency room for a problem that isn't really an emergency, anyone who arrives with a real emergency will be treated before you will. It's not uncommon to wait for several hours for emergency room treatment, and the longer you wait, the more you will realize your so-called emergency isn't an emergency after all. Besides, being treated in the emergency room is very expensive.

Here's a list of some of the problems that may warrant emergency treatment. If you are ever in doubt as to the severity of a problem, call your primary care physician or the emergency room to see what you should do.

Animal bites (see puncture wounds).

Bleeding that won't stop. If bleeding won't stop even when you put pressure on the wound, there may be damage to major arteries or veins. Worry only if you're bleeding profusely.

Blood poisoning or other infections. If you have an infected wound anywhere in the body that has caused you to have a fever, see a doctor immediately. Also see a doctor immediately if your wound smells bad and has thick pus. Wounds should get progressively better after an injury. If you find that a wound is getting worse rather than better, seek medical treatment.

Breathing difficulties. If you find yourself with shortness of breath that is not related to congestion due to colds, flu, or sinus infection, this is a medical emergency. Don't stop to make an appointment; go directly to the fast care center or emergency room—whichever is closer.

Broken bones. If you're not sure whether or not a bone is broken, it probably isn't. However, there are hairline fractures that don't even show up on x-rays until the break has started to "calcify" weeks after the event. But there are signs that suggest you've got a broken bone. If the limb is cold, blue, or numb, you may have broken it. If you're exhibiting symptoms of shock (cold sweats, thirstiness, paleness, or dizziness), the bone may be broken. If you do suspect a broken bone, it can just as easily be treated by your primary care physician or a physician at a fast care center. You don't need to go to the emergency room on a simple broken bone unless that's the nearest medical facility and you'd feel more comfortable doing so.

Burns. There's no question about it—burns hurt like crazy. But if they are not extensive, most burns do not require professional medical attention. Red spots are "first-degree burns." Blisters are "second-degree burns." Both first- and second-degree burns are the ones that hurt, but the serious burns are "third-degree burns." Third-degree burns are often painless, because they're so deep that the nerves have been damaged or destroyed. Usually you can see and smell charred flesh. If you have a third-degree burn, or a second-degree burn that covers a large area of the body (especially on the face or hands), see a doctor immediately. You can treat a less serious burn by immediately covering it with aloe vera gel and continuing the application until the burn doesn't hurt anymore.

Chest pain. There are many possible causes of chest pain, but heart problems are a big enough worry that if you have severe chest pain or a noticeably irregular heartbeat you should immediately go to the fast care center or emergency room—whichever is closer. Before you even sign in, tell the receptionist you're having chest pains. Chest pains are serious enough to take you to the front of the waiting line. Pain associated with heart problems may be located in the chest, jaw, or neck, or may spread to the insides of the arms and shoulders. It usually manifests itself as an uncomfortable pressure or a squeezing pain that lasts more than a few minutes. Along with the pains you may experience lightheadedness, fainting, sweating, nausea, shortness of breath, cold or sweaty skin, a pale complexion, and an increased or irregular heart rate. But in some cases you will experience none of these symptoms, so play it safe and get to the doctor immediately.

Choking. If you're choking and you can't talk, you're not going to make it to the emergency room. Your best bet is to go out in a public place and hope you find someone who knows the Heimlich maneuver. Before you panic, though, stop trying to breathe and see what happens. Whatever is lodged in your throat may pop right out if you aren't trying to force air into your lungs.

Eye injuries. If a foreign body gets in the eye and you can't get it out after flooding the eye with water, seek medical attention. This is especially true if there's a possible cut in the eye, if you can see blood in the eye, or if you've experienced a decrease in vision. If you can't see the foreign body, but you think it may be trapped behind the lid, seek medical treatment immediately. For chemicals in your eye see **poisoning**.

Gaping wounds. If a wound is dirty and you can't clean it out, seek medical treatment. If a chunk of you is missing so you can't bring the edges of the wound together, you should go to the nearest fast care center. If the cut goes deeper than the top layer of skin, and if it's long enough that you think you'll need stitches, see the doctor immediately. Always be more careful of wounds that are on the front of the hand or anywhere on the head or trunk of the body. These wounds should be given medical treatment unless they're extremely minor because infections in these areas are potentially serious.

Head injuries. Head injuries are potentially serious even if the skin isn't broken, because bleeding can occur inside the skull. With no place for the blood to go, the blood presses on the brain and could cause serious damage. If you lost consciousness, can't remember the injury, or had a seizure following the head injury, this is cause for alarm. Another sign of serious injury is blood or some other liquid coming from the ears, eyes, or mouth following a head injury. If you have any of these symptoms or even if you're just drowsy following a head injury, it's best to get to a doctor immediately. This is an instance where it's okay to go directly to an emergency room, although fast care centers can also help after this kind of injury.

Insect bites. Insect bites are only an emergency if you're allergic to the venom of the insect that bit you. If you start having breathing difficulties after you've been bitten or stung, get to a fast care center or an emergency room pronto. Other signs of allergic reactions include hives and abdominal pains. These, too, warrant emergency treatment. By the way, if you're bitten by a black widow or a brown recluse spider, seek medical treatment immediately. These bites won't kill you, but they can cause a lot of damage.

Loss of consciousness. If a person loses consciousness for any reason except a brief faint, seek medical attention immediately. Even a brief faint should be given medical treatment if it resulted from a blow to the head or other injury.

Poisoning. If you swallow something you shouldn't swallow, call or see a doctor immediately. If you can't contact your doctor, look for a poison control number in the phone book. Depending on the chemical composition of what you've swallowed, vomiting may or may not need to be induced. (Corrosive substances such as acids that burn on the way down will burn you again on the way up.) If you've swallowed a corrosive substance, wash it down with a whole lot of milk while someone contacts the doctor for you. And if you get a chemical in your eye that shouldn't be there, wash it out for about fifteen minutes in cool water as someone calls the doctor on your behalf.

Puncture wounds (including animal bites). If a puncture wound is not caused by an animal bite, you'll probably need a tetanus shot unless you're sure you've had one in the past five years. Tetanus is nothing to fool around with, so if you've had a puncture wound and aren't sure of the status of your tetanus shot, get the shot. If the puncture wound is caused by an animal bite, try to find out whether the animal has been vaccinated for rabies. If you can't locate the owner or (especially in the case of a wild animal) the animal has escaped, call your primary care physician and ask for advice. Unless the bite is extremely severe, this is not the kind of injury that should take you to a hospital emergency room.

Snakebite. Go to the doctor immediately. If you can take the snake (assuming it's dead) along with you to show the doctor, so much the better. However, a good description of the snake is probably nearly as good. Just don't go to the doctor and say you were bitten by a brown snake, or the doctor won't know how to treat you. By the way, if you're bitten by a snake in the United States, don't have a hissy-fit. You're far more likely to die from a car accident on the way to the doctor than you are from the snakebite itself, so calm down and *carefully* get yourself to the nearest medical facility.

Your Medicine Cabinet

When you're young and healthy, your medicine cabinet may be used for nothing more than makeup or aftershave lotion. This is as it should be. There's no sense in stocking up on cold medicines and laxatives just in case you might ever have a cold or constipation. For one thing, most medicines have an expiration date. If you stock up on an over-the-counter drug just in case you may need it one day, the odds are pretty good it will expire before you need it.

However, there are some basic things you may want to keep in your medicine cabinet, just in case you have a need for them. Pick and choose from the following list the items that make sense to you.

Adhesive tape. Good for holding gauze bandages in place. These days there are also tapes made of cloth and paper. These will work just as well and the paper ones are particularly easy to remove.

Aloe vera gel. This gel should always be in your household to treat cooking burns, but it's also valuable in treating sunburns.

Analgesics. "Analgesics" are pain relievers. These include aspirin, acetaminophen (Tylenol), ibuprofen (Advil), and Naprosyn (Aleve). Each has strengths and weaknesses. Aspirin and ibuprofen can be hard on the stomach lining. Whenever you buy aspirin, get the coated variety. Take aspirin or ibuprofen only with food. Ibuprofen is the best of the pain relievers for toothaches. Ibuprofen is also good for any sort of muscle pain or inflammation. Aspirin can prevent heart attacks if you take one a day, or it can lessen the effects of a heart attack if you have one. Acetaminophen doesn't have the stomach-irritating problems of aspirin and is a good all-purpose pain reliever. Naprosyn has only recently become an over-the-counter medicine, after having been a prescription medicine for many years. It's not necessarily better than the others; it's just newer.

Antibacterial ointment. Creams such as Neosporin can keep a wound from getting infected and can promote quicker healing.

Antibacterial soap. It's amazing how many infections you can ward off if you just use antibacterial soap whenever you take a shower.

Anti-itch medication. These types of medications are helpful for treating insect bites and rashes. The most effective creams and ointments contain 1 percent cortisone, but be careful how you use them. Continued use of cortisone creams causes the skin to get progressively thinner at the site where the cream was used. Once the skin gets thinner, it doesn't thicken up again.

Bandages, Ace. Eventually you or someone around you is going to sprain something. If you have a fresh Ace bandage on hand, you'll be ready when that happens.

Bandages, Band-Aid type or gauze. Despite what you may think, wounds are usually better off unbandaged. They heal better when exposed to the air. Bandages have their uses, though. They're helpful in keeping clean those wounds that are likely to get dirty. Plastic strips with gauze pads are also good immediately after a minor wound, to absorb blood that would otherwise get on your clothes or elsewhere. A third use is to keep a medicine in place over the wound, if you want to keep the wound medicated.

Betadine. Betadine—a great cleaning agent for wounds—is available behind the counter at pharmacies. It has an expiration date, so don't buy it till you need it.

Campho-phenique. A lifesaver if you have sores in your mouth.

Chloraseptic. Excellent for immediately killing the pain of a sore throat. The green stuff works better than the red flavor. By the way, Chloraseptic has an expiration date. It'll work beyond that expiration date but not infinitely beyond it, so you may not want to buy it until you get that first sore throat.

Cough lozenges. Invaluable when you get a cough attack in the middle of the night. By the way, if you don't have cough lozenges, hard candy will do just about as well.

Muscle cream. Muscle creams such as Ben-Gay will soothe muscles that are pulled during exercise or hard work.

Rubbing alcohol. Use it to clean wounds (even though it hurts like crazy).

Stomach medicine. Whether you use calcium-rich Tums or prefer a liquid such as Pepto-Bismol, stomach medicine is handy for occasional bouts of indigestion.

Tweezers. Good for probing for splinters and other things that get imbedded in the skin.

Understanding Health Insurance

In a perfect world, we would be able to go to any doctor at any time, without regard for how much that visit was going to cost. But the unfortunate reality of life is that doctors and medical procedures are expensive, and most of us don't have the money required to obtain medical treatment without seriously considering the costs. This means we have to deal with medical insurance and all the hassle and frustration that go along with it.

First of all, you would be foolish not to have medical insurance. Even if you have never been sick a day in your life, there is always a chance you will have a medical emergency or get into an accident that will put you in the hospital for an extended period. Such stays are not cheap, and you could easily run up a bill that would take you years to pay off, assuming you could ever make enough money to pay it off. No matter how frustrating it is to deal with health insurance companies, it is worth it for the peace of mind that comes from knowing you will be protected from such medical disasters.

When you first leave home, you may still be covered by your parents' medical insurance. Most such plans will allow you to remain covered for as long as you meet certain conditions. As you get older, you may be ineligible for such plans, or you may decide it would be better to get your own insurance. Fortunately, most employers offer health insurance to their employees, and the employer usually pays a portion of the cost. This can prove to be a real job benefit—those who are unemployed or self-employed can tell you horror stories about how much insurance costs when you are paying the entire bill yourself.

If you have several plans available to you, take the time to learn about them and choose the one that will be best for you. Although this may seem like a minor thing, making the wrong decision can cost you time, money, and even your health if you don't choose wisely.

Common Terms

When you get into the world of medical insurance, you will be exposed to certain terms that you may not understand. The explanation of many of these terms below will give you a better understanding of the rest of this section and will also help you when dealing with your insurance company.

Appeal. If your insurance company denies coverage on a certain expense, you usually have the right to appeal the decision and have them reconsider the facts. Try first to call the insurance company and talk with someone to explain the situation. If that doesn't work, ask the insurance company about the procedure you have to follow to file an appeal. This usually requires you to write a letter to explain the situation and why you think the payment should be higher. You may have to include an appeal form, and you should always include the explanation form that tells about how the claim was handled.

If your appeal is denied, you may still have the right to appeal to one or more higher levels within the insurance company. Check with your employer also to see if he can help you fight the decision. Many companies have people in their benefits department who are assigned to help employees work with the insurance company to resolve such issues.

Claim. Some plans require you to submit a claim form before they will pay for your medical treatment. This usually happens after you get the medical service. In such plans you will complete and submit the claim form to the insurance company along with a copy of the bill. Doctors differ in terms of how they handle medical claims. Some will file the claim for you, others expect you to file the claim but will not charge you until the claim has been processed, and others want their money up front and expect you to deal with the insurance company to get your money back.

Co-payment. Many plans will expect you to make a small fixed amount whenever you use a certain service. For example, some plans require you to pay $5 or $10 whenever you visit the doctor, and the insurance company covers the rest.

Deductible. Insurance companies often expect you to pay a portion of the costs of a medical treatment. This is called a deductible. For example, your policy may be written with a deducible so that you pay the first $400 of medical expenses in any given year. If you go to a doctor in January and he charges you $500, you would be expected to pay the first $400, and the insurance would cover the last $100. You may also be subject to deductibles for certain medical procedures. For example, many dental policies will cover examinations and cleanings, but will cover only 80 percent of the costs for cavity repair and 50 percent of the costs of crowns.

Exclusions. Read the fine print in your insurance policy carefully, because most companies have a list of procedures they will not cover. This list usually includes experimental treatments and alternate treatments such as acupuncture. But it may also include some elective procedures the insurance companies consider "cosmetic," such as breast enlargement. Many policies will not cover any procedure related to weight loss, even if that procedure is recommended by a doctor for a *bona fide* medical reason.

Maximum benefit. Some policies will have a limit to the amount that will be paid per person, either per year or during a lifetime. Many dental policies have a limit on the amount a person can per year, and many have a lifetime maximum per person that receive will be reimbursed for orthodontia.

Out-of-pocket maximums. Fortunately, many plans that have deductibles also have something called out-of-pocket maximums to help cap the amount you will have to pay. For example, your policy may have a deductible of $400 per family member per year, but it may also have an out-of-pocket maximum of $1,500 per family per year. Thus, the poor guy with a wife and eight kids would only have to pay $1,500 per year instead of a potential maximum of $4,000.

Premium. This is a fancy name for the money you pay each month to keep your insurance active. If you get medical insurance through your employer, the premium will usually be deducted automatically from each paycheck. Although some companies used to offer insurance to their employees at no cost, this is becoming less common because insurance costs have increased. Most companies will still pay a portion of the monthly premium for you, but most require that the employee also pay a portion each month.

Usual and Customary Charges. Most insurance companies calculate a maximum charge for a medical procedure and will not pay more than that amount. For example, there may be a guideline that a doctor in your city should charge no more than $25 to give a flu shot. If you submit a bill for $30, the insurance company will reject the last $5 as being excessive and will then apply your insurance to the remaining balance. Insurance companies are very secretive about the way these amounts are calculated. This has caused much controversy and many calls for reform.

Types of Plans

Now that you have an understanding of the terminology, we can jump right into a discussion of how the more common medical insurance plans work. All plans are unique, but most of the plans you will find fall into one of the following categories:

▶ Fee-for-Service

This is the most flexible kind of plan, but it is also the most expensive, and will probably be as extinct as a dinosaur unless things change dramatically over the next few years. This used to be the most common plan, but fewer and fewer employers are offering these because of the availability of cheaper managed care plans.

In a fee-for-service plan, you basically choose your own doctors, and visit them as often as you want. In terms of your choice of medical providers, this plan gives you absolutely the most flexibility. The downside is that this flexibility comes with a cost. Your monthly premiums will be very high with this type of plan (although your employer may be paying the lion's share of the premium). You will also have high deductibles, not only at the first of each year, but on each visit to the doctor. You may have to pay the first $500 each year, plus 20 percent of the cost of each doctor visit after that. You will also be subjected to the other standard limitations, such as Usual and Customary Charges, benefit maximums, and excluded procedures. But you do have your choice of doctors, and the insurance company will generally cover most of the charges.

If you can get this type of plan and money is no object, it will give you the most control over the type of medical treatment you receive and the doctors who provide it.

▶ Preferred Provider Organization (PPO)

This is similar to the previous plan—you still have control over how often you seek medical attention and some control over which doctors you will visit. The difference is that in this plan only those doctors who have consented to participate in the plan with your insurance company will be available to you. The insurance company maintains a list of "preferred providers," doctors who have agreed to participate in the plan, and you must choose from that list if you expect the insurance company to pay for your visits. Doctors who join the plan usually agree to be paid less than their standard fees for particular medical procedures. Thus, they are forced to work for less pay, but their association with the insurance plan will probably mean more patients.

This type of plan should be cheaper than the fee-for-service, but you should always expect your costs to be higher when you are given the power to choose your own doctors. With this type of plan, you should expect to see yearly deductibles, plus deductibles each time you visit the doctor. As with the previous plan, you will also be subject to Usual and Customary Charges, benefit maximums, and excluded procedures.

Whether this type of plan will work for you depends upon the doctors who participate. If all of your doctors participate, it will probably be a workable plan for you. One danger of this type of plan is that doctors may treat you as a second-class patient, because they are being paid less for treating you than for treating someone who uses another plan that pays the full amount they charge. If your doctor gives you less-than-adequate treatment, find another physician.

▶ Health Maintenance Organization (HMO)

Within the last few years, more and more of the types of health plans already described have been replaced by new plans that practice "managed care." The most common type of managed care plan is called a health maintenance organization, or HMO. Like other insurance plans, each HMO has a list of medical providers who have agreed to participate in the plan. When you join the HMO, you must review the list of doctors, and select one of them who will serve as your primary care provider (PCP). With an HMO, you are not free to visit the doctor of your choice, but you must always visit your PCP first. The PCP will try to solve your medical problems. If he cannot, he will give you a referral that will allow you to visit a specialist. This specialist must be one of those people who have agreed to participate with the HMO. The referral will usually allow you one to three visits with the specialist. After that, if you need to get more treatments from the specialist, you will need to get another referral from your PCP.

Make no mistake: managed care plans were developed by the insurance companies—not by the doctors. Most doctors hate HMOs and join them only because they have become so common that there are few alternatives. These are called "managed care" plans because the insurance company can manage the amounts they pay to medical providers. Most plans provide participating doctors with a fixed payment per month for each patient who selects them as a PCP. If you are as healthy as a horse, the doctor will make money on you, because he will get a payment each month even if you never visit. If you are sickly and visit the doctor each week, he will lose money on you. Some plans also penalize doctors if they give out too many referrals during the month.

Doctors also claim that more and more medical decisions are being made by the insurance companies (which are interested in saving money), instead of by the doctors who have the health of the patient in mind. As this was being written, the U.S. Congress was considering legislation that would provide doctors and HMO subscribers with more rights. Although we cannot predict what will happen with HMOs in the future, there is probably no going back to the older plans that did not involve some level of managed care.

Despite what doctors claim, there really are some advantages of joining an HMO plan. If you can get a PCP that you like and that features a good selection of specialists, you will probably be happy with the lower costs and administrative ease of such a plan. You will usually have to pay a small co-payment ($5 to $10) each time you visit a doctor in the plan, including your PCP. But there are usually no deductibles or claim forms to file, and there is less chance that a claim will be reduced or denied by the insurance company. If you like the plan but are unhappy with your PCP, ask friends or coworkers for their recommendations, and change your PCP until you find one that you like.

▶ Point of Service (POS)

Some employers give you the best of both worlds, allowing you to join an HMO but to also visit doctors that do not participate in the HMO. As you might expect, you will pay more for this kind of option, particularly when you visit a doctor outside of the HMO plan. But it does allow you more flexibility in choosing the medical services that you feel are right for you.

What Is Covered

No matter the type of health insurance plan you have, most of them will cover pretty much the same kinds of services. Listed below are the most common things that most plans cover. As all plans differ somewhat, read the details of your particular plan. Also, just because a service is covered does not mean it will not be subject to many of the deductibles, maximums, and limitations already discussed.

Dental. If you're lucky, your employer may give you an option to also receive insurance coverage for dental procedures. Your monthly premiums will probably be somewhat higher if you choose this coverage, but it is generally worth the extra money, especially if you have a large family or a lot of dental expenses.

Most policies will cover routine exams, X rays, and cleaning, and will pay a lesser amount toward such problems as cavities, crowns, and root canals. Some policies will also pay a limited amount each year toward orthodontia. As will any health policy, expect to find deductibles, maximums, and other limitations that apply to your coverage.

Doctor visits. Just about all policies will cover some of the charges related to doctor visits that are not related to medical emergencies. For example, if you have a skin rash or a sprained ankle, it is not unreasonable that you should be able to visit your doctor for treatment and expect the visit to be covered.

If you are in an HMO, you will probably have to make a small co-payment to the doctor. If you are in a regular type of plan, you will be subject to deductibles and possible benefits limitations.

Many health plans do not do a very good job of covering preventive medicine. Although your policy may pay for your doctor to fix a broken leg, it may not pay for him to give you an annual physical exam. There has been a general trend over the last few years to cover some of the more common preventive procedures, but check your policy before scheduling an appointment for such a procedure.

Emergencies. Most plans cover severe medical conditions that cause you to go to the emergency room of the hospital. Coverage for alternate emergency care facilities is not always provided, however, so check your policy before using such facilities. In fact, you're better off if you check the policy before the emergency occurs. In the event of a life-threatening situation, you should know what options are available without having to sit down and read your insurance policy.

Most HMO policies require you contact your PCP for advice before going to the emergency room, and they may insist that you visit a particular hospital that participates with the HMO. Having said that, most HMOs realize that the health of the patient is more important than following their clerical procedures, so most of them will cover any emergency room visit provided you contact the company within a certain number of hours after the visit. Make sure you check your policy, and contact your HMO as soon as possible after threatment so that you will not be stuck having to pay the bill yourself.

Hospitalization. Almost all plans will provide coverage if you are hospitalized for a serious medical condition. Coverage of hospital stays for less serious problems may have some limitations, so check the coverage of your policy before making plans for such procedures. Also, insurance companies sometimes have limitations on hospital coverage, such as paying only the amount charged by the hospital for a semiprivate room. If you insist on a private room, you will be expected to pay the difference.

Health, Mental. Most health insurance used to exclude coverage for mental health problems, but many companies are now realizing that mental problems can be just as serious as physical problems, and just as disruptive to the life of an employee. As a result, more and more policies are providing at least some coverage for treatment and counseling related to mental or emotional health. Many times this coverage is separate from the health care coverage, and you may have to follow different rules and use a different list of providers.

In many cases, it will be up to you to contact the mental health providers directly and make arrangements for your own appointments and your own counseling sessions. This is actually a good thing, because it is something you can do without anyone in your company having to know about your problems.

Emotional health is such an important issue that the section covers it in more detail. Meanwhile, if you decide you need professional help to cope with certain problems or feelings, make sure to check your health insurance policy to see if it covers such treatments. If not, you should still get the help, but you just need to be prepared to pay for it on your own.

Prescription drugs. Many medical policies will provide partial coverage for any prescription drugs you may be required to take. For HMO policies, this will often involve a co-payment, with you paying a small amount ($5 or $10) and the HMO covering the rest. For other types of policies, the insurance company will usually pay a percentage, such as 80 percent, and you will be expected to cover the difference. As with any coverage, expect to find certain maximums and limitations and be aware that certain types of drugs may be excluded from coverage.

Most health plans limit the quantity of the prescription to a thirty-day supply. This could cause you some financial hardship, if you have a condition such as diabetes that requires you to take drugs every day for the rest of your life. Many health plans have arrangements where you can order up to a ninety-day supply of drugs through a mail-order pharmacy, usually for a nominal cost increase over what you would pay locally for a thirty-day supply. See if such a plan is available if you have a need for prescription drugs on an ongoing basis.

Vision. Your employer may provide an option that covers certain procedures related to your vision. Eye exams are usually covered in full, but may be subject to deductibles and other limitations. Partial payment for glasses or contact lenses is also usually provided.

Your Emotional Health

Until now, we've focused on your physical health. Your mental health is every bit as important, however. No matter how well things are going for your physical body, life is miserable if you're unhappy. There's no magic pill that will make you happy, either. People often base their happiness on mistaken assumptions: "If I just had a boyfriend" or "If I just had more money" or "If I just had a nicer car." But people who make their happiness conditional usually find another reason to be unhappy if their first wishes are fulfilled.

Happiness depends on several factors, and none of them involves a new car. The first is a good self-image. If you like yourself, it's going to be a lot easier to wake up in the morning than it will be if you don't like yourself. If you don't like yourself, try to figure out why. If you're not educated, sign up for a class or apply yourself in your current classes. If you can't converse with people, start reading the daily newspaper to get up-to-date information that will give you something to talk about. If the problem is fixable, do what you can to fix it. If the problem isn't fixable, try to judge yourself by your good points instead of focusing on the bad ones. It's easy to tell you to like yourself, but that's not always easy advice to follow. One way to like yourself better is to be kind to others. If you're a blessing in the lives of others, their esteem for you may convince you—even if the mirror doesn't—that you're a friend worth having.

Another way to be happy is to look forward, not backward. Don't blame your unhappiness on things that happened in the past, because the past can't be changed. Plenty of people who had horrendous childhoods or have suffered debilitating accidents or have been dumped by a thoughtless fiancé are happy and productive citizens today. That's because they choose to look forward rather than dwell on the past. Don't find excuses for today's failures; instead, make up your mind to succeed despite your previous misfortune. If you spend your life looking back at life's unfairness, you're going to trip over the opportunities that lie ahead of you. Those opportunities are waiting for you to take advantage of them. Take the lemons life gave you and learn how to juggle.

Another important part of maintaining your happiness is minimizing stress. Worrying or getting angry about things never makes life better. In fact, it makes life worse because nervous and angry people alienate those around them. In addition, stress kills. It leads to heart attacks and strokes, to say nothing of automobile accidents and other potentially fatal situations. There are many ways to find peace in life, whether it be lying on the beach or losing yourself in prayer. Find a way that works for you and use it.

One of the most rewarding ways to be happy is to make friends. We're not talking about friends who will go out and party with you tonight but forget you're alive tomorrow. Make friends you can talk with or be quiet with. Make friends who will share your joys and your sorrows with you. If you don't know how to make friends, lose yourself in service. Perform acts of charity or get involved in a church calling. The friends you'll make when you're serving will be truer friends than the ones who want to see you only when you're ready to have a good time. In fact, if you forget about "making friends" and concentrate on others instead of yourself, friends will gravitate to you.

Yet another means of finding happiness is to explore the world around you. There's more in this world than you can possibly ever learn. Find things that interest you and learn about them. Find skills that intrigue you and become proficient in them. It's hard to sit around feeling sorry for yourself if you're too busy to schedule a time for it.

Handling Discouragement

Even if you're the happiest person in the world, you're going to have days when you're discouraged. You may have moments of homesickness. You may be disappointed by your friends. You may be betrayed by colleagues at work. Your roommates may drive you crazy, and your significant other may leave you for greener pastures. There's a word for such problems—*life*. Life is full of peaks and valleys. In fact, you can appreciate the peaks only because you have the valleys to compare them to.

If you find yourself becoming uncontrollably irritable or uncontrollably sad for no apparent reason and for a prolonged period of time, you may be experiencing clinical depression. Before you run off to a doctor, run off to a health food store and see what's available to help you. Kava kava may take the edge off your irritability, and St. John's wort may lift your depression. If the employee seems knowledgeable (and the employee is usually more knowledgeable if you're shopping at a corner store rather than one of the big chains), ask for advice. Try herbs for a month or so and see if they help. If you haven't seen any improvement by then, go to a doctor and describe your symptoms. Clinical depression is no longer a stigma that should embarrass those who suffer from it. You shouldn't feel any more shame about taking an antidepressant than a diabetic would feel about taking insulin shots. If your only option to treat long-term depression is with medicine, be thankful that medicines now exist that will quickly extinguish your symptoms without significant side effects.

I'm Still Clueless

? *How do I handle insurance claims if I get sick while away from home?*

You should always carry your insurance coverage card with you when traveling. Many insurance companies have toll-free telephones that are staffed twenty-four hours a day. Call an insurance company representative, explain the situation, and ask for his advice. If you are calling from an area where the company does business, he will probably direct you to a doctor or hospital in that area that is affiliated with the company's program.

In the case of a true emergency, it is more important that you get treatment first and worry about the insurance procedures later. Most insurance companies are understanding about such situations and will usually cover the costs—even if you visited a provider that was not in the company's plan. The key is to contact the insurance company representative as soon as possible. If you explain the situation early, the company will usually cover most emergency medical costs you incur while away from home.

CHAPTER 5

Tricks Mom Used to Do

★ **IN THIS CHAPTER**
- ✔ Knowing the Secrets of Buying Clothes
- ✔ Doing the Laundry Like a Pro
- ✔ Ironing to Help You Look Your Best
- ✔ Mending Clothes to Prolong Their Life
- ✔ Learning Why Cleanliness Is Better Than Slovenliness
- ✔ Cleaning the House Room by Room

Back in the old days when you were living at home, the kids who were really lucky were the ones whose moms did everything for them. Mom changed the sheets, did the laundry, mended the clothes, cooked the meals. She may have even cleaned the children's bedrooms. It only made sense. After all, Mom wasn't dating, or studying, or writing term papers, or going out to parties, or talking on the phone, or doing anything *important,* was she? It was her job to clean up after the family. If she hadn't cleaned up after her children, what else would she have done with her time?

But now that you're on your own, you may be seeing life from a different perspective. The kids whose moms did everything for them don't know how to cook, or clean, or wash their clothes, or do any of those other boring things. In fact, those "lucky" kids can be a pain in the neck as they leave a mess for roommates to clean up or let their laundry pile up until the apartment stinks or squander the week's grocery money on ice cream and Twinkies.

If you're one of the "lucky" kids, we're here to help you before your roommates kill you.

In this chapter, we're going to teach you how to leave your slothful ways behind you and turn into a responsible adult. We are extremely qualified to teach this because between us we have committed every housekeeping transgression known to man. As we move through this chapter, Kathy will tell horror stories about Clark, and Clark may reciprocate with a shocking tale or two about Kathy. Remember—do as we say, not as we do. We've made all the mistakes ourselves, so you don't have to.

Purchasing and Caring for Clothes

If you're typical of most people who are leaving home for the first time, your experience with purchasing clothing has probably been limited to pointing at something in the store and saying, "I want *that* one." You didn't care how much it cost or how difficult it might be to take care of. Why should you? *You* weren't planning on paying for it or taking care of it!

Now that you're responsible for your own wardrobe, you've got some hard lessons to learn. Having that designer name on your rear may not be quite so important when you realize it will lighten your wallet fifty dollars. And you're probably not going to enjoy that pleated skirt quite so much when you're the one who has to iron the pleats. Having clothes takes money and work. How much work and money it takes is entirely up to you.

Shopping Is Half the Battle

When you're dealing with clothing, shopping is indeed half the battle. If you buy things that are inexpensive but not cheaply made, and if you choose things that can be cared for without a lot of time or expense, you're going to make the best possible use of your clothing dollar.

There are three major factors in shopping for clothes. Although you may have thought of the first one on this list as being the only factor, or at least the most important, it's time for you to take a close look at the others:

Finding the look you want. When you were in high school, you may have been able to get away with wearing whatever you wanted to wear—whether that consisted of black clothes or a Mohawk haircut or strange rings to fill your assorted pierced body parts. Your look is part of who you are, and during no time does that look seem more important than it does during a person's teenage years.

Your look is also important after you leave school; but once you're out in the real world you have more people to consider than just yourself. Your ability to find employment may well depend on the way you dress. Most employers who pay above the minimum wage aren't eager to hire people who dress like teenagers. There are exceptions (writers, artists, and computer people come to mind), but unless you've chosen one of those careers, you may want to take note of what successful people in your chosen field are wearing and emulate them.

There's a wide range of material that is used for clothing these days, from the rubbery polyester double knit all the way up to natural cottons and silks. Natural fibers are more expensive and harder to take care of than synthetics, but they look better on the human form than the traditional polyester. Fortunately, these days there's an assortment of fabrics that fall between linen and double knit. Once you learn more about caring for your clothes, you'll be able to pick the fabric that enhances your appearance and that is relatively easy to care for.

Calculating the expense. Your clothing expense doesn't end when you've taken the garment home and hung it in your closet. Thirty dollars may not seem like much for a good blouse, but if it has to be dry cleaned at $4.95 a pop, that blouse is soon going to cost you several hundred dollars. Nor is thirty dollars a good bargain if the blouse will be out of style in six months or is made of such shoddy workmanship that you can wear it only a few times.

Before you buy an article of clothing, inspect it. Look at the tag to see what fabric was used in the construction and whether it has to be dry-cleaned. Look at the seams and see whether the pieces are solidly put together. If you can't tell the difference between a $1,000 suit and one you buy off the rack for $150, look at the features of the expensive model. Read the label to see what fabrics were used. Notice the colors and patterns. Like it or not, some colors and patterns are more acceptable in professional situations than are others. Inspect the reinforced stitching and the wideness of the seams. Check the weight of the fabric and crush it in your hand to see how it resists wrinkles. See how it lies on your shoulders and fits the form of your body. Look at the quality of buttons, zippers, or other fasteners—and how well they're sewed on. See if there are extra buttons hidden away for you to use later. All these things are a mark of good clothing. If you can find inexpensive clothing that has the features of top-of-the-line garments, you're getting the best possible value for your clothing dollar.

Another thing the smart shopper does when purchasing clothing is buy items that serve a multitude of purposes. For example, a blazer can be made to look like an entirely different garment, depending on what sort of shirt or blouse you wear with it and whether you add a tie or a scarf. If you purchase clothes that can be worn as part of an ensemble instead of having to be worn as a single unit, you'll be able to make more outfits out of fewer pieces of clothing. This is another way to stretch your clothing budget.

Matching your cleaning needs to your tolerance for cleaning. You've got to figure yourself out before you purchase clothing. If you perspire heavily, choose natural fabrics that can breathe and that won't show perspiration stains. Also, select sturdy clothing, because you're going to have to wash your clothes more often than do other people. If food jumps from your fork to the front of your shirt on a regular basis, you may want to select patterned informal shirts and blouses. Patterns don't show stains as readily as solids do, so you don't have to launder them every time a piece of rice lands on your chest.

Different fabrics serve different functions in your wardrobe. The weave of cotton allows the body to cool off. The tight mesh of polyester knits hold in body warmth. Cotton-polyester blends look more natural than polyester but are easier to care for than solid cotton. Rayon is a synthetic fiber that can mimic cotton in appearance, but that sheds wrinkles. Linens and silks make you look and feel pampered and expensive.

Just as fabrics serve different needs, they need to be cared for in different ways. Cotton is machine washable, if you allow for shrinkage. Cotton is also notorious for wrinkling. If you sit down on cotton once, you've got wrinkles in your clothes. This goes double for linen, which is also a natural fiber.

Polyester may not look as good as cotton, but it's low maintenance and virtually indestructible. The cheaper the polyester, the easier it is to take care of (and the more rubbery the look and texture). However, you may want to take note that the rubbery stuff (more commonly known as polyester double knit) increases perspiration and body odors.

Rayon and silks have traditionally been fabrics that are dry-clean only, but recent innovations make it possible to wash these fabrics in water. All the information you need for fabric care can be found on the label that's sewn into each piece of clothing. Before you buy an article of clothing, make sure you're willing to expend the energy that the clothing requires. When your decision between two articles of clothing is a toss-up, pick the one that's easiest to care for.

Laundry Day

The easiest way to have clean clothes is to keep from getting get them dirty. One way to do this is to keep a supply of around-the-house clothes on hand. You don't have to be dressed like a movie star when you're sitting around the house—and especially when you're cleaning or cooking or doing household repairs. If you can keep an old pair of sweats on hand for dirty work, you'll save your good clothes from a whole lot of extra wear and tear.

The less often you wash your clothes, the longer they're going to last. It's a fact of life. Water removes color from your clothes. Dryers weaken the fabric of your clothing little by little as they remove tiny fibers that are part of the weave of the material. The lint in your dryer's lint trap isn't dust. It's fabric that used to be part of your clothes, but that was shaken out by the dryer. You don't have to be a home economist to realize your clothes need that fabric more than your lint trap does.

This is not to say you should go without doing the laundry. Underwear is designed to be worn for no longer than one day at a time— at least if you're intent on keeping company with other humans. But outerwear can often be worn several times before it has to be laundered or dry-cleaned. You may have worn something once and thrown it on the floor for Mom to wash when you were in high school, but you're an adult now. As an adult, the goal is to keep your clothes in good condition so you can wear them more than once between washings. Inspect your clothes as soon as you take them off. If there's a stain that needs to be laundered, pretreat that stain immediately with a commercial pretreating solution. If it's a piece of clothing that must be dry-cleaned, mark the stain with a post-it note or a safety pin so you can point it out to the cleaner. That way the stain is more likely to come out when the clothing is laundered. If the clothing is free of stains or nasty smells, hang it up or fold it and put it away as soon as it passes inspection. That way wrinkles will have a greater chance of falling out before you wear the clothing again.

▶ Washing

 There are six big steps in washing clothes:

Sort the clothes. You might think sorting the clothes is a no-brainer. Darks go in one pile; lights go in another pile. (This is so colors from the dark pile won't "bleed" onto your lights.) But it's a little more complex than that. You may even want to go for four piles—darks, whites, mixed colors (such as stripes that have white in them), and special care items. You can determine what clothes go in the "special care" pile by reading the label. Anything that says it should be washed separately should be washed all by itself or with other items of the same color because the color will bleed. Anything that says "gentle cycle" is fragile and should be washed in the gentle cycle of the washer. Anything that says "dry-clean only" shouldn't be put through the washer at all.

There's one other category for "special care clothes"—clothes that need to be mended. We'll tell you about mending later, but for now it's enough to tell you that clothes should be mended before they're laundered rather than after. Tears only get bigger in a wash cycle, and loose buttons could fall off and get lost forever.

Pretreat stains. We're going to give you a handy chart for stain removal, but don't let the chart intimidate you. Most stains can be removed with a prewash stain remover, and several varieties of these are available at your neighborhood grocery store. (Zout is a particularly good variety.)

Handy Stain-Removal Chart

STAIN	TREATMENT
Adhesive tape, chewing gum, rubber cement	1. Put in the freezer or rub with ice. This hardens the residue so it can be scraped off with a table knife. 2. Saturate the area with prewash stain remover or treat with a citrus-based cleaning product such as Goo Gone or De-Solv-it. 3. Rinse, then launder in the hottest water that is safe for the fabric.
Beverages (soft drinks, juices)	Drink stains may dry clear, but don't be fooled. If there's sugar in the beverage, it will eventually discolor the fabric if it isn't washed out. If you spill a beverage on something, throw it in your dirty clothes hamper. Pretreatment isn't necessary unless you're dealing with grape juice. If you're dealing with grape juice, pretreat and hope for the best.

STAIN	TREATMENT
Blood	1. Pretreat or soak in warm water with a product containing enzymes, such as Era. 2. Launder. Several launderings may be necessary, but don't dry the garment until the stain is gone. If the stain refuses to budge, try a citrus-based cleaning product such as Goo Gone or De-Solv-it. If that doesn't work, wash with a fabric-safe bleach.
Chocolate	1. Use your favorite prewash stain remover. 2. Launder by washing in warm water with a product that contains enzymes, such as Era. If stain remains, rewash with a fabric-safe bleach.
Collars and cuffs	1. Use your favorite prewash stain remover. 2. Launder.
Cosmetics	1. Use your favorite prewash stain remover. 2. Launder.
Crayon	1. Treat the same as wax. Alternatively, you can dampen the stain and rub it with a bar of soap. 2. Launder using hottest water safe for fabric. *If a crayon contaminates a whole load of clothes,* rewash the load in hot water using a cup of baking soda in addition to your regular soap. If that doesn't help, soak in an enzyme-containing liquid such as Era and launder one more time.
Dairy products	1. Use your favorite prewash stain remover. 2. Launder with a product that contains enzymes, such as Era.
Deodorants, antiperspirants	1. Use your favorite prewash stain remover. For heavy stains, allow to sit for about 15 minutes. 2. Launder.
Dye bled from other clothes in the wash	There are products in the supermarket that are designed for this sort of thing. Find it in the laundry aisle and follow the instructions on the package label.

STAIN	TREATMENT
Egg	1. Use your favorite prewash stain remover. 2. Launder with a product that contains enzymes, such as Era.
Fabric softener	Don't be paranoid. Fabric softener was made to go on clothes. Just throw the article of clothing in the wash and launder as usual.
Fruit juices (see also Beverages)	1. Use your favorite prewash stain remover. 2. Launder with fabric-safe bleach.
Grass	1. Use your favorite prewash stain remover. 2. Launder with a product that contains enzymes, such as Era.
Grease and oil	1. Use your favorite prewash stain remover. 2. Launder in the hottest water that's safe for the fabric, using a detergent that advertises how great it is at removing grease. If the stain doesn't come out in the wash, you may need to try a professional cleaning fluid. Throw yourself on the mercy of your dry cleaner *before* you send the clothing through the dryer, and see what he suggests.
Ink	1. Use your favorite prewash stain remover. Ink is difficult and sometimes impossible to remove. You may want to find a prewash stain remover that's specifically formulated for the kind of ink in question. Laundering may permanently set some ink stains. 2. Launder.
Mildew	Launder in fabric-safe bleach and the hottest water that won't damage the fabric. It may be impossible to remove bad mildew stains, so don't get your hopes up.
Mud	1. Allow mud to dry. Then brush off as much mud as possible. 2. Use liquid laundry detergent containing enzymes to pretreat. 3. Launder in a detergent containing enzymes, such as Era.

STAIN	TREATMENT
Mustard	1. Use your favorite prewash stain remover. Look to see if there are any particular instructions for mustard, which is hard to remove. 2. Launder using fabric-safe bleach.
Paint, oil-based (includes varnish and wood stains)	1. Use the paint thinner recommended on the label or turpentine. 2. Rinse. 3. Use your favorite prewash stain remover. 4. Launder.
Paint, water-based	1. Rinse fabric in warm water while stains are still wet. 2. Use your favorite prewash stain remover. 3. Launder.
Perspiration	1. Use your favorite prewash stain remover. (If perspiration has changed the color of the fabric, pretreat fresh stains with ammonia or old stains with white vinegar, and then rinse.) 2. Launder in the hottest safe water for the fabric, using a detergent that contains enzymes.
Pine resin	1. Scrape resin off fabric. 2. Treat with a citrus-based cleaning product, such as Goo Gone or De-Solv-it. 3. Launder in the hottest water that is safe for the fabric.
Rust or iron stain	1. Use a rust remover recommended for fabrics. 2. Launder.
Shoe polish, liquid	1. Make a paste of granulated laundry detergent and water. Let it sit on the stain for ten minutes. 2. Launder.
Shoe polish, paste	1. Scrape solids off fabric with a dull kitchen knife. 2. Use your favorite prewash stain remover or treat with a citrus-based cleaning product such as Goo Gone or De-Solv-it; rinse. 3. Rub detergent into dampened area. 4. Launder using a fabric-safe bleach.

STAIN	TREATMENT
Tar	1. Scrape tar off fabric. 2. Treat with a citrus-based cleaning product such as Goo Gone or De-Solv-it. 3. Launder in the hottest water that is safe for the fabric.
Wax	1. Scrape off surface wax with a dull knife. 2. Treat with a citrus-based cleaning product such as Goo Gone or De-Solv-it. 3. Launder in the hottest water that is safe for the fabric. If any pigment from the wax remains, wash again with a fabric-safe bleach.

Set the washer. Once you've mended the clothes and pretreated the stains, it's time to set the washer. You'll need to determine the size of the load, the temperature of the water for washing and rinsing, and what kind of cycle you're running (heavy, permanent press, or delicate).

If you're unsure what temperature to use for particular fabrics, read the label. If you can't decipher the label, here's a little table for you:

TYPE OF LAUNDRY	WASH/RINSE SETTING
Whites	Hot/Cold
Light Colors	Warm/Cold
Dark Colors	Warm/Cold or Cold/Cold
Delicate Fabrics	Cold/Cold

Fill the washer. There's a proper order for filling the washer. First you add the soap, then you turn on the water, and then you add the clothes. There's a reason for this: Most laundry detergents are strong enough to leach the color out of your clothes. If you put the detergent in first and then add some water to the tub, that will dilute the strength of the detergent so you won't have pockets of detergent bleaching the color out of your clothes.

As for how many clothes to put in a washer, don't be unreasonable about it. Yes, you can probably stuff all your dirty clothes into one load if you work at it. But the clothes need room to move freely through the water. You're better off doing two medium-sized loads than one huge one.

By the way, you can wash hand-washable "delicates" in a washing machine. Take the clothes you want washed and put them in a pillowcase. Tie the end of the pillowcase so it won't come undone during washing. Then run the pillowcase through the "gentle" cycle of the washer.

Dry the clothes. Before you ever put your clothes in the dryer, you should check the clothes that were pretreated to make sure the stains came out. This may be hard to do, because wet clothing is naturally darker than it will be when it dries. Make the effort, though. Once you've dried a stain, it's probably there to stay. If a stain doesn't come out the first time around, run it through the washer again.

Once your clothes have passed inspection, throw them in the dryer along with a fabric softener sheet. (Fabric softener sheets take the static electricity out of clothes and make them soft enough to wear comfortably.) Set the dryer temperature according to the clothes you're drying—high heat for towels and for cottons that won't be ruined if they shrink, medium for "permanent press" and most of your clothes, and "air-dry" for delicate clothes that shouldn't be dried with heat. Turn the dryer on, and you're on your way to a finished project.

Most dryers have a lint filter that needs to be cleaned—usually after every drying cycle. Remove the filter from the machine, peel the layer of lint from the filter (it will look like gray cotton), throw it away, and return the filter to the machine. If you don't do this, your dryer will take longer to dry, and the eventual lint buildup could even cause a fire.

Put the clothes away. Part of the magic of using a dryer is that clothes that have been tumble-dried may come out of the dryer without wrinkles. This will take a little effort on your part. You should be standing at the washer when the washing machine shuts off. Immediately throw the clothes and a fabric softener sheet in the dryer. Then take them out of the dryer as soon as the dryer stops and immediately hang them up. If the dryer finishes its cycle before you can get to it and the wrinkles start to set, take a damp washcloth and put it in the dryer with the clothes for about five minutes. Then stop the dryer and quickly hang up the clothes before they get wrinkled. Ironing clothes is one of the nastiest jobs known to man, so you want to eliminate the ironing process if at all possible.

▶ Ironing

Ironing is such a boring, miserable task that it's not even fun to write about. Indeed, the ironing section got postponed until it was the last unfinished section in this book—that's how vile it is. However, unless you have funds to spring on a professional cleaner (and few of us do), ironing is a necessary evil. You can make it better by setting up the ironing board in front of the television.

The best way to iron is not to ever have to bring out the ironing board. Choose fabrics that shed wrinkles, or "crinkle cottons" that are supposed to be wrinkled. The less ironing you have to do, the happier you'll be when ironing day comes around. Another way to lessen the need for ironing is to stand over the dryer like a vulture and snatch clothing out of it as soon as the dryer stops. If you hang it up immediately, you may not have to iron it at all. In fact, even clothes that need to be ironed should be hung up as soon as they leave the dryer. That will help keep wrinkles from "setting," so that they're easier to iron out.

Other than a television or something else to distract your mind, there are only three things you need to iron: an iron, an ironing board, and a good supply of coat hangers. If you're planning to use the steam feature on a steam iron, the iron should be filled with water. Distilled water is the best water to use in an iron because there are fewer minerals in it to clog up the works. If you don't want to deal with buying or distilling water, you can set aside a spray bottle for ironing, and do your spraying directly from the bottle.

Some people like their clothes to have a starched look. Starch is helpful because it puts a light coating on the fabric that will protect it from stains when the clothes inevitably get dirty again. If you like starch, there are several varieties on the market. Pick one and have it with you when you begin your ironing experience.

The first thing to do when you begin to iron is to adjust the ironing board. You can stand or sit to iron, but you should be able to put your hand flat on the board without bending your arm or your back. If your ironing board is at the right height, the muscles in your shoulders won't get as tired.

➡ Next, set the temperature of the iron to the setting that's most appropriate for your clothes. Different fabrics need different temperatures, so you may want to iron all your similar fabrics in a bunch. If fabric temperatures aren't printed right on your iron, here's a quick guideline:

High—Cotton or linen
Medium—Wool
Low—Synthetics or silk

This applies to articles that are dry ironed. Most articles that are ironed with steam can be ironed on the "steam" setting. When in doubt, iron your clothes with a lower temperature. Once your clothes are burned, they're ruined.

When you start ironing, the best way to do it is to start with the things that get wrinkled the least. For example, if you're doing a shirt, start with the collar and cuffs. Then hit the button placket (the reinforced piece of material containing the button holes) and the space around the buttons. Then flatten those sleeves. Finally, hit the back and the front. The reason for this is that if you do the wide open spaces first, they're probably going to get wrinkled while you're doing the other parts so you'll be doing the same work over again.

You don't have to push down on the iron. It's the heat, or the heat combined with steam, that removes the wrinkles—not the pressure of your hands on the iron. Also, try to iron back and forth instead of in a circular motion that could stretch your fabric. Zippers should be closed when you iron around them. If you're using a plastic zipper, make sure the iron never touches the teeth of the zipper. If that happens, the zipper will melt.

If you find your fabric "shining" after you iron it, iron it again with a piece of fabric such as a handkerchief between the iron and the article of clothing. This "press cloth" should remove the shine.

As you iron, you'll notice that some things are simple, and others are a lot more complicated. The nastiest job on a piece of clothing is to iron around the buttons. There are plastic sleeves you can buy for irons that go over the hot spot, or "sole plate." These keep your iron from snagging on the buttons, so that you can iron right over the buttons instead of around them. Another advantage of the sleeves is that they protect the fabric so you iron everything on high heat and never burn anything.

If you don't use a plastic sleeve over your iron, delicate fabrics such as silk or velvet should always be ironed on the "wrong" side. This is the side that has the seams, or the side where the color is lighter. You may want to put a towel between the delicate fabric and the iron. Make sure you read the care label on the garment to see how it should be ironed.

Irons are dangerous objects. They should never be left unattended. You should never use an iron when a child or a pet is in the room. The cord should be placed so that you can't trip over it and knock the iron over. This next part is a no-brainer, but you don't want to be using that iron near a body of water it can fall in. It's also a good idea to unplug the iron before you fill the steam compartment with water. That way you'll be absolutely certain you're safe from electrocution. Electrocution is a pretty fast way to ruin your day.

Different fabrics have different personalities. Here's a handy chart to tell you what to do with each fabric you're likely to use:

FABRIC	CARE INSTRUCTIONS
Corduroy	Cover the ironing board with a towel and then iron the wrong side of the fabric. Steam helps remove the wrinkles from corduroy.
Cotton	Use either a steam or dry iron. Dark, solid colors should be ironed on the wrong side to avoid shine.
Decorations (Embroidery, Lace)	Iron over a towel, using steam but no pressure.
Knits	Press down on the fabric and then lift the iron rather than running the iron back and forth. This prevents the fabric from being stretched out of shape.
Metallic fabrics	Press with cool iron and a thin press cloth.
Polyester	Polyester is designed for little or no ironing. If you must iron, make sure to use an iron no hotter than the temperature settings recommended on the label. Otherwise, the fabric may melt.

▶ **Mending**

Mending is one of those chores that can greatly prolong the life of your clothing. The best way to do this is to catch small problems before they turn into big ones. It's far easier to tighten a loose button than it is to go to the store to find a replacement. Similarly, it's easier to sew a small rip than it is to mend it once the rip is three inches long.

There's not too much you need in the way of mending equipment. Buy a packet of needles in assorted sizes. Unless you're good at threading needles, you may want to choose embroidery needles that have bigger eyes. You'll also want to buy some spools of sturdy thread in assorted basic colors. Black, navy, white, and beige should do for most jobs.

When you're threading a needle, the end of the thread you put through the "eye" of the needle makes a difference. If you put the wrong end of the thread through the hole, the thread will knot when you're trying to sew with it. Don't ask us why. This is one of the mysteries of life. If you thread the needle while the thread is still attached to the spool, you won't go wrong.

Cut off twice the amount of thread you think you'll use, then put your needle in the center of it and knot the ends together. Using doubled thread will cut your mending time in half if you're sewing on a button, and it will prevent your needle from coming unthreaded while you mend.

When you're mending, do it from the "wrong" side of the garment so that your stitches won't show as much from the front. Take the smallest possible stitches, and involve the smallest amount of good fabric in the mending that you can get away with. Some fabrics ravel so that your stitches will soon pull out.

If your fabric ravels, or if you don't want to deal with a needle and thread, there are "mending tapes" and glue on the market that will allow you to mend your clothing without sewing. Ask a fabric store employee to recommend a good brand, and then follow the directions on the package. There are also iron-on patches that can save your clothing if you apply it to a small hole rather than waiting for the small hole to turn into a big one. Look around the fabric store to see what's available and go from there. You'll be surprised at the easy and inexpensive ways that have been developed to save your clothes from early retirement.

Keeping Your Home Clean

If you're like most young people, you probably think your parents are extremists on the issue of keeping the house clean. Since you left home, you have probably been happy not to have to put up with chores or reminders to make your bed and pick up after yourself. But after a week or two of dwelling in clutter and disorder, you may begin to wonder if your parents weren't onto something. This section will address the virtues of a clean home, habits that make cleanliness easy, and what to do when your home is in disarray, smells bad, and generally is a hazard to live in.

Why Keep Your Home Clean?

➡ Before we talk about *how* to keep your living quarters clean, the obvious question to ask is *why* you should keep your home clean. You may think you *like* being a slob. Even worse, being a slob may be such an ingrained habit for you that you may think you'll never be able to change. But there are several reasons why the place where you live should be clean and orderly, even if you have to suffer to do it. Pick the reason you like and focus on it. Let that be your incentive for keeping a clean house when you'd just as soon live in a pigsty.

▶ To Keep the Vermin at Bay

Human beings have been on the earth for a long time, but we only *think* we own the planet. Scientists, who know far more about such things than we do, refer to our era as the "Age of Insects." There are hundreds of thousands of varieties of insects who share the world with us. These range from cute little ladybugs to flies and roaches that spread disease. Spiders aren't insects, but they also outnumber human beings—and like insects, they inhabit houses and apartments. Mice and rats are other unwelcome guests that may find shelter in your home, especially as winter approaches.

All these vermin thrive on clutter. Every stack of papers or boxes gives unwanted visitors a place to hide. Every pile of clothes that stays on your floor is a good place for them to nest and breed. Every morsel of food that is left out will feed them and give them an incentive to stay in your home once they've found it.

▶ To Be Prepared for Surprise Visitors

Unless you're an extremely unpleasant person, you're going to have friends no matter where you live. Unless you're an extremely evasive person, you're also going to have home teachers or visiting teachers —or both. Unless you're an orphan, family members will expect to see you from time to time. Friends and family members and church associates have a habit of dropping by unannounced. If your house is clean, you'll be able to enjoy your visitors. But if you spend the visit trying to distract your visiting teachers' eyes from the dirty underwear that has been kicked under a chair, or trying to pretend your bishop doesn't smell the rank odor of used kitty litter wafting out from the kitchen, or if you're praying your grandmother doesn't have to use the bathroom, you're not going to be able to enjoy their visits. Keeping a clean house makes life a lot less stressful when unexpected guests come to call.

▶ To Impress Members of the Opposite Sex

It doesn't matter whether you're male or female: A filthy house is a major turnoff to the opposite sex. No potential suitor wants to see a pile of food-encrusted dishes in your sink, or wade through a sea of dirty laundry on the way to your sofa. You probably spend a lot of time looking in the mirror to make sure your intended suitor sees you at your best. But don't forget what else your potential significant other is going to see. Your living quarters don't have to be expensive, but it's just as important for your house to be clean as it is for you to be clean.

▶ So You'll Be Able to Find Things When You Need Them

If you always put your watch and your wallet on the nightstand, you'll be able to find them without even looking at the nightstand in the morning. But if sometimes you put your watch on the nightstand, and other times you put it on the kitchen sink, and other times you park it on top of the toilet tank, chances are you're not going to be able to find your watch when you're late for work and are on your way out the door.

As this chapter is being written, Kathy has slept in a cold bed for nearly a month. She took the down comforter off the bed when summer arrived, but she couldn't find it when the weather got cold again. You might think it's impossible to lose a queen-sized down comforter. Think again. It's not only possible, but it will happen if you keep a cluttered house. You don't really want to spend an afternoon looking for a blanket, do you? We hope you have better things to do with your life. If you don't want to spend your life looking for things, as Kathy does, keep your house clean enough that you know where to find things once you've put them somewhere.

Time isn't the only thing you waste by keeping a cluttered house. If you don't keep your things in order, you're going to waste a lot of money buying things you already have on hand. We can't count the packets of needles, or containers of Krazy Glue, or packages of mailing labels we have in our house. That's because it's always easier to go out and buy new ones than it is to look for the old ones. Kathy currently has enough needles to last for the rest of her life—except that next time she needs one, she'll probably have to run out and buy another packet of them because she can't find the ones she has. And that new packet will only add to the clutter.

▶ For Your Health

One of the reasons mice and roaches are so distasteful to us is that they carry disease. But your home can make you sick even if a household pest never crosses your threshold. Germs and bacteria grow on wet or dirty surfaces. You can pick up these germs and bacteria in the form of colds or other illnesses. Kitchens and bathrooms are especially prone to carrying disease-causing organisms.

Even if you keep your house free of germs, dust is going to collect on every surface. Dust is composed of a lot of things, but one of the primary ingredients is the fecal matter of invisible mites that live in your home and feed on the dead flakes of your skin. That's right: Your home is a giant toilet for dust mites. Many people are allergic to this fecal matter, so allergies to dust are extremely common. Even if you're not allergic to dust now, you may develop an allergy in the future—or you may produce children who are allergic to dust. You might as well get in the habit of dusting by beginning today.

If you don't think dusting is important, remember what those dust mites are doing. It's a great incentive to get out the dust mop.

▶ For Peace of Mind

You may not think you care whether your house is messy, but your soul cares. Like it or not, there is a spiritual dimension to cleanliness. The saying "cleanliness is next to godliness" is so oft-quoted because it's true. We read in 2 Corinthians 7:1, "Let us cleanse ourselves from all filthiness of the flesh and spirit." Doctrine and Covenants 42:41 adds, "And let all things be done in cleanliness before me."

But you don't even have to crack your scriptures to know there's godliness in cleanliness. Even the worst slobs in the world will tell you that there's something peaceful about clean and uncluttered surroundings.

How to Keep Your Home Clean

Now that you know *why* you should keep your house clean, the next thing is to tell you *how*. There's a huge, unknown secret to keeping a clean house. If you learn this secret and follow it, you'll never in your lifetime have to spend a weekend cleaning out a closet, or miss an appointment because you've lost your car keys. You won't have to shovel the living room and the kitchen before friends come over, and you'll spend far less time and money doing laundry because your clothes won't have to be washed so often.

Here's the secret: If you don't ever let things get dirty, you'll never have to clean them up. This may sound like a stupid statement, but think about it. Houses don't get dirty all at once. They get dirty a little bit at a time. Once the ball starts rolling, the whole situation falls apart. It takes a lot less time to keep the house clean than it does to clean the house once it becomes messy.

There are two challenges you'll face if you try to keep things clean. First, the task is a lot more difficult if you live with others. We know this from sad experience. Clark will be incensed with Kathy because of the clutter in their family room. When the clutter is finally separated into piles, Clark's pile is invariably the larger of the two. Similarly, Kathy can't understand why Clark won't keep junk off the dining room table. Then she cleans the table and learns that at least half the junk belongs to her.

You can get around this by keeping things clean. As soon as one thing is left where it shouldn't be, other things will gather to keep it company. Your job, then, is to keep the first item from being left where it shouldn't be. *Do not be obnoxious about this.* We know someone who snatches up a glass as soon as it's been put on a coaster, takes it to the kitchen, and washes it—even if only one sip has been taken out of the glass. You don't need to go that far. If you cheerfully say good-bye to visitors and then put the living room and the kitchen back in order, you can keep your friends and still keep a clean house.

If you need to give yourself little incentives to keep your house clean, by all means do so. Kathy once told a coworker that he could drop by her house at any time, and she'd give him a dollar for every item that was out of place. The gentleman in question never dropped by to make an inspection, but Kathy was sufficiently afraid he *might* drop by that she kept her apartment spotless as long as she worked with him. You might choose a different incentive, such as taking yourself to a movie if your house has been spotless for a week. Whatever it takes to keep your house in order, do it. Your whole life will be saner if your surroundings are in order.

Here is a quote that might help you in the quest for a clean house. If you see something out of order, ask yourself, "If not me, who? If not now, when?" At some time, someone is going to have to put that item away. If you automatically do it yourself as soon as you find something out of place, you won't have to live with the clutter, and your codwellers won't have to pick up after you.

If you're a naturally messy person, start small. Choose one room and get that room spotless. Then vow to keep that one room clean at all costs. You'll find it's so easy to keep the room clean if you put your mind to it that you'll soon want to expand your cleanliness zone.

As you're learning to clean a house, don't follow Clark's example. We had a tiny bedroom in our first house. There was barely enough space to walk around the bed, and a three-foot closet to hold all our collective clothes. Because of this, the room was always a disaster.

Our dining room was equally small. Once a year, we had a Christmas dinner for Clark's coworkers. Once we got the leaves in our dining room table, the only way the people who were going to sit on the far side of the table could get to their seats was to walk through our bedroom and down the hall, entering the dining room from the kitchen.

As we cleaned the house for one of these Christmas dinners, Clark realized he had to "shovel" the bedroom so people could walk through it. He worked for hours. He devoted a whole miserable evening to cleaning that bedroom, but eventually he was rewarded with a spotless room. It hadn't been so clean in years. Clark stood up, inspected the beautiful job he'd done, took off his sweaty clothes, and threw them on the bedroom floor. At that moment, Kathy sadly realized she'd better enjoy the clean bedroom while she had it, because it wasn't going to last.

➡ A challenge to keeping things clean is living in a place that is too small for your possessions. It's impossible to have a place for everything if there aren't as many places as there are things. There are two ways you can make room for your possessions. These methods may be easier to say than they are to do, but that's why so few people live in spotless surroundings. Here are the two ways:

Don't buy too much stuff. We live in acquisitive times. Americans are accustomed to buying whatever takes their fancy. This has resulted in mountains of debt—and mountains of clutter.

In all likelihood, your parents have been accumulating trinkets throughout their married life. If they have, they're probably drowning in clutter. In this instance, *do not follow your parents' example.* The people who say "less is more" know what they're talking about. If you don't believe us, talk to someone whose possessions were destroyed in a fire or flood. Although they all regret the loss of irreplaceable items such as scrapbooks or journals, many of those people say the tragedy was a blessing in disguise because it gave them the opportunity to start over. This time, they vow, they won't accumulate so much stuff.

If you have so many things that you have to spend your spare time taking care of them, you don't own them. *They own you.* You're young, and you probably don't have many possessions yet. Don't get in the habit of acquiring them. If you see something pretty, admire it just the way you'd admire a painting in a museum. Then walk away without taking out your wallet. If you're still thinking about it a week or two later, you can always go back and buy it.

Get rid of what you aren't using. Here's a good rule of thumb for you: If you haven't used something in a year, you don't need it. Do a good deed and give that thing to someone who does need it. In the process you'll help yourself as much as you help the other person.

The morning this chapter was being written, Kathy looked up from exercising to notice a corner of the bedroom that was full of clutter. As she looked at the mountain, she realized that she could see at least seven pillows in the pile—pillows that had been purchased, but which had never been slept on, because they were too firm or too high for Clark or herself to use. These seven pillows were only the tip of the iceberg. Kathy realized there were probably more than twenty unused pillows in the house. All of them were virtually brand new.

When Kathy realized she had to get rid of the extra pillows, she had the same reaction that she had last time she thought about getting rid of them. "I can't do that! I paid thirty-five dollars apiece for some of those things!" But then she realized that if she found a new home for the pillows, she'd reclaim a corner of her house—a corner that was big enough for a bookcase or a dresser or (best of all) open space that would make the bedroom feel bigger. When she thought of trading the pillows for all that extra space, getting rid of them seemed like a much better idea.

We have a wise friend named Lynne who takes a trip to the thrift shop every few weeks to donate items her family hasn't been using lately. Sometimes her family members notice something is gone and wail about the loss, but most of the time they never miss the things that have disappeared. Even though she lives in a family of pack rats, Lynne's house is always clean and uncluttered. The house is a peaceful place for her and her family, as well as for all who visit the home.

Additionally, by donating her excess goods to the thrift shop, Lynne accomplishes two purposes aside from having a cleaner house. First, she does a good deed. Many of the things she gives away are almost new when they're donated. Although her family no longer appreciates the items, they become valued possessions of people who wouldn't have been able to afford them when they were new, but who are glad to pay a few cents on the dollar to buy them in an almost-new state.

Another purpose Lynne fulfills by donating her used goods to charity is that she actually gets a tax write-off for the items she gives away. This is easy to do. When you donate a box of goods, write down what items are in the box, together with the "fair market value" of each of those items. Get a receipt for your donation, and staple the inventory to the receipt. Keep all your receipts and inventories, and claim them as charitable donations when you do your taxes next year.

If you're going to claim tax deductions for items you donate, there's one thing you need to keep in mind. "Fair market value" is *not* what you paid for an item; it's what the item will sell for in the used goods market. Thus, you can't claim a fifty-dollar deduction on the fifty-dollar shoes you've been wearing for six months. You can't even claim a fifty-dollar deduction on fifty-dollar shoes you took home and never wore. The shoes that have been worn for six months may be worth a dollar; the ones that were never worn may only bring five dollars in the used goods market. If you're unsure how to estimate the value of the goods you donate, visit a thrift store and check price tags on the items you find there. The amount on the price tag— however low it may be—is the fair market value of the item in question.

A Room-by-Room Cleaning Tour

If you've never cleaned a room in your life, there are whole books that can teach you how to do it. But here's a good start for you. The first thing to do when you enter a room is to get rid of the clutter. Put away things that have been left out, and that don't belong where they are. This is the most time-consuming part of cleaning a house. (If you *keep* your house clean, you won't have to do this part.)

Once you've gotten rid of the clutter, you're ready to clean. It's a good idea to assemble a "cleaning kit" to take from room to room. This kit can be stored in a large bucket with a handle, which will make the unit more portable. Cleaning fluids you may want to include in the kit are an all-purpose cleaning spray, a spray for cleaning glass, a powdered cleanser,

Sneaky Secret
One of the most important rules of cleaning is to consolidate your movements. If you find a spoon in the bedroom and take it to the kitchen, then return to the bedroom and take your dental floss to the bathroom, you're going to wear yourself out going back and forth. Put all the out-of-place items that belong elsewhere in a pile outside the door, so you can't leave the room without stepping over those things. Then concentrate on cleaning that room. When you finish the task, sort the pile of misplaced items according to their destination, and then make one trip around the house putting things where they belong.

some sort of toilet cleaner, furniture polish, and bleach or tile cleaner for cleaning the shower. Recently, some infomercials and salesmen are touting "super" cleaners that are allegedly good for everything from kitchen sinks to mirrors. If you find one of these that works, you may want to use it. You'll spend less money if you're purchasing only one cleaning liquid.

Cleaning implements might include clean white cloths, a clean abrasive sponge, an all-purpose brush to scrub showers and floors, an old toothbrush for cleaning corners, and a dust mop. (Old-fashioned feather dusters are pretty, but some of the new ones are made out of fabric that actually attracts dust and holds it rather than just spreading it around.) If you carry everything in a bucket or a multi-pocketed apron, you won't have to buy duplicates of all your cleaning items to put in the kitchen and each bathroom. This saves money, and it gives you more usable room under your household sinks.

When you're cleaning a room, always go from top to bottom. It makes sense, once you think about it. As you move things around in the upper part of the room, dust will settle down below. As you work downward, you can move the dust downward until you finally vacuum it away. (The only exception to the top-to-bottom rule is when you wash walls. If you start at the top, the cleaning solution will drip down to the lower part and make streaks.)

It also makes sense to go around the room, beginning at the door and going in the same direction. By the time you return to the door, the room should be clean. This helps consolidate your movements and makes the task faster for you to finish.

Kitchen

Having a clean kitchen is probably more important than creating order in any other room in the house. Even though germs abound in the bathroom, the kitchen is even more crucial because that's where we prepare the foods we eat. If there are germs on our preparation surfaces, those germs can easily find their way into our mouths. Many so-called cases of "flu" are actually mild cases of food poisoning that come from unclean food preparation.

Ironically, the most dangerous kitchens often look the cleanest. These are the kitchens where a sponge or a dishrag is always available to wipe off any smudge from the counter, range top, or sink. Dishrags and sponges are breeding grounds for germs. From a standpoint of cleanliness, it's better not to wipe off a counter at all than it is to wipe it off with a dirty dishrag or sponge that will only smear bacteria all across the surface.

There are ways to get around this. Antibacterial cleaners are a big help in the kitchen. Also, even though paper towels are less economical than sponges or dishrags, a clean paper towel is relatively germ-free. Unless you're willing to use a fresh dishrag or sponge for every cleaning job, you may want to consider using paper towels for your kitchen cleaning needs.

If you must use dishrags and sponges, make sure you keep them clean. Wash any sponges you've used in the dishwasher every time you wash your dishes, and run your sponges through a laundry cycle (including the dryer) at least once a week. If you're using dishrags, keep a big supply of them on hand so you can use them once and then throw them in the laundry. If you're scrupulous about doing this, you should be safe from food-borne illnesses.

When cleaning the kitchen, the first thing to do is to declutter it. Scrape any used dishes and put them in the dishwasher or wash them and put them away. Put food items away, or throw them away if they've been left out of the refrigerator too long. The decluttering has to come first; it makes no sense to try to clean a counter if the counter is stacked high with things that shouldn't be there.

After the room is decluttered, start at the door and make a circular cleaning tour of the kitchen. Look around doors and corners for cobwebs or dust, and get rid of it as you go. Look at the frames of doors and cabinets for fingerprints, and spray the smudges with a small amount of cleaning spray before wiping them off with a clean cloth. Attack the counters, first with spray cleaner and a cloth. Then go after the stubborn stains with dry cleanser and a scrubber sponge. If you still can't get rid of all the crud, bring out the paint scraper and use it carefully with a spray cleaner on counter surfaces.

Clean the sink, remembering to go from top to bottom. Sweep or vacuum the floor and then mop it, if necessary. Take a quick look around the kitchen. If everything is in order, rinse out your used sponges, squeeze out the moisture, and put them in the dishwasher. Now you're ready to reward yourself with a movie—or to go on and clean the bathroom, whichever sounds best to you.

Bathroom

Although the kitchen is the most crucial place as far as killing germs is concerned, bathrooms are a close second. You're not as likely to get sick from bathroom germs, primarily because these germs don't usually find their way into your mouth. However, one compelling reason to be careful with bathroom germs is that bathrooms that aren't clean have a tendency to stink. It's far better to get rid of the smell than it is to cover it with one of those handy little room deodorizers.

While we're talking about stinking, you may—or may not—want to think about the fact that odors are composed of tiny droplets of whatever it is you can smell. If you smell bathroom odors, you're actually inhaling whatever it is you smell into your lungs. These droplets don't just find their way into your nose—they also land on surfaces throughout the room. Think about that the next time you're tempted to leave your tooth-brush out in the open air of your bathroom.

If you use sponges when you clean your bathroom, it's essential to keep them separate from your kitchen sponges. We have a friend who almost lost his lunch when he learned his college roommate was using the same sponge to clean the toilet that he was using to wash the dishes—without bothering to launder the sponge between uses. You can avoid similar situations by purchasing sponges in two colors, always using one color in the bathroom and the other color in the kitchen. Be sure to launder your bathroom sponges after every use, but don't put them in the dishwasher with your dishes and the kitchen sponges. Bathroom sponges should be washed out by hand, using an antibacterial soap, and then thrown in the washing machine and dryer with a cycle of clothes.

When you clean the bathroom, the first thing to do is to get rid of the clutter. Put things away or throw them away. Hang towels neatly on the towel racks. Place any throw rugs outside the bathroom, laying them flat so you can vacuum them before you return them to the bathroom floor.

When the bathroom has been decluttered, start from the doorway and make a circuitous route around the bathroom. Look for any smudges on door frames and around light fixtures, and wipe them away with a small amount of cleaning spray on a cloth. Check for dust and cobwebs, too, paying special attention to the tops of the medicine cabinet and toilet tank. Remember—dust accumulates on flat surfaces, including the top of the molding around the bathroom floor. Cobwebs can be found in corners or anyplace where two surfaces meet.

Clean out the sink and tub/shower, starting at the top and then moving downward. That old toothbrush may come in handy for getting rid of the grit that accumulates around plumbing fixtures. You may need to get rid of mineral deposits or soap scum or mildew, which tend to accumulate in moist shower areas. Do this with bleach or with a tile cleaning spray, making sure it doesn't come in contact with your skin.

The toilet may seem to be a particular challenge, but it's pretty easy to clean if you know how to do it. Your toilet should be cleaned thoroughly at least once a week in order to keep the smells at bay.

When you set up your own household, do not rely on those cleaners that turn your toilet water blue. All they do is disguise stains; they don't get rid of the stains. Blue toilet water contraptions are similar to room deodorizers in that they hide the problem rather than doing something about it.

When you clean the toilet, there are three areas you may be tempted to overlook. Everyone can run a toilet brush around the inside of the toilet, but these other three areas are even more important because they're where germs and stains and smells collect. The first of these is under your toilet seat. Women don't ever raise the toilet seat when they use the toilet, so they may forget to lift the seat and clean underneath it. You'll be surprised how much junk accumulates on the underside of the seat and on the porcelain under the seat—junk that will be only too apparent to any male guests who may want to use your facilities. Don't ever clean the toilet without cleaning underneath the seat.

The second troublesome area can be found by lowering both halves of the seat and looking around the hardware between the seat and the toilet tank. This is an area that is particularly susceptible to grime if men are using the toilet, although you shouldn't ignore it even if only girls use your bathroom. The hardware that holds the seat in place tends to come loose, and germs find this area a convenient place to live.

The third trouble-spot is the outside of the toilet bowl, from the place where the seat rests all the way to the floor. If the only people who use your toilet are female, you don't have to pay too much attention to the outside of the toilet bowl and the floor in front of the toilet. If men are using the toilet, however, the outside of the toilet bowl is probably dirtier than inside the bowl. After all, the inside of the bowl is filled with clean water every time the toilet is flushed.

If men use your toilet and if your bathroom starts giving off an odor, the outside of the toilet bowl, together with the floor in front of the toilet, should be the first area you suspect. Wash it down with an antibacterial liquid. Bleach is a good germ-killer in this situation. If you make sure to keep this area clean, your bathroom will never smell like the inside of a bus on an August cross-country trip.

After toilet, tub, and sink are cleaned, your next target is the bathroom mirror. You don't need to soak the mirror (or any window you're cleaning) with window cleaner. A single light spray will be just as effective and will take a lot less time to wipe off.

Finally, turn your attention to the floor. Sweep or vacuum it. Mop it as needed, or at least once every week or so. (Otherwise it will collect huge mounds of dust.) Vacuum any floor rugs and replace them. Voilà! Your bathroom is clean enough to pass the most rigorous inspection.

Bedrooms and Other Rooms

The other rooms in your house aren't as complicated as the kitchen and bathroom. Remember to get rid of the clutter first, and then clean the room from top to bottom. The only difference in a bedroom is that the sheets will need to be changed on a regular to semi-regular basis.

Changing of sheets is purely a matter of personal preference. As far as Kathy is concerned, one of the big assets of staying in a good hotel is that the sheets are changed every day. But not everyone shares her opinion. During a tour of Clark's apartment when the authors were dating, Kathy received quite a shock when she saw the condition of Clark's sheets. Clark had been living on his own for quite a while, but apparently he believed sheets should be washed only in alternate leap years. He still swears he likes them "broken in." Clark's preferences notwithstanding, most people change their sheets weekly. If you have two sets of sheets and rotate them so that one set is always at rest, both sets will last longer.

When you're dealing with your bedroom, getting rid of the dust is essential. Any dust that remains in your room will be inhaled as you sleep, and as a result you may eventually develop dust allergies. Be sure to make sure no dust collects in curtains, on blinds, or on lampshades. You may also want to dust the walls as needed.

Grime, food, and other surprises accumulate under sofa cushions. Every month or two, take the cushions off the sofas and get rid of the litter. (You may make it a family rule that the person who cleans under the sofa cushions gets to keep all the coins that are found there.) Also make sure to vacuum under pieces of furniture that are big enough to get a vacuum underneath them. If you have pieces of furniture, such as sofas or beds, that lie flush to the floor, you don't need to move them and vacuum under them more than once or twice a year. After all, if people haven't been there, it's a good chance those areas haven't collected anything more serious than dust along the wall.

I'm Still Clueless

? *You write about mopping as though everyone is supposed to know how to do it. I've never mopped a floor in my life. Short of hiring a housekeeper, how do I do it?*

Mopping is a lot like dusting, except that there's water involved. If you read the section on housecleaning, you may remember there are two ways to dust—spreading the dust around with a traditional duster, or actually removing the dust with one of the new dusters that attract and hold dust.

The same is true for mopping. Traditionally, mopping was done with a mop that looked like—well, a mop. The yarnlike fibers picked up soapy water and spread it around the floor. The first time the mop dipped into the water, both the mop and the water were clean. But every time the mop was dipped into the water again, the water got browner and nastier. Soon the floor wasn't being cleaned—the dirty parts were just being evened out so that the whole floor was the same dingy color.

Fortunately, times have changed. Just as there are modern dusters, there are also modern mops. With just a flick of the wrist, the person doing the mopping can squeeze the nasty water into the sink, so that the mop can be filled with clean, soapy water from a bucket. There are probably a dozen different kinds of mops on the market, each with its own features. Find one that appeals to you.

The secret to keeping a floor mopped is to do it often. Just as it's easier to keep a room clean than it is to clean the room, it's easier to keep a floor clean than it is to clean the floor. Choose a mop that's so easy to use that you can whip it out and clear up spills as they happen. If the spills don't have a chance to harden on the floor, your job is half finished.

There are a lot of commercial floor cleaners on the market, and just about all of them will do a good job. However, if you have a no-wax vinyl floor, or if you have tile floors, you can save yourself some money by filling the sink with enough hot water to barely cover the mop head. Then add a cup or so of white vinegar to the mix. This is such a cheap alternative that when the water in the sink gets grungy, you can drain it and start over again with clean water. That way your floor will get even cleaner.

? *As long as you're talking about things Mom never taught me, I need some help with grocery shopping. Every time I go to the store I end up with a*

*whole lot of junk food and nothing to cook—yet my bill is astronomical.
What am I doing wrong?*

If you have trouble shopping for groceries, there are a couple of
things you can do to make life easier for yourself. The first is to plan your
menus a week ahead of time and use a list. Then don't deviate from that
list at all. Period.

When you're making your list, decide ahead of time that you'll allow
yourself a certain number of items of junk food per week. One sounds like
a good number, unless you aspire to become a sumo wrestler. This is one
area where you can allow yourself a little flexibility: If you decide ahead
of time to buy a half-gallon of ice cream but the homemade brownies
from the bakery are calling your name, feel free to change your choice.
That's *change* your choice, not add to it.

If you're not interested in making a list, the best advice we can give
you is to eat a full meal immediately before leaving for the grocery store.
People who aren't hungry don't buy as many impulse items. If you're
hungry, even the pickled pigs' feet will look tasty.

? *Mom also never told me about the birds and the bees. Can you help?*

Not on your life, Sweetheart. You're on your own. Maybe in a future
book . . .

CHAPTER 6

Dad and His Handyman Tricks

One of the nice things about apartment living is having a maintenance group who does repairs (even if the "group" might be so small that it consists of one old guy named Frank). If the toilet is plugged or the heat won't turn on, just notify maintenance, and the problem might even be magically fixed by the time you get home from work that evening. But don't be tempted to skip this chapter if you live in a rental property that has a repair crew. Even if you have a maintenance group to do the major repairs, there are still some repairs and projects where they won't be able to help you—or they'll be so backed up with projects that they might not get to your problem for a month.

And even if you don't need this information now, it will someday come in handy. Your level of responsibility over your home and appliances rises dramatically when you get into your own home or live in an apartment where you are responsible for repairs. How do you deal with a clogged sink or a broken electrical outlet? You can always hire a workman, but the amount they charge for a service call might break your budget. Your best bet is to learn some basic tricks and turn to the pros only when all else fails. Not only can you save your money by doing your own work, but you'll also get a feeling of accomplishment when you can hunt down a problem and fix it yourself.

Like any other skill, doing repair jobs around the house is something that can be learned. When we lived in Utah, Clark remodeled our kitchen, rewired the entire house, and installed a timed sprinkling system in the yard. He had no background in doing these projects, but just bought some books, studied them, and then proceeded through trial and error until the projects were finished. Even if you don't know a crescent wrench from a toilet auger, you can learn these things and then have the satisfaction of making your own repairs and saving money at the same time.

We will start the chapter by covering the common household repairs that just about every homeowner will have to face on a regular basis. After you have used those tried-and-true handyman techniques of cursing and kicking the offending object, there are tricks you can learn that will really fix them—or will at least allow you to calm down before calling in the repairman.

This chapter also covers the basics of common household projects you will often find yourself doing when you get a rainy Saturday. Sometimes, for no particular reason, we human beings just get tired of a particular room and need to rearrange the pictures or hang new curtains or put on a fresh coat of paint or new wallpaper.

Finally, we'll give you suggestions on how to make your home a safer place. Although we all like to think of our homes as shelters from the outside world, we sometimes forget that a good number of accidents and problems can occur right within our own four walls. These can range from problems that cause inconvenience, to those that can kill us. Fortunately, many of these types of accidents can be avoided just by taking a few precautions beforehand.

Handling Common Household Repairs

If you move into a new house or apartment, you'll probably be lucky enough to have a couple of years with no major repair jobs. But as your house ages or if you already live in an older home, problems with the your plumbing or electrical system will become a fact of life. If you suffer a serious mechanical breakdown, you'll need to call an electrician, plumber, or other professional. But you can fix many problems yourself using a little time, a little knowledge, and a few household tools. Those are the kinds of repairs we're going to cover in this section. Entire books have been written about household repairs, and we can't go into that sort of depth in one chapter. But we can give you some general hints that will fix the basic problems.

Plumbing

There are really just two major functions that plumbing performs. One is concerned with getting fresh water to you (such as filling the bathtub), and the other is concerned with getting rid of used water (such as draining the bathtub). A failure in either of these systems can make your life (and your bath) pretty miserable and frustrating.

Any amateur plumber should have a tool kit containing a few basic plumbing tools. Although you would need more tools if you were going to do major installing or remodeling, the tools mentioned here should be sufficient for simple repairs. An adjustable (crescent) wrench is handy for use on small pipes, and its big brother the pipe wrench is essential for use on larger pipes. You'll also need a sturdy plunger to help you get those pipes unplugged.

A drain auger (snake) and toilet auger are also necessary tools for clearing more stubborn clogs in pipes. Now that we have our tools together, let's look at some common plumbing problems, and how you would go about fixing them.

▶ Toilets

Although the design of your typical tank toilet is quite simple, there are a number of areas that can cause problems. Fortunately, most of these problems are also quite easy to fix once you have a little understanding of how the toilet works. This discussion assumes you have a tank toilet, which is the kind found in most American residences. This is the type of toilet that is composed of the bowl (that's the part where you sit) and a tank (that's the part you lean back against when you're reading the Sunday paper).

Fresh water enters the toilet tank through a plastic or metal supply tube that generally comes in through the floor or the wall. There is usually a hand valve connected to this tube, so that you may turn off the water flowing into the tank. On occasion, you may need to replace this supply tube. Just turn off the water at the valve, flush the toilet (to empty the tank), remove the supply tube where it connects to the tank and the valve, and replace it with a new tube by screwing the ends of the tube into the fixtures. Make sure all the connections are tight, then turn the water back on and check for leaks.

Water flows from the supply tube into the tank, filling it usually until the water is about one to two inches from the top of the tank. This might make more sense if you visit your favorite toilet, lift the top off the tank, and have a peek at the guts inside. See that cantaloupe-sized round object at the top of the tank? That's called the "float," and its job is to shut off the supply of incoming water when the tank is full. The float is connected by a metal rod to another valve. As the level of water rises in the tank, so does the float, lifting the rod with it, until it eventually causes the valve to close, stopping the supply of water. Just in case this doesn't work, an "overflow tube" sends the excess water down into the sewer instead of onto your bathroom floor.

If the float stops the incoming water too soon, there may not be enough water to clean out the bowl, leading to the old "double flush" problem. If the float does not stop the water before it reaches the overflow tube, you will hear leaking sounds and your water bill will go into the stratosphere as water continues to come into the tank and then immediately back out again. Both of these problems are easy to fix by gently bending the float rod up or down, so that the water will run for a shorter or longer period of time until the float shuts the valve. The other float-related problem is that the float may develop a leak and fill with water, causing it to sink rather than float. When that happens, just replace the float. If the valve connected to the float becomes defective, you may have to replace the entire mechanism. Just find a compatible one at the hardware store and follow the instructions.

Now, while you're still looking into the mysterious innards of your toilet, push the flush handle and have some real fun. When you push the handle, it will lift a rubber ball, or "flapper," at the bottom of the tank.

This allows the water from the tank to drain into the bowl. The contents of the bowl are pushed down the sewer by the fresh water that is draining from the tank into the bowl. When the tank is empty, the flapper should fall down again, blocking the exit valve into the bowl. Because the float is now on the bottom of the tank, fresh water should now be running in to fill the tank again.

Problems can be caused if the flapper falls back too soon, if it takes too long to fall back, or if it doesn't fall back at all. Most of these problems can be corrected simply by adjusting the various parts that connect the flapper to the flush handle. Because they're made of rubber, flappers tend to deteriorate every few years. As deterioration causes them to form a loose seal around the valve, you'll hear leaking sounds coming from the toilet as water trickles from the tank to the bowl and then more water comes in to fill the tank back up again. Just buy a replacement flapper from the hardware store, and follow the instructions.

As you can see, problems related to getting fresh water into the toilet are pretty easy to take care of. Unfortunately, problems getting waste water out of the toilet are probably more common, and are certainly more disgusting to fix. It'll take you only one session of unclogging a toilet to teach you to be extremely careful of what you try to flush.

If your toilet becomes clogged, your first line of defense should be your friendly plunger. The secret to using a plunger is vacuum, *not* brute force. Make sure the rubber end of the plunger is completely under water, and that it fits tightly against the outflow passage at the bottom of the bowl. Use the plunger to force water down the outflow passage, then pull the plunger backwards, letting it pop back to its original shape. Repeat this several times, until you can flush the toilet normally.

If a plunger won't do the trick, try a drain auger (snake). Put it into the outflow passage in the bowl, and as you rotate the snake, push it down into the pipes as far as it will go. Rotating the snake makes it go through the pipes easier and also removes clogs as it goes. Once the snake is in as far as it will go, pull it out slowly, again rotating it as you pull it out. You may have to repeat this several times.

You may find that it's difficult forcing the snake to navigate the various turns the pipe takes getting from the toilet bowl into the sewer. Consider investing a few dollars in a "toilet auger"—a special type of snake designed for toilets. With a toilet auger, the snake runs through a plastic tube that has a bend on the end. Pull the snake all the way into the tube. Then insert the curved end of the tube into the outflow passage, working the curved portion until it is fully in place in the passage. Now push and rotate the snake out of the tube and into the sewer pipe as with a normal auger. Having that curved portion on the end makes it easier to get around that first curve in the outflow passage.

Toilet still clogged? Keep reading to see if it may be a sewer problem.

▶ Sinks/Showers/Bathtubs

Most of the problems associated with sinks, showers, and bathtubs involve leaking water coming in or water that fails to drain out. Fortunately, these fixtures tend to have fewer problems than toilets, so you may not have to deal with them very frequently. Another plus is that even when the sinks *do* cause major problems, at least you're not wading through sewage.

We've all seen faucets that leak, and no matter how hard you turn the handle, there is still that regular drip, drip, drip of water. The leak usually comes where the pipe meets the fixture. The pipe screws onto a top that resembles the lid on a canning jar, with the pipe being the jar. The bottom of the lid is called a "valve seat," and the rubber ring that goes between the lid and the jar is called a "washer" when it's used in a plumbing situation. When the plumbing is new, there's a tight fit between the pipe and the valve seat. The washer assures there will be no water leaks where the two parts fit together. But the water that goes through the pipes has hard minerals in it that eventually corrode the pipe and the valve seat. In addition, the rubber of the washer gets hard and brittle as it ages. When the plumbing corrodes or the washer gets brittle, water leaks. The usual solution is to replace the washer—a cheap and easy thing to do. (Be sure to turn off the water before attempting even this simple procedure.) If this doesn't fix the problem, it's time to take a look at the valve itself. We'll tell you how to fix that in just a minute.

Another common problem is water leaking from around the handle when you turn on the faucet. This problem is caused by damaged "stem sealant" (either a stringlike packing material or a rubber "O" ring, depending on the type of faucet). This problem is treated just as you'd treat a corroded valve. For either of these problems, the first step is to turn off the water. When the water is off, disassemble the faucet to expose and replace the defective parts. If the valve seat is corroded, you can use a special tool called a "seat dressing tool" to smooth out the surface. Reassemble the faucet, turn on the water, and let it run through the faucet for a few moments to clean out any residue.

Clogged drains are easier to correct when you notice water draining slowly, rather than when the drain is completely blocked. If you have metal pipes, boil a large pan of water and pour it down the sink. For plastic pipes, try using a liquid drain cleaner. If you continue to work on the drain after using a drain cleaner, make sure to protect your eyes and skin from the harsh chemicals in the cleaner.

Your handy plunger may also be useful in fixing a clogged drain. As with a toilet, it's important to cover the rubber end of the plunger with enough water to make a good seal. Some sinks, especially kitchen sinks, feature overflow openings that defeat the action of the plunger by allowing water to escape each time you push on the plunger. You may be able to stop this by forcing a damp rag into the overflow opening.

Stubborn clogs may require you to call on your trusty auger (snake) again. For a sink, you may need to remove the drain stopper first. If you can't get access through the sink itself, you will have to use the trap, which is the U-shaped drain pipe under the sink. Some traps have a drain plug on the bottom through which you can insert the auger. For other traps, you may have to use your pipe wrench to remove the trap, exposing the drain pipe behind it. When using an auger in a bathtub drain, you may find it easier to insert the auger in the overflow opening than in the actual drain pipe. Just as you did when using an auger on a toilet, work the snake slowly down into the drain, rotating it as it is being inserted and removed. Repeat several times as necessary.

▶ Garbage Disposals

If a sink that is clogged contains a garbage disposal, this complicates things. If the plunger alone doesn't unclog the drain, you'll need to go through the sink trap as explained in the previous section. Be careful not to run the disposal too much while trying to remove the clog, because there's a built-in circuit breaker that will shut off the power if the motor overheats. If this happens, allow the motor to become cool to the touch before continuing. In some

units, the circuit breaker will reset itself when the motor has cooled. Other units may require you to press a reset button, often located on the top or the bottom of the unit.

Another common problem with disposals is that they get jammed and refuse to rotate, particularly if you try to dispose foods that are a little too challenging. "Too challenging" is the operative phrase here. As we've said before, builders and landlords are notorious for installing the disposals that are so cheaply made they can't handle eggshells. When the disposal gets jammed, you may turn on the switch and hear the motor humming, but the blades of the disposal will not turn.

If your disposal is jammed, you must first make absolutely sure the disposal is turned off. If you like your fingers, do not stick them down a moving disposal for any reason. Ever. Find a large wooden spoon that will fit down into the disposal chamber. Use the spoon to remove any residue waste, and then try to use the spoon to rotate the chamber. Some models have a large nut inside that you can rotate if you have a socket wrench with a long extension shaft (yet another handy thing to add to your ever-growing tool kit). Newer models have a place on the bottom where you can use an Allen (hexagonal shaped) wrench to rotate the chamber. Sometimes you can also wedge a stick or spare piece of wood (such as a broom handle) against one of the inside walls and force the chamber to rotate to clear a jam. When the chamber rotates freely, remove any tools used to free the chamber, turn on the water, cross your fingers, and give it another try.

▶ Sewer Pipes

A clogged fixture may indicate a problem further down in the sewer line, rather than within the fixture itself. If you suspect this, check other fixtures in the same area to see if they are having drainage problems, too. If both the bathroom sink and the bathtub drain are having problems draining, the odds are pretty good that the blockage is somewhere in the sewer pipe where they both drain.

Most systems of sewer pipe have a number of clean-out plugs where you can gain access to the pipe. For upstairs fixtures, these often stick out of the floor or wall, or they may be located in a closet that is close to the fixture. For fixtures on the main floor, the clean-out plugs are usually in the basement or under the house.

Start with the clean-out closest to the clogged fixture. Place a bucket or other protection under the clean-out, because waste water is likely to gush from the pipe when you remove the plug. If this happens, that's good news because it tells you the clog is somewhere between the fixture and that clean-out. If water doesn't gush out when you remove the plug, repeat the step with the next clean-out down the line towards the sewer. When you find the clean-out closest to the clog, use your auger to clean the pipe as far as it will reach. Replace the plug and try using the fixture again. You might also consider renting a "sewer rod" from a rental agency. This handy appliance will reach much further into your pipes than a typical auger. If none of this works, it's time to call your professional plumber and let him earn his keep.

▶ Frozen Pipes

If you live in cold climates, it may be a common problem during the winter months to have frozen pipes. The best way to deal with this is to take steps beforehand so the freezing does not occur. On particularly cold evenings, leave a small trickle of water running from each faucet. Do things that will increase warm air circulation around the pipes, such as using fans and keeping cabinet doors open. Obtain insulating material that can be wrapped around pipes that are especially susceptible to freezing.

If the pipes have already frozen, the best thing to do is to let them thaw by themselves, assuming they are in an area where the temperature is above freezing. If this is not possible, you will need to use a more aggressive approach. First, open the handle on the faucet so the water can drain as the ice melts. Then start working on the pipe as it enters the faucet, and work back toward the supply line. You can use heated cable or a heating pad that is designed to work in wet areas. Or consider using a hair dryer or a propane or electric heater that will heat the area around the pipes. Make sure none of these things gets wet when plugged in! If possible, have someone keep an eye on the faucet, so he can turn off the water when the pipes are thawed and let you know that the obstruction has been cleared.

Electrical Problems

Many people refuse to attempt any repairs to the electrical system of their house, thinking they will either electrocute themselves or burn down the house. Although such events are always possible, the probability of doing so will be remote if you follow a few basic guidelines and give electricity the respect it deserves. Although most communities require a permit and an inspection for major electrical projects, all of the repairs described in this section are considered minor household maintenance that should not require a permit.

Just in case you were sleeping during science class, let's review some facts about electricity. If you were to take a sledgehammer to an electrical appliance, you would probably find three different wires that perform different aspects of moving the electricity around in the appliance. The hot wire (usually black) supplies the energy to the appliance. It turns the motor, heats the elements, and does the other things that we associate with the work the appliance does. Once the electrons have done their magic, a neutral wire (usually white) will carry the electrons away. Although this may seem less important, any problem with either wire will cause the appliance to stop dead. Finally, a ground wire (usually green or bare copper) provides extra protection so that you will not get shocked.

Let's say you're using an electric dishwasher and something happens so that the black wire inside the dishwasher comes in contact with the metal on the outside. If you were to touch the outside of the dishwasher, the electrons would flow into you and give you a nasty shock. But the dishwasher will have a ground wire connected to the outside metal frame. If the hot wire comes in contact with the metal frame, the electricity will be carried away from the appliance where it will do no harm.

Before doing any electrical repairs, you should spend a few dollars for some basic tools. Plan to get a voltage tester, a wire stripper, some long-nose (needle-nose) pliers, some electrical tape, and a standard screwdriver. The voltage tester is used to test wires to make sure no electricity is flowing through them. The tester is about the size of a pen, and usually has a small light on the top and two wire probes on the bottom. The idea is to touch the probes to the hot and neutral wires of the appliance or outlet. If the light glows, it means there is power flowing through the wires, and you need to be careful. The wire stripper is used to remove the rubber or plastic insulation from wires, so that you can expose a bare portion of the wire underneath.

Now that we have our tools, let's talk about some of the basic repairs you should be able to perform with a little bit of practice.

▶ Tripped Circuit or Blown Fuse

Not all the electricity in your house comes charging down one huge wire. The wiring is divided into multiple "circuits," or sections, with each circuit being its own unique little power distribution network. One circuit might include the master bedroom and bathroom, while another could include the kitchen and dining room. Each circuit will connect to the master power panel, but not until it runs through a circuit breaker or fuse box (in older buildings). The idea of a circuit breaker is to cut off the power flowing through the circuit if too much power is being used, thus preventing such problems as overheated wires that could potentially cause fires. Remember our previous example about the broken dishwasher where the hot wire came into contact with the grounded metal frame? This is the kind of problem that would cause the circuit breaker to trip.

If you have a problem where just one major appliance or one section of the house is without power, it could be caused by a tripped circuit. Somewhere near the main power panel you will find a second panel that covers one or more rows of switches that look similar to the light switches in a room. Each switch should be clearly marked as to its on and off position. Look for any switch that is turned off, or seems to be right in the middle between on and off. In the latter case, turn the switch completely off. Then turn the switch on again. If it immediately switches off again, you have a problem with one of the appliances on that circuit. Unplug everything, reset the circuit again, and then plug things back in until you find the one causing the problem. If it stays on for a while but then trips again, you could have too many things connected to the circuit. Try connecting some appliances to outlets on other circuits, and see if that helps the problem.

Older houses have fuse boxes that are similar to circuit breakers. The difference is that when a fuse blows, you have to replace it with a new one. You can usually tell by looking at the fuse when it is blown, because there is usually a discoloration or burned metal inside the glass. Make sure you replace a blown fuse with a fuse that has the same AMP (ampere) rating: Look for a number such as 10, 15, or 20, and replace it with a fuse having the same number.

▶ Tripped GFI Outlet

Newer buildings are required by law to have special GFI outlets installed in bathrooms and outside areas. The GFI stands for Ground Fault Interrupt, and it makes the outlet sensitive to overload conditions that could cause lethal shocks. Having a GFI outlet is like having a small circuit breaker right in the outlet itself.

You can identify a GFI outlet because it will have two small switches in the middle, one labeled Test (or T) and one labeled Reset (or R). Pressing the Test button will cause the circuit to disconnect, and will simulate an overload condition. Pressing the Reset button will restore the power to the switch.

If you lose power in an appliance that is plugged into a GFI outlet, press the Reset button on the switch. If it immediately trips again, unplug the appliance and then try it again. If it stays tripped, then you may have a problem with the appliance. If the appliance works fine plugged into another GFI outlet, it could be that the first outlet is defective and needs to be replaced.

▶ Broken Wall Outlet

Sometimes after years of use a wall outlet will just wear out, and will fail to provide power when you connect an appliance to it. First, make sure the outlet is really the source of the problem. Take an appliance that you know is working and plug it into several different outlets in the house. If it works at all of the outlets but the suspect one, that will be a good indication that it is the outlet causing the trouble. Check for tripped circuits or blown fuses, and make sure that particular outlet is not connected to a wall switch that regulates power to it.

You must now locate the circuit containing the outlet to be replaced, and disconnect the power so you can work in safety. If you cannot locate the proper circuit or fuse, you may have to use the master switch to shut off power to the entire house.

Once the power is turned off, use a screwdriver to remove the outlet cover. It is usually held in place by just one or two screws. With the cover off, you should be able to look into the electrical box and see the switch and the wires that connect to it. All outlets and switches are installed in enclosed plastic or metal electrical boxes to protect them. The outlet should be screwed to the box with two screws on the top and the bottom. Loosen the screws until they are no longer connected to the box, and then pull the outlet out toward you. One type of outlet has two large screws on each side, and will have wires attached to two or more of the screws. The other type has holes in the back where the wires may be inserted, and a clamping mechanism that grips the inserted wires. Near where the wires are inserted, there should be a tab that may be pushed with a screwdriver to cause each wire to be released.

Disconnect the wires from the switch, either by loosening the screws or pressing the release tab as described above. Make sure to keep track of how the wires were attached so you can connect them correctly to the new outlet.

Obtain a replacement outlet. Now examine the bare end of each wire. If it has been bent out of shape, use your long-nose pliers to correct it. Wires that connect to screws should be bent in a loop, while wires that attach to the back of outlets should be straight. Connect the wires to the outlet in the proper position. When connecting to screws, twist the wire around the screw clockwise, so that the loop will close when you tighten the screw. Also, outlets with screws will have two screws that are brass in color, and two that are silver. Connect black wires to brass screws, and the white wires to the silver screws.

There might also be a bare or green ground wire that attaches to the bottom of the outlet. For metal electrical boxes, there may be a second ground wire that connects to the box itself. If you find these, just disconnect the ground wire from the old outlet, and connect it to the new one. If you are replacing an outlet in an older house where there is no ground wire, consider adding one. Just connect a piece of wire between the ground screw on the outlet and the metal electrical box. This will provide some degree of protection against shocks.

Once all the wires are reconnected to the new outlet, carefully push it back into the box, tighten the two screws, install the cover plate, and go turn on the power again. If the circuit or fuse immediately blows or trips, it means you wired something wrong and need to go check it again.

▶ Broken Light Switch

After flipping it a few thousand times, even the best wall switch will break and need to be replaced. The procedure for replacing a wall switch is similar to the procedure just described for replacing an outlet, so make sure you read that.

Disconnect the power. Remove the cover plate on the switch, and remove the screws that attach the switch to the electrical box. Pull the switch out and determine the type. This may be the most complicated part of the process because there are many types of switches (single-pole, three-way, four-way). The two things to look for are the number of connection screws on the switch (2, 3, or 4), and whether the words "On" and "Off" are printed on the handle of the switch. Obtain a replacement switch with the same specifications.

Disconnect the wires from the old switch, and then attach the new switch in the same manner. Remember to disconnect and connect the ground wire as well. If a ground wire is not present, consider running one from the switch to the metal box (not needed for a plastic box). Carefully push the switch back into the box, attach it, replace the cover plate, and go turn on the power. If the circuit doesn't trip and a fuse doesn't blow, cross your fingers and give it a try.

▶ Broken Plugs

Sometimes an appliance plug will get smashed or otherwise broken so that it cannot be used. For lamps and small appliances, it is a simple procedure to buy and install a replacement plug. Simply cut through the old power cord about an inch from where it goes into the plug. (Make sure the appliance isn't plugged in when you cut through the cord!) Next, cut the cord lengthwise so that the two wires inside it are separated for an inch or so. Most cords have an indentation running down the middle. If you use a sharp knife or blade to start cutting the end of the cord on the indentation line, you should be able to pull the two wires apart, just as if you were pulling a wishbone. The amount of wire that needs to be separated depends upon the type of replacement plug, but usually about an inch will be fine. Now use your wire stripper to remove about a half inch of insulation from the ends of each of the two wires.

The final step is to attach the bare wires to the new plug. Some plugs have a locking feature that will grab the wires, while others require you to attach the wires to the plug with screws.

Replacing a plug on a larger appliance with a grounded cord (where there are three prongs sticking out of the plug) is more of a challenge. See if you can buy a replacement cord that will attach inside the appliance, just like the old cord. If that doesn't seem possible, it might be time to call a professional.

▶ Broken Cords

Have you ever been a little careless with an electric knife and cut through the power cord? Or had your (late) dog chew through a lamp cord? Or had a cord get slammed in a door, so that the insulation was rubbed off, and the bare wires were showing through? All of these are occasions where the appliances can be fixed just by splicing the two ends of the cord back together.

Unplug the appliance and cut out any sections of damaged or frayed cord, so that you just have two clean cord ends that need to be reattached.

As you did when replacing a plug, separate the two wires that make up each cord, and strip about an inch of insulation from the end of each wire. Now you should have two cord ends, each with two wires sticking out that have been separated and stripped. Now you just need to connect the two wires from one cord to the two wires from the other. Look for some kind of line or pattern on the cord, so that you can tell which wires go together. If there are no such markings, it usually won't matter which wire is connected to which. Twist the bare portions of each wire slightly so they form a nice point, with no stray fibers of wire sticking out.

Lay the two cords out in opposite directions, coming together where the four wires are bare. Connect one wire from one cord to a wire from the other. Twist the bare portions of each wire around each other, much as you would do if you were braiding a rope. The more you twist the wires together, the stronger the patch will be, and the less likely the spliced wire will come apart when it is pulled.

Now you need to cover the spliced wire with electrical tape, so there will be no chance of anyone touching the bare wires and getting shocked. For now, don't worry about the other two wires that have not been connected. Start wrapping the tape around the two spliced wires, beginning about an inch down the wire from where the bare portion starts. Work slowly up the wire, wrapping the tape around it so that about half of each coil of tape overlaps the previous coil. Stop when you have reached a point one inch on the other side of the bare wire, but don't cut the tape just yet. The first splice should now be completely covered in tape, with no bare wire showing. It is now time to splice together the remaining two wires, using the same technique as before. Press the second spliced wire up against the first wire, with the tape preventing the bare portions of the two splices from touching. Continue wrapping with the tape, only this time make sure you cover both wires, and that you are working backwards toward the point where you started wrapping the tape around the wire. When you have reached that point, cut the tape and wrap the tape end tightly around the wire. Squeeze the taped area firmly in your hand to make sure the tape is sticking firmly to itself and to the cord. Make sure there is no bare wire showing through the tape.

▶ Plug Adapters

Here's a conspiracy theory for you: We believe the appliance makers have some kind of secret plot to drive homeowners crazy by introducing a new type of plug each year. You have the familiar grounded plugs with three prongs on them, plus some plugs where one of the two main prongs is larger than the other. All this can cause havoc, especially in an older house where the outlets were invented before the appliance dealers hatched their secret plots.

Fortunately, as an aid to the sanity of homeowners, you can buy a number of different adapters that will allow your 1999 CD player to coexist with your 1945 outlets. Although these adapters allow you to use the appliances, they often do so by circumventing the protections built into the new plugs. As a long-term solution, consider upgrading your outlets with new ones that will be compatible. Now that you've read this section, you should know how to do it.

Appliance Problems

With some minor exceptions, the repairing of large appliances is generally beyond the ability of the average homeowner. So usually the best thing to do is call a professional, and be prepared to pay for his expertise. Or if you have the aptitude to repair such things yourself, there are excellent repair guides available at your local library, bookstore, or hardware store. But before taking such drastic steps, there are a few things you can check yourself that may save you a service call.

If you have a problem where an electrical appliance seems to be dead, make sure there is electrical power available. First check to be sure the appliance is plugged in, then test the outlet to see if it has power flowing to it. As simple as this sounds, you would be surprised at the number of times people blame the appliance when the appliance is in perfect running order.

Similarly, if you have an appliance that requires batteries, make sure that fresh ones are installed properly. Dead batteries are a common cause of "breakage" for such items as remote controls and portable telephones.

Many large appliances contain their own fuses. If the appliance appears to be without power, check these. It may simply be a matter of purchasing and installing a new fuse. But if that fuse immediately blows as well, you may have bigger problems.

If you can find it, read the owner's manual that came with the appliance. Maybe you just don't understand the features of the product. There may also be a troubleshooting section that describes your exact problem.

Your owner's manual might also contain preventive maintenance tips that will keep the appliance from malfunctioning in the future. For example, most clothes dryers have lint filters that must be cleaned regularly. If you fail to do this, your dryer will not be as safe or efficient, taking longer to dry your clothes. Become familiar with the owner's manuals to your appliances, and you will have less frustration and lower repair bills in the future.

Don't be shy about asking friends and coworkers who might have had similar experiences with their appliances. Even if they cannot help you fix the product, perhaps they can recommend a repairman.

Even if you know nothing about the operation of a particular appliance, you can often discover problems just by giving it a thorough examination. Look for loose cords, broken or unattached wires, loose or broken hoses, missing bolts or screws, and other similar problems that may be obvious just through a visual inspection. Be cautious before getting too familiar with an electrical appliance, and disconnect the power just to be safe.

Minor Handyman Projects

Not all the projects you do around the old homestead will have to do with repairing broken objects. Sometimes you will do such things as painting and wallpapering, simply to improve the appearance of your dwelling. Other tasks you will perform include routine maintenance that will protect your home from the elements. This section will address some of these other minor projects.

Exterior Maintenance

One of the blessings of apartment/condominium living is that you have to do very little outside work. But those who lease or own homes are not so lucky, because there are all kinds of little maintenance projects that need to be done throughout the year. Some of these are required to protect your residence from the elements, while others are required to make your home inviting and safe to those who live there or come to visit.

The more temperate seasons (spring and fall) are a good time to determine if your dwelling needs any maintenance to prepare it for the more severe seasons of summer and winter. This may include outside cleaning and painting. Even brick dwellings usually have wooden trim that needs to be painted every few years. Other types of dwellings can benefit from a pressure wash every year or two to remove accumulated grime. At least once a year, it is a good idea to check the seals around chimneys, windows, and doors to make sure they will keep out the elements. If these have deteriorated, you will need to restore them using some caulk designed for exterior use.

If you live in an area where the winters are severe, you should perform some tasks to winterize your home for the coming cold season. This might include installing storm windows and draining outside water lines so they do not freeze.

In the summer, most of your outdoor maintenance activities will relate to work in the yard and garden. Any lawn you have will regularly have to be mowed, trimmed, weeded, and watered. If you have a garden, that will also need to be planted, weeded, and harvested.

If you have any exterior sidewalks, you should be a good neighbor and keep them cleared of snow in the winter. Many areas have laws that require you to clear your sidewalks after a storm.

Hanging Pictures and Curtains

Most people who move into a new home can hardly wait to add small touches that reflect their personalities and tastes. One easy way to do this is to hang pictures and other artwork on the walls. You may also want to hang curtains and window coverings, either to increase your privacy or to replace existing items that you don't like. If you are living in a rental unit, consult your landlord and read your lease to make sure you are allowed to make such changes. There are some landlords who won't allow tenants to do something as simple as drive a nail into a wall to hang a picture. If this is the case, you'd better find out what the rules—and penalties—are before you turn your home into a mini-Louvre.

Because similar hardware is used for hanging pictures and curtains, we will address both items in this section. Perhaps the best way to do this is to describe the various types of hardware used for hanging such items, along with the conditions under which you will use a specific piece of hardware:

Picture hangers. When hanging small to medium sized pieces of artwork on a plaster or sheetrock wall, using picture hangers is probably the easiest way to accomplish the task. Each hanger is held in place with a nail that is driven into the wall at a slight downward angle. With the hanger on the wall, it is simply a matter of hanging the artwork from the hanger and adjusting the artwork until it looks balanced on the wall. Hangers come in various sizes, and each size should have a recommended maximum weight for the artwork that can be fastened with that hanger. If the artwork is too heavy for one hanger, consider using two or three.

Wood screws. Much of the hardware used to hang curtains will be attached to the wooden moldings surrounding the windows the curtains will cover. If this is the case, simply use some high-quality wood screws to secure the hardware to the wood. If the curtain hardware is to be installed elsewhere (such as on the wall above the window), use one of the other fasteners described in this section.

Anchors. Use anchors when you're attaching heavy artwork or curtains to plaster walls, or when you're attaching things to brick or concrete surfaces. Each anchor is a cylindrical object (think of something about the size and shape of a pencil, but only about an inch or two long) designed so that a screw fits down the center of the cylinder. You remove the screw from the anchor, drill a hole in the wall, inset the anchor in the hole, and then insert and tighten the screw. As the screw is inserted, the circumference of the anchor expands, wedging the anchor very tightly into the wall.

Make sure you select the proper type of anchor for the surface you are using, because there are specific types of anchors for brick or concrete (called masonry anchors) versus plaster. The instructions should tell you the size of the hole to drill in the wall based on the size of the anchor you are using. When drilling into brick or concrete, make sure to use a masonry drill. Clean out the hole, remove the screw from the anchor, and then lightly tap the anchor into the hole until it is completely within the wall. If it will not go all the way, you may need to remove the anchor and drill the hole a little deeper. If you are hanging artwork, insert the screw and tighten it until the head is sticking out about one-third of an inch from the wall. Now hang the artwork on the protruding screw. If you are hanging curtain hardware, put the screw through the hardware and then screw it into the anchor until the hardware fits tightly against the wall.

Toggle bolt/Molly bolt. Both of these fasteners are used to hang very heavy objects on hollow walls, such as the plaster wallboard walls found in most homes today. The bolts are designed to expand once they get on the other side of the hollow wall, so that they may not easily be extracted. Start by drilling a hole in the wall large enough for the bolt to be inserted and then insert the bolt into the wall. The toggle bolt has spring-loaded "wings" that lie flat when being inserted in the hole, but then pop out from the sides once they are on the other side of the wall. The Molly bolt has sides that flare out when you tighten the bolt that runs down the middle. After either type of bolt has expanded itself, it is simply a matter of tightening the center screw to secure the fastener tightly in the wall.

Wall Repairs

This section is designed to help you repair all the damage you made while you were learning how to hang artwork and curtains. When you move or change the arrangement of a particular room, it is a common task to have to patch the areas where you previously had artwork or curtains hanging. Wall damage can also be caused by other things, of course, such as when the guys helping you move were not too careful about avoiding walls with your furniture.

Sneaky Secret

Sometimes the hardest part of hanging a picture is to get it to hang so it is level. Once you have it in place, step back a few steps and see how it looks. Move the picture slightly to the right or left to adjust the tilt. If you don't have an eye for such things, invest a few dollars in a small pocket level that can be placed on the top of the frame. Then move the picture until the bubble on the level is right in the center.

The first step is to remove any hardware that is still attached to the walls where you need to do the patching. Wood screws, picture hangers, and anchors can usually be completely removed. For toggle and Molly bolts, it is usually just easier to remove the inner screw, cut off the head of the bolt and then push it through to the other side of the wall. It will then just fall harmlessly down inside the wall, and you'll never see it again. If this won't work, just get a hammer and give it a solid hit to bury it into the wall, and then you can plaster over it. Once you have removed any hardware, remove any other loose plaster around the site.

Small holes and dimples in the plaster can usually be patched with a number of patching compounds that are found in hardware stores. Use wood putty for filling holes in wooden moldings, and patching plaster for filling holes in plaster walls. Put the patch material in the hole with a putty knife or screwdriver blade. Smooth most of the patch material off the surface, but leave a thin layer that rises just slightly above the surface of the wall. Once the patch material has dried, lightly sand the area until the patched area blends in with the surrounding wall. In some cases, it may be necessary to repeat the patching/drying/sanding sequence several times. Especially when patching large holes, it is better to build up the patch using two or three attempts, rather than trying to do it with one large patch done all at once. Once the patch is complete, paint the area so that it matches the surrounding wall.

For large patches, you may need to abandon the patching plaster and use wallboard compound. This is the material used when new wallboard is installed, and it usually comes in large buckets. It may take several applications to make the patch, but this is the method used to fill larger holes than patching plaster. As with the patching plaster, you need to apply, dry, and then sand as part of each application. For major wall damage, you may need to replace entire sheets of wallboard, or cut patches to replace portions of sheets. This is certainly not a project to be undertaken by the inexperienced, so you would be advised to hire a professional or to bribe some friends who have had experience doing such work.

Painting

You'll get a lot of painting practice when you own your own home. It can be done with minimal expense and experience, and yet it can really improve the look of dreary rooms. Even though you're less likely to paint if you are renting, landlords will sometimes allow you to paint selected rooms, often even reducing your rent or paying for some of the supplies if you will donate the labor. This is a good deal for them, because it improves the value of their property; it's a good deal for you, because it improves your surroundings. But make sure to get your landlord's permission first, unless your rental agreement specifically allows you to paint.

Although we can't go into a lot of detail about the fine art of painting, we can teach you some of the basics and point you in the right direction. The staff at the hardware or paint store where you buy your supplies should also be able to help with specific questions related to the materials you purchase from them.

▶ Surface Preparation

The secret for successful painting is to make sure the surface is properly prepared before the paint is applied. This is something we all tend to overlook because we're all more interested in doing work where we can actually see the finished product. First, follow the instructions in the previous section to fix any holes or otherwise damaged parts of the wall. Remove the panels around electrical switches and outlets, and remove any nails or picture hangers that are sticking out of the walls. Also, this is a good time to apply new caulk to the areas that will be painted, because it will cut down on drafts and moisture that come in around windows and doors. Any previous paint on the surface that is blistering or peeling must also be removed. In most cases, you can use a paint scraper or putty knife to remove the worst areas, and then sand the remaining painted surface until it's smooth. In some cases, you may wish to remove all of the previous paint before repainting. This can be done using sanders, scrapers, chemical paint removers, or devices that burn the old paint off with heat. Having done this several times ourselves, let's just warn you that getting all the old paint off is a lot harder than it looks in the television commercials for those miracle paint removal devices.

You also need to make sure the surfaces to be painted are clean. For most interior walls, wiping them down with a dry cloth should be sufficient. For kitchens, bathrooms, and other areas with particularly dirty or greasy surfaces, wash them with a household detergent, rinse them with clean water, wipe them dry, and then wait for an extra day to make sure all the moisture has evaporated.

As a final step before breaking out the paint, you should first protect the items in the room from paint splatters. Remove furniture or cover it with dropcloths. Things that cannot be removed should be covered by masking tape, newspapers, or dropcloths. These do not have to be the expensive dropcloths used by professional painters, but can be the plastic ones you buy for a couple of dollars. Also, make sure you cover the floor to protect it from dropped paint.

▶ Painting Equipment

A true snob of a painter will tell you to use a brush made of hog bristle. These are quite expensive, plus you will have to clean them thoroughly after each use. Most of us will do just a well with brushes made of synthetic bristles, or the newer kinds of brushes made of foam. These have the advantage of being cheaper— usually cheap enough

that you can throw them away instead of cleaning them. There are also many types of special-purpose brushes designed for painting in corners and other problem areas.

For painting larger surfaces, consider buying a paint roller. Standard rollers come in seven- and nine-inch roller widths, plus there are special models for painting corners and edges. You can also buy extension handles so the rollers can be used for painting ceilings or high walls. Take care when selecting the fabric roll that goes on the roller and is used for applying the paint. There are different kinds of fabrics made for different types of paints. Also, the texture of the fabric will determine whether the resulting painted surface has a textured or a smooth finish.

If you're going to be painting a large surface, consider buying a paint sprayer. You can buy one of these for a price that won't break your budget, yet the quality of the work they do is acceptable for most home projects. If you don't want to buy one, they're often available for rental. Paint sprayers are too much work to be useful on small projects but are a lifesaver if you are going to be painting a large area.

For minor painting projects, a small ladder will probably allow you to reach any surface that needs to be painted. For more major projects, you may need to construct a painting platform using several ladders or sawhorses, plus some sturdy wooden planks. If you are working near stairs, consider using the stairs to support one end of the plank. Make sure you open the ladders fully before you use them. Also, avoid using common household items (such as cardboard boxes or kitchen chairs) that will compromise the stability of the platform. When working around doors, lock or seal the doors so there is no possibility of someone opening the door and upsetting the platform (and the painter). Where the plank rests on a ladder or a sawhorse, make sure it overlaps by at least a foot, so there is no chance of it falling while you are painting.

▶ Paints

Before going to the paint store, calculate the approximate square footage of the surface to be painted. You need to do this before you buy the paint, so you'll be able to purchase as much paint as is indicated on the label (or as is recommended by the employee of the paint store). For example, if you were painting 200 square feet and each gallon would cover 75 square feet, you would need to buy three gallons.

There are many types of paint, depending on the surface you're covering, and the effect you're trying to achieve. Most interior painting is done with latex paint. Because latex is water-based, you use water for thinning the paint and for cleaning up afterwards. Latex paint also dries quickly, spreads easily, and doesn't have the noxious fumes of oil-based paints.

Some types of surfaces, particularly those found outdoors, are better suited to oil-based paints. Either paint thinner or turpentine must be used to thin the paint and to clean up afterwards.

No matter what type of paint you select, it is important to read the directions on the can. This will tell you whether the paint is appropriate for the type of surface you're painting. It will also indicate what type of surface preparation must be performed before applying the paint and how the painted surface may be cleaned when it gets dirty.

You'll also need to decide which surface finish to buy. Most walls and ceilings are painted with a flat finish—which means the surface has a somewhat dull appearance and does not reflect light back off the surface of the paint. In contrast, select a semigloss or high-gloss enamel finish when painting furniture, woodwork (doors and window frames), kitchens, bathrooms, and other high-traffic areas. Enamel paints lend themselves to cleaning, so they are better choices for areas where you expect a lot of traffic and dirt.

If you're painting a wooden surface such as a floor or a piece of furniture, another option is to use a stain or varnish. Unlike paint, this does not completely cover the wood, but protects it and brings out its natural grain.

Another big choice is determining the color of the paint. In general, if you plan to mix colors in the same room, select a light color for the ceiling, a darker color for the walls, and the darkest color for the trim. Another thing to keep in mind is that lighter colors make a room appear larger, while darker colors make it appear smaller. Also, avoid the temptation to use colors that are too radical. A red kitchen or a black bedroom may seem exciting, but we can almost guarantee that you will tire of it quickly and will soon be returning to the paint store for a more conservative color. When choosing between colors, you should remember that paint always looks a lot darker once you have a whole room of it than it looked on the miniscule paint chip in the store. It's a good rule of thumb to buy paint that's several shades lighter than you think you'll need.

▶ Applying the Paint

Some paints should be stirred before use, and others should not. See the instructions on the can. If you need to stir your paint, use a wooden paddle and make sure there are no traces of pigment on the bottom of the can. If the paint is too thick, thin it with either paint thinner (oil-based paints) or water (latex paint). Paint used in a sprayer must be thinner than usual, so follow the instructions supplied with the sprayer.

Some surfaces paint better if you apply a primer coat first. For example, sheets of new wallboard tend to absorb paint, and may require a primer coat. Also, a primer coat may also be necessary if you are making a drastic color change or if the surface to be painted is quite rough. Paint stores sell special primer paint that may be used for the first coat, or you may wish to just apply a second coat of the same paint.

Paint ceilings first, then walls, then the floor, if applicable. When painting a ceiling with a brush, work across the narrow dimension of the room, painting a swath no more than two feet wide per pass. This means you will have to move your ladder more often, but it allows you to overlap your previous swath before the paint is dry, allowing you to blend the seams easier. When painting a ceiling with a roller, use a brush first to paint all the edges, and then use the roller to work in from the sides to the center of the ceiling. Make at least two passes over each area, running the roller in different directions (for example, north to south, and then east to west) to better cover the area.

When painting walls with a brush, start at the ceiling and work down to the floor, painting a swath about three feet wide. Then start a new swath and blend it in with the first. Use short brush strokes and vary the direction of each stroke. When painting a wall with a roller, use a brush or an edging roller to paint all the edges, and then use the roller to finish off the middle part. As with a brush, divide the wall into vertical swaths three to four feet wide. Start painting each swath with an upward stroke of the roller, followed by a downward stroke, and then paint in horizontal stokes in both directions until the area is covered and blended into the previous swath.

While painting, keep people and pets out of the room, and minimize the amount of walking you do while painting. Such motions tend to stir up dust particles that will stick to the wet paint and produce a rough surface.

▶ Cleaning Up

After a long day of painting, avoid the temptation to postpone cleaning for a later time. No matter how tired you are, the best time to clean up after yourself is right after the painting. Remove excess paint from brushes and rollers by rubbing them against old newspapers. Clean your equipment with turpentine or paint thinner (oil-base paints), or with soap and hot water (latex paints). Place your cleaned brushes and rollers on another piece of newspaper, and let them dry for at least a day. Store them in a plastic or paper bag to keep them clean until you need them again.

Examine the areas under the dropcloths to check for paint spills, because they will be easier to clean while the paint is still wet.

After the paint is dry, remove any masking tape that was applied to protect fixtures from the paint. Determine if a second coat is needed. Touch up areas that may have been missed with a small hand brush. Remove the dropcloths, install any removed items such as electrical outlet covers and start enjoying your new room.

Wallpapering

Although it is more difficult than painting, applying wallpaper can really make a room look classy. There is also no rule that you have to use one or the other—the two can often be combined together for even more dramatic effects. We have one room that has paint on the ceilings and on the lower third of the walls, with wallpaper starting at about waist height and running up to the ceiling. The secret of using this technique is to use smaller accent rolls of wallpaper that overlap where the paint and the wallpaper meet.

▶ Surface Preparation

Most of the preparation that applies to painting will also apply to wallpapering. Repair any wall damage, make sure walls are clean, and remove all fixtures, electrical outlet covers, and picture hangers. Is it less important to protect surfaces from splatters, because excess wallpaper paste can usually be removed with just a damp sponge.

If you are going to put wallpaper over new plaster or wallboard, you should prepare the surface first with a coat of wall sizing. This is a mixture that seals walls and prepares them to receive wallpaper paste, and is usually applied with a brush or a paint roller.

You can usually paper over a layer of existing wallpaper, provided the old paper is sticking tightly to the wall. If any portions are peeling off, cut the loose pieces off with a razor blade, and sand the edges down so they are flat and smooth. There are some papers that will not look good when placed over existing paper—ask someone at the hardware store if your combination will work. If there are already two coats of paper, or the existing paper is peeling badly, or the new paper you are using does not work well over other paper, you need to be safe and remove all the layers of existing paper. This can be done using a chemical and a scraper, but a better method is to rent a steamer that is designed to remove old paper. This can remove several layers at a time and is much less work than the chemical and scraping method. It's no barrel of monkeys, though. Prepare yourself for some messy work.

▶ Buying Supplies

There are a few specific tools you will need for wallpapering, but none of them is too expensive to purchase. You will need a smoothing brush, scissors, a trimming knife, a seam roller, a plumb line, and a water tray. We will talk more about each of these as we use them.

Most wallpaper comes in standardized rolls that are 27 inches wide, although you may find some rolls that are twice that wide. The lengths are also standardized—they come in regular, double, and triple rolls. As you might expect, a double roll is twice as long as a regular roll, and a triple roll is three times as long. In general, the double and triple rolls are better because you are less likely to end up with a lot of roll ends that are too short to be usable.

When estimating the amount of wallpaper to buy, calculate that every regular roll will cover about thirty square feet of surface. Thus, if you have a wall that is ten feet long and nine feet high, that represents 90 square feet (10 x 9), so you should be able to paper it with three regular rolls or one triple roll. Some walls contain features that will not be covered by the wallpaper, such as doors and windows. For a standard size door or window, reduce the amount of wallpaper you will need by approximately one-half regular roll. When in doubt, buy more wallpaper than you think you'll need. We can tell you from sad experience that it's better to have extra wallpaper than to run out of paper in the middle of the job. If you have to buy extra, you'll have to match the dye lot numbers on your pattern. Otherwise you may end up with two rolls of wallpaper that are allegedly identical, but that are actually different colors.

Most wallpapers come with patterns printed on them. Although this makes for an attractive result, patterned wallpaper is more difficult to hang because you must hang each strip so that the pattern is aligned with the previous one. Consider this when buying wallpaper, especially for your first project. Buy plain wallpaper or paper with a pattern that will be easy to align.

Most wallpaper these days is prepasted, meaning the wallpaper paste has already been applied to the back—much like a postage stamp. All you need to do is get the paper wet, and it's ready to hang on the wall. At least for your first project, you may want to avoid wallpaper that is not prepasted because it is more work, is harder to use, and creates a bigger mess.

▶ **Hanging the Wallpaper**

When starting a room, you need to determine where the first strip of paper will be hung. In general, start in a corner or next to a vertical edge (the side of a window or door), and work toward the far wall. Strips of wallpaper are always hung vertically, each strip running from the ceiling to the floor. The only exception to this is the border paper you may install horizontally to cover the places where the wallpaper meets the ceiling or floor.

Cut the first strip of paper to be about six inches longer than the height of the wall. Hold the paper up to the wall, just to make sure that it is the correct length. Now cut a second strip of paper to be the same length, but before doing so, line up the strips so that any pattern in the wallpaper will meet along the edges. Doing this may cause there to be an inch or two of extra paper on the top or bottom of the strip, but that's one of the joys of wallpapering. Remember—it's always better to have the second strip be too long than too short. This is the procedure you will follow for all the strips you cut: Align each new strip with the previous strip, cut it to the proper length, and then hang the previous strip. It is easier to align the patterns when you have the paper on the floor than when the strips are hanging on the wall.

You must make sure the first strip you hang is exactly vertical. Even though you will run the strip along the edge of a corner, you cannot assume the corner will be exactly straight and vertical. This is where the plumb line comes in handy. We hope you know what a plumb line is, because they're hard to explain. This is a string that hangs from the ceiling to the floor to help you determine true vertical, much as a level will help you determine true horizontal. Attach the string, which is coated with colored chalk, to the ceiling; the weight at the bottom of the string will cause the string to fall in a true vertical position. Hold the string taut and then twang it against the wall, much as you would a guitar string. The chalk will put faint marks on the wall to indicate where the edges of that first strip of wallpaper should go.

Fill the water tray with water, and place the first strip of paper in it, rolled up. If you don't want to buy a tray, your bathtub will do in a pinch. Let the paper soak in the water for about thirty seconds, unless you are told differently by the instructions. Then pull the paper from the tray by one end so that the strip unrolls as it's removed. Do this slowly to ensure there are no dry spots on the back of the paper.

Start in a corner but hang the paper so it overlaps about an inch onto the previous wall. Again, because corners are seldom exactly square, don't be surprised if the amount of overlapping paper varies from top to bottom. As long as the paper covers the corner, don't worry. The final strip of paper will cover any imperfections.

Hang the first strip at the top of the wall and line it up with the chalk line you drew previously. Don't press the paper against the wall too vigorously at this point, but give it a couple of brushes in the center of the paper with the smoothing brush. Remember, you cut this strip longer than the wall, so both the top and the bottom should overlap several inches onto the floor and ceiling. Continue working down the wall, lining up the edge of the paper with the chalk line, and using the smoothing brush to press the center of the paper against the wall. Barely pressing the paper against the wall allows you to completely remove it and start over if necessary. Once you are satisfied that the strip is positioned properly, take the smoothing brush and go over the entire surface of the strip, working from top to bottom. Start in the center and then work out towards the sides. Press firmly this time, to force the paper against the wall, to remove wrinkles and air bubbles, and to force extra paste out around the edges. Use a sponge or wet cloth to wipe up any excess paste that is forced out from under the paper. Use the smoothing brush to force the paper tightly into corners, especially where the paper meets the floor and ceiling. You now need to trim off this overlapped area where the paper meets the floor and ceiling. Put a metal ruler on the wall so it touches the ceiling. Then run a sharp razor blade or the trimming knife along the top of the ruler to cut off the excess paper at the point where the wall meets the ceiling. Another option is to force the paper into the corner with a putty knife, then pull the paper away from the wall and cut it with scissors along the line made by the knife. Repeat this same procedure for the overlap where the wall meets the floor. There are special trimming tools for cutting in corners that might do a better job. Once the excess paper is removed, brush the top and bottom again to flatten the paper and remove paste.

Once the first strip is hung, follow the procedure of matching and cutting the third strip, and then hanging the second strip. Always have two strips cut and ready to go before you hang the first one. Instead of matching secondary strips to the chalk line, you should align the seams (edges) with the previous strip. The most common way to do this is called a "butt seam," where you run the seams up as close together as possible, without overlapping. You actually can use an "overlap seam," where the seams overlap slightly. This is more difficult to do, and you might not want to try it until you have wallpapered at least a couple of rooms. When hanging secondary strips, you also need to remember to line up the pattern if the paper has one. After the secondary strip has been on the wall for about fifteen minutes, run a seam roller over the seam between the two strips of paper. This will press the seams down tightly, as well as closer together, and will also force out excess paste. Seam rollers should not be used with some papers, so read your instructions.

When you come to a corner, paper around the corner and then draw another chalk line to determine how closely the last strip aligns with true vertical. If it is close, then just keep going. If not, cut the last strip so that it overlaps about an inch onto the new wall. Hang a new strip along the new chalk line, so that it fits tightly into the corner without wrapping onto the previous wall. Even though there may be some variation in terms of how closely the paper fits into the corner, the overlapped portion should not make this noticeable.

When papering around windows, doors, and other objects, use scissors to cut away most of the paper, leaving about an inch to overlap onto the casing of the object. Use the smoothing brush to force the paper into the point where the wall meets the casing, and then overlap the paper onto the casing. Once the paper is in place, trim off excess paper using the ruler and the trimming knife. Paper over any electrical boxes, and then cut the paper away where the paper meets the edge of the box.

When you have papered all the way around the room, cut the last piece so that it will fit into the corner as closely as possible. Because you started with a slight overlap, this does not have to be exact.

Do not be too disappointed when the wallpaper pattern cannot be matched exactly, especially when papering around corners, doors, and windows. It is almost always impossible to get it to match everywhere, so just do your best. Once the room has been papered for six months, you will probably neot notice.

▶ After the Fact

Watch the paper as it dries, because it will sometimes shrink or move slightly. If you see this, you can often use the brush or the seam roller to correct the problem.

Look at the paper from the side under a strong light, and be especially alert for air bubbles under the paper. If you see these, try moving them out to the closest seam with the brush or seam roller. If that doesn't work, you can use a syringe to inject wallpaper paste into the bubble. Then use the seam roller to force the air and excess paste out the hole made by the needle.

Use a sponge and clean water to clean up any excess paste on the surface of the wallpaper. Reinstall your electrical outlet cover plates and other fixtures, move your furniture back in, and start enjoying your new room. If you have scrap pieces of wallpaper, keep them in a safe, dry place. These can be used to patch the paper if you have future problems.

Preparing for Household Emergencies

➡   If you haven't already read chapter 4, it might surprise you to learn that accidents are the leading cause of death for those under thirty-five years of age. According to the National Center for Health Statistics, the four most common causes of accidental death are as follows:

1.   Automobile accidents
2.   Falls
3.   Poisonings and overdoses
4.   Fire

Fortunately, there are some simple things you can do around your home to reduce the chances of you contributing to these statistics. Even though most of these things don't take a lot of time to do, most people still neglect to do them on a regular basis. They are not as fun as hanging a picture or remodeling a room, but they might be more important to your future. Following the hints suggested in this section will reduce the odds of your being hurt or of your possessions being damaged—so please pay attention.

Falls

The elderly are the most susceptible to injury from falls because they have reduced coordination and bones that are more brittle. But younger people may also be injured from falls if they don't follow the proper precautions.

It is not uncommon to have to stand on something to reach the top shelf of a closet, or to finish a household project such as painting. When you have to do this, avoid using such objects as chairs and beds. Ladders and stools are specifically designed to accommodate standing. Also, make sure you use these devices properly and follow the manufacturer's recommendations.

If you have loose rugs placed on top of wooden or tile floors, they may also slip out from under you and cause a fall. If you have a slippery rug, use a carpet pad or adhesive strips under it so that it will not slip.

Also be aware that certain things you take into your body can affect your balance and judgment; these can make you more susceptible to a fall. Although it's a no-brainer that consuming alcohol and illegal drugs will affect your mind and body detrimentally, be aware that many legal drugs such as over-the-counter allergy medications can have similar effects on your body and mental faculties. Not only is it good advice to avoid driving when taking certain medications, but it is best also to avoid any activity that would put you at risk of injury if your balance, coordination, and judgment are impaired. Read the label of any medication you may be taking before performing an activity that could put you or others in danger. And then take extra caution. Recent studies have shown that people who do not think they are impaired by such drugs are often just as compromised as people who know they're under the influence.

Poisoning

You should also be careful to always take the correct dosage of medication. Many people accidentally poison themselves on prescription drugs and over-the-counter medications. Always follow the instructions included with such products, especially the warnings related to particular side effects that may appear. *Read the fine print!* If you transfer such products to different containers, make sure they are labeled and that you keep the instructions with the new container. If you have any doubt about the contents of a container, discard it. And never use a prescription that was intended for someone else.

If you think or know you have been poisoned, look in the front of your phone book for your community's poison control number or simply dial 911. If you are not able to get to a phone, have someone take you to the nearest hospital emergency room.

Fire

The cheapest way to prevent major fires is to use smoke detectors. Although they are required by law in new buildings, consider buying your own if you live in an older dwelling that doesn't have one. There should be one detector on each floor, and one should be located close to the bedrooms. Test each detector at least once a month, and replace the batteries at least once a year. Read the instructions that came with your detector for more specific instructions.

Consider buying one or more fire extinguishers and placing them in areas prone to fires, such as the kitchen, workshop, and basement. Buy an "A-B-C" type extinguisher, which is designed to extinguish most of the types of materials that would be involved in a home fire. Before you can use your extinguisher, you generally must pull a safety pin. Then point the nozzle at the base of the fire, squeeze the handle, and move your arm from side to side to soak the entire area.

After a period of time, extinguishers will lose pressure and need to be recharged. This can usually be done for a small fee by your fire department. Some extinguishers have a gauge that indicates when a recharge is required.

The use of supplemental room heaters (such as wood-burning stoves, kerosene heaters, gas and electric space heaters) can lead to fires if they are not used correctly. Locate the heater in an area where it will not tip over or come into contact with clothing, furniture, or other potentially flammable objects. (Some of the newer models of heaters will automatically turn off if they are knocked over.) Follow the instructions that came with your heater to make sure you're using it correctly. Never try to use an alternate fuel source, such as gasoline, in a kerosene heater. Do not leave such heaters burning if you are leaving the room or going to sleep. Make sure heaters are used in a well-ventilated area, because they can produce potentially lethal fumes if there is not enough air circulating around them. Try not to use extension cords with electric heaters. If you must do so, use a heavy cord designed to handle the current loads these heaters require.

The burning of wood causes a substance called creosote to form in the chimney, which can lead to chimney fires. If you have a stove or fireplace that burns wood, you should have your chimney cleaned every few years to prevent creosote deposits.

It is estimated that approximately 25 percent of all home fires are caused by those who are careless with cigarettes or other smoking materials. If you have friends or roommates who want to smoke in your home, try to convince them to step outside before lighting up. If all else fails, at least provide them with ashtrays and make sure they don't smoke while in bed or around flammable material. Don't put ashtrays in places where they may be knocked over, and make sure nothing is burning in the ashtray before dumping it in the trash.

Avoid storing flammable or combustible items close to the kitchen range, particularly above the range where they could fall down on the cooking surface. When cooking, turn handles of pots and pans towards the back of the range so there is less possibility of knocking them off. Avoid wearing long-sleeved clothes when cooking, particularly loose sleeves that could catch on pot handles or touch the burners. When cooking greasy foods in a pot or pan, always keep the lid nearby. If a fire starts, you can put the lid on the pan to suffocate any flames. Also, having either a box of baking soda or a carton of salt near the range is useful because these substances can be dumped on small fires to extinguish the flames.

Store flammable substances (such as gasoline and oil) in the containers designed for them, and make sure they are properly labeled and tightly closed. Store them outside of the house if at all possible. Avoid storing, opening, or using such substances in areas where there are open flames (including gas pilot lights) because the fumes from such substances can travel to flames and cause a fire or explosion.

Devise a fire escape route that could be used to escape from any room in your dwelling. This is especially important if you live in a large apartment or condominium building. Review the routes on occasion and make sure you could find your way along it even if blinded by darkness and smoke. Never try to call the fire department from inside a burning building. Exit the building first and then call the fire department from another phone.

Leaking Natural Gas

If you have ever smelled natural gas, you know that it smells vaguely like rotten eggs or garlic. It may surprise you to learn that this smell is added by the gas company, just so you will have a warning if there ever is a gas leak in your home. There are strict codes regulating natural gas lines and the appliances that use natural gas. But even though the odds of you ever having a dangerous natural gas leak are low, it still makes sense to know what to do.

When you first notice the smell of gas leaking (other than the minor fumes that are often present around gas appliances), make sure everyone is evacuated from the dwelling immediately. Don't do anything that would create a flame or a spark, such as lighting matches or candles, or even flipping electric light switches. On your way out of the house, open the windows and doors so that the air circulation will reduce the concentration of gas inside.

When the dwelling is empty, use a neighbor's phone to call 911 or the gas company. If your gas meter is outside, look for a large shutoff valve that is placed in the middle of one of the gas pipes, usually right where the supply pipe comes out of the ground and runs into the meter. Borrow a pipe wrench or adjustable wrench from a neighbor and try to shut off the gas with this valve. Turn it one-quarter turn, so that the stem you gripped with the wrench is vertical, not horizontal. Wait outside until the gas company arrives, and don't return until the professionals have declared your home safe.

Leaking Water

You should know the location of the valve that turns off all the water coming into your home. You may not ever need to use this information, but it comes in handy if you wake up one morning to find a broken water heater and a foot of water on the basement floor.

Depending on the hardness of the water in your area, water heaters may last only ten to fifteen years before mineral deposits in the water cause them to rust through and develop a leak that converts your basement into a pool. This would be a pretty reliable sign that it's time to shut off your water and to buy a new water heater. If there is a valve that just affects water flow to the water heater, you may not need to turn off all the water in the house.

Other appliances, such as washing machines, may also develop water leaks in the rubber supply hoses that bring water to the appliance. By replacing these hoses every few years, especially when you see signs that the hose has become brittle or cracked, you may lessen the chance of springing a leak. You may also want to replace the rubber hoses with more sturdy hoses where the rubber is encased in a metal sheath.

If you are going to be away from your home for an extended period, consider turning off the water at the main supply valve.

Electrical Problems

If you have a gas leak or a severe appliance malfunction, you may need to turn off all the electricity in your home until the problem is fixed. Being able to shut off the current is another one of those pieces of information that is good to know, even if you may never have to use it.

You learned earlier in this chapter about circuit breakers, and how they can be used if you want to turn off the electricity to just one portion of your dwelling. This is what you would use, for example, if you were replacing an electrical outlet in the kitchen, and needed to turn off just the power in the kitchen.

Near the circuit breaker panel—perhaps even as part of the same panel—there should be a large master switch that can be used to turn off all the electricity to all the circuits. This is what you should use if you have a sudden emergency and need to kill all the power to the house. Practice flipping this switch a couple of times just to make sure you can operate it and that it does cut the power. Now go around and reset your

VCR and all your digital clocks, taking some satisfaction in knowing that you learned something new today.

Although you probably already know most of the rules for personal safety around electricity, take special care when using electrical appliances around water. Never use electrical appliances when sitting in the bathtub or when standing in water, or even when standing near a water-filled bathtub or sink. This increases the ability of electricity to travel through your body and into the ground and has the potential for turning a minor shock into a lethal jolt.

Home Security

There are some basic things you can do to improve your home security without spending a lot of money on an expensive security system.

Have the locks on your apartment doors changed if you suspect that a previous tenant may still have keys. If your door has only one lock (as part of the doorknob), consider adding a dead-bolt lock, which is more difficult to open without a key. If your outside door contains panels of glass, consider using a dead-bolt lock that can be unlocked only from the inside with a key. This will make it impossible for a burglar to unlock a door after breaking the glass and reaching inside your home.

Like most of us, the average burglar is lazy and is looking for the house that requires the least amount of work to burgle. If you don't give him an easy and safe point of entry, he will usually pass you by and find a house that is more inviting. Make sure the locks and fasteners on all doors and windows are working, and check them regularly to make sure they are locked. Trim or remove outside landscaping that would make it easy for someone to work on a door or window without being observed.

When you're away from home, do your best to make it appear that someone is there. If you have an extra car, park it in the driveway or in front of the house. If you're planning on being away from home for several days, arrange for a neighbor or friend to pick up your mail and newspaper each day. If you are going to be gone over a trash collection day, have them put out your trash cans and bring them in the next day.

I'm Still Clueless

? *Is it difficult to install your own carpet or kitchen tile?*

Although those projects require a little more skill and practice than painting or wallpapering, there are certainly many people who are not afraid to tackle them, and even more difficult projects such as adding new rooms and doing major remodeling. As we confessed in the introduction to this chapter, over the years we have tried many serious projects that others might leave to the professionals. (Carpet installation was not among those projects, however!) It's just a matter of whether you are willing to invest the time to learn the skill and practice it to the point where you can do a professional-quality job.

One thing to keep in mind is the cost of the tools that will be required to do the work you have in mind. The tools needed for painting and wallpapering can be purchased without a major investment, so more people are willing to give those tasks a try. Other do-it-yourself projects may require an investment of several hundred dollars in tools, which may discourage those who are not very confident in their abilities to learn the task. One option might be to rent the tools or to borrow them from a friend.

If you decide you wish to tackle an ambitious project, visit your local library or bookstore and find a book that will teach you what you need to know. Also, ask for help from a friend or acquaintance who has experience in doing such a task for help. Most friends are usually more than willing to invest a night or two toward your project, often asking nothing more in return than some free pizza and soft drinks.

Keep in mind that some local governments require you to get a permit for certain types of major remodeling projects. This is one advantage of hiring professionals to do the work—they usually know all the laws and will obtain the permits before starting to work. Plus, they will handle all the inspections throughout the process to make sure the project is being done in accordance with the local regulations.

? *What if I run out of paint before the end of the project?*

When buying either paint or wallpaper, it's important that you buy enough to finish the job the first time. If you go back to buy more, there's a chance that what you buy will not exactly match the color or pattern of the previous materials. This is especially a problem if you buy a paint color that is custom mixed at the paint store or if you buy a roll of wallpaper that was not manufactured in the same batch as the previous wallpaper. Most stores will allow you to return extra cans of paint and extra rolls of wallpaper, provided they have not been opened, are still in good condition, and that the paint is not a custom color or a special order. If the store will allow returns, overestimate the amount you will need and return it as necessary. Even if the store will not allow returns, it's better to overestimate and have materials left than it is to run short. You can always use the extra materials for future repairs.

Getting from Here to There

Many of the rites of passage between childhood and adulthood are associated with the automobile. Most teenagers count the days until they are old enough to get a driver's license. The next milestone is that first solo ride, when you drive around the neighborhood and hope that all your friends will see you in complete control of several tons of steel as your parents develop ulcers at home. Of course, the ultimate rite of passage is that fateful day when you get to abandon the family buggy for your own car. You can travel as far as you want, provided there are roads and your gas money holds out. You now truly feel like a citizen of the world.

As you move away from home and start being more self-sufficient, there are many new freedoms and opportunities that will open up to you—the opportunity to have your own place, cook your own food, have your own job and money, and travel where you want. But as these opportunities have unfolded before you, you have probably begun to realize that each of these opportunities also comes with its own set of responsibilities.

This marriage of opportunity and responsibility probably relates more to automobiles than to anything else. Failure to be a responsible driver can cost you dearly—it can even cost you your own life. Failure to be a responsible owner can also provoke a whole range of financial and legal problems. If you don't believe this, just pick up any newspaper and read the headlines. You'll find stories about people being sent to jail or being sued for millions of dollars because of reckless and irresponsible driving. You'll also find the obituaries of people killed in accidents because the driver was having a little too much fun when he should have been watching the road.

In this chapter, we'll teach you the basics of buying, operating, and maintaining a car. Although it may seem a bit odd, we'll start this chapter on cars with a discussion of the ways you might avoid having to have one. This idea may seem like blasphemy to some people your age, but many people find themselves living in situations where car ownership may be either impractical or unaffordable. If you still aren't convinced that car ownership is not a requirement for the continuation of life as you know it, you can read on as we explore the various ways of acquiring your own vehicle.

As any car owner finds out, the expense of owning a car does not end when you drive the car away from the dealership. This chapter will familiarize you with the various fees and expenses that you will have to pay, and will offer some suggestions as to how you might be able to lower those costs. Car repairs can also quickly drain your budget, and we will explore some ways you can save money, either through preventive maintenance or by making the repairs yourself. By the end of this chapter you'll be well prepared to drive away into the sunset (well within the legal speed limit, of course).

Alternatives to a Gas Guzzler

No one can doubt the positive effects of the automobile in modern life. Cars have greatly increased our options as to where we can live, work, and play. They have allowed us to travel inexpensively and see more of the world around us. They have allowed us to expand our circle of friends beyond just family and immediate neighbors.

But there are also negative aspects associated with a society so tightly tied to its cars. In many households, a common source of arguments between parents and children relates to the use of the family vehicles. Automobiles can also become a bottomless sinkhole, consuming both time and money. We once lived in an apartment where one of the tenants spent every day washing and waxing his car, which was no beauty. He would spend hours each day making sure every inch of the car was clean and shiny, while his daughter sat miserably by and watched him take care of the car—and ignore her.

Purchasing a car can also significantly strain your budget. Here's how most people pay for their cars. They usually save up a few dollars for a down payment, and then finance most of the cost of the car through a bank or through the car dealer. That means that the dealer or the bank is paying for most of the car, and expects to be paid back—with interest. Each month, the owner makes a car payment of several hundred dollars, most of which goes to cover interest on the money loaned for the car. After several years of high monthly payments, the owner may eventually pay off the loan. This is usually about the time the owner gets tired of the car, so he trades it in on a new one and starts the whole process over again. Paying several hundred dollars a month for transportation is no longer a temporary condition, but is something that will eat away many people's income every month for the rest of their lives. The only thing they can do is try to reduce the payment.

Contrast the person described above with the prudent person who pays cash for his first car. Even after the car is purchased, this wise owner continues to pay a couple hundred dollars a month into some type of savings account. The only interest he deals with is interest he earns, rather than interest he pays to someone else. (We'll talk all about interest and investments in chapter 8, so be patient if these terms are a little confusing.) After several years, this person also gets tired of his car and trades it in for a new one. But in his case, the money from the savings account can now be used to pay for all of the new car—avoiding the need to finance the car through the dealer or a bank. Just as our first person is stuck in the cycle of always having to finance his next car, the second person is caught in a good cycle of always having the money available to be able to pay cash for a vehicle.

When you compare the two people in these examples, you will find the first person will be throwing away thousands and thousands of dollars throughout his lifetime in unnecessary interest. Because the second person is not paying interest, he will have no monthly auto loan payments, he can trade in his cars more often, and he can drive nicer cars than the person in the first example.

So the secret to becoming a smart car owner is to be able to come up with enough money to purchase your car without having to finance it. How do you do that? One way is to get by without having a car for a couple of years while you are saving the money. We'll give you some ideas in this section about how you might do that. If you absolutely cannot get along without a car, consider buying a cheaper used model that will get you around until you can save the money for your first "real" car. Yes, such a junker will not impress your friends who are driving around in their new late-model cars, but you'll be the one who laughs all the way to the bank.

Public Transportation

Certain urban areas have excellent public transportation systems, and you can get almost anywhere you want with a little bit of planning. In areas such as New York City, for example, most residents do not own cars, but rely on the bus, train, subway, and taxi to get them anywhere they need to go. Before you automatically assume you'll need a new car before moving away from home, check out the public transportation in the area where you'll be moving to see if it has a system that will meet your needs.

You may think that public transportation is too expensive, and you may complain at having to pay five to fifteen dollars each day to commute between work and home. But if taking public transportation will avoid the need to have a car, such an investment will be minor compared to all the costs of car ownership.

Foot Power

If you locate a residence that is convenient to your work, school, church, and friends, you may be able to solve a lot of your transportation needs using your own foot power. (Foot power includes using roller blades, bicycles, or any other form of nonmotorized transportation.) Not only will your transportation costs be low, but you'll get regular exercise and improve your health in the process.

For you who live in areas with severe weather, resign yourself to the fact that you will not be able to use foot power when the weather is bad.

Rely on public transportation, rides from friends, and even taxi service when necessary. This may seem expensive, but will still be cheaper than owning a car.

Ride Sharing

Perhaps you have a friend, coworker, or relative that will allow you to ride with him. If you do this, always be on time and go out of your way not to be an inconvenience to them. You should also regularly offer to contribute money to help with the maintenance of the car and gas costs. If the owner will not accept money, try to convince him to allow you at least to fill the tank with gas on occasion. But you and he may want to look into the legal ramifications of this first: If you pay for your chauffeur's gasoline, he may have legal problems at tax time or in the event of a traffic accident. Without any risk to the person who is giving you rides, figure out some way to help that person so that both of you will be better off because of your association.

One problem with ride sharing is that you're at the mercy of the driver's schedule. Sometimes you may have to stay late and may not be able to meet your ride; or your driver could become ill or have an emergency that requires him to leave early. When this happens, try to get a ride with someone else, or resort to using public transportation or a taxi.

Getting Some Wheels

Even if you don't own a car now, you will probably want to buy one eventually. If you do own a car, it will be only a matter of time before it wears out and needs to be replaced, or you just get tired of it and want to be driving something different. This is not a decision that should be made hastily. Next to buying a home, buying a car is probably the biggest purchase you will ever make—and you don't want to do anything you will regret later.

The first piece of advice is to buy a car with your head, not with your heart. For many people, buying a car is something governed by emotion rather than intellect. They wake up one morning and decide they want a new car. They go to the closest dealer and find the car they want. They probably pay more than they need to pay for it, and they may select a model that is totally impractical for what they need. Resist the urge to be a macho cowboy when buying your car. This applies equally to women who, although they may not be cowboys, are often just as impractical when car shopping.

Buying a New Car

When you buy a new car, you will have to go to a dealer that specializes in the make of car you wish to purchase. All of the major auto manufacturers enter into arrangements with dealers to market their cars in specific local areas. A dealer will commonly deal in several different car makes, often built by the same manufacturer. For example, Ford, Lincoln, and Mercury are all made by the Ford Motor Company, so it isn't unusual to find a local dealer who specializes in all three cars. Keep in mind that there might be multiple dealers in your area who sell the same make of car, so you have the advantage of being able to comparison shop among the different dealers.

The new cars you see on the floor of the dealership will always have a price sticker pasted to the window. This sticker lists the various costs for the options on the car, as determined by the car manufacturer, and should have a final total for what the car will cost. This price is known as the MSRP (Manufacturer's Suggested Retail Price), more commonly called the "sticker" price. With one exception defined below, keep in mind that *nobody pays this full price for a car.* It is the starting point for negotiation with the salesman. We'll talk about the negotiation process involved in buying a car in a few minutes, but for now, just remember that nobody pays the full MSRP. If you're naive enough to walk into a dealer showroom and write a check for the full MSRP, the dealer will be laughing all the way to the bank.

There are some manufacturers who are trying to change the way that new cars are sold. They know that many people hate the negotiation that goes on to determine the purchase price, so they start by pricing their cars at a more reasonable level, and they expect you to pay the sticker price as shown on the car. Although you might end up paying a little more money than you would after some shrewd bargaining at a regular dealer, you avoid the hassle of having to haggle with the salesman over the price of the car.

Buying a Used Car

In most cases, the first car purchased by many young people will have had a previous owner. With new cars now costing what houses used to cost, it is unlikely that most people just moving away from home have the financial resources to buy a new car the first time around.

Up until a few years ago, buying a used car was something that many people wouldn't do. Getting a used car was viewed by many as "buying someone else's troubles." To some degree, this view was justified because cars didn't used to be as reliable as they are today. A car with more than 50,000 miles was often viewed as being ready for the junkyard.

Increasing car prices and vehicle reliability have changed many people's attitudes about used cars. It is not uncommon for newer cars to log more than 150,000 miles before giving up the ghost. Also, many used cars are being sold with better warranties that will protect you if the car develops major mechanical problems.

When buying a used car, you can go to either a new car dealership or a seller who deals only in used cars. Because new car dealers accept older cars as trade-ins, they will often run a used car department that cleans up the traded cars and sells them to the public. The used car sales are just a side business for these dealers, and this means you can sometimes get better deals here than you would if you went to a seller who deals exclusively in used cars. Another advantage of buying from the used car lot of a new car dealership is that new car dealerships always have a service department to perform repairs on vehicles of that make. You can take advantage of this service department to perform maintenance on your own vehicle that is still under warranty. Even after the warranty has expired, you may be able to get better service on your car—and at a lower price—than you could get elsewhere.

For the reasons mentioned above, be very cautious of buying a used car through a small seller who deals only in used cars. Because the small seller's overhead is higher and because all his income must be derived from used car sales, you will usually pay more for your car. In addition, you may get a car that is worse because the dealer doesn't have the means to fix problems before he puts cars on the lot. The history of most cars sold through such lots is also more dubious. These vehicles are usually purchased from car auctions, so you will have no idea how many previous owners there have been, or whether the car has been repaired after sustaining serious damage.

As with new car dealerships, most used car dealers will quote a "sticker" price on a particular car, but will then be willing to negotiate for a lower price. The sticker price is sometimes written on the car, but often you will have to ask a salesman.

Just as some new car manufacturers are refusing to play the variable price game, there are a few large used car brokers who price their cars at a fair price, and then expect you to pay the quoted price if you want the car. Many of these lots carry thousands of cars, and allow you to do computerized searches of all the cars on their various lots. As you can with the prices of new cars, you can probably beat the prices offered by these used car sellers if you wish to play the negotiating game. But some people think paying a little extra is worth the price for avoiding negotiation and getting a reliable car from a seller they trust.

Planning Your Car Purchase

Other than the differences described above, buying a new car is pretty similar to the process of purchasing a used one. In either case, there are rules you can follow to make sure you get the car you want for a reasonable price. There's no reason to be at the mercy of the car salesman who does not have your interests at heart. A little knowledge on your part will allow you to be the one who controls the transaction. After all, it's your money. Be sure to leave plenty of time for planning your car purchase. If you wait until your existing car is falling apart, you will be rushed to get a replacement and will likely make bad decisions. Plan to devote at least two weeks to the entire process of planning, shopping, and purchasing your car.

Before you ever set foot on a car lot, it is important that you first do some planning for the kind of car that you want to buy. Yes, this isn't as fun as going to the lot and kicking the tires, but it's probably the most important step in making sure you buy the correct car. As part of this planning, be prepared to answer the following questions:

▶ What Kind of Vehicle Will Best Meet My Needs?

Honestly evaluate the transportation needs you have, and determine the best vehicle to meet those needs. Failure to do this will end up costing you time and a lot of extra money, as you may have to trade in the car within a year or two for something more practical. Try to project into the future and predict your sneeds for as long as you plan on owning the car.

If you currently own a vehicle, identify the things you don't like about your present car, and make sure you don't make the same mistakes again when shopping for a new one.

▶ What Will Be the Resale Value of the Car?

Unlike a house, which appreciates in value over time, any car you buy will depreciate in value. That means it will be worth less than what you paid for it. New cars usually depreciate the fastest, which is another good reason for buying a used car. But there is quite a variation in the amount different cars will depreciate each year. Some will be worth thousands of dollars less, and others will depreciate only a few hundred dollars.

Visit your local bookstore or public library and look for the *Kelley Blue Book,* the *N.A.D.A. Official Used Car Guide,* or a similar book that reports average used car prices. Each of these books should list a retail or "market" price and a wholesale or "trade-in" price for each car model. Find the car make and model you want and then compare the average retail price for each year over the past five years (assuming the model has been manufactured for that long). This exercise should help you determine how much depreciation will occur each year for each particular manufacturer and model.

▶ How Much Is My Trade-In Worth?

If you're planning to trade in your current car, you need to calculate approximately how much you'll be able to get for it. The books that you used to answer the previous question should also prove useful here. In this case, you'll ignore the retail price, but use the wholesale or "trade-in" price (sometimes also called "actual cash value") for the make and model of your current car. This is the amount you're likely to get for your car when you trade it in.

Keep in mind that the prices quoted in these books are just estimates, and there is no guarantee you'll be able to obtain the quoted prices. Make sure the book you're using is for the current year, and read the explanations in the books for factors that may raise or lower the price you'll get for your particular car. For example, if you have more mileage on your car than typical cars from the same year, expect the amount you will get for it to be slightly lower. If different books show different prices, compute the average—your trade-in price will be somewhere in the middle.

If you still have a car loan outstanding on the car you're trading in, you need to deduct the amount still due on the loan for the amount you expect to get on the trade-in. The holders of the car loan can tell you how much you have remaining on your loan.

If there is a great difference between the wholesale and retail price of your trade-in, you may do better by selling your old car in a private sale. You can then apply the money to your next car. Although you can usually get more money from this type of sale than from a trade-in, you'll need to consider the cost and hassle of selling the car privately. This would include such activities as running ads in newspapers, answering phone calls, giving test drives, and waiting for the potential buyer to get his own financing.

▶ How Much Is My Down Payment?

If you're buying your first car, you won't have a car to use as a trade-in and will therefore need some money for a down payment. Try to make the down payment as large as possible, because that will reduce the amount you'll have to borrow and will ultimately reduce the amount of money you'll pay in interest. Many lenders who make car loans will give you a lower interest rate if your down payment is at least 20 percent of the price of the car.

Even if you have a trade-in, consider saving some extra money to apply to the purchase price of the car. As noted above, this will reduce the interest you pay and shorten the time it takes to pay off the car loan.

▶ How Much Can I Afford Each Month?

Analyze your monthly budget carefully, and calculate the maximum you can afford to pay each month toward a car payment. (If you don't know anything about budgets yet, read chapter 8.) Unfortunately, most people take the opposite approach—they find the car they want and then try to work their budget around it. A better approach is to determine the amount you can afford, and then select the car based on what you can pay.

▶ Which Cars Are the Most Reliable?

Magazines such as *Consumer Reports* regularly report on the average repair costs of various car makes and models. This will give you a good idea of the cars that, on average, will cost less to keep on the road. Of course, these are just averages, and there is no guarantee the car you buy will not be a "lemon," costing you more than you expect to keep it running. But at least look at what the testers have to report.

If you have friends or coworkers who own the same make and model you're considering, you might ask them what their experience has been and what things they like and don't like about that particular car.

▶ What Features Are Most Important to Me?

The features you'll want on your car will depend on who you are, where you live, and your circumstances at the time. For example, Clark used to think standard transmissions were "cool" and that automatic transmissions were only for wimps. (Most young men think this way.) Another of Clark's long-held opinions was that the only air-conditioning anyone needed was an open window. (This opinion was not shared by Kathy.)

Then we moved to the Washington, D.C., area, which is notorious for bumper-to-bumper traffic. Clark soon realized that in start-and-stop driving a standard transmission was no longer an attractive option. It also took his move to Washington to convince him that automobile air-conditioning was a necessity, not a gas-guzzling frippery. Clark's opinions, which were solidly in one camp when we lived in Utah, took a 180° turn when we moved to another part of the country.

Kathy's mind runs in different directions. She has always driven faster than she should, so she's particularly mindful of safety features. Four-door cars withstand accidents better than do two-door cars because they have an extra beam of steel running up both sides of the car; so Kathy naturally lobbied for a four-door vehicle. She was interested in air bags long before they became standard equipment, and she always checks the ratings to see how well a particular car model will withstand a head-on collision. In addition, turning a steering wheel is painful for her, so she looks for cars with power steering. These are Kathy's preferences—not Clark's, and not necessarily yours. If you do a little research to see what's available and why specific features are incorporated into specific cars, you'll be able to purchase a vehicle that's much better suited to your needs.

▶ Who Will Handle the Financing?

If you've ignored our previous advice to always pay cash for cars, you need to determine how you're going to finance your purchase. Contact your bank or credit union about getting a car loan, and find out the maximum amount you can borrow, and the interest rate you'll be charged. There are many Internet sites that allow you to shop and apply on-line for car loans.

Before shopping for a car loan, you may want to get a copy of your credit history and make sure there are no negative items that will cause you to be refused for a loan or will result in a loan that is less attractive. Read more about this in chapter 8. If there are negative items that are in error, you should get them removed prior to shopping for a loan.

Just because a bank is willing to lend you a certain maximum amount for a car loan doesn't mean you should borrow that amount. Have the loan officer calculate the estimated amount of your monthly payment, and see how that matches your own estimate of the maximum amount you feel you can pay per month.

Keep in mind that anyone selling you a car will also be more than happy to also handle the financing—in fact, they usually hope you'll choose to finance the car through them. But doing your own research first will allow you to have an alternative to seller financing, and will set off warning bells if the seller proposes a financing plan that is way out of line from what you can get elsewhere.

▶ How Much Will Insurance Cost?

You may not realize this, but insurance companies don't charge the same amount for each car they insure. If a particular model costs a lot to repair, the insurance company will charge you more to get insurance for that car. Also, certain models that have the reputation for being "sporty" will probably cost more to insure, because the owners of such cars tend to drive faster and get in more accidents. They also get more traffic tickets, because policemen expect sporty cars to speed and are more likely to catch them in the act, and that drives up the insurance rates even more. In addition, you will find that your insurance costs might increase based on certain features of a particular vehicle, such as a more powerful engine.

When you get to the point where you've narrowed your choice down to one or two models, call your insurance agent and see what the costs will be for each of the options you're considering. All things being equal, select the option that will cost you less on your insurance.

▶ What Will Be the Other Monthly Costs?

In addition to the costs already mentioned, try to determine other things that will affect your total cost of owning the car. For example, having a larger vehicle with a larger engine will result in a larger gasoline bill than having a compact car that is more fuel efficient. Also, you may want to consider how much it will cost to have regular maintenance and repair work done on the car. Clark has a friend who once bought a very expensive sports car, thinking he could barely afford the monthly payments. What he didn't consider was that this particular make of car needed to have the engine tuned every other month, and the dealer charged several hundred dollars for every tune-up. This car owner learned a very expensive lesson about considering all the costs before you purchase a vehicle.

Finding the Right Car

If you've done your research and answered the questions in the previous section, you'll have a pretty good idea of the particular car you wish to purchase, the maximum amount you can afford to pay, and the amount that a reasonable seller should charge you for that car. If these last two amounts aren't in the same ballpark, you need to figure out a way to raise more money, or start over and find a different car more in line with your budget.

Now it's time to start visiting the car lots. Visit the dealers in your area that carry the particular car model you want. Even if you are buying a used car, a new car dealer for that same model will very often have a number of those models in the used car section. This speaks well for that particular model, because it means previous owners are trading in their cars for newer versions of the same model.

If there are multiple dealers in your area that sell the same model, visit all of them so you can see all the options available to you. Avoid the temptation of buying the first car you see. As silly as that sounds, it happens more often than you may think. Take your time in looking at all the available models at all the available dealers. Then you can make an informed choice based on all the cars available to you.

If you don't want to be bothered by a salesman yet, consider visiting the lot after it is closed. Or, politely but firmly tell the salesman that you are "just looking" for now. Eventually, you'll probably want the attention of the salesman after you have narrowed your field down to a handful of cars. Other than asking about the price for a particular car (assuming there is no price sticker), avoid issues related to price at this early stage. Concentrate more on the features of the cars you like. Ask any questions related to features, the operation of the car, or its previous owner history.

If you're really interested in a particular car, ask that you be allowed to take it for a test drive. When you're test driving, make sure you test the car in a wide variety of conditions. How does it drive on the freeway? on a residential street? How does it handle corners? Is the turning radius good enough that you can perform a U-turn without stopping and backing up the vehicle? Is the braking smooth? Does the vehicle have good acceleration, especially when passing? Do the heating, air-conditioning, sound system, and electrical system all work properly? Do the tires, battery, and fan belts look new, or will they need to be replaced soon? If the salesman goes with you on the test drive, ignore his patter and any questions he might ask. Remember—you and the salesman have different agendas. As far as you're concerned, the purpose of the test drive is for you to evaluate the car. But the salesman is using that test drive to find out things about you that he can use to his advantage during the sales negotiations. You're in the driver's seat literally and figuratively; ask the salesman to please be quiet and to let you concentrate on your driving.

If the salesman helping you is typical, he'll end the test drive by suggesting that you "go inside and write it up." Avoid being pressured to purchase at this point; first, you want to make sure you've asked all your questions and looked at all your options. You're most likely to make a bad deal right after you take a test drive. This will be the time when you are most attached to the car and are not yet thinking with your head. Take some time off and go to lunch, then come back later. That will help you be more objective, and will put the salesman at a disadvantage.

Even if you've found the dream car that you cannot live without, avoid showing too much excitement around the salesman. If the salesman knows you must own a particular car at any cost, it will put him in a much better position during the negotiation phase. Discuss each car in a very objective manner. *If anything, act bored.* That throws the salesman off-kilter, and you're more likely to get a better deal. Feel free to bring up any concerns with the salesman and point out any defects or problems you see with the cars you consider. Remember: Buy with your head, not your heart.

Once you have completed this exercise, you will have hopefully found at least one car that will meet your needs and also your budget. If not, perhaps you need to revise your criteria, or perhaps you just need to look in more lots. If you've found the car you want, it's time to proceed to the negotiation stage.

Items to Check on a Used Car

In addition to the items mentioned above, there are extra steps you'll need to follow if you're buying a used car. If a car has been previously owned, pay special attention to the following signs of possible problems. If these problems are serious enough, you may want to have your mechanic check the car before proceeding.

- Check for signs of rust, particularly on the fenders and bumpers, in the wheel wells, under the doors, and under the carpet in the trunk.

- Check for signs of damage that has been repaired and then repainted. Look for unusual welds, parts that don't fit tightly together, and different paint colors in such areas as the inside of the doors.

- Make sure the hood, trunk, and doors all open and close smoothly, and fit tightly when they are closed. Something not fitting well suggests that the car was previously damaged.

- Check for unusual signs of tire wear, particularly on the front tires. This may indicate either bad alignment or other problems that are more serious.

- Push down on one corner of the car and then see how it bounces back. Excessive bounce indicates worn shock absorbers.

- See if the battery has an installation date written on it. If it is more than two years old, or if there is powdered residue around the terminals, it may need to be replaced soon.

- Check the tailpipe for unusual accumulations of black soot and grime. These could indicate a car with engine problems.

- Check all the fluid levels to make sure they are correct, and that the fluids are free from sedimentation, rust, and unusual odors.

- When driving the car, be alert for unusual noises, vibrations, excessive smoke and odors.

- Check the interior carpets, seats, and operator pedals for unusual wear. This usually indicates a car that has experienced hard driving. If the car has low mileage, it may also indicate that the odometer has been illegally rolled back.

- Once you have the vehicle identification number (VIN) from the car, you can use some Internet sites (or ask the seller) to determine if the car has ever had a "salvage" title. This means it was in an accident, was "totaled" by the insurance company, and then was later rebuilt. Not only do such cars often have serious mechanical problems, but some lenders will not write you a car loan for them.

Negotiating the Purchase

Most people would rather go to the dentist for a root canal than go through the process of negotiating a price for a car. This negotiation process is an elaborate mental game, where the salesman and the customer both use their best psychological moves to come out with the best deal. The customer wants to purchase the car he has chosen and come away having negotiated a bargain price. The salesman wants to make the maximum profit for the sellers, all the while making it seem that the customer is taking advantage of the poor salesman. In reality, most deals are a compromise somewhere between these two extremes. Remember that the salesman plays this game every day, and he's an expert at what he does. But you can even the odds a little bit if you've done your research and if you understand the various approaches the salesman may use. If you have never purchased a car before, consider taking a parent, relative, or more experienced friend with you for both advice and moral support.

Consider Horace and Poindexter. They both want to buy a $20,000 car, and they both have a car to trade in that is worth $5,000. Getting a good discount off the sticker price is important to Horace, and the salesman immediately picks up on this. The salesman knocks $4,000 off the sticker price, but tells Horace he can give him only $3,000 for his trade-in. Horace thinks he's done pretty well as he writes out his $13,000 check and drives his new car home.

Horace's friend Poindexter is proud of how well he has maintained his current car, and is sure he can get a better than average price when he trades it. The salesman sees how important a good trade-in is to Poindexter, so he praises Poindexter on how well he took care of his previous car. He's quick to tell Poindexter that even though used cars like his are usually worth only $5,000, Poindexter's car is in such great shape that the salesman is going to give Poindexter $6,000 on the trade, and will knock $1,000 off the sticker price on top of that. Poindexter congratulates himself on making such a shrewd deal as he writes out his $13,000 check and drives his new car home.

In both these examples, the car seller made the same profit, and both customers left thinking they had made themselves a pretty shrewd deal. The salesman was the shrewd one, however, because he was smart enough to identify each customer's "hot buttons" and manipulate the deal to push those buttons. Horace was not too concerned about losing a little money on his trade-in, because he got a big reduction in the sticker price. Poindexter was proud of getting more money on his trade-in, but he got a smaller reduction in the sticker price. The obvious solution to being a shrewd buyer is either to hide your hot buttons, or not have any hot buttons the salesman can push.

➡ Here are some variables a salesman may manipulate to make a deal that pushes your hot buttons while making a profit for the seller:

▶ Sticker Price

Unless you're at a dealership that features nonnegotiable prices, you should always expect the salesman to discount the sticker price shown on the car. If a used car has no sticker and you have to ask for the price, you can usually still expect to negotiate a lower price than the first one you're given. Everyone knows the salesman has some latitude as to how much he can reduce the price. Because everyone knows this, you need not be afraid to ask for a generous discount to start things off.

For a new car, you should ask to see the factory invoice that lists the actual amount the dealer paid the manufacturer for the car. If the salesman will not provide a copy of this, you can get the approximate cost from another dealer, consumer guidebooks, and even some Internet sites. Even if the salesman is willing to provide you with the invoice, it is still a good idea to verify its accuracy through some of these other sources.

Even when you've finally determined the factory invoice price, there is no guarantee it's accurate. Most manufacturers will reduce the invoice price even further with dealer incentives, rebates, and allowances for advertising costs. These reductions usually amount to several hundred dollars, but can be more in some cases. You may also try asking the salesman how much the "dealer incentive" or "factory allowance" was for the particular car you want. Although the factory invoice price may not be accurate, it will at least give you a starting point. Once you have the dealer cost, minus any incentives or allowances, you might take the approach of saying, "I realize you have to make some money on this deal, so I'm willing to pay you 5 percent more than your true cost for this car." You should also ask if the manufacturer or dealer is providing a rebate for this particular car, so you can take advantage of that.

When buying a used car, your research should have provided you with the approximate wholesale and retail costs for the model you want. That will give you an approximation of how much the car dealership paid the previous owner, and how much they expect to get when they sell it. Although there is always some variance between the dealer price and the prices in the used car books, the smart shopper will shy away from any deal where there is too much variation between the two, regardless of the explanation given by the salesman.

▶ Trade-In Value

Once again, if you have done your research first, you will know how much your old car is worth—and you should not expect too much variation in how much money you will be given when you trade in your old car. Try to avoid discussion of the value of your trade until you have established a reasonable price for the new car. That will lock the salesman into one price and will prevent him from playing one number against the other.

Don't let the salesman reduce the value of your trade-in by using such tactics as saying, "Our mechanic has looked at your old car, and it will need $2,000 in repair work before we can sell it." Even if the car does need that much work, you should take into account that $2,000 is the retail repair cost you would have to pay—their repair department can perform the repairs for much less. Also, there is no guarantee they will perform the repair work before they sell the car. If they can knock $2,000 off your trade-in, then discount the car $1,000 and sell it "as is," they will still make $1,000 extra on the deal. If the salesman tries this tactic, take your old car to your mechanic for an opinion. If he agrees that the repairs are necessary, consider adjusting the value of the car accordingly, but less than it would cost you to make the repairs.

▶ Financing Options

The salesman will be more than willing to let you finance the car through the dealership. In fact, he is hoping that you will. He will be glad to arrange the financing and then add on some fees or higher interest rates for his efforts. Once again, if you have done your research first, you will know how the car dealership's rates compare with the financing you can get elsewhere. If the seller's financing is reasonable, go with the dealership because the salesman will be more likely to cut you a better deal in other areas. If the financing offer is outrageous, don't hesitate to mention the terms you were able to get on your own. That may force the dealer to come up with a better offer when he realizes you have other alternatives.

It's to your advantage to negotiate the price of the car before you ever mention financing. If the salesman thinks you will finance through the dealership, it's more likely he will offer you a better deal. You don't need to be untruthful about this. If the salesman asks about financing, simply say you'll probably finance part of the purchase, and that you're more than willing to go through the seller if he offers you a competitive deal. You don't need to volunteer that you have already researched your financing options. For that matter, you don't need to tell the salesman if you plan to pay cash for the car. Just leave the issue of financing open until the price has been determined. If the salesman knows you're planning to pay cash he will drive a harder bargain in other areas.

If you select financing through the seller, make sure the dealership doesn't attempt to add any unreasonable fees as part of getting the loan. Also, if you've never made a major purchase before, don't allow the dealership to charge you a higher interest rate or purchase loan insurance because you have no credit history. Once again, doing the proper research on financing before you set foot on the lot will give you ammunition against many of these schemes.

If you do finance a portion of your car purchase, design the loan so that it will be paid off in four years or less and so that your monthly payment will be as high as you can afford. This will pay off the car faster and result in your paying less interest. It will also give you more equity in your vehicle if you sell the car before the loan is paid off.

▶ Dealer Add-Ons

Especially with new cars, dealers often will attempt to make you pay fees and charges in excess of what is listed as the sticker price of the car. Right on the sticker itself, there is often a brazen attempt to add hundreds of dollars to the MSRP for such items as "transportation fees" and "dealer preparation." Even if these fees are not on the sticker, you can be sure they will be mentioned by the salesman after you have agreed to a purchase price for the car. The salesman may tell you that "there is a $200 office processing fee for every car that leaves the lot, and as a salesman, I have no authority to waive that fee." This is rubbish. It is like buying a hamburger and being charged an extra dollar for handling and packaging. All other businesses include the cost of their overhead in the price of the items they sell, and there is no reason that a car dealership can't do the same. The salesman is attempting to show that he is really on your side, that he doesn't agree with the policy either, and that there is nothing he can do about it.

You should identify and determine each dealer fee, question it, and ask to have it removed or at least reduced. If the salesman stands by the argument that he has no power to remove the fee, ask that he compensate by reducing the sale price or giving you some other concession. Perhaps he'll agree that the service department will give you several free oil changes in return for your paying the fee.

Avoid having the dealer install other options as part of the sale, such as air-conditioning or a car stereo. You'll always be overcharged when these options are installed by the dealer, so you're better off having an independent mechanic do the installation after you buy the car.

▶ Post-Sale Add-Ons

Once you've agreed to purchase the car, and the price and financing options have been set, you will be sent to a "business manager" who will finalize the sale. He will draw up all the papers, have you sign them, and give you instructions for leaving your old car and driving the new one home. He will also give you instructions for properly registering the car, including getting license plates and any required state or county permits.

But this final session is also another opportunity for the seller to squeeze more money out of you. As part of the sale, you'll be pressured to purchase such things as rust-proofing treatments for the car, an extended warranty to cover more repairs than the existing warranty will cover, and all sorts of bogus garbage. The last time we bought a car, the business manager brought out all kinds of expensive repair bills to show us how much we might have to spend if we didn't buy the extended warranty. Don't fall for any of these additional warranties and treatments. Most research shows that, on average, they aren't worth the extra money you pay for them. The majority of new cars already come with a thirty-six-month warranty, which should be adequate. If you want an extended warranty beyond that, it can be purchased from other sources who will probably give you a better rate than what the seller will charge.

The seller may also try to get you to agree to buy auto insurance as part of the contract—another rip-off. You'll do better to find your own insurance agent who is not affiliated with the car dealership.

Make sure you carefully review all the charges that are listed on the contract you'll be asked to sign. If there is something that doesn't agree with what the salesman said or if there are additional charges you don't understand, make sure to raise questions on these items. *Don't trust the dealership's math.* Bring your own calculator to double-check the seller's calculations. If the seller promised you a certain percentage rate on a loan, make sure he didn't use a different rate by "mistake."

Keep in mind that some additional expenses may be valid, particularly expenses associated with transfer of title and registration of the car. Many states that have sales taxes will require that such taxes be paid when cars are sold. Sometimes the seller will cover these fees, sometimes he won't. It's usually not worth your time to question these fees, unless you feel you are being charged more than you would be charged if you were buying the car from another owner. You can always check with the proper government authorities to determine the going charge for the same service.

Make sure you get everything in writing. If the salesman promised you three free oil changes and a free case of soda pop, make sure you get those promises in writing, too.

If the salesman is doing his job properly, he will make you feel as though every price concession he makes is taking food from the mouths of his children. You'll think he's cutting you such a sweet deal that he will get no commission, he will probably lose his job, and his family will be out roaming the streets because of you. If you start feeling sorry for the poor guy, just consider that he would never agree to a deal that would lose money for his employer. He has a certain amount of profit that he must make on each sale, and there's no way he'd ever agree to a deal that would reduce that profit margin. Despite what he tells you, you can be sure he will always get a commission on the sale. He will have some latitude in terms of negotiation, and you may talk him into getting a smaller commission than he'd like, but he'll always get something for his efforts. It does you no harm to request lower prices and the removal of fees; the worst that can happen is that the salesman will say no.

Your best two weapons in the negotiating process are to let the salesman know you're an informed consumer and to show that you're willing to leave if you don't get a fair deal. Keep your emotions out of the process (remember our first rule of using your head?). Be polite and informed, but firm. If the salesman won't agree to a certain concession, try another approach. He has several levers for making you feel you're getting a good deal, but there is nothing to prevent you from using those same levers to your own benefit. If all else fails, you should always be ready to thank the salesman for his time and walk out of the dealership. The salesman will try awfully hard to prevent you from doing that. He'll try to make you bond with your prospective new car, convincing you this is the only car that will meet your needs. Remember—it's his job to make sure you don't leave the lot unless it's behind the wheel of a new car. You need to look at the car as a means of transportation rather than as an object of affection, stoutly resisting the impulse to fall in love with the car until after you've taken it home with you. Only if your emotions are detached will you be able to leave at any time during the negotiations if you feel you have reached an impasse. If you're able to walk away from the car without looking back, and if the salesman knows you have this attitude, it will put you in a much better position for negotiation.

Having said that, we urge you to keep in mind that the seller is running a business, and it is not unreasonable for him to expect to make a profit on your purchase. You want him to be fair to you, but you need to be reasonable with him as well. Once again, if you've done your planning before you visit the seller, you'll have a pretty good idea of the kind of deal that you can expect to be fair to both sides.

You also need to be flexible and realize how much your own time is worth. Perhaps you've negotiated with the salesman for three hours, and you're still $200 away in terms of agreeing on a price. If you stick by your principles, you could walk away and start the whole process over on a different day or with a different dealer. But is it worth three more hours of your time for an additional $200? Most of us usually just get worn down and agree to pay the extra cost. You can either view this as a victory for the salesman or just realize that your own time is worth something, too.

Beware of Dirty Tricks

After reading the previous section, you probably think we hate all car salesmen, and that they are the lowest life form on this planet. Actually this isn't true, and we like to think that the last couple of car salesmen who sold cars to us were pretty decent. Either it's possible to find an honest salesman or the ones we were dealing with were better salesmen than we thought! In any case, you should at least start out treating every salesman like a human being and giving him the benefit of the doubt until he proves himself otherwise.

➡   Car salesmen are put under tremendous pressure to produce. If you have a salesman who's resorting to dirty tricks, it may be that he's working for a dishonest seller who expects devious behavior. Underhanded dealers have several dirty tricks that may be played on you in an attempt to close a sale, in addition to the ones described in the previous section. Be cautious of a salesman who tries any of the following:

Let me talk to the sales manager. This is a common trick that just about every salesman will try. After you've agreed on a price, he'll say he has to make sure his sales manager will approve of the deal. He then leaves the room (probably to go out for a drink), only to come back and report that the deal was too good, and his manager insisted he couldn't let that car go unless you paid at least "X" more dollars. This makes it seem that the salesman is really on your side, and it's his evil manager who's the bad guy.

While the salesman is "talking to his manager," don't discuss anything related to the deal with anyone who may be shopping with you. As Kathy learned the hard way, some salesmen are so sleazy that they'll bug the office and listen to your conversation while they're away from the room. If you discuss the pending deal with your friend when the dealer is away, he can easily use that information against you. If you must discuss the deal, give the salesman a taste of his own medicine by telling your friend that you're not crazy about the car and you're ready to walk. If the salesman overhears your lack of enthusiasm, his "sales manager" may magically agree to better terms than you otherwise would have received.

This offer is only good for today. Research shows that if you leave the lot without buying a car, the salesman is unlikely to see you again. Because of this, salesmen will apply all kinds of pressure to force you into buying today. One trick is to say, "I've been authorized to give you 'X' dollars off my best price, but that offer is good only for today." Do you really think if you came back the next day, he wouldn't offer you the same deal, if not a better one?

I think I have a buyer for your old car. You may be told that the seller already has a buyer for your trade-in and that the dealership will be able to give you top dollar because the buyer really wants your old car. The motivation behind this trick is to get you to agree to the sale immediately, thinking that you will get less money for your trade-in if you let this offer pass you by.

Someone else is looking at that car. This is another trick to get you to buy immediately, and perhaps to get you to pay more than you normally would. The salesman tells you that someone else is looking at the same car you want, that the other customer is very anxious to buy it, but that you have the first right for purchase.

This car has already been discounted. Some car manufacturers offer value package discounts that are shown on the new car sticker. Don't let the salesman try to tell you that this discount keeps him from offering any other discounts on the car.

Perhaps we need to find you another car that costs less. If negotiations aren't going well, the salesman might try appealing to your ego by suggesting you might consider another car more within your pathetic budget. Don't take the bait and fall for this one.

Let me have you talk to someone else while I take this phone call. Don't let the seller pass you on to another salesman, hoping he will be more effective in getting a better deal for the dealership. If your business isn't good enough to deserve the full attention of the salesman, it's time to walk.

Cars starting as low as $9,999. You need to learn early on that newspaper ads for car lots can never be trusted. You can be sure there is always some fine print, or that the cars advertised in your price range will always seem to be gone before you arrive. Use the ads to find the sellers for the model you wish to buy, but don't expect the prices to reflect reality.

I haven't been selling cars for that long. If a salesman tells you this, he's probably the biggest shark on the lot. The salesman gives you this story so you'll feel at ease with someone who you think doesn't know all the tricks yet. In fact, if he's good enough he may arouse your compassion so you want to help him as much as you want to get a good deal for yourself.

This will add only a few dollars to your monthly payment. Don't let a salesman switch into the mode where he talks about cost in terms of what your monthly payment will be. He may tell you that adding a certain option will add only a few dollars to each monthly payment. What he won't tell you is that the monthly payments might continue for a year longer than before. Insist that all negotiations be done in terms of total costs, not monthly payments.

Leasing

It has become popular lately for people to lease cars instead of buying them. With a lease, a bank or leasing company actually buys the car, and you lease it on a monthly basis. Think of it as being more like a long-term car rental. When you have leased the car for the required number of months, you'll usually have several options such as terminating the lease, paying an extra fee to buy the car, extending the lease, or entering into a new lease for the same car or a different one. If you want to get out of the lease early, you must expect to pay a severe financial penalty.

Leasing a car probably isn't a good idea for most people who are just leaving home for the first time. There are a few cases, however, where it might make sense. Leasing is generally a better option for those who like to trade in their cars every couple of years. If you plan to get a car and drive it until the engine falls out, purchasing the car is your better option. Leasing also makes sense for those who need a bigger car than their budget can afford (notice we said "need" and not "want"). For example, you have a spouse and five kids and really need a huge van for hauling them all around. In this case, the monthly lease payments will usually be less than if you were to buy the van and make monthly car payments. Finally, if you are driving a car that is worth less than what you owe on the loan (a condition known as being "upside down" in the car business), you can sometimes roll the difference into the lease price, pay off the loan, be driving a new car, and still be paying less per month.

If you think a lease would work for you, make sure you do your research carefully before signing anything. Understand the various fees you will be charged both at the start and at the end of the lease. Determine if there is a limit to the number of miles you can drive per year and what the penalty for exceeding that limit. If there is any chance that you would not be able to complete the lease, research the penalties for early termination.

Keep That Wallet Open

Although having that nice new car will give you a feeling of freedom, you will soon come to discover that car ownership actually robs you of some of your financial freedom. Even after you survive the shock of buying the car, you'll find that other car expenses just keep coming.

This section will introduce you to other costs that come with automobile ownership and explore ways that you might be able to reduce those costs.

The Shock of Insurance

If you're young and single and if you drive an expensive, sporty car, don't be surprised if the cheapest insurance you can get is going to cost from $150 to $250 per month. Young single males probably pay the highest insurance rates of any group, with young single females following close behind. These rates, however unfair they may seem, are based on what it costs insurance companies to insure young drivers. When you get a little older, get married, and establish a good driving record, your rates will go down.

High rates notwithstanding, don't think for a minute that you can get by without having auto insurance. In most states, you must have a minimum level of insurance coverage on a car before you can drive it. Even if your state doesn't require insurance, you'd be foolish to go without it. Without insurance, you could be sued for millions of dollars if you caused an accident that injured someone.

As we already pointed out, the make and model of your car will have the greatest effect on keeping your insurance cost low. If you bought a modest car and did your homework before buying, you should be able to buy insurance without breaking your budget. Get estimates from several companies because there's often quite a difference in rates. Up to a certain age, you may be able to add your car to your parents' insurance policy (with you paying for your car's insurance, of course).

There are a couple of things you can do to help bring your rates down. If you're in school, be aware that some companies offer discounts to students who maintain good grades. Additionally, the careful driver can count on paying less than his accident- or ticket-prone counterpart. Being involved in accidents and receiving traffic tickets can increase your rates dramatically and even result in the cancellation of your insurance policy.

One final way to reduce your insurance bill is to change the coverage provided by your policy. Some people don't realize that a car insurance policy actually consists of several different types of protection, and the policy may be adjusted to increase, decrease, or eliminate certain of these protections—which causes your cost to go up or down.

The most basic kind of insurance protection is called liability coverage. Minimum liability protection limits are required by most states, although it is often smart to obtain more protection than the minimum required by law. Liability coverage will pay for medical expenses and property damage related to an accident you caused. It will also protect you in court if an injured party decides to take legal action.

Collision protection is designed to repair your own car from damage sustained in an accident you caused. (If the other person was at fault, his insurance will cover the damage to your car.) Comprehensive protection covers damage to your car from causes not related to an accident, such as fire, theft, storm damage, and vandalism. Your insurance bill can be lowered if you apply high deductibles to both collision and comprehensive protection. For example, if your car catches on fire and you have a comprehensive coverage with a $500 deductible, you will pay the first $500, and the insurance company will pay the rest. Also keep in mind that the coverage offered by both of these options is limited to the cash value of the car. If you're driving an old car that is worth only $500, that's all the insurance company will pay if the car is destroyed. When a car gets to the point that it has little cash value, you may be better off to drop collision and comprehensive coverage on it, and just take your chances.

Although most states require insurance, there are still some people who break the law and drive without it. Or they may have only the minimum level of insurance, which will not cover all your damages if they cause an accident involving your car. You can avoid these problems by adding another type of protection, called "uninsured motorist" or "underinsured motorist," to your own policy.

Before making any changes to your insurance policy, you should call your agent and have him explain all the options. It's nice to save money on your insurance bill, but you don't want to expose yourself to a situation that could cost you dearly.

Taxes and Fees

Just as you paid certain government fees when you purchased your car, your state and local governments will probably require you to pay additional fees each year as part of the cost of car ownership. You should account for these taxes and fees when you are calculating how much it is going to cost you to own a particular car.

Most states require that you renew the car's registration once each year, often on the anniversary of the day you purchased it. This can usually be paid at the local motor vehicles department or through the mail. The registration fee is usually a fixed price somewhere in the range of $20 to $75. In the Dark Ages, states used to send out new license plates each year. These days, most just provide an expiration date sticker that can be applied to one corner of the plate. Some counties or cities may also require you each year to buy a sticker that must be placed on the windshield or in some other visible location.

A few states require vehicle owners to pay a yearly property tax, similar to the property tax charged to homeowners. The tax is usually calculated as a percentage of the current value of the car.

Many states have regular vehicle inspection programs designed to keep unsafe cars off the road. Once every year or two (depending on the state), you may be required to take your car to a service station or inspection station that will perform the inspection for a small fee. If your car doesn't pass inspection, you'll need to get it repaired. When the car passes the inspection process, you'll usually be given a sticker that must be displayed somewhere on the car. Also, to identify cars that are producing an excessive amount of pollutants, many states require emissions testing. Cars that don't pass the emissions inspection must also be repaired.

It will be your responsibility to learn about the fees and taxes that apply to your area and to make sure they're paid on time. Inquire at the motor vehicles office, or ask a current resident what is required. Failure to do this will cost you a fair amount of money, and a whole lot of inconvenience.

Here Comes Trouble

One cost that we did not mention above is the cost of keeping your vehicle in good operating condition. Even if you bought a new car, there are certain things that you should be doing regularly to keep the car running at its best.

If you feel comfortable working around cars and your objective is to save money, there are a number of regular automotive maintenance tasks that you can probably do yourself, rather than taking the car to a mechanic or a repair shop. But there are other, more complicated procedures that are better left to the professionals. Over the past few years, many of the major systems of the automobile have been redesigned to use newer technologies, such as computer microprocessor chips. This has been a mixed blessing. Although computerized systems are more reliable and less likely to have problems, those problems that do arise are generally more difficult to diagnose and repair. Thus, there are fewer tasks that you will be able to do yourself and more that will need to be done by your mechanic and his expensive diagnostic computer.

Preventive Maintenance

Although people usually go to the doctor because they're sick, sometimes they go just for a checkup so that potential problems may be found and corrected even before symptoms appear. Similarly, you can give your car periodic checkups, diagnosing potential problems before disaster strikes. No one wants to be stranded at the side of the road with a broken belt or an overheated engine, and these kinds of problems can be corrected before they occur if you perform preventive maintenance on your car. You may be tempted to forget preventive maintenance because you don't have time to deal with it or you don't have the money. This is a big mistake. When dealing with cars, ignoring small problems that are easy to fix will usually result in bigger problems that are expensive to correct.

Your bible for doing preventive maintenance should be the owner's manual that came with your car. If you did not get a manual with your car, you should be able to order one from the dealer for only a few dollars. These books usually contain a maintenance table that shows the various tasks that need to be done and tells how often they should be done. For example, you might be told you should change the oil every 5,000 miles or every six months, whichever comes first. Brakes, on the other hand, might be inspected every 10,000 miles, regardless of the time it takes to accumulate those miles. The maintenance schedule is usually different depending on driving conditions. For example, if you make a lot of short trips or if you drive in dusty conditions, you might be told to change the oil filter every 3,000 miles. Otherwise, you might be told to change it every 6,000 miles. Not all the items on the log will be things that need to be replaced. Sometimes you'll just need to check the condition of something. For example, it's a good idea to check tire pressure and the levels of all the fluids about once a month.

When planning a lengthy driving trip, take your car to a mechanic and have it checked before you leave. Most mechanics don't charge much for this service, which may uncover potential problems that could result in a breakdown if they are not corrected. The repairs the mechanic might suggest usually aren't very expensive, such as replacing a worn belt or a cracked hose. If such problems are not discovered until you break down, they will end up costing you much more in both time and money.

When you have preventive work done on your car, note the work performed, the date, and the mileage of the car. Record this in the back of the owner's manual or in a separate notebook that you keep in the same place.

Diagnosing Car Problems

There is no worse feeling than being stranded far from home, late at night, with a car that either won't start or won't run properly. For serious problems, you may have no choice but to call a tow truck and have the car fixed by a mechanic. But sometimes you can do things yourself that will either fix the problem or allow you to get home so that you can drive the car to your own mechanic.

It used to be that when you had a problem on the road, all you had to do was drive (or push) the car to the nearest gas station. Although a few gas stations still have service departments, most have replaced them with "convenience" outlets that sell diapers, soda, cigarettes, and junk food to go with your gas. If you drive a lot, you might consider investing the few dollars a year it takes to belong to an auto club, such as AAA. Not only do auto clubs provide emergency towing and repair service, but they also provide hotel discounts, maps, and other services for travelers.

Sometimes you know you're having problems because the car will not start or is not operating correctly. More often, your first sign of trouble will come from one of the warning lights or gauges on the dashboard. If you don't understand these, refer to your owner's manual. Some warning lights indicate serious problems, but others warn of minor problems that should not stop you from driving the car.

➜   Listed below are some of the common problems that you might experience and some of the things you can do to correct them:

▶ Flat Tires

Make sure your car has a spare tire, a jack, and the tools needed to replace a flat tire. Remember to check the pressure in your spare tire when you check the pressure in the other tires. When you get a new car, practice changing a tire so that you'll know how it's done. It is far easier to acquire this skill in your driveway on a sunny day than on a dark road in the middle of a snowstorm.

If you're not going to learn how to change a tire no matter what, at least consider purchasing one of the aerosol cans on the market that will fill a flat tire for you. Read the instructions—the aerosol can may fill the tire with some sort of goop that will force you to purchase a new tire. However, using the aerosol option is better than sitting at the side of the road because you don't know how to change a tire or can't get the jack out from its "convenient" location underneath your car.

Unless you have no other option, don't drive the car when one of the tires is flat. This will bend the rim of the wheel and make it much more expensive to repair.

Most spare tires are smaller tires, which allow you to drive the car to the closest tire repair shop. They aren't designed to be tires you use from day to day. Get the flat tire repaired as quickly as possible so you won't need to drive on the spare longer than necessary.

▶ Brake Problems

Fortunately, most brake problems occur gradually, giving you plenty of time to get them fixed before a serious failure occurs. If warning lights come on when you brake, if you hear a grinding noise, or if takes longer to stop than normal, you should visit your mechanic without delay. One thing you can do is to check the level of brake fluid in the master cylinder and add fluid if the level is low.

Moisture reduces brakes' effectiveness. If you are in a severe storm or if you drive through standing water, you may find that the brakes are sluggish and are not working well. Drive slowly and apply the brakes lightly as you drive. This should eventually dry the brake pads and linings and fix the problem.

▶ Engine Temperature

The most common temperature problem you'll have is an overheated engine. This usually happens on a hot summer day when you are stuck in traffic and have the air conditioner running at full blast. Although an overheated engine could be a sign of serious problems, it usually only means that the cooling system of the car is overwhelmed. If you're stuck in traffic, try taking an alternate route that will allow you to move rather than just sit and idle the engine. If that isn't possible, place the transmission in neutral and press on the accelerator to run the engine at a higher speed. This will cause the fan to turn faster, pulling more fresh air into the radiator. Turn off the air-conditioning and turn the heater on high. This will be miserable for you, but it will put less strain on the cooling system. If none of this works and the temperature gauge continues to be in the "red" zone, turn off the engine and don't drive any further—unless you don't mind severely damaging your engine. *Do not attempt to remove the radiator cap while the engine is still warm—you might be severely burned by steam and boiling water from the radiator.*

Regular overheating that is not related to a cooling system failure may mean that your radiator needs to be flushed or that your level of coolant is too low. Once the engine is cold, take off the radiator cap and check the fluid level. If it is low, add more coolant. Most cars are designed to use a mixture composed of equal proportions of antifreeze and distilled water.

Sometimes you have the opposite problem—your car engine will never warm up. When you run the car heater, you never get any warm air. This means your thermostat is stuck in the closed position. Replace it yourself, or let your mechanic do it.

▶ Electrical Problems

The electrical system of your car is powered by the car battery. When the engine is running, the fan belt also turns the alternator, which recharges the power in the battery. Like your home electrical system, the electrical system in your car is divided into several circuits, each of which is protected from electrical surges by a fuse. If only one headlight or taillight is not working, the culprit is probably a burned-out bulb that needs to be replaced. If multiple items aren't working, your problems probably stem from a failure in one of the circuits—either an electrical short or a blown fuse. Your owner's manual should list the items that are on each circuit, and help you locate the fuse box so you can replace the fuse. If none of the components of the electrical system in your car is working, you probably have a dead battery—perhaps because the lights were left on after the car was last driven. Use jumper cables or a battery charger to get the car started, and then run the engine so that the alternator can recharge the battery. If the problem happens again, either the battery needs to be replaced or you have more serious electrical problems and should seek a mechanic's help.

Sometimes a gauge or warning light will indicate that the alternator is not functioning properly. This often means the drive belt that powers the alternator is slipping or broken, but it could also indicate a problem with the battery or the alternator.

▶ Problems with Starting the Engine

Cars with automatic transmissions will not start unless the transmission is in the "park" or "neutral" setting. If you are sure your transmission is set properly but the car still won't start, the first thing you should suspect is a weak or dead battery. Turn on the headlights and then try to start the car. If the lights won't come on at all or if they dim significantly when you try to start the car, you've probably got a weak battery. A starting failure on the first cold day of winter is another sign, because batteries lose much of their power as the temperature drops. If this is the reason your car won't start, sometimes just waiting until the temperature rises during the day will fix the problem—at least until the next cold day.

If you suspect a battery problem, first try cleaning the two terminal posts that connect the battery to the cables. Sometimes corrosion accumulates on these terminals and prevents a good connection. Remove the cable clamps, clean the terminals and clamps with a wire brush, and then reattach the cables and try again. Most batteries contain six acid-filled cells that you can check. The level of the acid should come up almost to the bottom of the filler hole for each cell. If any cell is low, add distilled water until it is at the proper level. You're working with battery acid here, so protect your eyes, skin, and clothing and wipe up any spilled water or acid when you're done.

If the battery is weak or dead, you may need to use a battery charger or jumper cables to get it started. After starting the car, drive or run the engine for approximately thirty minutes to recharge the battery. If the battery fails again in the next day or two, it may be time to replace the battery, or you may have electrical problems that are causing the battery to be discharged when the engine is not running.

If the engine turns over well but it just won't start, there's a possibility you're getting either too much or too little gas to the engine. Try pressing the accelerator pedal all the way to the floor and starting the car. If that doesn't work, try starting it without pressing the pedal at all. If *that* doesn't work, let the car sit for thirty minutes or so, and then try again.

▶ Oil Pressure

The oil pump moves oil through the engine to keep it well lubricated, reducing the wear of friction and heat on the moving parts. It takes only a few minutes for an engine to be destroyed if oil isn't flowing. The oil pressure gauge or the oil warning light may be used to tell when the oil pressure is too low.

If the oil pressure drops when you're sitting in traffic but then corrects itself when the engine is running faster, the level is probably low. Check the level, and add oil until it reaches the correct level. If it has been a while since the last oil change, it may be time to do that as well. If the oil pressure is still low even when driving and the oil level is not low, get the car to the shop, driving it as little as possible.

▶ Roadside Emergencies

When your car begins to malfunction, pull off to the side of the road as far as you can to keep from blocking traffic. Turn on the emergency flashers, so other motorists will see you and reduce their speed. If the problem occurs during daylight hours, lift the hood of your car and tie a white or bright-colored cloth on the car where it can be seen easily. If it's dark, put flares or reflective signs behind your car as a warning to other motorists. Also, wear light clothing if possible so that others will see you. When you get out to examine your car, stand on the passenger side of the car if possible. This will protect you from oncoming traffic and will also give you some protection if someone runs into the rear of your car.

If you own a wireless phone, now would be a good time to use it to summon help. If you're in a remote area or you don't feel safe walking for help, lock the car and stay inside until help arrives. Be cautious of strangers who stop and offer to help, and don't unlock your doors until you're confident that the person can be trusted. You might roll down your window just enough to request that the Good Samaritan drive ahead to get help.

▶ Traffic Accidents

No one likes to think about being involved in a traffic accident, but sometimes they happen. Because you aren't likely to be doing your best thinking after an accident, it pays to know ahead of time about the laws in your area. Some states require you to call the police for every accident, but others do not require police involvement when there is only minor damage and no injuries. Some states expect you to leave the car at the scene of the accident, while others request you pull the cars off to the side of the road before calling the police. To determine the specific laws and regulations in your area, you should contact both your motor vehicles department and your insurance company. Request a copy of the rules for your area, and consider keeping a copy with the other important papers in the car.

Regardless of your local laws, there are some things that you should always do after an accident. First, make sure there are no serious injuries, either to yourself or to others involved. If there are injuries, call 911 for help before worrying about anything else. Determine if the police should be involved; if so, contact them. If there is any question about whether the police should be called or if you and the other driver disagree about calling the police, it's best to be safe and make the call.

While waiting for the police (or if you decide not to call them), you should exchange information with the driver of the other car. You should each produce your driver's license, car registration, and proof of insurance. Many insurance companies provide small cards that list the name of the insurance company and your policy number. Write down all the information about the other driver and his vehicle. If there are witnesses to the accident, record their names, phone numbers, and addresses.

When the police arrive, each of the drivers who were involved in the accident will be asked to fill out an accident report form, and the police will want to talk to each driver individually. If the officer determines that a

Sneaky Secret

Always keep your important automotive papers in the car in a place where you will be able to find them. This includes insurance information! (The one exception to this is your title to the car, which should be kept in a safe place at your home.) Anytime you have an accident or a traffic violation, you'll need these papers. Consider placing them in a small carrying case that will fit in the glove box. This will keep all your papers together and will protect them until you need them.

law was broken or that one driver was primarily at fault in the accident, a traffic citation may be issued. The outcome of the police investigation will usually lead to a conclusion about which driver was at fault, if any. This is important to help the insurance companies decide which one has to pay. Some states have no-fault insurance laws, which means that each company will fix the car that is owned by the company's customer, regardless of who is to blame for the accident.

One thing you should never do is leave the scene of an accident. This is a serious crime that may result in severe penalties. Even with a minor accident, stop and talk with the other driver before leaving. When both drivers agree the matter has been resolved, then it is safe for both of them to leave.

Driving in Adverse Weather

Even if you're the world's best driver, all the rules change when the weather turns ugly. Although you should always be careful while driving in bad weather, there are a couple of situations that should cause you to pay special attention:

You just moved to a new area. Each location seems to have its own particular driving challenges, and those who are new to the area may not know how to handle them. Our area gets snow a couple of times per winter, and we have a lot of people moving into the area who have never driven in snow. The first snowstorm of the year always looks like a demolition derby.

You're driving an unfamiliar car. Each car handles a little differently when it comes to driving in bad weather. Until you get used to it, you won't know what to expect.

If either condition applies to you, proceed with much caution when driving in bad weather. You might want to pull into an empty parking lot and just drive around until you get a feeling for how the car handles in bad weather.

Because snowy and icy conditions seem to be the most deadly form of adverse weather, here are some general ideas for safer driving in those conditions:

- Go slower than usual, and be more gentle when braking, turning, or accelerating.

- If you do a lot of driving in snowy conditions, consider getting snow tires, chains, or a vehicle designed to handle well in the snow.

- Be cautious when driving over bridges and raised structures, because ice tends to form on them faster than on the surrounding roadways.

- If your car starts to fishtail, take your foot off the accelerator and turn the steering wheel into the direction of the skid (for example, if the back end of the car has fishtailed to the right, turn right).

- During the winter, keep an emergency kit in the car's trunk. This should include such items as sand or gravel (for putting under the wheels), warm blankets, food, water, flares, and tow straps.

- Before winter weather arrives, have your mechanic check your tire pressure and the condition of your radiator and coolant. These steps will give you better traction and protect you against some radiator problems during the winter.

I'm Still Clueless

? *Couldn't I just avoid dealing with car salesmen by buying a used car directly from another owner?*

That's certainly one option, and thousands of cars are sold this way every year. Once you've done your research, you should know the approximate retail price of the model you want and be able to determine a fair deal when you see one. The classified section of the newspaper is a good source for used cars, and the list is usually arranged by make and model so it's easy to see what's available. Of course, you will be dealing with the owner directly, so you'll be responsible for contacting him, making an appointment, driving to his location, test driving the car, and negotiating the purchase. There is usually less negotiation on price when dealing directly with the owner, but you should still suggest a lower price if you think the price is too high.

There are a couple of potential problem areas when buying cars directly from previous owners. Unless the car still has a manufacturer's warranty that can be transferred, you'll have no warranty on the car. You can protect yourself by asking a mechanic to check the car and give you an evaluation of any major problems he finds. Your mechanic should be willing to perform the inspection for a modest fee. The previous owner should not object to this. (If he does, that probably means he knows the car is a lemon.)

You should also make sure the paperwork associated with the transfer of the car is handled correctly. This isn't a problem when buying through a dealer, because dealers handle these issues all the time. Because regulations differ from state to state, contact the Department of Motor Vehicles in your area before buying a car from an individual. The DMV can tell you the steps you'll need to follow to make sure the car gets correctly transferred to you from the previous owner.

? *How can I get the maximum amount when I trade in my old car?*

Most appraisers will look all around the exterior and interior of the car, and will then take it for a test drive. Concentrate on the items that will make the car appear nicer and drive better. Clean the inside and outside of the car, vacuum the carpets, and clean the upholstery or install seat covers. Replace anything broken on the car that would be obvious from an external inspection, such as tires and windshield wipers. In general, don't spend a lot of money fixing things that can't be seen (oil change, brakes), unless it affects the ride of the car. Keep in mind that any money spent on the car will probably not increase the value of the trade by the same amount. Installing $400 worth of new tires will probably not increase the value of the car by $400. Concentrate on making improvements that can be done cheaply and that will improve the appearance of the car.

The value of your trade-in will also decrease for each increment of 10,000 miles. A car that has been driven 32,000 miles will be worth less than one driven 29,000. If possible, trade before hitting the next increment.

? *Is the Internet valuable when shopping for a car?*

Yes, yes, yes! Much of the research that you should do before buying can be done on-line. You can determine the dealer's actual cost for a new car and the trade-in value of your old car. You can also read owners' reviews for various car makes and models and determine what the owners like and dislike about a particular car.

In addition to doing research, some Internet services will actually let you avoid a lot of the hassle of buying the car. Some of these will give you a free quote and will also give you a list of sellers in your area who will honor the quoted price. If you think the price is fair, you can visit the seller and be home with your new car within an hour. If this trend continues, it could revolutionize the way cars are bought and sold.

When you're ready to finance a car purchase, there are on-line companies that will arrange car loans at reasonable rates. There are also companies that deal in such products as extended warranties.

Be sure you search carefully and find a number of different sources before making a decision. Some sites pay big premiums so that popular search engines always seem to find their sites first. Dig deeper, because these sites usually cannot offer you the best deals when they are paying so much in advertising.

? *How do I use jumper cables to start a car with a dead battery?*

➔   Invest in a set of good jumper cables and keep them in your trunk. Then when you have starting problems, all you need to do is find another friendly driver willing to "jump" your battery and get you on your way again. Take precautions when working around batteries, which are filled with acid that can burn your skin and clothes. Batteries can even explode under some conditions. These are the general steps to take to jump-start a battery:

- Have the other driver position his car so the two batteries are close together. They need to be close enough for the jumper cables to connect the two batteries.

- Turn off both engines, put the transmissions in "park" or "neutral," and set both parking brakes.

- Identify the positive and negative terminals on each battery. The positive one will often be connected to a red cable, or will have a plus sign or the letters "POS" next to the terminal. The negative one will be connected to a black cable, or will have a minus sign or the letters "NEG" nearby.

- Connect one end of the *red* jumper cable to the clamp on top of the *positive* terminal of the good battery. Connect the other end of the *red* cable to the *positive* terminal on the dead battery. Make sure there is a good connection between the jumper cable jaws and the clamps.

- Connect one end of the *black* jumper cable to the *negative* terminal of the good battery. You can connect the other end of the *black* jumper cable to the negative terminal on the dead battery, but this may cause the battery to explode in rare cases. It is safer to attach the cable to a "grounded" part on the dead car. Just look for an unpainted metal part, such as an engine clamp or a part of the frame of the car.

- Make sure all cables are clear of moving engine parts, and then start the engine of the car with the good battery. Race the engine a couple of times. Now try starting the car with the dead battery. If it doesn't start after a couple of tries, the problem may not be related to the battery.

- With both engines running, remove the jumper cables in the opposite order from when they were attached. Close both hoods, thank the other driver, and be on your way. In order to charge the battery again, make sure to run your engine for at least thirty minutes before turning it off.

? *Can I trust my auto mechanic?*

You can trust a strange auto mechanic about as much as you can trust used car salesmen. Honest ones exist, but they're more precious than gold. Choose your mechanics wisely, based on references from friends or consumer groups. Even then, approach the auto mechanic shop with caution. Even if the firm has a good reputation, the mechanic who earned his shop that reputation may have been replaced by a scoundrel.

Just as used car salesmen have scams that jack up the price of their cars, auto mechanic shops are notorious for their own money-making schemes. A common one is to offer a standard job such as a tune-up or a radiator flush or an oil change for a cheap price. When the mechanic goes in to do the work, he will "accidentally" find several other problems (usually expensive ones) that absolutely "must" be fixed before you drive away. *Don't fall for this scheme.* If a mechanic tells you there's expensive maintenance that needs to be done on your car, get a second opinion before you let him do the work. And if you find yourself being given a list of expensive car repairs every time you get a tune-up, you may want to find yourself another mechanic.

CHAPTER 8

Making Cents of
Financial Stuff

★ **IN THIS CHAPTER**
- ✔ Opening and Using a Checking Account
- ✔ Balancing Your Checking Account
- ✔ Using Credit Cards Wisely
- ✔ Understanding Other Types of Investments
- ✔ Practicing Wise Money Management
- ✔ Utilizing Your Employment Benefits
- ✔ Learning the Sad Truth about Taxes
- ✔ Planning Your Financial Future

When you first get out on your own, you'll probably think that managing your money is no big deal. You get a regular check from work or from home, trade it at the bank for a wad of cash, and then pull out the wad whenever you see something you want to buy. If you get the things you wanted and have any cash left over when you get your next check, then you probably consider yourself a financial wizard.

After you've been on your own for a while, you'll probably start to wonder if there might be a better way. Spending money as you make it may always give you cash to buy a pizza or take in a movie, but don't even think about buying that new car. And if you live from paycheck to paycheck, your dreams of owning a home someday may never be fulfilled. In fact, you may not even be able to go on a spur-of-the-moment weekend trip with friends unless you've set some cash aside to plan for that rainy—or sunny—day.

Matters are complicated by a phenomenon that you may or may not have yet experienced. We call it "the amazing shrinking paycheck." When you get out on your own and get a part- or full-time job, you can't wait to

COME ONE! COME ALL TO SEE THE AMAZING SHRINKING PAYCHECK!

receive your first paycheck so you can go out and celebrate. But when you look at your long-awaited paycheck, you'll be shocked to see how little money you were paid.

"There has to be some kind of mistake here," you might say. But as you examine your check stub, the sad truth is only too clear. You were paid exactly what you should have been paid, but a number of greedy people got their hands on your paycheck before it ever reached you. In addition to many types of federal, state, and local taxes you must pay, still more of your earnings may be extracted by your employer to cover some of your benefits. And don't forget the huge chunk that goes to Social Security!

There are three ways to fight back against the amazing shrinking paycheck. You can get a promotion and get paid more money, you can make choices so that less money is taken out for taxes, or you can manage the remaining money so that it goes further. We can't help you with the promotion, but we will try to teach you to use the other two techniques in this chapter.

We'll cover such topics as opening and managing checking and savings accounts, acquiring and using credit cards, budgeting your income, and paying taxes. We'll also briefly look into ways that you can start to prepare for the future. So before you open (and empty) your wallet, take a peek at our suggestions on managing your money.

The Check Is in the Mail

Even if you ignore all the other advice in this chapter, it's a pretty good bet that you will probably have a checking account at some point in your life. Although more and more businesses are accepting credit cards as a form of payment, there are still places where paying by check is definitely the way to go.

Using a Checking Account

You open an account with a bank by putting some money in the bank in your name. When you want to pay someone, you write a check, which is a request for the bank to extract the specified amount of money from your account and give it to the person. Fortunately, the person who receives the check does not need to go to your bank to get the money, because banks have an agreement to honor checks written against other banks. After giving the person the amount indicated on the check, his bank does the work of arranging for the same amount to be transferred from your account to his bank. Or if the recipient prefers, the money can simply be transferred from your checking account into his.

Figure 8-1 is an example of a typical blank check. Notice that the name and address of the owner of the account are printed on the check. This is not required. In fact, the "starter checks" you get when you open your account won't have anything printed in that area. But you will find that many merchants are hesitant to accept a check without this information, so printed checks are an asset. Each check also has a unique number (200 in the upper right corner in this example) to help you keep track of it. There are also blanks on the check for the date, the name of the "payee" (the person to whom the check is written), and the amount of the check. To prevent fraud, the amount is written twice—once as a number, and once in words. You will see an example of this shortly. At the bottom of the check is a line for your signature and a "memo" area you can use to write a note to yourself, in which you can describe what the check was for if you wish. The very bottom of the check contains some funny numbers that will be used by the bank's computers when the check is processed.

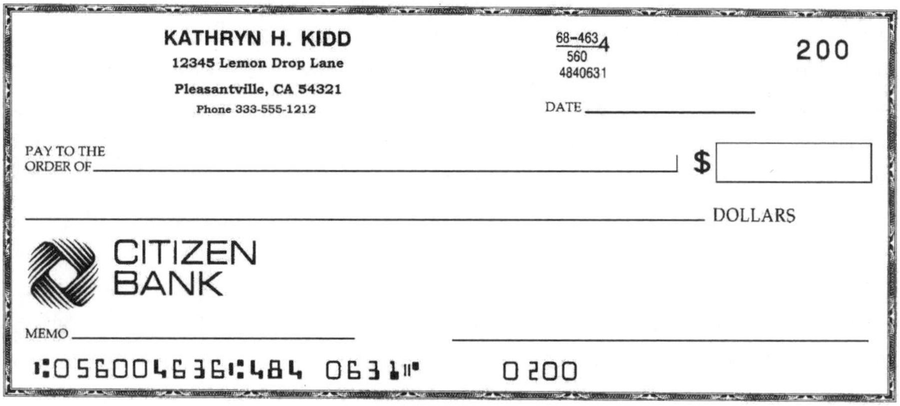

KATHRYN H. KIDD
12345 Lemon Drop Lane
Pleasantville, CA 54321
Phone 333-555-1212

68–463
560
4840631
4

200

DATE _____

PAY TO THE
ORDER OF _____

$ [_____]

_____ DOLLARS

CITIZEN BANK

MEMO _____

⑈0560046361⑈484 0631⑈   0 200

Figure 8-1

Now that you have seen what a blank check looks like, refer to Figure 7-2 for a view of the same check after it has been written to someone.

KATHRYN H. KIDD
12345 Lemon Drop Lane
Pleasantville, CA 54321
Phone 333-555-1212

68–463
560
4840631
4

200

DATE *Oct. 30, 1999*

PAY TO THE
ORDER OF *The Atomic Chili Company*

$ **45.66**

Forty-five-and-66/100--------------------- DOLLARS

CITIZEN BANK

MEMO *Chili for Halloween Party*

Kathryn H. Kidd

⑈0560046361⑈484 0631⑈   0 200

Figure 8-2

Pay particular attention to how the amounts are written in the completed check shown above. The dollar amount is bounded by asterisks so that the number cannot easily be modified. Where the amount is written out in words, a line is also drawn through the rest of that area so that additional words cannot be added. If you make a small mistake while writing a check, you can cross out the mistake, write the correct information, and then place your initials next to the correction. For larger mistakes, it's better to just tear up the check and start over.

Your typical checkbook is designed to hold a pad of checks on one side, and a check register on the other. The register is the record where you keep track of all your account activity, so that you can make sure there is always enough money in the account. An example of a register is shown below in Figure 8-3.

Number	Date	Transaction	Payment	X	Deposit	989.56
174	5/3	Bay View Apartments/Rent	600.00	X		600.00 389.56
175	5/7	Jack's Garage/New Tires	138.79			138.79 250.77
—	5/15	Deposit/Paycheck		X	1076.20	1076.20 1326.97
ATM	5/15	Cash/Movie with Jill	20.00	X		20.00 1306.97
176	5/20	VOID		X		—— 1306.97
177	5/20	Corner Market/Groceries	33.75			33.75 1273.22
178	5/25	Pacific Power/Electricity	51.33			51.33 1221.89
—	5/31	Deposit/Paycheck			1076.20	1076.20 2298.09

Figure 8-3

Your typical check register will probably not look this neat, but we wanted you to be able to read it! Note how the top of each page will show you how much money you have in your account at the beginning of the period. (In this case it's $989.56.) Each page of the register will record all the things you do that affect the money in the account—in this case, during the period from May 3rd to May 31st. Everything you do to change the amount of money in your account should be reflected in this check register, including writing checks, making deposits, and withdrawing cash via ATMs (automated teller machines).

For each check that is written, you should record the check number, the date, a description of why the check was written, and the amount (listed in the "Payment" column). Recording the check number will help you when you "balance" your checkbook. It's also helpful to record the check numbers as you write checks, because this will show you when you have forgotten to record a check. If for some reason you have to tear up a check, create a "Void" entry in the register, similar to the one you see in the illustration next to check number 176. This will give an accounting of that particular check number in your register, so you won't have to worry about whether you forgot to record a check. Don't leave any of the sections on your check register blank, because all of the information is vital for your records.

If you don't think it's important to record check numbers, dates, and the recipients of the checks, your first call from a company that has not received your payment will convince you otherwise. If you can tell the irate woman from the electric company, "I mailed you a payment for $51.33 on May 25th. It's check number 178," she's a lot more likely to believe you than if you just tell her, "The check is in the mail."

The right-most column of the register is used to keep a running balance of how much money remains in your account. In Figure 7-3, the amount at the top, $989.56, was the amount carried forward from the previous page. As you record each item in the register, you record the amount in the Payment/Deposit columns, but you also carry it across to the top part of the last column. Then you add (for deposits) or subtract (for checks and ATM transactions) the amount from the number on the previous line. For example, the balance before writing check number 174 was $989.56; then we wrote the check for $600.00, which we subtract for a current balance of $389.56. Just remember to always *add* the Deposit column, and *subtract* the Payment column. (Just ignore the "X" column for now; we'll cover that later.)

When you wish to deposit money into your account, you'll use the deposit slips found at the back of each pad of checks. On each slip there is a place to put the date and also an area where you list all the cash and checks that you're going to deposit. List each check separately, by amount. Use the back of the slip if you're lucky enough to have too many to fit on the front. Total up all the different amounts you are going to deposit. There is also an option that lets you keep some cash, rather than depositing all of it. For example, you may wish to deposit all of your pay-check except for $50 for gas and spending money.

If you're including some checks with your deposit, there is one thing more that you will need to do before making the deposit. You'll need to "endorse" each check, which is a fancy way of saying you need to sign them. The signature goes on the back of the check, on the left side. There are usually lines on the back that indicate where to endorse the check. Sign your name exactly as it appears on the front. Even if your friends call you "Chuck Jones," if the check says "Charles Bartholomew Jones," that's the name to use when endorsing that check.

When someone writes a check and puts your name on the front, those funds are pretty safe. If the check is stolen or you lose it, the person who comes up with it will have a difficult time cashing it without some sort of phony identification. But once you endorse that check, it becomes just like cash. To make sure this isn't a problem, write "For Deposit Only" under your name. This means that the check cannot be cashed—it can be deposited only to an account that has your name on it. Another option is to leave the check unendorsed until right before you deposit them.

Many employers allow you to deposit your paycheck directly to your checking account. This avoids the inconvenience of going to the bank, and also eliminates the possibility of loss or theft.

When you have a checking account, you'll occasionally want to withdraw some cash for yourself. One option is to get some "cash back" when you make your deposit. Another is to write a check to yourself or to "Cash." But keep in mind that usually only your own bank will cash such checks. Probably the best option is to request an ATM card. These come as an option with most checking accounts, and there is usually no extra charge for obtaining such a card. After you request a card, the bank will send you one in the mail, along with a PIN number, which is often mailed separately. The PIN number is like a password, and you use it along with your card to obtain cash from an ATM machine. Make sure to record all ATM transactions in your check register. At some point you'll also have to record the fees you're charged for each use of the ATM, but we'll go into more detail on that later.

It is possible to open an account where multiple people are autho-rized to write checks on the account. This is known as a "joint account," and is most often used by married couples. But you may also find joint accounts to be useful when dealing with relatives, organizations, and business associates. If you are in a joint account, make sure you're deal-ing with someone you trust. It's perfectly legal for someone who is part of a joint account to take all the money out of the account and spend it—even if he's not the one who put the money in the account in the first place.

Opening an Account

➡ Before you open a checking account, it's wise to check with several different banks to see what types of checking accounts are available to you. Your goal should be to find an account where you won't be charged any extra monthly fees for the privilege of having that account. If you look hard enough and are willing to follow certain conditions, you can usually find such accounts. In general, most banks offer three different types of checking accounts: fee accounts, free accounts, and interest-bearing accounts.

▶ Fee Accounts

This is the type of account you want to avoid if possible. The bank charges you a monthly fee, usually about $5, for maintaining your account. The fee is deducted from your account balance every month when you get your statement in the mail. Thus, if you opened an account with $100 and never deposited any money or wrote any checks, the bank would have all your money after twenty months. Some banks offer student accounts that have lower fees.

▶ Free Accounts

This is a better account, because there is no monthly fee deducted from your balance. But to qualify for free checking, you usually have to maintain a minimum balance in the account—commonly $500 to $1,500. Thus, your checking is free as long as your balance doesn't drop below this minimum. If you drop below the minimum, you'll be charged a monthly service charge (usually $8 to $12). Opening this type of account is a bit of a gamble. If you're not sure you'll be able to maintain the minimum balance, it may be wiser to open a fee account and endure the monthly charges.

▶ Interest-Bearing Accounts

This best kind of account is even better than the free account. Not only does it offer free checking, but in this arrangement the bank actually

Sneaky Secret

To remove the temptation of dropping below your minimum balance, consider excluding the minimum amount from the balance in your register. For example, if you need to maintain a minimum balance of $500, and you open your account with $700, just write a starting balance of $200 in your register. If you pretend the minimum balance is not there, you're less likely to spend it. The only time you need to "remember" the extra funds is when you balance your checkbook.

Some types of free accounts also have other restrictions. You may be limited to a maximum number of checks you can write per month and be charged a service charge for each check beyond that limit. With the rise of Internet banking, some banks are offering accounts that are free as long as all of your transactions are done electronically. If you actually go into a bank for a transaction, you will be charged a service fee.

pays you for banking with them. The word interest, means a fee that is paid for using someone else's money. Interest may be something you pay (bad), or something you earn (good). The interest in this kind of account is good, because the bank is paying you for the use of your money. Interest is usually expressed as a percentage that is paid over one year. Thus, if you open a checking account that pays 3 percent interest, you will earn $3 for every $100 that you leave in the bank for a full year. You will not get rich from an interest-bearing checking account because they usually pay very low rates of interest (1 to 3 percent), but it beats getting nothing back or having to pay a fee.

As with a free checking account, you usually qualify for an interest-bearing checking account by keeping a minimum balance in the account. This will usually be a larger minimum amount than for a free account and can be as high as $3,000.

You'll find that banks are quite different from each other in terms of the types of accounts they offer and the minimum deposits they require you to keep in the account. It's worth your time to check all the banks in the area until you find the one that will work for you. Often, smaller banks will offer better deals than larger banks, because they are working hard to get customers and grow larger. Some large banks are interested only in business accounts and discourage personal accounts by charging heavy fees. Also, organizations such as credit unions are less oriented toward making money and are more likely to offer accounts with lower fees and more reasonable restrictions.

When selecting a bank, also consider the availability of branches and ATM machines in your area. You can get money from any ATM if you're in a pinch, but you may be charged a fee if you use an ATM that isn't connected with your own bank. Those fees add up, so don't make a habit of using ATMs in supermarkets or other places that aren't affiliated with your bank. Thus, it's important to choose a bank that will be convenient to work, school, and your home. Otherwise, you may find yourself driving clear across town for cash every time you decide that you need ten dollars to go to a movie.

When you have selected a bank and the type of account you want, it is time to visit a local branch bank and open your account. Go to one of the branch officers who has a desk in the branch, usually located near the teller windows. Choose somebody who looks friendly, and tell him or her you wish to open a checking account. You'll have to answer a series of questions, which the bank employee will record on your application. You may have to show some kind of identification, such as a driver's license. You will be given a checkbook containing a pad of starter checks and a blank check register. There are usually about ten starter checks—just to get you by until your real checks arrive. These won't have your name or address printed on them, so you should write that information neatly in the proper place before writing each check. As noted earlier, be aware that some businesses are hesitant to accept such checks, so use them sparingly until your real checks arrive.

When you open your account, you will also be asked to sign a signature card, which the bank will use to verify the signatures on your checks. (Make sure you sign the card the same way you are going to sign your checks.) The bank employee will also show you a book of check styles, and you can choose from these styles for your first order of real checks. This is a chance for your real personality to shine through. You will find check styles ranging from the simple to the bizarre. Note that there is often a charge for the checks, and that charge may vary depending on the style you like. Make sure you ask the bank employee how much, if anything, you will be charged for a particular style of check.

Sneaky Secret

Kathy was recently surprised when she ordered 200 new checks and found that the bank had charged her a whopping $42. You can eliminate this "middle man" fee by ordering directly from companies that print checks. These companies usually advertise in magazines, through mail advertisements, and in the Sunday newspaper. Just send them a voided check (one of your starter checks is fine), the information about the checks you want to order (style and quantity), and your payment.

In two to three weeks, your real checks will arrive in the mail, and then you will be all set to write checks with abandon. Once a month, your bank should send you a statement showing all the activity against your account. Most banks will also return to you the checks you wrote that were processed against the account. Keep these checks for at least three years, because you can never tell when you may need an old check to prove that you paid something.

The Old Balancing Act

As noted above, your bank will send you a monthly statement showing all the activity against your checking account. This statement is not just junk mail; it should be used to make sure your records and the bank's records are the same. This process is known as "balancing" your checkbook and should be done every month, as soon as possible after the statement is received.

Kathy was never taught how to balance a checkbook, so she made a habit of ignoring the statements that arrived regularly each month. She simply subtracted the amount of her checks from the total she thought she had in the bank, but because she didn't take bank fees into account when she did so, there was always less money in her account than she thought she had. Soon her checks would start to bounce because of insufficient funds, and she ended up with even less money in her account because the bank charged her twenty to twenty-five extra dollars every time she bounced a check. Every couple of years, her account would become so confused that she would simply close the account, and take whatever money was left to start a new account at another bank. Clark says it was good she met him when she did because she was running out of banks.

There's nothing mystical about balancing a checkbook. It is simply the process of making sure the bank's records and your checkbook register are in agreement. Doing this monthly will help you catch and correct lots of errors, such as unrecorded checks or deposits, amounts that were recorded incorrectly, and even mistakes made by the bank. Once when we bought a house, we wrote a check for $25,000 that the bank subtracted from our account twice. Needless to say, a number of other checks bounced, and there were several people who were not very happy with us. But we had a good bank that paid all the fees and wrote letters to other banks and merchants telling them the errors were caused by the bank and not us. Everything was eventually corrected, and it didn't cost us an extra penny. If in balancing your checkbook you find that your bank has caused a similar problem, you should expect—and demand— the same type of treatment.

The back of your bank statement will usually have tables and instructions that you can follow to balance your account. These differ from bank to bank, but the process will usually go something like this:

☐ 1. Review all the entries in your check register since the last time you balanced your account. Make sure the math is correct, and make sure all checks and ATM withdrawals were subtracted and all deposits were added to your balance.

☐ 2. For each check processed by the bank, find the matching entry in the register, and make sure the amount is the same. Check the amount written in the "Payment" column and also the amount carried over to the far-right column. Make sure each check was subtracted from your balance. If you find a check that is not recorded, record it now and subtract it. If a check was recorded for the wrong amount, make a new register entry for the difference. For example, if you recorded the check as $10 but it was actually $15, make a new entry that shows a new $5 "Payment," and subtract it. Similarly, if you recorded a $15 check, but it was really only $10, you will need to add a new $5 "Deposit" to correct for the previous error.

☐ 3. Now we come to the part where we use the mysterious "X" column shown in Figure 7-3. As you are checking the amount of each check against the entry in your register, place an X or a check mark in this column for each check that was processed by the bank. If you added any register entries to correct for wrong amounts, mark an X for those as well. Follow this rule: If the bank knows about it, there should be an X in the column. If the bank doesn't know about it (such as a check written after the statement was printed) the column should be blank.

☐ 4. Repeat the same process for each deposit or ATM transaction shown on the statement. Find the entry in your register, make sure the amount is the same, and place an X next to the transaction.

☐ 5. If your account earns interest, record the amount of interest paid as a "Deposit," add it to your balance with an X. If you are charged a fee for check printing, or for the number of checks you wrote, or for a returned check, treat that as a payment, subtract it, and mark it with an *X*.

❏ 6. Now go through your register looking for all the entries that do not contain an *X*. These are called outstanding items—things you know about but that the bank doesn't. Make one list containing all the additions (deposits) and one list of all the subtractions (checks and ATM withdrawals). Add up the amounts on each list.

❏ 7. The last step is the easiest. Take the ending balance shown on your bank statement. Add the additions, and subtract the subtractions. Now compare that number with the ending balance in your check register. These numbers should be the same. If they are, give yourself a pat on the back and go get a big bowl of ice cream. When you come back, draw a heavy line under the last entry used in your register. This is an indicator of where the register ended when it was last balanced, and you will use it as the starting point the next time you balance the account.

➔   If your first attempt at balancing a checkbook is a failure, don't bang your head on the table in frustration. This happens to the best of us on occasion. Here is a checklist that might fix the problem:

❏ Check all your math again.

❏ Make sure each amount was recorded properly.

❏ Make sure a transaction was not added when it should have been subtracted, or vice versa.

❏ Make sure that every bank charge on the statement was properly recorded in the register.

❏ Make sure each item on the statement has an *X* in the register.

❏ Make sure you have included all outstanding items (without an *X*) in your Additions or Subtractions list. Do you have a very old check that still hasn't been processed? Did you recently change registers, and are there any outstanding items in the old register? Compare the outstanding items found when doing last month's balancing.

❑ Compute the difference between your calculated balance and your actual register balance, then cut that number in half. Now look for a check or deposit in that amount. If you find one, make sure it was added or subtracted properly.

Possible Problems

A checking account is a necessity of modern life and if managed correctly, it will be a convenient tool for managing your finances. But checking accounts can also cause you to lose a lot of money and gain a lot of frustration if you don't understand some of the finer details of how to manage them. Here are a few things that will save you a lot of grief:

- About the worst thing you can do with a checking account is write a check for more money than you have in the account. The technical name for this situation is having "insufficient funds," which is commonly referred to as "bouncing a check." This is a serious situation. You can be sent to jail if it can be proved that you have knowingly done this. Usually, however, people bounce checks because they aren't sure how much money they have in their account. When you bounce a check, the bank will charge you a penalty of $25 to $50, and the payee of the check will often charge you a fee as well.

- Most banks require checks deposited to your account to be held in your account for several days before you can use that money. If you write a check that dips into those funds, the bank will either refuse the check or charge you a penalty. Find out about the bank's "hold" policy before you open your account. Many banks will place no hold on payroll checks if you tell the cashier it's a payroll check when you deposit it.

- After you have a checking account for some time, you will start to play the "float" game. This allows you to take advantage of the fact that checks take several days to make it back to your bank after they are deposited. For example, you may write a rent check knowing you have insufficient funds to cover it, but also knowing that you will be paid next week, and that the paycheck will be deposited before the check is returned for payment. We all play this game a little, but don't cut it too close. The computer age has drastically cut down "float" time. Checks that used to take a week or more to clear may actually be processed the same day you write them.

- Make sure you always sign your checks in approximately the same way. Banks may refuse to accept a check if the signature is too different from the one on the signature card created when the account was opened. This is known as an "irregular signature," and can cause you some extra fees.

- Make sure you deposit checks on time. Some checks have small print that indicates they must be cashed before a certain date. Aside from that, most banks will not accept a check if too much time has elapsed since it was written.

- Avoid writing checks that can be easily altered. There is a story about some IRS employees who started a dummy business called IR Septic Tank Service. When they received a tax return with a large check addressed to the "IRS," they would add "eptic Tank Service" and deposit the check to their own phony business account. Obviously, they would avoid the checks that were written to the "Internal Revenue Service." We don't know if this is a real story or folklore, but it does make the point about how careful you should be when you write your checks.

- Consider having such items as your social security number and your driver's license number included with the preprinted information on each check. Many merchants require such information on checks, and having it printed there will save you and the employee time. There is a downside to this, however, because it increases the risk that someone would obtain this information for dishonest activities.

- Be cautious of the fees you may be charged when using an ATM. Most banks still allow unlimited access to their own ATMs with no fees, but charge you a fee if you use an ATM from another bank. Some banks are getting even more greedy, and are charging noncustomers a fee to use their machines. Thus you may pay $2 to another bank to use that bank's machine, and then your bank will charge you an additional $2 for processing the withdrawal. Paying $4 to get $20 out of a machine is not a good investment.

If your account gets hit with unreasonable charges, you can always call the bank and ask them to reconsider. They do not want to lose a customer and in many cases will consider removing the charges—especially if you have a good reason why you think the fees were unjustified. It doesn't hurt to ask, especially when one phone call could save you $40 or $50.

Paying with Plastic

Credit cards are very popular these days and are accepted as payment in more and more places. This is good, because they are easier to use than a checkbook and are less of a hassle than cash or traveler's checks. You can go on a vacation these days with only $20 in your pocket and pay for everything else with the trusty card.

It has recently become easier for young people to get credit cards. When we were in college, few students had them, and offers for credit cards usually didn't come your way until you had reached your mid-twenties.

Using a Credit Card

The good news about credit cards is they are easy. If a merchant accepts your particular credit card, all you've got to do is present the plastic, make sure you're being charged the correct amount, and sign on the dotted line. Be sure to keep a copy of the transactions for your records.

Every credit card account has a "credit limit," which is the maximum amount you can charge on the card. If you hit the limit, you must stop using the card until you have paid the account balance back under the limit.

Now the bad news. Once a month the credit card company will send you a statement listing the money you spent during the previous month. From the time you get the statement, you'll have approximately two to three weeks before you have to send in a payment. If you have the money, you can—and should—pay the entire amount that is due on your account. With most cards, if you do this you will not be charged a penny more than what you have already paid. Thus, the credit card company has generously loaned you some money for up to a month without you having to pay anything for the favor. Don't feel too sorry for the credit card company. Every time you buy something with a credit card, the merchant pays a small percentage of the charged amount to the credit card company. Thus, even if you never pay a penny extra, the merchants are paying for the privilege of letting you use your card.

But what if you spent more than you had thought, and you don't have the money to pay for all you purchased? The credit card companies have a ready answer. On each statement, you will see a "minimum payment" amount. This looks like an attractive option. Why should you pay off the full amount of $900, when you can pay a minimum of only $50? The answer is "interesting." The credit card company will charge you interest on every unpaid dollar on your account, and the interest rates are usually pretty steep. It only makes sense that credit card companies hope you will take the minimum payment route every month.

Remember when we said earlier that interest can be good or bad? Credit card interest is the worst sort of interest because you are the one paying it. Before you get a credit card, make sure you read the rest of the information in this chapter about credit cards and interest. If they're used wisely, credit cards can be a blessing; but more often, they become a trap that can keep you in financial bondage throughout your life.

How to Get a Credit Card

You usually don't have to look very hard to find a credit card—credit card companies are pretty good at finding you. They want your business—especially if you're the type of person who doesn't pay your bills in full every month. Once you have established a permanent address, you will start getting offers in the mail on a regular basis. If you don't receive an offer to get a credit card and want one, contact your bank. As someone who already has a checking or savings account there, you're probably eligible to apply for a credit card as well.

Be cautious of ads that promise to get you a credit card even if you have bad credit or no credit history. Many of these charge you a hefty fee to get a card, or they make you pay your account in advance before you can charge anything. For example, they may require you to pay $500 and then give you a card with a $500 credit limit.

Avoiding Big Trouble

Before you get your first credit card, we want to scare you with some cold, hard facts. These facts come from Debt-Free America, a company whose sole reason for existence is to help get consumers out of debt.

- The average person who uses credit cards has already accumulated more than twenty years' worth of debts.

- By the time people pay their debts, they will usually have paid back three times the amount they originally charged. You may think that a new TV is a bargain at $300. Would you still buy it if you knew you'd eventually pay $900 to own it?

- Recently, American credit card balances have been rising 20 percent per year. This is more than three times the current rate of inflation.

- Fewer than 30 percent of all credit card holders pay their account balance in full each month.

- Credit card companies share their information with other lending institutions, and indebtedness could come back to haunt you. The amount of money you owe on credit cards could keep you from buying a home or a car when the time comes.

- Credit card companies do not want you to pay off your bills. They make it easy for you to pay the minimum amount so they can continue to collect interest from you.

- If you pay only the minimum monthly payment on a credit card, you can expect to spend anywhere from ten to thirty years to pay off your bill. Here are some examples of how long it would take to pay off a credit card balance, depending on how much you pay every month:

Creditor	Amount Owed	Monthly Payment	Percent Rate	Pay-Off Time
A	$2,047	$39	17.7%	34.83 years
B	$617	$15	21.0%	10.58 years
C	$491	$10	19.8%	8.50 years
D	$1,421	$86	17.2%	5.41 years
E	$1,816	$31	18.0%	57.16 years

Many young people get themselves into terrible trouble with credit cards. Having never used such things before, they often forget that a credit card is simply a short-term loan that must be paid back. The biggest mistake you can make is falling into the trap of paying only the minimum monthly payment. The interest rates you pay with a credit card are among the highest allowed by law; some cards charge well over 20 percent a year. This means that for every $1,000 you charge on your card and don't pay off, you will pay an extra $200 *per year*. Most minimum payments are designed so that most of the money you pay is going toward interest, with very little going to actually pay back the money you borrowed for your purchases. Thus, while that monthly payment of $75 may seem reasonable, consider that only a small portion of that, maybe $5, is going to pay down the debt, while the other $70 goes into the pocket of the credit card company. *At this rate, even if you don't charge anything else on the account, you will be paying $75 a month for another 40 years.*

The worst kind of trouble happens when someone gets multiple credit cards, runs each one up to its credit limit, and then pays only the minimum payments on each account. Then they wake up one day to find they are paying $500 a month in payments for credit cards that are now useless to them because they have been charged to their maximum.

If you find yourself in such a mess, the first thing you must do is stop making new charges. Destroy your cards if you have no self-control. Then find the card with the highest interest rate and concentrate on getting that one paid off. Pay the minimum on the other cards, but pay as much as possible on that one card. When that one is paid off, follow this procedure for the card with the next highest rate, and so on.

Sometimes you will receive offers for new cards that offer a low introductory interest rate for the first three to six months. If so, get one of those cards and transfer the balance on the expensive cards to the new one. This will give you a few months where just about all your payment will be going toward the debt, and not toward interest. Sometimes you can play this card transfer game for years, always transferring the balances to new cards with lower rates.

If you are so far in debt that you cannot see the light at the end of the tunnel, call a debt counseling service. These services are invaluable to people who are overloaded with debt. Not only can debt counselors help you plan a budget and payment schedule, but they will often work with the credit card companies to get you lower interest rates while you are paying off the cards. Several of these companies are nonprofit organizations, which means they'll help you at no charge.

Another thing to avoid is a credit card that charges an annual fee for the privilege of owning a card. There are plenty of no-fee cards out there that you can find. It makes no sense to pay sixty dollars or more every year for the privilege of using a credit card, when you can get the same service elsewhere for free.

Places to Stash Your Cash

A checking account is great, but it should be used only as a temporary holding place for the money with which you pay your bills. Other accounts are better for storing excess funds when you're saving your money for a house or for some other major purchase. Even if you are lucky enough to have an interest-bearing checking account, the interest you will earn is far less than that which you could earn with accounts that are specifically designed for saving money. Some of these alternate accounts are quite safe; the safest accounts, however, pay the smallest amount of interest. Other accounts carry more risk, but they can also produce more spectacular results.

Savings Accounts

Once very popular, savings accounts are not used as frequently today because of the increase in other savings options. Nevertheless, many banks still offer the old standard savings accounts. You can open these accounts with a minimum deposit and then add or remove money from the account as often as you want. The interest rate you earn will be better than that earned by an interest-bearing checking account, but less than you would receive from some of the newer types of accounts. This is because the minimum amount to open the account is usually far less than that for other accounts, often being as low as $50.

Savings accounts will often pay different interest rates depending on the amount of money in the account. For example, you may be paid 1.00 percent on balances below $1,000, 1.10 percent on balances between $1,000 and $2,500, and 1.20 percent on balances above that.

Certificates of Deposit

A certificate of deposit is more often known by the term CD—not to be confused with the musical or software variety. The bank will pay you more interest on a CD than on a savings account. The catch is that you must promise to keep the money in the bank for a predetermined period of time. The longer you leave your money alone, the higher rate of interest you'll get. At the time this was written, one local bank was paying

3.30 percent on a thirty-day CD, 4.15 percent on a one-year CD, and 4.20 percent on a four-year CD. You can cash a CD in early if you have an emergency, but you will be forced to pay a penalty that will wipe out most of the interest. If you aren't sure you can leave the money in the bank for the required time, either choose a CD with a shorter life, or put your money into a different type of account.

When you open a CD, you'll specify the amount you wish to deposit (usually a minimum of $1,000) and the time limit of the CD. When the CD is near its expiration date, the bank will send you a notice. If you don't respond to that notice, the CD—along with any earned interest—will "roll over" to create a new CD with the same life as the original. The new CD may or may not have the same interest rate, because interest rates go up or down depending on the prevailing interest rates at the time. If you don't want the CD to roll over, you have a certain number of days to visit the bank and close out the CD.

A CD is considered a very safe investment, but one in which you have little chance of making a fortune. If you are looking for an investment where you will never have a chance to lose money, but where you'll still make a little more money than you would with a standard savings account, a CD is a good choice.

Stocks

We're sure you've heard stories of fortunes that have been won and lost in the stock market. Despite the fact that a few people make fortunes quickly in the stock market, the majority of people looking for the quick payoff end up with the quick loss. This does not mean buying stocks is not a good investment, but the secret is to buy carefully and to hold the stocks for the long term. People who have historically followed this strategy have done well, even though you won't see their names in the headlines.

If you don't understand how the stock market works, here are the basics. We won't try to give you everything you need to be a stock expert, but we will teach you enough that you'll be able to decide if investing in the stock market appeals to you. If so, there are hundreds of investment guides that will teach you everything you need to know.

When you buy shares of stock, you're buying a portion of a public company—a business that is actually owned by the public. Let's say you want to open a lemonade stand, but you don't have the money you need. You estimate you'll need $100 to get started, so you print up 100 shares of stock in your company and offer them for sale at $1 per share. Two of your friends think there's potential in your business and want to invest in it. Bill buys forty shares of stock for $40, and Sam buys the remaining sixty shares for $60. After three months you're doing so well that you decide to reward your investors. You decide to pay your investors .10¢ for every share of stock they own. Thus, Bill gets a check for $4, and Sam gets a check for $6. This is called a "dividend." After a year, your stand is doing so well that other people become interested and want to invest in your business by buying shares of your stock. But there are no stock shares available, neither will there be unless Bill or Sam can be persuaded to sell theirs. As an incentive, the potential investors offer Bill and Sam $1.50 for each share if they will sell, which they both decide to do. Thus, Bill has turned his initial $40 investment into $64 (including the dividend), and Sam turned his $60 investment into $96.

This imaginary example shows how it is possible to make money by investing in stocks. Some companies pay dividends, which are calculated and paid quarterly (every three months). Many give you the option of joining a "dividend reinvestment program," which allows the money from your dividend to be used to buy additional shares of stock. The second way to make money is if the share price of the stock rises, because people are willing to pay more for your shares than you paid. Of course, if the company does poorly and people lose faith in it, the share price will fall, and you could lose money.

A third way of making money is through a "stock split," which occurs when those who manage the company decide it would be a good idea to have more shares of stock available. When this happens, you will be notified of the split and you will be sent extra shares of stock absolutely free. This does not mean you have automatically made more money, because the price per share is usually adjusted downward accordingly when a split occurs. But if the company continues to do well, the share price should continue rising, and you will benefit.

On any given day, the radio or newspaper may say that the market that day was "up" or "down." This means that, on average, stock share prices went either up or down during that day's trading period. There are a number of ways to calculate this, with the most common being the Dow Jones Industrial Average. In such averages, the closing share prices of the stocks of several large companies are compared with the previous day's average. The values of these averages have nothing to do with your own investments, unless you happen to own stock in the same companies used to compute the averages. But in general, if the big stocks are going up or down, then the smaller stocks will follow.

Although the analysis of whether a stock will increase or decrease in price can be very scientific, you will find that most often the stock market is driven by emotion. If people get nervous about a certain company or about the economy in general, they may sell shares of a stock and its price may drop like a rock. On the other hand, sometimes a company will appear to be "hot," causing share prices to rise far out of proportion to the value of the company. For each stock, look for a number called the P/E, or the "price-earnings ratio." If this number is high, it probably means the stock is popular, and is selling for more than it's worth. This doesn't mean you can't make money from it, but just that you should be careful. Check the financial section of the daily newspaper for closing stock prices, P/Es, and all those other numbers printed in tiny print.

If you wish to buy or sell stock, you must first open an account. You can do this the old-fashioned way, by telephoning a stock broker, or you can open an account with one of several Internet services that allow you to buy and sell on-line. You will be charged a fee each time you buy or sell stock. This is usually based on the number of shares traded, and minimum and maximum values usually apply. If you trade too often your profits will be eaten up in service fees, so watch them carefully. There is a wide variation in the fees you will be charged at different services, so shop around for the best.

How do you make money in the stock market? First, avoid "hot tips" and other deals promoted by brokers and casual associates. You may certainly take the advice of financial experts, but you should check out each company yourself and make sure you're comfortable with its product or service—as well as its potential for growth. Buy stocks with the expectation that you will hold on to them for several years. Not only is this a good investment strategy, but it has tax advantages. Don't be too anxious over the minor dips and jumps that occur in the stock market. You're in it for the long haul. Finally, diversify your investments by buying a number of stocks, rather than putting all your money into just one. No matter how well you research, you can't foresee everything that will happen.

Having several stocks will help you average a better return even if some of them don't perform well.

Before investing your hard-earned money in the stock market, do as much in-depth research as you can. Go to the library and find several books designed to help people who are considering investing in the stock market for the first time or do your research on the Internet.

Bonds

When governments or large corporations wish to raise large amounts of money, they do it by selling "bonds." You may have heard about "U.S. Savings Bonds," which are probably the bonds that are the best known. Let's assume your local county government wants to build a new high school that will cost fifteen million dollars. To raise the money, the county might issue bonds that will mature (or reach their full value) in twenty years and pay 6 percent interest. If you have some cash that will be lying around for that long, you might think that's a pretty good deal and so you use it to buy some bonds. Over the next twenty years, the county will make regular 6 percent interest payments to you and will also pay back the amount of the original loan after twenty years.

Although bonds are not as secure as a CD, most bonds are pretty safe investments. The interest rate paid by the bond will depend on current market conditions and the reputation of the organization issuing the bond. For example, the U.S. government will pay lower interest than many bonds, because the bond is very likely to be paid back. Some governments or companies are not as stable, however, and they have to pay a higher interest rate to attract investors.

Most investors like to have some of their money in stocks and some in bonds, because the two markets tend to react differently. Sometimes bonds will be doing well, and stocks will be doing poorly. At other times, the opposite will be true. Having money in both places will help you average out your gains and losses. In general, bonds tend to be less sensitive to economic and market conditions, and therefore they tend to have fewer ups and downs than the stock market.

Although you can purchase bonds directly, most people purchase them through a mutual fund. Which, conveniently, leads us into our next topic.

Mutual Funds

When you were reading the section on stocks, you may have found yourself thinking, "Now, if I just knew an expert who would tell me the stocks to buy." You're in luck, because that's the idea of a mutual fund. Those who run such funds proclaim themselves to be experts in deciding which stocks and bonds are going to do well and then proceed to buy those investments. When you invest in a mutual fund, you're actually buying fractional parts of all the investments the fund owns. Each day the fund calculates its "Net Asset Value" (NAV) by dividing the total value of all its investments by the number of shares in the mutual fund. The value of the NAV will follow the value of the investments in the fund—if the investments do well, the NAV will go up, but if they do poorly, it will go down. Let's say you invest $1,000 in a fund when the NAV is $100, which buys you ten shares. A year later, the fund has done well, and the NAV is now $150. If you sell your shares, you'll get $1,500. Think of investing in a mutual fund much as you would think of buying stock. But instead of buying shares in one company, you're pooling your cash with other investors and buying shares in many corporations.

The fact that there are approximately 7,000 mutual funds attests to their popularity. But not all mutual funds are alike, because each fund will have its own objective as to the types of investments it purchases. The four major types of funds are as follows:

Stock or equity funds. As the name implies, these funds deal mainly in stocks. These funds will have the most volatility (movement up or down in value), but they have historically been the best performers over a long term. If you're planning to leave your investment alone for ten or more years, put it into an equity fund.

Even among equity funds there is a lot of variation. Some funds are known as income funds, because they buy stocks that pay good dividends. Growth funds are less concerned with dividends, but want the share price of the individual stocks to increase. Funds may also target specific types of companies, such as technology stocks, medical stocks, or stocks outside the United States.

Bond fund. A bond fund will invest most of its money in bonds. Some funds will try to purchase mainly short-term bonds, while others buy bonds that typically have longer expiration dates. There are also funds that buy tax-free bonds (which are free from all tax penalties except for federal, and in some cases, state income taxes). The returns from these funds are typically lower than the taxed funds, but you have to consider that the proceeds are worth more because they aren't taxed.

Balanced fund. This type of fund will try to be ready for any occasion by buying both bonds and stocks. If the stock market is doing poorly, the income from the bonds will help offset it. This type of fund is for the cautious investor. It offers the thrill of buying stocks, but also produces steady income if the stocks are doing poorly.

Money market fund. We'll talk more about this fund in the next section, but just keep in mind that a money market fund is really just a different kind of mutual fund.

Running a mutual fund is not done as an act of charity, and those who run them extract a certain amount of the profits from the fund to pay their expenses. You should make sure the fund you choose charges reasonable expenses. Details about all fund expenses are contained in a legal document called a "prospectus." According to federal law, a company selling mutual funds must provide a prospectus to any potential investor. The typical prospectus is written in legal gibberish, but you should at least read the section that discusses fees. Avoid "load" or "loaded" funds that apply a sales charge (or front-end charge) each time you invest in the fund. What you want is a non-load fund, which does not charge this type of fee. Some funds will also charge fees on reinvested funds, or redemption charges (back-end charges), or account maintenance fees. Some fees, such as maintenance fees, are charged by all mutual funds, but you should be wary of a fund that tries to charge any of these other fees.

Just like a stock, most mutual funds will regularly pay some type of dividend or interest on your investment. You will usually be given the option to automatically reinvest this money into the fund. If you can afford it, this option will buy you more shares and cause the value of your investment to increase over time.

When choosing a mutual fund, make sure to compare its performance against a stock index, such as the Dow or the S&P 500 (Standard & Poor's 500). If the mutual fund does not regularly outperform the index (many do not), consider a different mutual fund or an "index fund," which buys the same stocks contained in the index and usually has lower fund expenses.

Money Market Funds

Remember we said that bonds are long-term loans made by you to governments and corporations? Sometimes governments and corporations would rather borrow money for shorter periods of time. Rather than buy a bond, they will use a "money market instrument." These loans typically pay a decent interest rate and are designed to be fully paid back within thirteen months. The only problem is that these loans tend to be for very large sums of money, so that the average investor with a few extra dollars would not be eligible to take advantage of them.

All this was changed a few years ago when money market "mutual funds" were introduced. These gave the average investor the opportunity to benefit from the money markets without having to mortgage his house to do it. Unlike other mutual funds, most money market funds keep their NAV at a constant value of $1.00. This means that you benefit from the interest paid on the loans, but there is no chance of your investment losing value over time. It is the safest type of mutual fund, and the high interest rates it pays will typically beat your average CD or savings account.

Most money market funds require a minimum investment such as $1,000 to open your account. Once open, you can send in additional checks to add to your investment at any time. Interest is usually paid and reinvested into the account once per month, and you can take money out at any time via checks or telephone redemption.

Exotic Investments

Think long and hard before you invest in anything not already mentioned in this section. There are all kinds of people eager to get you involved with "hot" stocks, rare coins, generous tax shelters, and other exotic investments. This is one area where we are definitely qualified to give advice, because there's probably not a scam we haven't fallen for at one time or another. Over the years, we have invested in coins, silver bars, artwork, investment gems, hot stocks, oil and gas leases, solar leases, and audio master leases. In every case, we were told that there was "big money" to be made in all these investments. There was big money to be made all right, but unfortunately not by us. Even though some of these investments were legitimate, they left us with items that were difficult to sell. Even if a gold coin has doubled in value, does it do any good if you can't find a buyer?

If someone approaches you with an offer that seems to be true, ask yourself, "If this investment is really that good, why is this person trying to sell me on it, rather than investing in it himself so *he* can get the profit?"

You would also do well to avoid multilevel marketing programs (MLMs). These are programs that work on two levels. First, you sell products (usually ones that people are reluctant to buy because they're sold at an inflated cost). But the big push is for you to recruit other people to sell the same products, on the theory that you get a cut of everything your recruits eventually sell.

If you get invited to a "pitch" for such a program, you will be put under a lot of pressure to join. In fact, we once attended a pitch that was allegedly being presented to a group of people, only to learn that everyone else in the group was already part of the MLM and the entire meeting had been held specifically to convert us. It all sounds good, because the pitchmen will give you examples of people who have become fabulously wealthy through the program. There's no denying that a small group of people can make a lot of money when these first start. But the laws of probability are against you, so save your time and your money.

Managing Your Funds Wisely

Although making money is important, it is equally important, and in some ways more important, to manage that money wisely. The "Smiths" can illustrate that. They make tons of money, and yet they always seem to be broke. They live from paycheck to paycheck, worry a lot about how the bills will be paid, and have no money saved for times of emergency. The "Browns," on the other hand, have a more modest income, yet seem to enjoy life quite a bit more, without having to worry about bill collectors. They take nice vacations, have nice things, and have plans in place for retirement and for sending their children to college. Mr. Smith's pay stub might hint that the Smiths would be more secure financially than the Browns. But the Smiths waste a lot of their money paying interest and fees, they buy things that are expensive and unneeded, and they have no investments to generate new income for them. In other words, they throw away a lot of their money by giving it to banks, credit card companies, and the good old IRS. The Smiths need to follow the advice in this section. They have learned to generate a good deal of money, but now they need to learn how to make that money work for them instead of for someone else.

Your Credit History

You may not realize it, but there is someone out there who keeps track of how you make and spend your money. Actually, there are a lot of someones in several national organizations called "credit bureaus." These credit bureaus work closely with banks, credit card companies, department stores, mortgage companies, and other organizations that loan you money. The goal of each credit bureau is to build a financial profile of you—a report card of how well you manage your money. Forget to pay your credit card bill on time? The credit bureau will be notified. Default on your car payment and have the bank take your car? You can be sure they will hear about that.

Other organizations that loan money can contact the credit bureau for a copy of your profile. They will use that as one of the factors to determine whether they want to loan you money or open an account for you. If you have a bad credit history, they probably won't be too eager to have you as a customer.

Keeping a good credit history is important. You don't want to be denied a home or car loan just because of some old bills that you forgot to pay . . . which leads us into our next topic.

Paying Bills

You don't need an advanced degree to see the logic in paying your bills on time, but it is surprising how many people get into financial trouble because they're habitually late in making payments. Failure to pay bills on time will result in late fees, extra interest payments, possible loss of service (such as having your phone turned off), and lots of other minor frustrations.

When you're on your own for the first time, it may be difficult to get into the habit of paying bills. Here is a trick that might work for you. First, find a specific place, such as a drawer or table, where all bills will be placed when they arrive. Second, when you get a bill, write the date the bill must be paid on the front of the envelope. Third, get into the habit of reviewing all your bills once a week. When you review the bills, use the dates to select the ones that must be paid that week. Then write out the checks, get the payment envelopes sealed and stamped, and put them where they will be mailed.

Some companies will make arrangements with your bank to have the amount of your bill automatically deducted from your checking account on a certain day of the month. This saves you from having to remember to pay the bill, provided you always have enough money in your account to cover it.

Even more depressing than forgetting to pay a bill is knowing a bill is due, but not having the money to pay it. This is another reason to have some extra savings socked away somewhere, so you can use the extra money to pay for unexpected expenses. If you find that you cannot pay a bill, the worst thing you can do is to just ignore it. Call the company and explain the situation. They can usually work out alternate arrangements for payment, and you might avoid late fees and negative entries on your credit history.

Budget Is Not a Dirty Word

If you find yourself unable to meet some of your financial goals, one of the ways to make a course correction is to establish a budget. For some people, the word *budget* invokes visions of living on bread and water and of never spending any money on anything fun. Actually, a budget is nothing more than a study of where your money goes and a plan for reordering your spending priorities. You certainly don't have to cut all the fun out of your life to follow a budget.

Before you can plan a budget, you need to have an accurate record of where all your money goes each month. That's easy if you always pay by check or credit card, but a little more difficult if you spend a lot of cash. If you do the latter, start keeping a record book close by, and record all the times you spend cash for anything—even the purchase of a package of gum should be recorded.

Once you have a spending record, you need to analyze all your spending to see where the money comes from and where it goes. Some expenses, such as rent, are called "fixed" expenses, because they will be the same amount each month. Other expenses, such as utility bills and groceries, are "variable" expenses, because the amount will change each month. To get a handle on variable expenses, you will need to follow them for several months and then compute an average per month. Now figure out, on average, how much you are spending each month by expense category (rent, tithing, transportation, utilities, food, entertainment, and so on).

Once you have this done, you'll have a pretty good idea of where the money is going and where you can make adjustments. For example, you may decide to start saving $100 per month to buy a new car. That adds $100 to your budget, so you will need to either find a way to increase your income by that much or cut existing expenses by that much. Fixed expenses such as rent cannot be cut unless you do something drastic, such as finding a roommate or considering a move to a cheaper apartment. Most of your cuts will have to come from variable expenses, such as entertainment or groceries. Perhaps you'll decide these cuts will be too drastic, and you will have to reduce your savings goal to $50 per month.

When you have adjusted your expenses to reflect your new priorities, you can also rank the expenses in order of priority. After essentials such as rent and tithing and utilities, your new savings program should be your highest priority.

Even after you have set your budget, it is good to tune it up on occasion, making sure the expense amounts are still close to what you are actually spending. You will also want to adjust your spending priorities as your needs change.

Income and Expenses

As mentioned earlier, your income and expenses are the two levers you can use to adjust your financial situation. If you're having a hard time making and following a budget, you can make things better either by bringing in more income or spending less of it, or both. As simple as that sounds, it is one of the fundamental keys of financial management.

There are many ways to cut your expenses. Consider taking in a roommate or trading in your car for one with a lower monthly payment. Perhaps you can get rid of your cable TV or use a telephone billing option that will cost less each month. But cutting your expenses does not always have to be this drastic. One friend discovered she was spending $30 each month by stopping at a convenience store each morning for a large soda. Substituting cans of soda purchased from a discount shopping club saved her more than $20 each month. You can almost always find ways to cut your entertainment budget. Try going to more inexpensive restaurants or renting videos instead of going to movies. Don't overlook the money you can save by being a smart shopper. Consider using coupons, shopping at discount stores, and buying in bulk when items you normally use are on sale.

Increasing your income is more difficult, but not impossible. If you're in the position to be paid for overtime work, you could consider working more overtime. There is also the radical step of changing jobs if you find an employer who pays better. Outside of your primary job, you can make more money by taking a second part-time job or developing a skill with which you can generate income. If there is a lot of junk around the house, consider having a garage sale and turning some of that clutter into cash.

Avoiding Debt

If debt doesn't cost you anything, then it doesn't have to be a bad thing. For example, many merchants will offer programs in the autumn that allow you to purchase major items and not owe anything until the next spring. This is not bad debt, because the merchant is loaning you the money interest free. Provided you can actually pay off the bill when it comes due, this could be a good deal for you.

Unfortunately, most debt comes with the heavy price tag of interest. Any money you pay in interest goes into the pocket of the lender—and gets you nothing. Some debt is unavoidable. Unless you're wealthy, you will obtain a mortgage when you buy a house. Mortgage debt isn't all bad, because it has the advantage of reducing your taxes based on the interest you pay. This is not the case for interest on charge cards and similar accounts, which are obscenely high but aren't even tax deductible.

Most debt can be avoided if you stop purchasing on impulse, and if you exercise a little self-control. For example, you want to buy a new $1,000 audio system, but you don't have the money. Why don't you save $250 a month for four months and buy the system outright? Yes, you have to defer your gratification for a few months, but that gives you more time to anticipate the purchase and decide on the options you want. When you make your purchase in cash, not only will you have saved the interest charges, but you'll have actually earned interest as you were saving the money. By exercising a little self-control, you can get your system, avoid paying interest, and even get a little financial bonus for doing it the right way.

Now consider the alternative. You are in the mall one night and see a system you really like. You whip out your magic plastic card and take the system home with you. Now instead of making a cash payment before the purchase, you will make monthly payments to the credit card company. Assuming your card charges you interest at an APR (annual percentage rate) of 18 percent, here are your payment options:

Monthly Payment	Months to Pay	Total Paid	Interest Paid
$ 250.00	4.2	$ 1,038.97	$ 38.97
$ 200.00	5.2	$ 1,047.26	$ 47.26
$ 100.00	10.9	$ 1,091.57	$ 91.57
$ 50.00	24.0	$ 1,197.81	$ 197.81
$ 25.00	61.5	$ 1,538.58	$ 538.58
$ 20.00	93.1	$ 1,862.22	$ 862.22

The first option isn't bad, because it will still take you just over four months to get out of debt, and you'll pay a penalty of only $38.97 for your impulse purchase. But look at the last example, where you pay only the minimum payment of $20 per month. It will take you almost eight years to pay off the debt, and you'll be throwing away $862.22 as the penance for your sin of instant gratification. The moral of this story is clear—plan for major purchases so they don't cause debt. If you have to incur some debt, you can minimize that by paying as much as possible each month and by avoiding the temptation of making just minimum payments.

Fee Frenzy

As if the interest rates they charge were not obscene enough, most banks and credit card companies have recently gone crazy in terms of the fees they charge you for various "sins" against your account. If you go over the assigned credit limit on your charge card, expect to be assessed a fee of up to $30. Expect a similar fee if you send your payment and it arrives even one day after the due date.

Some lending institutions are crafty about those due dates, too. It used to be that if your payment was mailed and postmarked by the due date, it was considered to be an on-time payment. Now we have several charge card companies who don't process checks for up to two weeks after the checks are received. Say your payment is due on the first of the month. Your check sits in their office on the first of the month. But the company doesn't bother to process the check for a week or even more after the check was received—and then has the audacity to charge you a late fee. This is illegal, by the way. Nevertheless, credit card companies who are trying to squeeze just a little more money out of the customer are doing it more and more often.

You can avoid such fees by understanding the rules of your account and making sure you follow them. On the rare occasions where you make a mistake and get assessed a fee, you can often call the company and get the fee removed if you have a good explanation. If the company is obnoxious and refuses to budge, pay the fee but consider moving your account to another bank or company. Life is too short to have to put up with such abuse from the people who benefit from your business.

Understanding Employment Benefits

It is estimated that an average employer pays each employee benefits equivalent to 30 percent of his salary. Put another way, if you have a job that pays you $50,000 per year, your employer will be spending another $15,000 on your benefits! If you're not using some of these benefits, you're throwing that money away. Do yourself a favor and become acquainted with the benefits your employer offers. Most employers will provide you with some type of benefit book. If not, contact your human resources or personnel office.

➡ Here are some of the common benefits that you might find that can have the effect of increasing your income if you use them wisely:

Health insurance. Because of the high cost of medical care, everyone should be covered by medical insurance. Your employer will usually pay most of the monthly cost, but you will be expected to pay something, too. Coverage often includes medical, dental, vision, and sometimes counseling for emotional problems.

Medical and child care reimbursement. The government will let you put a portion of your salary into a fund that may be used to pay child care costs and medical costs not covered by insurance. The good news is that you don't pay taxes on this money. But there is bad news, too: You have to specify at the first of the year how much to contribute; the amount cannot be changed during the year; and anything left at the end of the year will be lost.

Tuition reimbursement. Many companies will pay for you to take work-related classes at local training schools or community colleges. Usually, you have to get approval before your enroll and you must get a good grade from the class.

Retirement benefits. You will probably find several options that allow you to put aside money for retirement. We will talk more about this subject later in this chapter.

Stock purchase plans. Many public companies have plans in place to allow employees to purchase shares of the company stock through payroll deduction. Look into these options carefully. The risk is usually quite low, and the plans usually allow you to purchase stock at a rate discounted from that of the rest of the public.

Stock options. Some public companies reward valued employees with "stock options." This allows you to buy company stock at a future date for a specific price. For example, you may be given the option to buy up to a thousand shares for $5 each anytime over the next three years. If the price goes up to $10, you can immediately buy

1,000 shares for $5,000, and then turn right around and double your money by selling them. If the stock price doesn't go up, just don't exercise your option and keep your money.

Vacation and sick leave. Although we don't normally think of this as a financial benefit, some companies will allow you to be paid for these days if you don't use them. Nobody wants to lose a vacation, but it may be an option if you're really strapped for funds.

Death and Taxes

Everyone complains about taxes, but then we just get back to work and pay them anyway. As we were writing this section, Clark was sent an e-mail message containing the following joke:

> A little boy desperately wanted $100.00. He prayed for two weeks but nothing happened. Then he decided to write God a letter requesting the $100.00.
>
> When the postal authorities received the letter to God, they decided to send the letter to the president. The president was so amused that he instructed his secretary to send the little boy a $5.00 bill. The president thought this would appear to be a lot of money to a little boy.
>
> The little boy was delighted with the $5.00 and sat down to write a thank-you note to God, which read: "Dear God: Thank you very much for sending the money. However, I noticed that for some reason you sent it through Washington, D.C., and as usual those jerks deducted $95.00 in taxes."

If you don't see the humor in this, we're sure you will after you've been a taxpayer for a couple of years.

Let's introduce you to some of the various taxes you'll "get" to pay at one time or another.

Federal Taxes

When you start a job, one of the many forms you will complete will be a form called a W-4. This tells your employer how many people you support, so they can calculate how much to withhold from each paycheck for federal taxes—taxes that go to the United States government. (Obviously, this won't apply if you live outside the U.S., but most major countries have similar taxes.) Make sure you complete a new form whenever your family situation changes, such as through marriage or the birth of a child.

You'd think that taking a pretty good slice out of each paycheck would keep the federal government happy, but it doesn't. You'll also be required to complete a tax return at the end of the year, at which time you may have the privilege to pay more taxes, or you may be lucky enough to get some money back as a refund.

Sneaky Secret

The first few months of a new year, check your mail carefully for any statements that report taxable income. Don't lose these, but keep them with the other materials you will use to do your taxes. If you lose a paper and don't list the income on your taxes, the IRS will eventually notice the error, and you will be charged the extra tax, plus interest and penalties for having made the mistake.

Even though your tax return will cover a complete calendar year, it does not have to be filed with the IRS (Internal Revenue Service) until April 15 of the next year. Your employer will give you another form called a W-2 that lists your salary for the year, and also the amounts held out of your wages for various taxes. If you received any interest (from banks), dividends (from stocks or mutual funds), or other types of income, you should also receive forms reporting that income. These need to be included as you calculate your taxes.

You may have heard friends or parents complaining about how complicated the tax forms have become, or you may have simply noticed that sleepy, haggard look they have after too many late nights around tax time. Lucky for you, your taxes will probably not be that complicated when you first move away from home. You can probably figure out the forms yourself, have a tax person do it for a small amount, or use some of the excellent tax software that has been on the market for the past couple of years.

When your return is complete, make a copy of it and keep it in a safe place. Then mail the original so that it is postmarked by April 15. Keep your copy of the tax return, plus all the forms and records used to calculate your taxes, for at least three years.

State and Local Taxes

Most states also levy their own income taxes, which are collected to pay the expenses of running the state. Just as with federal income tax, state income tax is usually deducted from each paycheck, and appears on your W-2 form at the end of the year. States with income taxes usually require that you file a state income tax return once a year, similar to the federal return. Depending on the state, this return may be due along with the federal return on April 15, or it may due two to four weeks later.

Many state tax returns are based on the federal return. In order to compute your state taxes, you take some numbers off the federal return, do some calculations with them, and arrive at the amount of state tax you owe. As with your federal return, you may get a refund, or you may have to pay more depending on the amount of taxes that were withheld.

A few areas also charge a local tax in addition to state and federal tax. As with the other types of taxes, you will probably have money withheld and will also have to file a tax return at the end of the year.

> **Sneaky Secret**
> If you have never filed your taxes before, you might wonder how you go about getting the forms for tax returns. Although you can call the IRS or your state tax commission, most public libraries and post offices also have copies of the most common tax forms. Once you have filed your first return, you should be mailed the forms automatically in following years, although the IRS is trying to eliminate paper forms in favor of electronic filing over the Internet.

Other Payroll Taxes

As you survey the damage done to your paycheck, you should also see a couple of other taxes that you are paying. One of these is the Social Security tax, which is used to fund the federal retirement program. The other tax is for Medicare—the federal program used to provide health care to those who are retired. These programs are the subject of much controversy, with many young people saying they are paying into programs that won't be around when they are ready to retire.

Both Social Security and Medicare are pyramid schemes, where the people who are working now fund the retirement of the previous generation and hope that the generation after them will return the favor. However, the general belief is that the postwar baby boom generation will bankrupt both systems, because so many people will be demanding benefits at the same time. There have been many ideas proposed for improving these programs, but Congress seems unwilling to tamper with the programs and risk the wrath of current and future retirees.

Unlike other payroll taxes, you don't need to file a separate yearly return to account for Social Security and Medicare.

Sales Tax

Many state and local governments raise money by imposing a local sales tax. Such a tax is charged whenever something is sold, and it usually runs somewhere in the range of 3 to 9 percent of the purchase price. Thus, if you buy a new car for $10,000, you will pay $300 to $900 extra in sales taxes.

Some states have their laws written so that certain items are not subject to sales tax. These items generally include the necessities of life, such as medicines, clothing, and food items purchased from grocery stores.

Property Tax

Most counties also raise money by assessing a "property tax"—a tax you pay for owning certain kinds of properties. The most common type of property tax is assessed on land and buildings. Thus, when you finally buy that new house, one of the new expenses you will have each year is property tax.

The rate of property tax is usually based on the value of the property. For example, you may be assessed a tax of $1.00 for every $100 the property is worth. Both the tax rate and the valuation of your property will tend to change each year, based on the sale of similar houses in your neighborhood. If all your neighbors are selling their houses for $150,000, your house will probably be valued at that amount for tax purposes. If the assessed tax is $1.00 for each $100, you will have to pay property taxes of $1,500 for that year.

Although you cannot change the assessed rate, you can challenge the valuation of your property. There is usually an appeals process, and someone will decide if the value placed on your property is correct. Be careful about doing this, however, because the valuation of your property could be raised rather than lowered.

There are also states that assess property taxes on other types of properties, such as automobiles, planes, and boats. As with the property tax on land, these rates are usually based on the estimated value of the property.

Planning for Later Life

When you first start working, your retirement is about the last thing you'll have on your mind. Retirement probably won't be an option for forty years (practically an eternity to young people), and you certainly won't want to concern yourself with any of those details for at least another thirty years. Or will you? Although you may not believe it, the decisions you make early in your working career can have a significant effect on the quality of your life when you retire. In this section we can't cover everything you'll need to know about retirement planning, but we'll try to impress upon you the importance of preparing for your golden years. For more details, find books in your library about long-term investing and retirement planning.

Start Early

The secret for building a good retirement is to start early, and then allow interest and the clock to work for you. Consider the following example. Four friends all decide to start saving $250 per month in their retirement accounts that are earning 10 percent interest per year. One will retire in ten years, one in twenty, one in thirty, and the youngest will not retire for forty years. How much will they each have saved in their accounts when they are ready to retire? Here's the answer:

Years to Pay	Monthly Payment	Amount Available for Retirement
10	$250.00	$51,211
20	$250.00	$189,842
30	$250.00	$565,122
40	$250.00	$1,581,020

At first glance, you might be tempted to say, "Well, certainly the account of the youngest worker will be larger, because he will be contributing for forty years instead of ten or twenty." While that is true, there is more at work here than just the number of years contributions are made.

Logic should tell you that the person who saves for forty years will end up with four times the amount of the person who saves for ten. But if you multiply the account of the ten-year investor by four, you end up with $204,844, which is only about 13 percent of the size of the benefits that will be earned by the forty-year contributor. The rest of the money will come through the miracle of "compound interest." As money earns interest over a long period of time, each interest payment increases the value of the account, which then results in a larger amount of money on which interest will be paid the next time. This produces a snowball effect as the balance grows larger and larger over the years.

If you find yourself saying, "But I don't have the time or money to think about my future right now," consider that every dollar you don't contribute today will require a $5, $10, or $20 contribution later in your life. Start that money working early, so that the magic of compound interest will fund the lion's share of your retirement.

Understanding Retirement Benefits

The most common plan in use today is called a 401(k), named after the section of the IRS tax law that allows the accounts. Employees of some types of organizations can contribute to 403(b) accounts, which are similar.

Under a traditional 401(k) account, an employee can contribute up to 15 percent of his gross (before deductions) salary to his personal retirement account. Most companies will also match your contribution up to a certain percentage. For example, your employer may pay 1 percent for every 2 percent you contribute, up to a maximum of 5 percent. Thus, if you contribute 10 percent of your salary to your account, your employer will kick in another 5 percent of your salary. This is like getting a 5 percent bonus on each payday, except that you can't spend the money just yet.

Most 401(k) accounts offer a variety of different investment options, and allow you to specify how your money will be invested. You don't have to pick one option from the menu, but can choose a percentage of your money to be assigned to any number of options covered by your employer's plan. You can usually change these allocations later, if you decide you want to try something a little safer—or a little more aggressive.

One final advantage of a 401(k) is something you will appreciate when you file your tax return. The taxes on any money paid into a 401(k) do not have to be paid until you start taking the money out.

If your employer offers no retirement benefits, you can still prepare for your retirement by opening one of several types of accounts, the most common of which is an "IRA" (individual retirement account). The traditional type of IRA account is similar to a 401(k) and allows you to invest up to $2,000 per person per year into an investment of your choice, and have the investment deducted from your income that is taxed. The newer Roth IRA allows a similar account, but allows the tax savings to occur when you take the money out, rather than when you contribute it. The Roth accounts also allow you to save money for such things as the down payment on a house.

If you choose to start investing money for your retirement—and you should—keep a few things in mind. First of all, just as you shouldn't put all of your eggs in one basket, don't put all your money in one investment. There is always the potential for any investment—no matter how secure it seems—to fail. You can protect yourself from major losses by spreading your money into many different promising investments. Also, remember that you have a long time to let that money sit. You should consider putting your money into more risky, higher-interest bearing accounts. You can be more aggressive with your money than can someone who has only a few years remaining until retirement. Even if the market were to have a major downswing, it would almost certainly correct itself by the time you are ready to take your money out.

But before you make any major investment plans, talk with someone from human resources at your work or do some independent research to help you know where and how much to invest. You can also look in your local library or bookstore for one of the monthly personal finance magazines. These typically will rate the funds and banks that are paying the best rates and producing the best returns for their clients. They will also have advertisements for many funds, most of which have toll-free phone numbers and Internet websites. These businesses want you to invest with them, but they will be more than happy to send you all kinds of information that will educate you about investing in general.

There are also independent organizations, such as Morningstar, that track the performance of most mutual funds. In addition to providing rating systems (such as Morningstar's one- to five-star ratings), they will also provide useful information such as the name of the person managing each fund and the names of the major stocks being held by the funds.

I'm Still Clueless

? *What is a debit card?*

A debit card looks similar to a credit card, and as with a credit card, you can use it to buy goods and services. The difference is in what happens after you make the charge. With a debit card, the amount is deducted from an account you already have—most commonly a checking account. Many banks will give you an ATM card that also doubles as a debit card. You can use the card to get cash from the ATM machine or to buy that expensive dinner for your date. The amount you charge will be deducted from your account, just as if you had written a check (so make sure to record it in your check register).

From a purely financial standpoint, a credit card is better because you are borrowing someone else's money for up to thirty days, interest free. But a debit card is nice for those who cannot get a credit card or for those situations where you are short on cash and need to make a purchase from a merchant who will not accept checks.

? *I was turned down for a credit card. What can I do?*

The bank or credit card company is required by law to tell you why you were refused. If you were denied a card because of negative information they received from a credit bureau, they must tell you the name and address of the credit bureau.

Although credit bureaus will usually charge you if you want to see a copy of your file, they must provide you with a free copy if you are denied credit based on their information. In this case, you should write to the credit bureau as soon as possible. In your letter, ask for a copy of your file and be sure to enclose a copy of the refusal letter sent by the credit card company.

When the file arrives, examine it carefully to check for any errors. If you find major errors in your credit file, write to the credit bureau, explain the errors, and provide documentation (if possible) to prove your point. Ask that the errors be corrected and that you then be sent a corrected copy of your report. Once your credit file is accurate, contact the credit card company again and ask to be reconsidered.

? *I don't have a driver's license. What do I use for identification when I'm opening a checking account or cashing checks?*

Relax. You're not the first person in the world who hasn't had a driver's license by the ripe old age of seventeen. Many people have valid reasons for postponing the decision to drive, and they cash checks every day without any trouble. If you go to your local Department of Motor Vehicles (the people who issue the driver's licenses), you can pay a small fee and have a nondriver's identification card made for you. This will look exactly like a driver's license (it's even got the horrible picture), but it will not license you to drive. Once you have this card, you can use it for any purpose where you'd otherwise show your driver's license to identify yourself.

? *My grandma always put her spare money in U.S. Savings Bonds. Is that a good idea?*

The only two reasons for investing in Savings Bonds are to be patriotic and to put your money in an absolutely safe investment. Some of the newer bonds have better interest rates, but the returns are still far less than you would get from investing in a mutual fund with even an average level of return. In fact, sometimes the rates for savings bonds are so low that over the life of the bond you'll actually lose money because inflation is higher than the rate of interest. Another problem is that bonds have to be held several years before they mature, which makes it hard to get your money out if you have a crisis and need the funds. Bonds may have been fine for Grandma, but you can probably do much better.

CHAPTER 9
Our Daily Bread

★ **IN THIS CHAPTER**
- ✔ Preparing for Your Career
- ✔ Writing an Effective Résumé
- ✔ Finding the Right Job
- ✔ Surviving the Job Interview
- ✔ Evaluating a Job Offer
- ✔ Keeping Your Skills Current

This chapter focuses on preparing for a career and finding, getting, and keeping a job. Unlike the previous chapters in this book, this chapter may not have immediate relevance when you first move away from home. If you're going away to become a student, a missionary, or a soldier, your future career may seem like a distant reality. If you're moving away because of employment, then you're probably already employed and hope that you will not have to think about changing jobs for a while. But even if you don't need this information today, it will be of great concern for most of your adult life. Remember this chapter is here, and read it when you're ready to use the material.

Some young people devote very little attention to their eventual careers, thinking that everything will fall into place when the proper time arrives for them to be employed. This can be a big mistake, because a good deal of your enjoyment of life as an adult will relate to your employment or your spouse's employment. When you consider that about 35 percent of an adult's waking hours will be spent at work, you'll realize you should certainly devote as much time to planning your career as you would to planning your education or your wedding. Wouldn't you rather spend a third of your life doing something that is challenging, rewarding, and financially profitable, rather than having an unpleasant job that you tolerate only because you have to pay the bills?

One of our friends is quite intelligent, yet often has a childlike view of how the world works. He has a lucrative career that fascinates him, and he's always telling us about the different projects he's doing. He recently told us about a convention he'd attended, where in the process of talking to the other attendees he met several people who hated their jobs. He had never considered that someone might actually not enjoy working, but just do it to pay the bills. We hope that all of you will be able to plan a career that you will enjoy as much as our friend enjoys his.

Don't be tempted to skip this chapter if you're a woman. We grew up in a time where education for women was often thought to be less important. The theory was that because women were expected to do the housework and raise the children, they would have very little need of formal education. That philosophy may have worked in an earlier time, but it doesn't apply today. Even if a woman wants to devote most of her time to mothering and domestic interests, there are very few couples these days who can survive on one income. Many modern wives and mothers work part-time or run their own businesses from home in order to supplement the family checking account. You must also consider the possibility that even if you're lucky enough to get married and have children, divorce or the death of your husband will throw you into the role of being the primary breadwinner for the family. Older women whose children have left home often have a desire to return to the workforce, too. For all of these reasons, modern women should put as much emphasis on education and job skills as their male counterparts. Think of your education and job skills as an insurance policy. Even if you never have to use them, you'll be more secure in knowing you would be able to provide for those you love if the need did arise.

Preparing for Your Career

A career doesn't just happen. Just as you prepare for other important events in your life, a career is something that should be planned. This doesn't mean you need to know your intended profession when you enter kindergarten, but certainly you should have been thinking about potential careers when you were in high school. Remember that your goal is not just to get a job, but to plan a career that will reward you in many ways other than just a regular paycheck.

Higher Education

In order to get a career and not just a job, your first goal should be to graduate from high school and then attend college. We can hear you now: "You sound just like my parents!" Sadly enough, this is yet another area where your parents have the facts standing behind them.

According to the Census Bureau, 89 percent of the jobs being created today require skill levels beyond those possessed by a high school graduate. Back in the early 1980s, a college graduate could expect to earn 38 percent more money than someone who had only a high school diploma. This trend has become even more pronounced since then, with the gap in salaries currently at 73 percent. If you stretch this difference in income over a lifetime of employment, you'll be talking about a difference that can easily be in the millions of dollars.

Unfortunately, the costs of attending college have also risen over the years. You can reduce your college costs by getting good grades in high school and then applying for scholarships. If you already know the particular career you wish to follow, there are some organizations that give scholarships to students who are majoring in certain fields—yet another advantage for doing some career planning while you're still in high school. If you're not lucky enough to get a scholarship, there are always the traditional ways of paying for college—student loans, part-time jobs, and summer jobs.

Another way to save money is to attend a local community college rather than an out-of-state school that may be more expensive. Some will argue that students attending a high-priced, prestigious college will earn back the investment through higher paychecks. Some recent research casts doubt on this, suggesting that a person who has the drive to attend a prestigious school will use that same drive to be successful in his career. Check out the lesser-known schools that are cheaper but that still have a reputation for placing graduates in good positions.

Technical Schools

You may not realize this, but most students who attend college spend the first two years attending general education classes. In order to graduate, the typical college student must master a wide variety of subjects, such as math, English, history, art, and physics. The idea is not just to produce a well-rounded graduate, but to expose the student to several different types of careers that may be of interest to him. Thus, the first two years of college offer a general education and expose you to the possible careers that are available. By the time you've reached the end of your sophomore year, you should have a pretty good idea of your "major" (the area you wish to study in more detail) and should spend the final two years of your college life working toward that career. If you already know what career you want to pursue, you may be able to attend a technical or business school and reduce your four years of higher education to two.

If you're interested in attending a technical school for at least part of your higher education, check with employers who hire graduates in your chosen field. If they're willing to hire employees with a two-year degree, you may ask them to recommend some schools who do a particularly good job training people for that career. Not all specialty schools are equal. Some use misleading advertising and have a poor record of placing graduates in decent positions. Make sure you choose a school that comes highly recommended both by former students and employers.

Advanced Degrees

Some people believe that if one college degree is good, then having a handful of advanced degrees is even better. These "professional students" expect the spouse to watch the kids, run the house, and earn the money while they spend their time attending school. Based on our experience, a marriage where one of the partners is a professional student is fraught with strain. There's a huge potential for resentment in the spouse who is doing most of the work.

Some professions require an advanced degree to get that first job, but most don't. If you're a student who has a family to support, your best plan would be to get a job after graduating from a four-year college program and then pursue an advanced degree while you're working. Although this will keep you busier than just being a full-time student, it will put less pressure on your family. You may also have the advantage of having your employer pay for all or most of your advanced degree. Many companies will pay your tuition expenses when you take classes that relate to your career.

If you and your spouse decide together that you should be a full-time student, be considerate of your spouse by working a part-time job, taking a full class load, and attending summer school. This will get you graduated and out into the workplace quicker, making it easier on every member of your family.

Internship Programs

Many companies have internship programs that allow students to work as a summer intern while school is not in session. Check with your school for information about the availability of such programs in your area. If you can secure one of these internships, you can earn money while working in the same career you wish to pursue after graduation.

The advantage of being an intern is that it gives you valuable "real life" experience to complement the principles you're learning in school. You'll find it easier to understand certain concepts if you see them actually in use, rather than just as a theory in the classroom. Another plus is that it gives you some related job experience, which will give you an advantage when you go looking for that first job and will give you an opening to those businesses where you served your internship. If you like the company and they are impressed with you, there is a good chance that you might be offered a full-time job when you graduate.

Writing Your Résumé

When applying for all but the most menial jobs, the potential employer will usually ask that you send a copy of your résumé. Think of the résumé as being something like an advertisement for yourself. Rather than selling tires, cars, or frozen dinners, the purpose of your résumé is selling your skills as an employee and getting those with job openings to hire you rather than the next guy. Thus, you need to write a résumé that will impress people with your abilities and make you stand out from the other twenty candidates who sent résumés for the same job.

It's important to remember there is no standard for résumés. Each book or article that you read will give you different advice about what to include. You need to come up with the format that you think will be most effective. When writing your résumé, here are some points to keep in mind:

- Start the résumé by giving your name and mailing address. Make sure this is a street address where an employer can reach you and not a temporary address or a post office box number. Make sure all phone numbers include an area code. Because e-mail is becoming more common, list an e-mail address if you have one. A fax number may also help.

- Many businesses get so many résumés that they don't even read them, but load them into a database of résumés that can be searched for specific keywords. Once you know this, you can pepper your résumé with words that will cause it to pop out when someone is searching for a particular skill.

  A friend of ours who hires hundreds of people each year tells us the key to having a good résumé is to write it specifically for the job you want. We all want to be lazy and send out a one-size-fits-all résumé, but a custom-tailored one gives you the advantage.

- Don't ruin a good résumé with grammar, spelling, or typographical errors. Make the résumé neat and sharp looking, but don't make it too busy with different fonts, borders, or other effects. Print the résumé on high quality paper with a good printer.

- The "objective" section is optional. These days, this information is usually included in a cover letter instead of on the résumé. Regardless of where you put this information, it should be brief but informative and should summarize the job you want and why you think you are qualified for it.

- The "qualifications" section is also optional, but can sometimes be effective. It serves as a summary of the reasons you think you're qualified for the job. If you think you have strong qualifications, list them here. Otherwise, omit this section.

- An "education" section should summarize the education you've had. Include any degrees that were awarded, the date you graduated, and the name and location of the institution. If your major and minor subjects are relevant to the job you seek, include them as well. You should also list any workshops, seminars, or special class projects that relate to your qualifications. Calculate your GPA (grade point average) for all classes and for the classes within your major. If either of these exceeds 3.0, consider listing the highest one on the résumé. Don't forget to list any awards you won during your days as a student. You need to pay special attention to this section if you have had little actual work experience.

- A section on employment experience should always be included. If you have limited work experience, list your involvement with other training events, such as internships and relevant volunteer work. For example, if you're seeking work as an accountant, you could describe your experiences with a volunteer program that helps senior citizens prepare their tax returns. What this section should convey to the employer is the skills you possess that will be useful in doing your job. For each previous job, include your job title, the name and location of the employer, and the dates that you worked for him. Also include a few short sentences that describe your responsibilities, putting emphasis on your most impressive achievements.

- The "other experience" section is particularly important if you haven't had a lot of previous employment experience, or if there are gaps in your work or education history that need to be explained. Emphasize those activities that provided you with skills that will be valuable for the particular job you want.

- The "additional information" category is useful information that doesn't really fit in any other category. Because many jobs expect some level of computer expertise, it's common to list those skills here—particularly your familiarity with specific software products. Other skills that may be listed include the ability to speak additional languages. Some people like to list interests and hobbies, believing they add more of a human touch to the person behind the résumé. Also list any activities that demonstrate ambition or leadership abilities, such as election to an office, work as an officer in a volunteer organization, or service as a full-time missionary. Put any item here that would demonstrate your character and skills to your potential employer.

- Remember that the goal of the résumé is to get yourself invited to a job interview. It is not intended to be your life history, which can be explored more fully during the actual interview. Write your résumé in such a way that it will attract the reader's attention, and will make you stand out from the other applicants.

- In order to make your résumé readable, limit the length to two pages. Use short, choppy sentences, but not sentence fragments. Choose words that convey a sense of action, because that will be more impressive to the reader. For example, the phrase, "I developed a training program that increased sales and reduced the number of returns," is more impressive than saying, "I was part of a program designed to improve profit margins."

- When categories include multiple events, include the most recent event first and then work backward in time. For example, list the most recent job you held, and then the one before that.

- Avoid including any limitations or restrictions that would cause your résumé to be rejected before an interview. For example, you should never say, "I'm looking for a sales job, but I refuse to work on weekends." Even if that statement is true, sell yourself first and then work out the details during the job interview.

Figure 9-1 illustrates these principles:

BECKY ELLEN SMITH
425 Casper Road, Apartment 410
Walnut, Virginia 20123
(540) 555-1212
bsmith@techworld.net

Qualifications
- I have more than three years' experience in a customer service environment.
- I received the "Customer Service Employee of the Year" award in 1998.
- I possess excellent communication skills, both oral and written.
- I have a familiarity with the most common customer service software.

Education
I was awarded a B.S. in computer science with a minor in English, June 1995, from Taylor University, Williamsburg, Virginia.
- My GPA was 3.67.
- I was secretary of the Campus Computer Club.
- I was a member of Phi Delta Phi Honor Society.
- I am a July 1989 graduate of Washington High School, Dallas, Texas.
- I wrote software to assist in the layout of the yearbook.
- My science fair computer project won "Best of Show" award in 1998.

Employment Experience
- Senior Customer Support Representative;
  Acme Software, San Francisco, California (May 1997–Present).

I was promoted to a senior position after less than 18 months of employment. I developed a training guide for new support employees and am frequently asked to lead the team when the regular team leader is away.

- Customer Support Representative;
  Circle Products, Orlando, Florida (July 1995–April 1997).

I was hired as a trainee but promoted within six months. I consistently maintained one of the highest scores in terms of customer satisfaction. In addition, I helped convert the customer database from an older software program to a Millennium 2000 system from Saturn Software.

Other Experience
I served my church as a missionary to Mexico City for 18 months. This experience taught me to communicate well with others and empathize with their problems. It also taught me to speak Spanish—a skill that I have maintained.

Additional Information
- I'm experienced with most word processing and spreadsheet software.
- I have developed several pages for use on the World Wide Web.
- I also have some experience with desktop publishing software.
- My hobbies include softball, golf, poetry writing, and photography. I am also studying judo and hope to get my brown belt this year.

References available upon request

Figure 9-1

Finding a Job

With your résumé in hand, you are now ready to find a job. Depending on your circumstances, this is a process that may take from one day to a year—or longer. Much of this depends upon your qualifications, and the number of job openings that exist for someone with those skills.

There are a number of ways to find job openings:

- Contact any previous employers in the field where you're seeking employment. Perhaps you had a summer internship, or you worked part time for a company while attending school. If you liked the company and they liked you, see about the possibility of a full-time job. Even if the company has no openings, you may be referred to another company who might be hiring.

> **Sneaky Secret**
> Don't feel shy about asking acquaintances to submit your résumé to their employers. Many companies have employee referral programs that pay a bonus to an employee who refers someone who is hired. If so, your friend will probably be more than happy to forward your résumé, knowing there is a chance he'll make some money in the process.

- Your network of family, friends, and associates is probably one of your most valuable assets in terms of getting a job. The successful candidate for many jobs is often the one who has some type of contact on the inside. Don't hesitate to ask for help from any of your contacts who may be in a position to know of such openings.

- Check the "Help Wanted" section in the newspaper classified section, particularly in the Sunday paper. Avoid ads that give little information about the company or the job or that require you to call a phone number or send your résumé to a post office box. Watch out for ads that sound too good or that promise a lot of money without requiring many skills. Sometimes ads are also run by employment agencies, who are simply trying to get you as a client who will pay them a fee to find you a job. If you do see an ad that looks good, respond quickly before the job is filled.

- There are many Internet sites that allow you to search for job openings in their databases. Some of these will also allow you to post your résumé on their system, allowing prospective employers to view your résumé. Many large newspapers also have Internet sites that allow you to search for jobs in their Help Wanted sections. These have the advantage of allowing you to search the newspapers in locations far away from your residence.

- If you have an idea that you might like to work for a particular company, do an Internet search to see if it has a website. Many companies have a section on their website where they list current job openings. If you can't find an Internet site, call the company directly and ask how you apply for a job.

- Most states provide an employment service, usually found by looking in the state government section of the phone book under "Job Service" or "Employment." These agencies will try to match available jobs with those seeking employment and will also provide free services that will help you do such things as write a résumé and prepare for an interview.

- Private employment agencies also try to match job openings with applicants, but they do so for a fee. Some of these require you to pay this fee—often a portion of the salary you make your first year—while others are paid by the companies who are looking for workers. Try to avoid the ones who expect you to pay, unless you can be provided with a list of their satisfied clients, and unless you fully understand how much you will be expected to pay. Some of these agencies specialize in specific types of jobs, such as engineering or computer science, and their employees are usually called "headhunters."

- If you're in college, a placement service often works with companies who recruit on campus for graduates with certain skills. The placement service may also provide other services such as help in writing a résumé or being interviewed.

- If there are any trade journals or professional newsletters that cater to your particular profession, check them to see if they contain any Help Wanted ads.

- If you're interested in a government job, the availability of such jobs is usually announced through civil service announcements. Contact the proper government agencies to see when and where such announcements are posted. Because completing the various forms for a civil service job can be confusing, enlist the help of a friend or relative who understands the process.

- Sometimes there are job search programs that exist for certain groups, such as veterans, the handicapped, youth, or low-income families. Check with the proper federal, state, and local government agencies to see if you're eligible for any of these programs.

- Community agencies such as churches, libraries, and volunteer organizations will sometimes maintain job listings and offer help in finding a job.

When you find a company that interests you, send a cover letter along with a copy of your résumé. It should be in standard business format and should summarize your qualifications and describe the job that has caught your attention. Address the letter to the person who is coordinating the applicants for the job (usually identified in the ad). Name the specific job opening, including the job title and job opening number. Review your qualifications in several short sentences, and request a job interview. Include all phone numbers where you may be reached, along with an e-mail address if applicable.

Many of the résumés you send will probably be answered by a postcard or form letter, telling you that the company has received your résumé and that it will be kept on file to consider for future openings. This is usually a polite way of telling you to look elsewhere for employment. Avoid the urge to call a company and ask whether your résumé has been received, because it's unlikely you'll find anyone who knows the answer to that question.

Don't be discouraged if you send out a dozen résumés and get a dozen rejection letters. It takes time for the process to work, and sometimes it's just a matter of being patient until a job opens that is right for you. Some people make the mistake of applying for only one job and doing nothing until they hear back on that application. Use many sources to look for job openings, and apply to all the jobs that look interesting. If more than one company responds, you'll have more options when it comes to interviewing and selecting a position.

Surviving the Job Interview

When your résumé finally generates some interest, the potential employer will contact you and arrange for you to come in and have a job interview. Make sure you ask how long this will take, because it will give you an idea of how intense the interview will be. Most interviews last about one to two hours, but Clark has been through some all-day marathons where he was grilled by five or six different people. The depth of the interview process will depend on the company and the type of job you are seeking.

Regardless of the type and length of interview, here are some steps for surviving it and impressing the employer:

- Learn about the organization where you will be interviewing. You'll be much more impressive to the interviewer if you can talk intelligently about the organization's products and activities. You can usually obtain this information from the public library or from the company's Internet website.

- Bring a copy of your résumé with you. Prior to the interview, most employers will have you fill out a job application. Most of the information on the application will be found on your résumé, so you can copy directly from that and save yourself some effort.

- As part of the interview process, you may be asked for a list of references. These references are people who would be willing to answer the prospective employer's questions about your skills and abilities. References are often classified as either professional (those who can talk about your work-related skills) and personal (those who can talk about your general character). Most résumés no longer list references, but usually contain the expression, "References available upon request." You should prepare a separate list of typed references, and take them to your job interview. Provide three personal and three professional references, and make sure to include each reference's name, job title, employer, address, and both business and home phone numbers. Obviously, you should check with these people first to make sure they are willing to be used as a reference. Avoid using relatives as references unless you have no other option.

- Determine ahead of time which position you want. If an employer has several openings, determine the one that would be most interesting and the best fit for your skills. Don't go to the interview without a specific job in mind.

- Review the skills needed for the position you want and compare them with your own abilities. Be prepared to talk with the interviewer about each required skill and your experience in that area. If there are skills you don't have, do some research in those areas. Then you can honestly say, "I haven't done much in that area, but I have read about it, and I would love the opportunity to learn more."

- Prepare yourself to answer a wide variety of questions both about your qualifications and your work habits. Expect such questions as "What is your greatest strength?" "What is your greatest weakness?" and "What particular talents would you bring to our organization?" Although you will not be able to anticipate all these questions, it will help if you do some thinking about such topics before the interview. Some interviewers will even ask you such bizarre questions as "If you could be any animal, what animal would you be, and why?" If you get one of these, try not to laugh. The employer is trying to determine how you think, and he believes he's asking you a valid question—even if you believe he's full of malarkey.

- Practice an interview with a friend or relative, who can play the part of the interviewer as you respond.

- Dress properly for the interview, and be well groomed. Even though many organizations are moving to a casual dress policy, it usually doesn't hurt to wear a conservative suit or dress for the interview. Although you may show up dressed better than any of the employees, it shows them you think enough of the organization to dress respectfully. You can break out the jeans and the T-shirts after you get the job.

- Avoid habits that might annoy the interviewer. Clark once interviewed a woman who pulled out a cigarette in the middle of the interview and blew smoke in his face. Any bets about whether she got the job? Obviously, as a Church member you shouldn't be lighting up anywhere, but watch out for other habits such as chewing gum that might be equally annoying to your prospective employer. Also, go light on the perfume and aftershave—some people are allergic to them.

- Arrive ten to fifteen minutes before the scheduled interview. Aside from demonstrating your promptness, this will allow you a few minutes to relax. This time can also give you a chance to see how the organization works and whether the employees seem to be enjoying their jobs.

- Be on your best behavior during the interview. When you meet each person who interviews you, shake his hand and remember his name. Look at the person as you talk to him, and avoid looking at the floor. Don't use profanity or slang, and be sure to use proper grammar. When you're finished, thank the interviewer for his time. Exit with a sincere and positive comment, such as, "Thanks for taking the time to talk with me today. I've enjoyed learning more about what this job involves, and I hope we may work together in the future."

- Try not to be nervous. Convey a positive attitude and show confidence in your own abilities. It will be easier to sell the employer on you once you have convinced *yourself* that you're the best person for the job. If you get nervous, just remind yourself that this is only a job interview, and the worst that will happen is that you won't get the job.

- Employers realize you may lack some skills they would like, but will be more concerned about your ability to learn new things and be excited about the projects you are given. You don't need to pretend to know everything, but express a willingness to be adaptable and to learn new things.

- The two main things the interviewer will try to evaluate are your job skills and your ability to work with others. Even the most talented person in the world will not be hired if he has an obnoxious personality (unless perhaps the interviewer is equally obnoxious). Take every opportunity to emphasize your skills in working with others, and don't dwell on any previous problems you may have had in this area.

- Try to answer each question fully, but avoid going into too much detail or talking about things that aren't relevant. The interviewer will ask another question if he wants more detail. When appropriate, you should also ask questions you might have about the organization or the job position. The objective of the interview is for you and the organization to both decide if you are right for each other.

- Unless the interviewer mentions them, avoid talking about salary or job benefits. Even then, do not spend a lot of time on these issues. Your objective is to sell them on you and to work out the details later.

- When you get home from the interview, immediately write thank-you notes to all the people who interviewed you, and drop them in the mail that same day. This is not done as often as it used to be, but it's a nice touch. Writing thank you notes may make the difference in whether you get hired, particularly if the interviewers have some minor doubts about you.

The Job Offer

If the organization thinks you are qualified and would be a good employee, someone will make you a job offer. This may occur right after the job interview, although it usually happens after there has been time to evaluate you and any other candidates who may have applied. Someone will usually notify you by phone and will then follow up with a written offer if you accept. You'll usually be given a couple of days to decide whether you want to accept the position once it has been offered to you.

This waiting period can be agonizing, but some organizations move excruciatingly slowly when hiring new employees. Don't put your life on hold while you wait for the offer, but move on and work on other possibilities. You might receive multiple job offers, which gives you even more options in getting the job you want.

If a potential employer decides not to hire you, you will usually receive a form letter within a week. Sometimes you'll be notified by phone. Some organizations don't have the courtesy to notify you, assuming you'll understand that no response means no job. After a week of no contact, it's acceptable to call the organization and ask to speak to the person who interviewed you. This shows you're still interested and may influence them toward hiring you if the decision still hasn't been made. If the interviewer always seems to be busy and doesn't return your calls, it's a pretty safe assumption that you should look elsewhere.

When you have a job offer firmly in hand, that is the time to address issues such as salary and benefits. If you think the salary is too low for the position, do some research on similar positions in the same area. If the salary is too low, contact the person who issued the job offer, tell him about your research, and ask him in a nonconfrontational way why the salary you've been offered is so much lower. If you do this in a pleasant manner, you may end up with a better offer. How much room you have to negotiate better terms depends on the job situation. If a dozen qualified people applied, the employer can pretty much tell you to take the job or leave it. If you're the only qualified candidate, then you probably have more room to bargain. Keep in mind that some benefits are set by policy, and the employer can't change them no matter how much you threaten. Remember to be unfailingly polite and reasonable, because you don't want to antagonize or alienate other employees before you even start work.

If you found your position through a private employment agency (recruiter), the recruiter may be invaluable to you during this negotiation process. The employment agency's commission depends on you getting the job and on how much salary you will make. Thus the recruiter's interests parallel your own. The recruiter can often work as the middle-man between you and the organization, giving you advice about how far you can push and then working with the organization to see what arrangements can be made.

There are many factors that go into the decision of whether or not you'll accept the offer. These relate not only to the enjoyment of the job you would be doing, but also whether you'd be happy with your fellow employees and the culture of the organization. You should have been able to answer these questions while you were interviewing. If you still have doubts or unanswered questions, feel free to call the organization and get those issues resolved before you make a decision.

Here are just a few of the questions you should consider when deciding whether you'll be happy with the job that has been offered:

- Are the salary and benefits fair and acceptable to you?
- How often will you receive performance and salary reviews?
- Would the work be interesting and challenging?
- Are there options for you to be promoted or moved into other positions?
- Will the job help you further your career goals?
- Will you develop skills making you more valuable to other organizations?
- Does the company have a training program for your position?
- Can you get along with the other people in your section or group?
- Can you get along with the person who will be your manager?
- Are you impressed with the organization and its goals and culture?

- Is it a stable and financially sound organization that will still exist in a year?
- Does the company deal in a product or service with a good future?
- Will the office location require a move or a long commute?
- What do current and former employees say about working there?
- Does the company have an unusually high turnover rate?
- Are you comfortable with the size of the organization?
- Are you comfortable with the working hours and working conditions?

Once you've made a decision, you need to notify the prospective employer as soon as possible. If you're accepting the position, you'll usually receive a written offer and will be contacted by someone who will finalize some details such as your salary and starting date. Read the agreement carefully before signing it—it is a legal document that will bind you. Resolve any questions or make any revisions before signing it. Make a copy for yourself, send back the original, and then enjoy a few days of freedom before starting your new job.

If you don't get the job or you decide not to accept it, go back to the search process and start over. This can be very discouraging, but try not to let it get to you. Finding the right job often takes longer than you want, but you just have to be patient and keep trying.

Maintaining Job Skills

Clark's father worked his entire career for the same company. He started there after college and worked there his entire life, except to serve a mission and to fight in World War II. For better or worse, this kind of dedication is dead and probably won't return. Both employers and employees seem to have given up any pretense of loyalty, and they often part company for the most minor reasons. If you're just entering the job market, you can probably expect to have at least half a dozen jobs before you retire. This gives you the responsibility of keeping your job skills up to date, so you can exist in the job market if you leave your current job.

Work hard at being a good employee and at getting along with others. You may be surprised to learn that most dissatisfaction with employees is caused by their behavior rather than their lack of job skills. If a manager has to lay off an employee, he will probably fire one who is obnoxious and disagreeable instead of one who is pleasant but not as talented. Stay on the good side of your manager and coworkers.

Look for warning signs that your company is in trouble. These include such things as disappointing earnings, hiring freezes, pressure to reduce expenses, and the downgrading of benefits. Also look for signs that your company might be acquired, merged, or forced out of business. These signs don't mean you need to jump ship, but you may want to start keeping an eye out for other opportunities.

Pay attention when you're given job reviews. Pay close attention to areas that are critical of your performance. Work on fixing those areas so you'll be considered a more valuable employee.

Regularly evaluate your situation to determine if your current job is moving you toward your eventual career goal. Where do you want to be in five years? Did you make any progress in that direction during the past year? If you are not making the desired progress, either get your management to make changes or consider another employer.

Sneaky Secret

Get in the habit of revising your résumé once a year, even if you have no wish to change jobs. This will help you focus on your career plans, and will also update your résumé with last year's accomplishments while they are still fresh in your mind. More importantly, you will not have to waste time if you suddenly lose your job or have the need to find another job quickly.

Always keep your skills current so you'll be valuable to someone else if you have to leave your current job. Don't let your employer stick you in a position where you'll learn nothing new and have nothing to offer another employer. Continually compare the skills you're developing on your job with the skills in demand in the job market. Work with your employer to provide the training you need to stay current. If your employer refuses to train you, find a more reasonable employer or learn on your own through trade journals, magazines and books, and training courses.

I'm Still Clueless

? *What happens if my résumé is not exactly truthful?*

Anyone with any résumé experience knows résumés are written to present the job candidate in the best possible light. A person who spent the last decade in prison might easily write a résumé stating, "I have spent the last ten years as a state employee working in a challenging and stressful environment, with a diverse group of coworkers." Even though such claims are almost expected on a résumé, one of the purposes of the interview is to see if the candidate is as talented as his résumé claims.

Although you should use the strongest language you know to describe your achievements on your résumé, don't say anything that will come back to haunt you later. The résumé is to get you in the door. The interview gives you the opportunity to show your good qualities that a résumé won't convey. Be sure you are perfectly honest during the job interview. Many organizations will immediately terminate your employment if they find you lied on your résumé or during the job interview—even if you're an outstanding employee in terms of job performance.

? *How will I ever get my first job without any experience?*

With proper planning during school, you should be able to have some experience before you need to get your first full-time job. Seek out internships or summer jobs in your area of study. Also consider being involved with volunteer programs and training workshops. These may not be paid positions, but they count as job-related experience.

Many organizations want to hire people just entering the job market. These employers can give you an entry-level position that pays less but still gives you an opening into the workplace. If they see your talent, you will likely be promoted into a better job. If that doesn't happen, you can go somewhere else and still have the experience on your résumé. Your school placement office is a good source for these types of jobs.

Some organizations like to hire employees without previous experience so they can mold the employee to their own organizational culture without any "contamination" from previous workplaces. They find it is easier to teach people "our way of doing things" if the people have had no earlier experiences with other employers.

? *If I'm desperate for money, should I accept a job I don't want?*

That depends on how hard up you are for money. If the cupboard is bare and the landlord is at the door, you should take any job you can get. It also depends on the likelihood of getting other job offers. If this is the first offer in six months of looking, you may want to think hard about taking it.

Having a job—even one you don't like—will remove the financial pressure so that you can look for another job while under less stress. But the downside is that you will have less energy and time to look for a better job.

Taking a job is always a gamble. Some people take what they consider to be dream jobs, only to leave a short time later because they were miserable. Others have taken jobs they didn't want, only to be surprised when it turned into a career they really enjoyed. If the job is close to what you want, but not an exact fit, take the job anyway and see what happens. Maybe you can eventually work yourself into a better situation. If not, you will at least have a job while you look for a better one.

? *Now that I've got the job, how can I balance my responsibilities at work with my other interests in life?*

Single people who like their occupations are tempted to work at all hours of the day and night, and even on weekends. This dedication is fine, and there are some fields where it may even be demanded of new employees. Although you may be so excited about your new career that you want to jump in with both feet, there are occasional drawbacks to this behavior. The biggest one is that instead of being grateful for the extra work you're doing, your employer may expect this same level of dedication from you even after you've found other things to do with your leisure time.

Both of us were workaholics when we were single and not in a dating relationship, but after we met each other we wanted to spend our leisure time away from work. Kathy eventually lost her job over this. She'd been working until 1 A.M. many nights and had worked all day most Saturdays—just for the fun of it. When she cut back to a forty-hour week, her productivity dropped off so dramatically that her editor decided she was a slacker. Kathy knew she was working just as hard as ever, so she was puzzled by the editor's loss of esteem. What she didn't realize until years later was that the editor was used to eighty hours of work from her per week. When her output dropped by half, he couldn't help but think she was malingering on the job.

You're young and healthy. This is the time for you to develop hobbies and interests that will last for the rest of your life. Take up skiing or painting, take on a demanding church calling, or do something else that interests you on your hours away from work. You'll meet more people by doing something different during your off hours, and you won't be setting unreal expectations that your employer will count on forever.

CHAPTER 10
Managing Your Life

★ **IN THIS CHAPTER**
- ✔ Managing Your Time
- ✔ Living as a Single Person
- ✔ Developing Spiritual Connections
- ✔ Dealing with Roommates and Neighbors
- ✔ Selecting a Compatible Roommate
- ✔ Choosing Your Friends
- ✔ Finding the Perfect Spouse

As you left home, your mind may have been on the physical aspects of your future. Where were you going to live? Where were you going to work? How much money were you going to make? How were you going to spend that money? How were you going to survive doing your own cooking?

So far, we've tried to address these physical concerns. We've taught you how to shop and how to cook, how to buy clothes and how to mend them, how to be your own physician, how to invest your money wisely, and a number of other things. But even having all your physical needs met is no fun if you don't feel fulfilled in life.

There are many ways to find fulfillment in life, and the ways differ somewhat for each person. But generally, people find fulfillment from similar sources. These sources of fulfillment include using time wisely, learning, developing spirituality, getting along with those around you, making true friends, and pursuing romantic relationships. In this chapter we'll tackle these issues and try to help you discover ways to make your life meaningful.

Time Management

If you're like most people, you'll work for eight hours and sleep for eight hours every day. That leaves a third of your life for you to fill with other activities. How you fill that last third is up to you. Either you can waste that time or you can use those eight hours to enrich your life and to benefit the lives of others. The choice is yours.

Back in the days when you were living at home, your time wasn't your own. You awoke when your parents rousted you out of bed in the morning, you left the house to catch a bus or a ride, you ate dinner when Mom put it on the table, and you went to bed at night when your parents demanded lights out.

Now that you're on your own, you're responsible for your own schedule. Unless you're cooking for roommates, you can eat breakfast or dinner whenever you want to—or not at all. You can stay up as late as you want, and you can sleep all day on weekends if that's what you want to do. In fact, you may be tempted to do all those things, *just because you can.*

But here's something you may not have considered: The things you do determine who you are. If you're tempted to spend your days watching television and your nights going to parties, think about it. You may have more "fun" than the person who grinds away at a job five days a week or spends his evenings in the library. But this kind of fun lasts only a little while. Eventually your sloth will eat away at your self-esteem until the fun isn't fun anymore. People who really have good times are the people who've earned their fun. You'll like yourself better if you do the things you're supposed to be doing and set aside leisure activities for the hours after your work has been satisfactorily completed.

Managing Your Time in School

If you're living in a dormitory, the temptation to stay up all night and carouse with your friends may be almost overwhelming. There may be a party just down the hall every night of the week, and nobody wants to pass up something that may be exciting. But if you stay up having fun every night, you'll eventually suffer, physically and academically. Whether you do it consciously or by default, part of your role as a student will require you to choose between horsing around and participating in school activities. It's better to decide ahead of time why you're going to college and to gear your activities toward the fulfillment of your goals.

Your parents have probably told you that you're going to school to get an education. This is true, but there are many forms of education. Some people do indeed go to school primarily to get the knowledge that accompanies that magical diploma. Others go to school to be part of a campus community, complete with theatre departments, the daily newspaper, and campus politics. This is an education that is just as important as is anything you can get from books. Still others think of college as a four-year party. These people are being educated, too.

Kathy's understanding of education was broadened even before she began her first day of college classes. She'd been an honor roll student in high school and assumed she'd continue to do so, right up until the moment she heard the journalism advisor talk about how to succeed in journalism.

The journalism professor said that journalists record life and that successful journalists need to know about life in order to do a good job of reporting it. He said that any journalism major who focused only on getting good grades would do so at the cost of missing other experiences that were more important to journalists. He even predicted that the straight-A students would probably never get jobs in journalism.

This was the best news Kathy could have heard. Although she wasn't someone who wanted to spend a lot of time at parties, she thought there were a whole lot of things in life that were more interesting than studying the required journalism curriculum. So she took the journalism professor at his word. Instead of taking a lot of journalism-related classes, she took the classes that sounded interesting to her, studying farm animals and dinosaurs and medicine and law and crime and world religions, and anything else that took her fancy. She didn't bother to get decent grades in the classes that didn't interest her, but instead spent her study time working in campus politics or on the school newspaper. Indeed, she got notice that she was on academic probation the day she received her college diploma.

But the journalism teacher had been right. Kathy left college and went directly to work for a large metropolitan newspaper. Her study of farm animals helped her when she became agriculture editor; her study of world religions helped her when she became religion editor; her study of law helped her when she covered the federal courts. She also wrote stories about dinosaurs and medicine and all the other things she'd studied, and had a great time doing so.

One day she received a phone call from a former classmate who was in tears. "It's not fair," she said. "All you did was goof off in college. I got straight A's. Now you're a reporter and I'm a waitress at Denny's. What went wrong?"

The only thing that "went wrong" was that Kathy's classmate had been indoctrinated into believing that grades were the only worthwhile measure of an education. Kathy had taken the lazy way out, and in doing so she accidentally educated herself in the only way that mattered to someone in her field.

If you're majoring in medicine or law, do not follow Kathy's example. Some fields of study really *do* require good grades. The point of this story is not to give you permission to goof off, but to teach you that there's more than one kind of education. If you're wise, you'll determine what your actual goals are and will attend college with those goals in mind.

If you're going to school just to find a husband, focus on activities that will allow you to find the right husband, but at the same time take classes that will teach you to be a good wife and mother. (Don't forget that more and more mothers are finding it necessary to work outside the home. Part of your training should give you skills to work outside the home if necessary.) If you're going to school just to find a wife, focus on activities that will allow you to find the right wife, but at the same time take classes that will teach you to be a good husband and provider.

If you're going to school just to train yourself for a career, you may want to take extra classes so you can get into the workforce even faster than most students. If you're going to school just to get away from your parents and stay up late every night, by all means save yourself some money and skip school altogether. Get yourself a job where you don't have to think during the day. That way you'll have the money to support yourself as you waste your life in riotous living.

No matter why you choose to go to school, you can still learn things in every facet of your life. Indeed, life is worth living only as long as you're still learning. The day you decide you've learned all from life you needed to learn is the day you might as well dig a hole and throw yourself in. But don't fool yourself into thinking that learning comes only from books. You're learning things even when you don't know it, simply by virtue of the things you do and the company you keep.

Clark once questioned his father about the value of college, reasoning that most of the knowledge he was learning would be obsolete when he finally got a job. His father replied that people go to school to learn how to learn, rather than to just memorize a list of facts that will soon be out of date. Keep this in mind as you attend school. The productive habits you learn while being a student will be of more value than any of the facts found in your textbooks.

Holidays and Vacations

Most people look forward to holidays and vacations, but single people may find them traumatic. On one hand, you may feel too old and mature to go home for Christmas, where you'll naturally be treated as your parents' child instead of as an adult. But if you don't go home, where else are you going to go? Nobody feels lonelier over holidays and vacations than a person who is midway between childhood and marriage. Indeed, the suicide rate goes way up during holiday periods, precisely because so many people feel unloved and alone.

If you don't know what to do with yourself on holidays, forget yourself and think about others. Sponsor a Thanksgiving dinner for the homeless—or even for single people from church who are in your situation. Organize a Sub-for-Santa project and take Christmas gifts to children who would otherwise receive no presents. Take flowers to a rest home on Mother's Day. Get the kiddies in your neighborhood together for a July Fourth parade. Dress up as a witch and scare the socks off trick-or-treaters. If you're out among others, your holidays can be full of joy even on days that are designed for families. Remember—there's always someone who's worse off than you.

As for vacations, the time will come when you'll regret the opportunities you missed in your single years. After you're married, your family will find ways to spend all your extra money and your career will tie you down to one place. Right now you're portable and unattached. If you've always wanted to join the peace corps or spend Christmas in New Zealand, it's now or never.

Before Kathy was married, she dreamed about traveling all over the world with her husband. Then she married someone who has no earthly interest in trying to find his way around countries where the people don't speak English. If she'd had a brain in her head, she would have traveled when she had the opportunity. After she was married, she could have taken Clark back to those places and acted as tour guide. Because she didn't have anyone to tell her what we're telling you now, her passport is almost empty. She'll never visit Egypt or Russia or any of the other places of her dreams, because she didn't do it when she had the chance.

While Kathy was dreaming of foreign travel, Clark was postponing missionary service because he wanted to do missionary work with his future wife. He had—and still has—dreams of serving at a visitors' center in a historic site or serving a temple mission. Then he went and married someone whose body was not built for the rigors of missionary life. The only way he'll fulfill his dream is to knock off Wife Number One and serve a mission with Wife Number Two. Kathy doesn't think this is a good idea.

There's a lesson in this. Don't let *your* dreams go unfulfilled because you're saving them up to share with someone else. Fulfill the dreams you can fulfill today and let tomorrow's dreams take care of themselves.

Church Participation

If you grew up in a churchgoing family, the chances are pretty good that church attendance wasn't an option. Church was something your family did together, and "together" meant you were part of the ritual of worship. If you stayed out late on a Saturday night and wanted to sleep in on Sunday, it didn't make any difference. You went to church anyway because your parents made you go to church or out of habit (which amounts to the same thing).

Once you're on your own, one of the first things you'll realize is that nobody is going to make you go to church on Sunday. For maybe the first time in your life, you have the freedom to go to church or to stay home. Many people, particularly young men, take advantage of this freedom by missing church for weeks or months or even longer, while they decide how deep their religious streak runs and whether they want to continue attending church now that the decision is their own. *This isn't all bad.* Most of the young men we know—Clark among them—who stopped going to church when they went out on their own soon learned that there was a void in their life without church attendance. When they came back to church of their own free will, they became stronger church members than they had ever been before. Once they realized they had their own spiritual roots, they decided that church was going to be a lifelong commitment, and they settled down into being good church members.

The key here, especially if you're trying to help someone come back to church, is that each person should decide for himself. Although encouragement is certainly permitted, attempts at coercion will only alienate those who are hesitant to return. And a person who is bullied into returning to church will never develop the spiritual roots he'll need to sustain him through the trials of life.

If you take a sabbatical from church when you leave home for the first time, do yourself a favor and do some thinking while you're on your vacation. First of all, ask yourself why you don't want to attend church. All too often, young people stop going to church solely because their parents go. If church is important to Mom and Dad, some sons and daughters want to make sure church isn't important to them.

If you think about it, that's not a great reason to stay away from church. Your parents do *some* things you want to do, don't they? They drive cars. They spend money. They go grocery shopping. They breathe in and out. If you decided to stop doing all those things just because your parents do them, you'd be in big trouble. It's the same way with church, except it takes longer to notice the effects if you stop going to church than it would if you stopped breathing.

Once you've honestly determined you aren't skipping church just to spite your parents, there are other questions you should be asking. Why is religion so important that your parents and other relatives have made a lifelong commitment to church attendance? What have church and God done for you? How well would you thrive without these influences in your life? What effect would it have on your future children if they grew up without being taught the principles of the gospel?

Once you've considered these questions, read the scriptures and pray about your decisions. If you're sincere in your quest, your prayers will be answered. When you return to church—and you *will* return to church if you ponder and pray about this decision—it will be because you know within yourself that it's the right thing to do.

Church Activities for Singles

Once you make up your mind to go to church, you're going to be able to get a lot out of your church activity. For one thing, being a religious person will bolster you up when you're going through times of trouble. For another, serving in a church calling will allow you to concentrate on the needs of others rather than focusing on yourself. And don't discount the social aspects of church. This is where you'll likely find your truest friends and the best candidates for marriage.

Depending on where you live, you may have a choice of what congregation to attend. If you're going to school, there may be a student ward available to you. In these wards, every person is a student (except for the bishopric, which is usually made up of faculty members or other adults from the community). Some students may be married with young children, but all of you will have your studies in common.

Singles wards can be found in areas where there's a high concentration of single adults. The difference between singles wards and student wards is that you don't have to be a student to attend a singles ward.

There are advantages to going to church in a student/singles congregation. Many young people feel a strong spirit in the meetings and draw from the enthusiasm and spiritual conviction of their peers. Also, in a student/singles ward you may have the opportunity to serve in any number of callings. In a student ward there are often two elders quorums and two Relief Societies, which means there are also two elders quorum presidents and Relief Society presidents and a set of counselors for each. You could also be called as the Sunday School president or as a Gospel Doctrine teacher. In some wards a student is even called to be a member of the bishopric.

Additionally, because student/singles wards are composed exclusively of people who are roughly the same age, there's a much bigger pool of people for you to consider as friends or eternal companions. Meanwhile, the activities are a lot more fun because they're geared to your age and interests. Going to church in a student/singles situation has great advantages, and you may want to do so for a time if the opportunity presents itself.

But while you're looking at churches, don't overlook the advantages of the resident wards. Resident wards, also known as family wards, offer you other opportunities to serve. In a ward full of families, there are plenty of ways to use a single person—particularly if you're young and energetic. As a young person, you can have a significant impact if you're assigned to teach young people because your tastes and experiences are similar to theirs. As a Primary teacher or nursery worker, you won't be inhibited about getting down on the floor and acting silly with children. But you may be even more valuable in working with teenagers. Teenagers will listen to you because you're a real person—not just somebody's mother. If you're given the opportunity to work with the Young Women or the Scouts, take advantage of it. These may be some of the most significant callings you'll ever have. As a teacher of young people, you can change lives.

But let's face it. Going to a resident ward as a single person isn't always going to be a bed of petunias. Every once in a while you may run into someone who thinks there's something wrong with you because you aren't married and who treats you that way. *That is their problem, not yours.* Don't let their ignorance get you down.

In all areas of life, people who condemn others usually do so because they're insecure. They put you down because they don't know any other way to build themselves up. Don't let their insecurities influence your self-esteem. God is no respecter of persons, and God is the only one who counts.

Living with Roommates and Neighbors

If you're typical of most young people, one of the reasons you were so excited about leaving home was that you could be your own boss. You longed for the day when you could play your stereo as loud as you wanted to play it, talk on the phone for as long as you wanted, keep your room as messy as you pleased, stay up and watch television all night long, and leave the lights on when you left your room for five minutes without being nagged to go back and turn them off. You dreamed about the day when you could live under your own rules. Your new home would be your castle, and you'd be the ruler of that castle.

And you were right. You *are* the ruler of your own castle. Unfortunately, your castle is surrounded by other castles that are governed by their own rulers. If there's another castle in the next apartment from yours, or in the next bedroom from yours, or—heaven forbid—in the bed across the room from yours, your kingdom ends where somebody else's kingdom begins.

It's sad, but true. All those years, your mother wasn't telling you to pick up your clothes or to be nice to your little brother just to hear her lips flap. She was teaching you how to live in a civilized society. For the rest of your life, you're going to be working among—and even living among—people who will not be of your own choosing. You'll love some of these people; others will be thorns in your flesh. But even the ones you love will have habits that occasionally send you up a wall, just as you will do things that drive your loved ones crazy.

Despite what you may have previously believed, now that you're on your own you don't have the right to turn up the stereo as loud as you want (or even play it whenever you want, unless you use earphones), because other people have an equal right to sleep whenever they want to sleep. You don't have the right to tie up the telephone line for hours on end unless you're exclusively responsible for paying for that line, because other people's calls are as important to them as your calls are to you. You don't have the right to keep your living quarters as messy as you want—not when the mess in your room can attract roaches that will infest the room or the apartment or the house next door. You can't even do anything as simple as leaving the lights on all the time—not unless you're solely responsible for paying the power bill. And you certainly don't have the right to haul off and whack the people who annoy you, even if you were in the habit of whacking your little brother whenever he got out of line. In these litigious times, those you whack are likely to take you to court for assault.

As you'll soon learn, Mom was right. The real world is just like your family home, only bigger. Your freedom really does end where the nose (or the ear) of your neighbor begins. Whether you're dealing with a roommate across the bedroom from you or a neighbor across the street, your life will be considerably more pleasant if you govern yourself. Otherwise, you'll have to be governed by landlords or homeowners' associations or even the local police, who are going to be considerably less gentle about it than Mom was.

Living with Roommates

Many years ago, parents in many cultures used to pick out their children's mates. Deals were often made when boys and girls were babes-in-arms, and when the time came for the son or daughter to leave the nest, that son or daughter obediently went to live in the household of a spouse who was often a total stranger. This custom is still practiced in parts of the world. Although it seems barbaric to have to marry someone you've never met, people who study those cultures report that arranged marriages are surprisingly successful. In fact, the success rate for arranged marriages seems to be about the same as for marriages that are entered into out of love. Although strangers to one another at the time of the marriage, these husbands and wives go on to develop a love for one another despite any personality differences they may have brought to the union.

Moving in with a roommate is similar to entering an arranged marriage. Chances are pretty good that some of your roommates will be strangers to you at first. But even if your roommate was your best friend in high school, you don't really know someone until you live with that person day in and day out. Your former best friend in the world may turn into the roommate from hell. On the other side of the coin, the stranger sharing a room with you may become a lifelong friend.

If you're moving into a college dormitory or into an apartment you found from a note on a bulletin board or especially if you are a full-time missionary, you're pretty much stuck with what you get. We'll give you some suggestions in the next section about how to deal with these "arranged marriages." But if you're lucky enough to be able to choose a roommate ahead of time, do it with your eyes open. It's not enough to like somebody. You should also find somebody whose lifestyle is similar enough to yours that the two of you will complement each other, not kill each other. *This goes double if the two of you are sharing a bedroom.*

Don't room with an extravert just because you've always wanted to be more extraverted or with a person who is cleaner than you are just because you think that cleanliness may rub off. All too often, the thing that attracts you about the potential roommate may turn you off to such a degree that you end up with less of the good quality than you would have had if you'd lived with someone who was naturally more like yourself.

Kathy had many roommates, and she knows whereof she speaks. She once roomed with a person whose religious nature she had admired from afar. It was only after the two were living together that she realized how rigid the person was. This particular roommate was so strict that she believed anyone who drank a Coca-Cola was going straight to hell. There were no mitigating circumstances; the consumption of Coke, all by itself, outweighed every other human characteristic.

When Kathy moved in with this roommate, she was not a Coke-drinker. She didn't have a taste for Coke. But the roommate was so rigid about her position that Kathy found herself bringing home Coke bottles she'd found on the street, washing them out, and leaving them around the apartment just to make the roommate think she had consumed them. (Kathy freely admits that she is an evil person.) Eventually it just got easier to buy the Coke and drink it than to wash spiderwebs out of used bottles. Kathy has been a Coke-drinker ever since.

Following are some areas that may cause conflict between you and a roommate as well as some suggestions for resolving differences. Needless to say, the potential for conflict will be much greater if you are sharing an actual bedroom than it will be if everyone has a private retreat. A room of one's own covers a multitude of sins.

▶ Begging, Borrowing, or Stealing

You may have grown up in a household where people wore each other's clothes, raided each other's cupboards, used each other's computers, or listened to each other's music, but your roommate didn't necessarily do so. Before you borrow that first compact disc, lay down some ground rules for borrowing and lending. More than one friendship has broken down because a roommate borrowed—and lost or broke—a five-dollar item. If you set up guidelines ahead of time that cover breakage and replacement or even determine what you're willing to lend and what you aren't, your relationship is more likely to survive the inevitable catastrophe.

▶ Cleanliness

There are as many degrees of cleanliness as there are roommates who share a living space. Some people maintain their living quarters with military precision; others consider their housekeeping a success if they manage to keep the roaches under control. As messy people will point out, there's a difference between clutter and filth. You may find that clutter is acceptable, or maybe not.

If you find your roommate has different expectations from yours, set guidelines before one of you kills the other. You may decide that the kitchen and living room should be kept "company fresh" at all times, but the bedroom is meant to be lived in. And remember that compromise on *both* sides may be in order.

▶ Cultural Differences

Unless you've hand-picked your roommates, you'll be living in a cultural grab bag. Not even in Minnesota can you expect that everyone will be tall and blonde and of Swedish extraction. Your roommate may be of any color or of any faith. You're not even guaranteed of living with someone of your own nationality. After all, the student from Lesotho or Yemen has to live with *someone*. That someone might just as easily be you.

The cultural differences between you and the roommate may be subtle, but even so can be unsettling. Kathy once lived next to an apartment that had one roommate of Spanish extraction. Although Americans believe in maintaining at least eighteen inches of space around every person, this roommate's culture had taught her that people should stand much closer together. She habitually stood less than ten inches from the face of the person to whom she was speaking, and she often hopped in bed with them and lay with her head on their shoulders. This was more than a little disconcerting to the Americans, but the roommates eventually reached some compromises that allowed everyone to live together in relative comfort.

If you find yourself living with a person from another culture, don't panic. More likely than not, you will find yourself enriched by the experience.

▶ Differing Expectations of the Role of a Roommate

There's a whole spectrum of expectations that people have when moving in with a roommate. At one end of the spectrum, some people expect their roommate will be their new best friend. They anticipate a situation where roommates will eat together, go to movies together, take the same classes, and socialize with the same people. *There is nothing wrong with this.* Roommates can be one of the joys of life, and strangers can quickly develop into lifelong friends.

At the other end of the spectrum, some people want a roommate to share expenses—period. These people plan on maintaining their own friendships, their own eating schedule, and the privacy of their lives. To such people, a roommate is a necessary burden that allows a person to live in a place that would otherwise be too expensive. *There is nothing wrong with this, either.* Seeking a roommate solely to share expenses is a valid reason for sharing living quarters with that person.

The conflict comes when a roommate at one end of the spectrum tries to force his expectations on the roommate who resides on the other end of the spectrum. Nobody can force a friendship, but some people are willing to try.

After one of Kathy's roommates got married, leaving her in a two-bedroom apartment without a roommate to share it, she let it be known in church circles that she was looking for someone to live in the other bedroom. One day she got a call from a person she had seen in church, but had never done more than smile at in the halls. This person was severely physically disabled, which in itself would not have been a problem. But the person's telephone call left Kathy's chin on the floor.

"I've decided to be your roommate," she said. "I'll be moving in at the end of the month. Of course I can't cook for myself, so you'll have to be home to get my dinner to me by six. I'll want my breakfast, too. You don't need to come home for lunch—you can leave me a sack lunch. You'll need to be home all night after dinner with me and also on weekends in case I need you. You'll have to take out your furniture to accommodate my wheelchair. I don't have a car, so you'll be driving me around. I can't move my things, so you'll have to do the moving. And you certainly can't expect me to pay for half of the apartment, because I don't have a job."

Needless to say, Kathy did not accept the potential roommate's kind offer.

Although the brazenness of the caller was more than a little appalling, at least the potential roommate told Kathy well in advance exactly what kind of roommate she was expecting. If you're looking for a roommate, make sure you and your potential roommate understand what you're each seeking before you go out and buy matching towels for the kitchen.

▶ Financial Problems

Depending on your living situation, you may or may not have financial ties with your roommates. If you're living in a dormitory, your roommate's financial situation probably won't have an effect on you. But if you're living in an apartment or a house, one roommate's inability to pay bills could drastically affect everyone else who lives with that roommate.

The phone company doesn't care if three out of four people in an apartment are paying their share of the phone bill. If the phone bill isn't paid in its entirety, service is cut off. If one roommate doesn't pay his share of the rent, everyone in a shared house could be evicted. A power bill that's left unpaid results in a loss of power—even when it's ten below outside and you're relying on electricity to keep you warm. *And the credit rating of the roommate whose name is on the bill will suffer even if the unpaid portion of the bill is the fault of somebody else.*

If you're living in a situation where expenses are shared, your roommate's finances are your business. When choosing a roommate to live in a shared-expenses situation, the payment of bills should be discussed ahead of time. By the way, it's not as important to look for a rich roommate as it is to look for a roommate who honors his or her commitments. A lot of people with big incomes duck their financial obligations at every opportunity.

▶ Guests

Everyone wants friends, but some people like occasional visits and others want people around them at all times. Kathy, who is a strong introvert, once shared a bedroom with someone who was a friend to all. Everyone knew they could call this friend for help at any hour of the day or night—and they all did so. Guests frequently arrived well after midnight or called to unburden their problems at 3:30 in the morning. As long as they were sharing that one bedroom, Kathy had to accept that people could show up at any time. Eventually Kathy and her roommate got a two-bedroom apartment.

▶ Personality Differences

If you make an honest effort to like your roommate but you just can't stand each other, that doesn't mean you're an evil person. It doesn't even mean your roommate is an evil person. It just means the two of you are different. Face it—sometimes roommates have such different personalities that they're like oil and water. You may both be good people, but being good people doesn't guarantee you'll like each other.

Don't fall for the myth that if you're both good church members you'll get along. We may indeed, as the Apostle Paul said, be parts of one body in Christ—but you don't see the pancreas going out for dinner with the Achilles tendon.

The pancreas and the Achilles tendon work independently of one another, being members of the same body only by virtue of the fact that they're encased inside one piece of skin. They don't waste energy arguing with one another; they just concentrate on doing their jobs. By the same token, you and your roommate may be enclosed by the four walls of a single room. There's no sense in condemning the pancreas that sleeps in the bed across from yours. You do your job as an Achilles tendon, and let the pancreas work out his own agenda. Trying to force a close friendship when there's no common ground may be counter productive for both of you. Be kind to your roommate no matter how different he is from you, but don't feel guilty if the two of you aren't friends for life.

▶ Pets

Most on-campus housing prohibits pets. But if you live in off-campus housing or in an apartment or house that isn't connected with a college or university, pets could be a big issue.

If a roommate wants to bring a pet into the household, the first thing you should do is check your rental agreement. Many rental agreements prohibit pets altogether. Other rental agreements require a large extra deposit to be made to cover any damage the pet might make. Even if your rental agreement doesn't prohibit pets or if the pet owner agrees to pay the damage deposit, the remaining roommates need to have given their consent before a new pet is brought into the household. This isn't a case where majority rules. If most of the roommates are willing to go along with a pet but one is strongly opposed, a pet should not be brought into the environment.

After it has been agreed that a roommate can have a pet, the room-mates may need to set some ground rules to determine what kind of pets can be allowed, how many pets should be allowed, and how those pets should be cared for. There should also be rules determining how reimbursements will be made if the pet does any damage to property belonging to someone else. Any decisions you don't make now are going to come back and haunt you later, so don't forget this step of the procedure.

If you move into an existing household, it's up to you to follow the preferences of the people who were there before you were. If you feel strongly about taking your pet into the situation, it's your responsibility to find out before you move in whether a pet would be agreeable to the people who are already there. If you don't like the answer, find another place to live. By the same token, if you're a pet-hater who sees a pet in residence when you inspect a potential place to live, it's your responsibility to find out before you move in what rules are in place regarding that pet. If you can't live with the rules, don't move in. Nobody should be expected to give up a dog who has been a companion for twelve years and who has already found a place in the household just to satisfy the bias of a newcomer.

▶ Petty Annoyances

If you ever shared a room with a brother or sister, you know that even if you love the person his quirks may drive you crazy. When you move in with a stranger, you have no built-in affection that will keep you from going after that stranger if his habits annoy the life out of you. It doesn't matter what nasty habit drives you up a wall—a roommate who eats constantly, or eats noisily, or snores like a trucker, or clips his toenails at the dinner table—annoyances that seem petty could turn into huge bones of contention when two people are trying to live together.

If your roommate's habits are driving you to thoughts of mayhem, remember that even though you're almost perfect, you're certainly doing *something* that's annoying your roommate just as much. It may be more fruitful to have a civilized discussion about the problem than it would to bring out nuclear weapons at the first sign of conflict.

▶ Promptness or Procrastination

Your roommate's tendency to be late for everything may have no effect on you if the two of you aren't expected to do things as a team. But often, people choose to room together because they're taking the same classes in school, or because they work together, or because they go to church together. If you're considering living with someone for one of these reasons, you may want to find out if that roommate is usually prompt. This is especially true if the two of you intend to share transportation. Remember—a roommate's procrastination can get you fired. If your life depends on promptness, you may want to choose a roommate who can read a clock.

▶ Respect for Order

Everyone who has ever lived with roommates knows that some people go crazy when they get out from under their parents' thumbs. Rules of all kinds go out the window when there's nobody to lay down the law, and almost anything can happen. Some people stop attending church; others experiment with forbidden practices or substances; others do nothing more harmful than staying up all hours of the night.

To some extent, it's natural for kids to try their wings when they're out on their own. But some people go way too far and may have trouble finding their way back. If you're a rule-follower who is paired up with a scofflaw, you could have conflicts in a roommate relationship. The potential for conflict goes both ways, though. Some people get even *more* strict when they leave the parental nest, saddling themselves (and others) with more rules and regulations than Mom and Dad or even the Church ever did and driving their roommates nuts.

▶ Significant Others

Although guests can be a trial at any time, at least guests usually visit all the roommates at once, rather than singling one of them out.

Once a guest becomes a suitor, however, all rules seem to be off. There's no one more oblivious to the needs of others than a person in love. And heaven help you if your roommate gets engaged! If you're the odd person out, you may soon learn that your presence is not welcome even in your own apartment.

Both Clark and Kathy have had the dubious honor of enduring roommates who were engaged. In Kathy's case, she'd lived in the apartment first. The name on the contract was hers; the furniture was hers; the cooking equipment was hers; the television and stereo were hers. But the day her roommate got engaged, Kathy was no longer welcome in her own living room. It was made abundantly clear to her that if the roommate and the fiancé were in residence, she was to remain out of sight. She eventually spent more than one night in the ladies' lounge of the newspaper company where she worked, because there was no other place for her to go.

If you think Clark and Kathy are wimps, think again. But roommates who are in the final stages of the courting period can be extremely intimidating. Before you choose a roommate, determine whether this roommate will grow fangs if he or she meets The One, or if you'll be able to continue living in your own living quarters without feeling like an interloper.

▶ Sleeping Habits

If one roommate is a morning person and the other is a night owl, troubles may arise. This is especially true if the roommate who is awake insists on carrying out traditions that were developed when the roommate had a room to himself.

Kathy once had a roommate who got out of bed at 7 A.M. each day but set her alarm clock for 5 A.M. Every morning, seven days a week, this roommate was awakened by country-western music that played for two hours straight until she bothered to roll out of bed. Although three girls lived in this room, no amount of reasoning or pleading would convince this roommate to set her alarm clock for 7 A.M. For the entire school year, the other two girls in the room were awakened every day at 5 A.M., just to satisfy the routine of one inconsiderate roommate.

▶ Study Habits

If you're leaving home for the first time in order to attend school, your study habits—or lack of them—may offer a potential conflict with a roommate who shares your bedroom. As long as both roommates are willing to compromise, this is a fairly easy problem to overcome. If you and your roommate aren't willing to compromise about when the room should be quiet and when it should be open for entertainment, you're never going to be able to work through some of the bigger potential problems. Remember, the party can occasionally be moved elsewhere—and you can occasionally move your studying to the library.

▶ Telephone Sharing

When you lived at home, you were lucky if there was one phone line for the adults and one for the kids. You probably won't be so lucky now

that you're away from home. In a dormitory, there will probably be one telephone line per bedroom for two (or more) of you to share. This is usually also true in apartments and other shared housing.

If one person is paying the phone bill, the rules are easy because the person who is paying for the phone line makes them. If the phone owner wants you to use the phone only between 3:36 and 5:03 A.M. on the morning of a full moon, he has the right to do so. Rules get a little more complex, though, if all of you are paying equally for the use of the phone. This is especially true if there are competing long-distance courtships, when one of you may want to talk to a significant other and someone else wants to keep the line free so his own significant other can get through.

▶ Television and Radio Habits

There are two kinds of television watchers. Some people turn on the television when they have a specific show to watch, and turn the television off again when that show is over. Other people turn on the television when they awaken in the morning and go to sleep with the television on at night. Television is entertainment to some people, and it's company for others. The same is true for radio. If people from different camps find themselves rooming together, fireworks could result.

It's not just frequency of noise, however. Quality of noise is also an issue. If your tastes run to Bach and your roommate wants to listen to Garth Brooks, you could be heading for trouble in a roommate situation. The same is true if there's one television in your living quarters, but the two of you have strong attachments to shows that occupy the same time slot. By the way, if the television or stereo belongs to one roommate, that roommate should have first choice over how it's used. If the television or radio is shared, compromises may be in order.

Kathy once had a roommate who had to be at work by 5 A.M. This roommate got up shortly after 3 A.M., giving herself plenty of time to fix her hair and put on her makeup. From the moment this roommate awoke, the radio was on. The knowledge that Kathy was trying to sleep in the next room was not the slightest deterrent to a girl who played the radio every waking hour of her life. She could not even comprehend that some people prefer silence to noise.

It wasn't that the roommate was bad and Kathy was virtuous. There's nothing wrong with using a television or radio for companionship. But people with differing philosophies may find themselves at each other's throats if they try to live together. If you're considering a roommate who must have the television or radio on in order to be happy—or one who cannot stand the noise of a television or radio when you want to enjoy it—you might want to rethink your choice of roommates.

▶ Transportation

There are definite advantages to having a car. A car allows you to leave campus for recreational pursuits. If you want to see a movie in town, go shopping at the mall, or even stop by the local fast food outlet for a hamburger, you're out of luck unless you have an automobile. Automobiles represent freedom, and lucky is the man or woman who owns one. But that freedom may soon sour if you find yourself living among a group of roommates, and you have the only vehicle. If you find yourself in that situation when you leave home, prepare yourself with three simple rules:

1. Nobody drives your car except you. This will sound harsh to a roommate who claims that he would certainly let you use his car,

if the situation were reversed. Prepare yourself ahead of time by finding a valid reason why nobody can drive your car except for yourself. You may need to look no farther than your insurance policy. A lot of policies may not cover a vehicle if it is involved in an accident with any driver who is not the policyholder. And by the way, you don't have to be nasty about making this rule. Don't announce it the moment you meet your roommates. Wait until someone asks and then quietly say you can't allow others to drive your car—giving that valid reason.

2. Your car is not a communal vehicle. Roommates should not expect you to drive them places. If you're all going to church at the same time, that's one thing—although even then you aren't obligated to give anyone a ride if you've got other people you'd rather take. But if your roommate wants to go shopping and you don't, don't feel guilty.

3. Have a little compassion. If you were the one without the car, you'd want people to consider your feelings. Volunteer to do the weekly grocery shopping, if others will do the cooking chores for you. (Carrying home sacks of groceries from a supermarket that may be two miles away is no picnic, even in the best of weather.) Take a sick roommate to the doctor. Give your roommates a ride to campus if they're going the same time as you are. If a roommate finds himself in a jam, bail him out by giving him a ride. You can be kind to people without letting them take advantage of you. After all, if you were the one without the car, you'd want people to be kind to you.

If you don't own a car but your roommate does, you're in the beggar's seat. Don't think of that vehicle as being available to you—not even if you overslept and are late for your final exam. If your roommate offers to drive you somewhere, that's one thing. But chauffeur service is a blessing, not a right. Don't even consider it as an alternative unless your roommate is the one who makes the suggestion. (Hinting is not allowed.)

If your roommate does drive you places, be grateful for it. Show your gratitude by occasionally putting gas in the car. If you don't have money to buy gas, wash the car (even in the winter), do your roommate's dishes, or clean the bathroom when it's your roommate's turn to do so. There's always some way you can return a kindness. One happy result when you return a kindness is that kindnesses will be extended to you again.

By the way, if you're lucky enough to have a roommate who acts as your chauffeur, be considerate of the driver. Don't keep the roommate waiting. Don't mess up the roommate's car. Your roommate may be the driver, but you're not a passenger in a limousine. Treat the driver as you would like to be treated, and you may get another ride in the future.

▶ Unequal Division of Labor or Goods

If you and your roommate are sharing one room of a dormitory, it's pretty easy to divide the labor. Each of you is responsible for keeping his half of the room clean. It's the same thing with household goods—if you're living in a dorm, the dorm provides the toilet paper and the electricity, but each roommate is responsible for his own toiletries.

Once you move into an apartment or a house, though, the lines aren't as clearly drawn. You may find yourself in a situation where one roommate expects the other roommates to pay for household supplies and to clean up after the privileged character. He eats food from the refrigerator but doesn't replace it. He never washes his own dishes or cleans up after himself in the bathroom. He doesn't do his laundry and then raids the closets of unlucky roommates who are approximately the same size. If cleaning the living room were up to him, he'd let guests sit on his crumpled, dirty clothing. In this case, "he" can refer to male or female roommates.

If you're able to choose your own roommate, look for signs of selfishness. Does your friend expect to be treated every time you stop at the local fast food establishment? Does he try to copy your homework? Does he borrow things and then forget to return them? If he does, he's more than likely to turn into a roommate who expects you to pay for his share of household goods and do his share of the work.

▶ Wacko Roommates

You will quickly learn that people don't have to pass a normalcy test to enter a roommate situation. Sometimes you may find yourself paired with a roommate who is intellectually or emotionally underdeveloped, just a little off-kilter, or even seriously mentally ill. Roommates aren't guaranteed to share your moral standards, either—even if you go to a Church-sponsored school.

We can't give you any blanket suggestions in dealing with problem roommates because there is no one solution. Kathy once had to buy locks to protect her possessions from a kleptomaniac. She once had a roommate who was an undiagnosed sociopath, another who was manic-depressive, and yet another who was a pathological liar. She thrived in some of these situations, she endured others, and she handled at least one of them pretty badly—but she learned things from every one of those roommates.

Your roommates will mirror people you'll have to deal with for the rest of your life. Employers. In-laws. The traffic policeman who pulls you over even though you were going only two miles above the speed limit. Think of a roommate situation as a training ground. If you can get along with the worst roommate life can throw at you, you can get along with anybody. Make an effort to learn something from every roommate you have and to find some good in each one of them, and you'll be able to deal with a lot of the nasty situations you'll face in the future. Persevere—and when you can persevere no more, find another roommate.

Avoiding Problems

Your best chance of avoiding problems with your roommates is to anticipate them before they start. When you're entering a roommate situation, go into it hoping for the best but prepared for the worst.

You may want to practice what we call "defensive living." Humbly admit to your roommate right up front that this is a new situation for you and ask if it might be productive to talk about your individual expectations before you get too far into the relationship. If you do this in a non-threatening manner—preferably over pizza—your roommate will probably be more than happy to visit with you. (If you pay for the pizza, it's almost a sure bet that you'll have a cooperative audience.)

At this first meeting, find out what you can about your new roommate and try to focus on his positive traits. Candidly tell your roommate about yourself, including your strong points and your interests as well as your faults. If there are potentially serious areas of conflict, suggest that both of you think about ways you can compromise and that you talk about possible compromises at a later date. You don't want to be setting rules at this first meeting. Rules and regulations may not ever be necessary, so don't spring them on a new roommate before you've even memorized each other's names.

If you're moving into an existing situation, such as filling a vacancy in an apartment where others have already lived together, it's your job to adapt to the other roommates rather than their job to adapt to you.

Learn what the customs and rules are before you get into any established household. If you don't like the rules but everyone else is satisfied with the status quo, you're not going to have much luck if you try to get everyone else to change their ways.

If you and the other roommates are equally new in a situation, all roommates have an equal say in how the room or the apartment should be run. If there are more than two of you, votes may come in handy. If there are only two of you, both of you are likely going to have to make some compromises. Don't expect your roommate to make the big adjustments, while you live your life exactly as you please. Huge compromises may be necessary on both sides in order for you and your roommate to be able to live together in harmony.

When living in a roommate situation, the Golden Rule is the most important guideline. This also applies when dealing with your neighbors next door. Be the kind of roommate or neighbor you'd want for yourself. Remember: If others hear you, or smell you, or have to navigate around personal items you've left in a common area, or step in what your dog left on the sidewalk, you're out of line.

You may think it's your business what music you listen to, or when you listen to it. This is true only if you're living in a room by yourself. Even then, your noises shouldn't be audible outside your room. If someone in the next room—or the next apartment, or the next house—can hear you, it's your responsibility to turn the noise down or off. It isn't their responsibility to learn to live with it.

If you live in a house that has a yard, you may think it's your own business if you and your roommates neglect to mow the lawn or keep the place tidy. Guess again. The property values of all the houses on the block will go down if your home looks ragged. This will not make your neighbors happy.

Unpleasant odors aren't the only smells you should avoid. These days, many people are allergic to perfumes, hairsprays, incense, or even cleaning products that are sprayed in the air. Remember—if someone else who doesn't want to smell it can smell it, you're in the wrong. Before you use something that has an odor or a fume, ask permission. If someone asks you not to use the perfume or the hairspray or the aerosol can, cheerfully go outside to use it or don't use it at all.

If you make sure you're inoffensive as a roommate, you've probably guaranteed that your roommate will have no feelings about you that are worse than neutral. But if you're going to thrive as a roommate, you'll probably want to go farther than that.

Kathy once had a roommate who knew how to go the extra mile. Occasionally on Sunday afternoons, Kathy would sigh that she was in the mood for chocolate chip cookies but that since she didn't have any chocolate chip cookies she was going to take a nap instead. Almost invariably, the roommate baked chocolate chip cookies while Kathy was asleep. Needless to say, Kathy thought this roommate walked on water. It's almost impossible to dislike any roommate who does kind things for other people. If you go the extra mile for others, they're going to be a lot more tolerant of your little personality quirks.

Be careful not to overdo it, though. If you act possessive of people or gush over them or constantly do favors for them or buy them presents, it's eventually going to make them uncomfortable. Be friendly, be kind, be helpful—but don't be a clinging vine. And don't expect people to fawn over you or to reciprocate every time you do something kind for them. If the only kindness you get in return for all your good deeds is that you get along better with your roommates and neighbors, that should be reward enough.

Dealing with Problems

Despite all your good intentions, you and your roommate are going to have conflicts. Every human being is different. Even if you're identical twins, you and your roommate are going to do some things differently.

Having a roommate is different from having a friend in high school. You saw your high school friends when you wanted to see them, and when you weren't in the mood for company all you had to do was go home. Roommates are much harder to avoid. They're around when you want to sleep, when you want to study, when you want to daydream, and when you want to be alone and to cry into your pillow. And you're around when they want to do those same things.

The conflicts we've just mentioned are going to occur even if you and your roommate are crazy about each other. But sometimes a roommate situation doesn't exist on that happy note. You and your roommate may not be crazy about each other to begin with. If you and your roommate aren't on good terms anyway, little disagreements could turn into huge arguments.

If you have a problem with a roommate, ponder the situation to determine what portion of the problem is caused by you. In scriptural terms, look for the beam in your eye before you point out the mote in your roommate's. If your roommate has been playing his stereo at eighty decibels, maybe he's doing it to cover up the mushy conversations you're having with your significant other. If your roommate used all your shampoo, make sure he isn't retaliating because you squeezed his toothpaste tube in the middle. Try to figure out the underlying cause of your roommate's behavior. If your actions have contributed to it, changing your own behavior will probably eliminate your roommate's objectionable actions.

If after sincere and unbiased thought you still believe the fault isn't yours, the next item on your agenda should be to determine how important this issue is to your peace of mind. Is it worth the conflict? Will discussing it only engender bad feelings between you and your roommate? Will a confrontation result in your roommate being less tolerant of your own annoying quirks?

If after careful consideration you still believe you can't live with the problem, the first person you should go to is the roommate who is causing it. Don't go to other roommates and try to drum up support for your cause. This is tacky. Go directly to the source in a friendly and non-confrontational way and say that the two of you seem to be having a conflict, and that you'd like to find a way to reach a compromise that's acceptable to both of you. Don't point fingers or cast blame. There is rarely a right and a wrong in these situations; the conflict more than likely comes from a difference in your habits or personalities.

If the two of you are unable to resolve your differences, ask the roommate if a mutual friend can be your "Judge Judy." You can make a game out of it if you want to—and in fact, trying to solve problems with humor could strengthen your ties to your roommate rather than widen the rift. The two of you can present your case to the neutral source and agree to abide by the decision of the "judge." Then the winner can take the judge and the loser out for pizza, just to show there are no hard feelings.

The preceding suggestions apply in situations where both of you are decent human beings who would rather live without conflict. Unfortunately, this isn't always the case. Not all roommates are reasonable or decent. Occasionally you may find yourself living with a roommate who is going to do what he wants to do, and if you don't like it you can drop dead.

If you're living in campus housing, consider yourself fortunate. Dormitories and other on-campus housing units cater to people who are away from home for the first time. Visit your housemother or senior resident or whatever person is in charge of arbitrating between roommates, and explain the situation. If the roommate is in the wrong to a degree that the authority figure believes some intervening needs to be done, he or she will intervene on your behalf. If the problem escalates even after the intervention, the authority figure should have the power to move one or the other of you to another room.

If you aren't lucky enough to have a built-in authority figure on the scene, other roommates may be brought in to vote on the situation. This is a great solution if there are other roommates, and if they aren't divided as to which of you is in the right. However, this method of conflict resolution is effective only as long as you and the other roommate agree to abide by the decision made by the others. If the loser doesn't change his ways, this could be grounds for asking the troublemaker to live elsewhere.

If the relationship has deteriorated to the point that you and your roommate are no longer on speaking terms, the time may come when one of you should move out. Roommate situations are extremely fluid, and nobody will think less of you if you decide you've endured a bad roommate as long as you can, and it's time to move along to a different environment.

If there's any silver lining when living with unpleasant roommates, it's that it will teach you how to adapt to stressful situations. This is great preparation for missions and marriage and parenthood. Endure it as long as you can, learning as much from the situation as you can, and then move on to another roommate.

Choosing Your Friends

Now that you're away from home, you're going to discover that the world is a large place. Your varied experiences will make it possible for you to make a wide variety of friends. In fact, one of the nifty things about being an adult is that you will have different circles of friends based on your different interests.

You may have one set of friends who take the same college classes as you do, another set who participate in the same set of extracurricular activities, and still another set who go to church with you. Once you embark on a career, you're likely to make friends at work. And don't forget the friends you can make in your own neighborhood. You'll find it's no longer important that all your friends look the same and dress the same and even talk the same. Now that you're an adult, you can pick and choose your friends just as you'd pick and choose desserts at a buffet table.

When we were young, our bishop once told us that friends come and go, but the friends we'd end up keeping were the friends who weren't like anyone else. He was so right. The people in a clique are almost interchangeable, but you're likely to have only one friend who does a killer imitation of a toaster. Because he's unique, that weird friend endears himself to you. He expands your mind by bouncing ideas off you that you would never have considered on your own, or he takes you to places that never sounded interesting until you saw them through your friend's eyes.

As you can imagine, choosing friends who are different from you is a double-edged sword. It's one thing to have a friend drag you to the Buddhist festival for the dead, but it's quite another thing to have a friend drag you to a bar. When you're choosing your friends, you need to keep in mind who you are, and you need to know yourself well enough to gauge whether a friend's attitudes will influence you in ways you don't want to be influenced.

Face it. When you put a rotten apple in a bunch of good apples, the good apples don't make the bad apple good. The rotten apple makes all those good apples bad. By the same token, you may think you can influence a wayward friend to choose the right, but more often it's the wayward friend who will prevail. After all, it takes a lot more effort to walk up the ladder than to slide down the banister. And sliding down the banister seems like lots more fun.

It's important to pick your friends with care, because in all likelihood you're going to end up married to one of those friends. If going out dancing at the cowboy bar every weekend sounds fun to you, look at the people who go to the cowboy bar and see if you'd want to spend eternity with one of them. There's nothing wrong with people who go to a cowboy bar, mind you. But if you're a young girl who's hoping to marry a handsome prince who'll take you to the temple and put you in a castle and support you while you raise a house full of children at home, you've probably come to the wrong place.

Finding Your Better Half

We don't want to sound cynical, but finding your Own True Love is a crapshoot. If you're in your late teens or even in your early twenties you most likely have no idea whom you should marry, because you have no idea who *you* are. You may feel mature right now, but trust us. Right now you're probably attracted to an entirely different sort of person from the kind of person who will attract you five years up the road. Your body may be an adult's body and your mind may be an adult's mind, but your tastes are still changing.

Just as your tastes in food and television are evolving, your tastes in people are also changing little by little. Let's use girls for an example. In high school, most of the girls are attracted to the good-looking jock with the big smile and the nice car. By the time girls get to college, they start considering a boy's mind rather than just his body and automobile. For the first time, boys who were pimply-faced geeks in high school start getting dates. By the time they're thirty, the jocks have peaked and are on the downhill slide. The geeks, on the other hand, are ready to take the world by the horns. It's the girls whose tastes evolve who end up with the winners.

Because you're still in the process of deciding what qualities are important to you, it's a mistake to run off and get married just because all your friends are doing it. But all too often, people get married because their friends are, or because they just got home from a mission, or because they're unhappy or bored and another birthday has passed and they don't know what else to do. Here's a news tip for you: Forget about birthdays. Forget about your biological clock. Your biological clock does not have your best interests at heart. Your biological clock only wants you to reproduce. It doesn't care whether you're happy once you've done it.

To a degree, the same thing can be said of anyone who tries to talk you into marriage when you're not sure you want to do it. This includes suitors who say God has given them a sign. It includes parents who tell you they want grandchildren. It includes friends who want you to be married just because they are. If you're not ready for marriage, wait until you are. And if you're not sure about the person you're marrying, call off the engagement—even if you're in the car on the way to the temple.

We can't tell you whom to marry, but we can tell you one thing: Being unhappily married is a whole lot worse than not being married at all. So play the field. Date a whole lot of people. And when the time comes that your whole heart and soul tell you it's the right person and the right time, *then* get married.

This may sound snobbish, but make sure you don't even go on a first date with someone you wouldn't consider marrying. Love has a way of hitting you over the head when you least expect it, and when you fall in love your brain is going to fly out the window. Somebody you'd never consider in the cold light of morning can seem like a match made in heaven when you are looking through the blinders of love. Do everything you can to prevent a disaster by setting high standards for the people you go out with, even on a casual basis.

When you're looking for a spouse, go about it in the same way you'd look for a friend. Find people who share your interests. Even more important, find people who share your values. Yes, ladies, it's possible to find a returned missionary at a convention of Harley-Davidson bikers or at a NASCAR race—but don't count on it. If you put yourself in places where people you'd want to marry will naturally congregate, you're more likely to find someone you can proudly take home to meet Mom and Dad.

Once you decide the time has come for you to get married, the best thing you can do is to tell the Lord you're ready and then forget about it and let him take care of the details. Nobody is less attractive than a man or a woman who is desperate. You've seen that hungry look on other people; make sure you don't see it when you look in the mirror. If you want to make people run from you, being desperate is the best way to do it.

It's not easy to tell someone to just have faith that these things will happen in their own due time, but that's exactly what we're telling you. In the first place, if you're out in the world living your life, you're considerably more likely to meet that eternal companion than you will be if you're pining away at home waiting for him to come to you. In the second place, if you've been living your life instead of putting it on hold, you're going to be more attractive to that eternal companion when you do meet him or her. To paraphrase the scriptures, the best way to find yourself is to lose yourself. Concentrate on others—not just as potential husbands or wives, but as people. Perform acts of service. Put yourself in places where you're learning new things. Develop new hobbies and new skills.

Above all, be happy. You may think it's a nice face and a good body that's going to attract your spouse, but happiness is far more important. A person who is happy and optimistic when single is far more likely to be happy and optimistic when married. People who are unhappy before they're married and are looking for marriage to make them happy are going to find an excuse to be unhappy even after they're married. In fact, if you aren't happy now you should make it a goal to be happy before you're married. Marriage is hard enough without bringing somebody into the equation who expects marriage to be the solution to life's problems. It's not fair for you to rely on your husband or wife as your source of happiness. And if your potential spouse is dependent on *you* for happiness or for success or for inspiration, run. Fast. Don't stop running. Marriage should be an equal partnership. One person can hold the other one up for a week or a month or maybe even a year, but nobody is strong enough to do that over a lifetime—especially when children and household crises are added to the mix.

I'm Still Clueless

? *Nobody ever told me about all the backstabbing that goes on in the real world. People at work take credit for the work I've done. Friends gossip behind my back. My girlfriend's mother hates my guts, for no reason I can see. What can I do about people like this?*

When you were growing up, your family may have been something you took for granted. If you had older brothers or sisters, you could never remember a time when they weren't a part of your family. If you had younger brothers and sisters, you had at least nine months to adjust to them before they arrived on the scene. You may have liked some family members better than others, but you learned to live with them anyway. If you weren't particularly crazy about Uncle George, you learned early on that you were expected to treat him kindly despite your personal preferences. After all, as your parents may have told you, blood is thicker than water.

Now that you're out on your own, you're learning that much of the rest of your life will be spent dealing with people who don't have those blood ties to you. Some of them will be roommates; others will be employers; others will be in-laws. You'll take an immediate liking to some of these people. But some of these people won't ever become your friends, and indeed you may find that a small minority of them may try to undermine you in social, business, or even church settings.

You may be tempted to write such people off if you don't develop a liking for them. You may be especially tempted to lash out at people who treat you badly. It's okay to have these impulses. After all, you're only human. But it's *not* okay to act on those feelings, and indeed you may find that your success as a human being may ultimately be measured on the way you treat people who can't help you, or who don't like you, or who treat you unfairly.

This is tough news, but we're not making it up. The Savior himself in no uncertain terms said to "love your enemies, bless them that curse you, do good to them that hate you, and pray for them which despitefully use you, and persecute you" (Matthew 5:44). The Apostle John said it this way: "If a man say, I love God, and hateth his brother, he is a liar" (1 John 4:20).

Mom and Dad Learn Quickly

American humorist Mark Twain allegedly said, "When I was a boy of fourteen, my father was so ignorant I could hardly stand to have the old man around. But when I got to be twenty-one, I was astonished at how much my father had learned in seven years."

Whether or not Samuel Clemens ever said those words is really not relevant. But no matter who said it, this quote fits the way many of us view our parents as we age. In our teenage years, our parents are all too often an embarrassment to us. They're totally out of step with the world and the important things in it—at least, they're out of step with the things that are important to us. They're too strict, they make us do things for no good reason, and they really don't know how to have fun. We can't wait to escape from their omni presence and their rules and regulations.

When we start life on our own, our perspectives begin to shift. We learn that running a household involves a little more than just being the "boss" and making all the rules. Maybe Mom and Dad knew a little more than we gave them credit for. They played the roles of chef, maid, purchasing agent, tailor, cleaner, handyman, painter, mechanic, chauffeur, financial planner, doctor, social secretary, and counselor. In their spare time they dealt with their own employment, church activities, hobbies, family activities, and community service. Once you start trying to do all those things yourself, you may wonder how they ever had any spare time at all to spend with each other or with the children.

What we have tried to do with this book is provide you with an "owner's manual" for living on your own. We have given you some advice, pointed you in the right direction, and warned you about some of the problems you should avoid. Obviously, no book can teach you everything you need to know. Knowledge can be gained from a book, but wisdom comes only from a lifetime of experience.

But as you've read this text, we hope you have developed a little more self-confidence, along with an understanding that although you may not know everything, there's nothing you can't learn or accomplish if you have the proper drive and attitude. That is the real secret for running your own household or achieving any goal in life—realizing that while there are limits on what you know, there are no limits on what you can achieve. If you learned nothing else in these pages, we hoped you learned that.

Ultimately, finding happiness in life has nothing to do with how you look, where you work, or how many possessions you own. And even though we hope you learned some practical lessons from this book, baking the perfect cake or balancing your checkbook the first time does not guarantee happiness either. What really matters are the relationships you develop with other people and the service you render to family, friends, neighbors, coworkers, and your community. That may sound like something out of a Sunday School lesson, but it's true.

You may work hard for a promotion, only to realize that it brought you less happiness than watching your son play baseball. You may have saved every penny for a new sports car, only to realize you would have had more fun using the money for a family vacation. You may have spent all your weekends remodeling the dining room, only to realize that you no longer have any friends to invite to dinner. When you realize your priorities have not brought you happiness, you have the power to reevaluate those priorities and make the changes necessary to get yourself back on the proper course.

As you spread your wings to leave the nest for the first time, resolve to learn the things you need to learn, do the things you need to do, and remember the truly important things in life. And on your way out the door, give your parents or guardians a big hug. Thank them for all they have taught you, and resolve to be the kind of spouse, parent, and neighbor that they have been. That may not be an easy thing to say now, but you'll be surprised at how much they are going to learn in the next seven years.

Index

About the Authors

Clark and Kathy Kidd know all about self-sufficiency because they are older than dirt, and they both moved away from home more years ago than they care to remember. They hope that you, the discriminating reader, will be able to benefit from their successes and failures on the road to adulthood. (For example, adding chocolate chips to a tuna casserole makes for an interesting treat, but may not impress your date as much as you'd hoped.)

Residents of Northern Virginia, the Kidds have written three previous books for Bookcraft—*A Convert's Guide to Mormon Life*, *A Parent's Survival Guide to the Internet*, and *Food Storage for the Clueless*. Kathy also dabbles with writing LDS fiction in her copious free time.

The authors appreciate the kind support of their readers and are full of gratitude while spending their generous royalty checks on exotic trips and such household luxuries as toilet tank flappers.